Praise for *A Widow's Walk*

"Gripping. Fontana's firefighter husband died in the World Trade Center. Her narrative skill draws the reader in." —*The Washington Post*

"Every survivor of 9/11 has a story to tell, but Marian Fontana seems uniquely qualified to tell hers and in doing so, embraces every victim's spectrum of loss, grief, and closure that seems just out of reach. As a comedienne, actress, and writer, she brings to *A Widow's Walk* an articulate presence, at once a compellingly readable love story, a slice of American history, and a hefty dose of the spunky determination that made her into an activist for improved working conditions for firefighters and other emergency responders, and president of the 9/11 Widows and Victims' Families Association. There has been, and there will be, much more written about the events of September 11, 2001, but readers owe it to themselves to share Marian Fontana's remarkable and inspiring story, with its clear message of hope, not despair, in the face of the unthinkable." —Mary Garrett, *The Advocate*

"Deeply affecting, terribly poignant memoir."
—John Marshall, *The Seattle Post-Intelligencer*

"The author's passionate, irreverent persona comes through on every page. Her book has the addictive appeal of a smartly paced novel, and readers will close it wanting more."
—Michelle Green, *People* magazine's "Picks & Pans"

"Marian Fontana has written a spectacularly beautiful, insightful, and wrenching memoir detailing the year that followed her personal, and collective, tragedy." —*Parent + Teacher Exchange*

"Fontana manages to infuse her book with enough humor, anger and observation to make the anger and loss fresh again."
—Ann Hood, *The Washington Post*

"Fontana's own story is one of almost unbearable grief, slow recovery, and, ultimately, personal growth. She is a graceful writer, and the book is emotional without being maudlin."   —David Pitt, *Booklist*

"*A Widow's Walk* manages to make an exhaustively covered public event into a riveting private narrative. Fontana, who's written and performed comedy, has a sharp eye for detail and filled her account with rich characters, vivid scenes and a vast range of emotions. There's her desperate, volcanic heartbreak, of course, but she's also a keen recorder of the nuances of human feeling and behavior; she even gives her sorrowful story unexpected flashes of irreverent humor."
                              —Cathleen McGuigan, *Newsweek*

"Fontana's keen eye and ear make for an absorbing account of the first year of coping with historic tragedy. . . . With its built-in drama and pathos and excellent pacing, this book should bring Fontana to the attention of talk shows nationwide."   —*Publishers Weekly*

"Intelligent and insightful, honest and humorous."
                              —Anne Neville, *The Buffalo News*

"Compelling, gorgeously detailed and unsparingly honest. . . . Fontana's gifts for storytelling, dialogue and characterization make the memoir a pleasure to read, even as it rips you apart."
                              —Marion Winik, *Newsday*

"In her courageous book, *A Widow's Walk,* Marian Fontana brings us into the life of a firefighter's wife and shows us a mother's love that transcends all hurt, and a widow's love that preserves the memory of her husband, Dave—as beautiful a husband and father as can be found. This book is an homage to him, and to all those who lost their lives at the World Trade Center. There is literary greatness in this book which even the best of today's fiction cannot stand up to. . . . We see a woman who resolves to bring the 9/11 families together to protect their interest—the country's interest—in preserving the honor that accompanied our greatest tragedy. There is no better way to mark that honor than to read this story."

—Dennis Smith, author of *Report from Ground Zero*

"*A Widow's Walk* is not only a deeply moving portrait of familial grief, a tribute to the firefighters who died on 9/11, a call to action for justice for those most affected by the tragedy, and an insider's bracing take on the political machinations that followed—but also a snapshot of our country at a time of crisis. The miracle of Fontana's tale is that it is somehow funny—painfully funny—and true-to-life and redemptive. It makes you wonder how we, as a nation, have gone so long without this book."

—Elissa Schappell, author of *Use Me* and *The Friend Who Got Away*

"Fontana tugs at the heartstrings in this engrossing, inspiring 9/11 memoir."   —*Kirkus Reviews* (starred review)

"More than a chronicle of grief, more than a tale of how tragedy prompted courageous activism, *A Widow's Walk* is a love story. How sweet and wonderful that Marian Fontana introduces us not just to the hero firefighter that perished in 9/11, but also to the loving husband, doting father, and steadfast friend that Dave Fontana so clearly was."

—Philip Van Munching, author of *Boys Will Put You on a Pedestal*

"A memoir remarkable for its keen, close descriptions and characterizations, its humor and strength, and its great, hope-filled heart."

—*Elle* magazine

"But more than anything, Fontana exhibits in her writing and through her dedication and work with the 9/11 Widows and Victims' Families Association an indestructible spirit and a deep love for one of the many men who gave everything they had."   —Helen Ubinas, *Herald News*

A Widow's Walk

Marian Fontana

Simon & Schuster Paperbacks
New York   London   Toronto   Sydney

SIMON & SCHUSTER PAPERBACKS
Rockefeller Center
1230 Avenue of the Americas
New York, NY 10020

First Simon & Schuster paperback edition 2006

SIMON & SCHUSTER PAPERBACKS and colophon are registered trademarks
of Simon & Schuster, Inc.

For information about special discounts for bulk purchases,
please contact Simon & Schuster Special Sales at
1-800-456-6798 or business@simonandschuster.com

Designed by Jeanette Olender

Manufactured in the United States of America

1   3   5   7   9   10   8   6   4   2

Library of Congress Cataloging-in-Publication Data
Fontana, Marian.
A Widow's Walk / Marian Fontana.
p.   cm.
1. Fontana, Marian.   2. September 11 Terrorist Attacks, 2001—
Personal narratives.   3. Fire fighters' spouses—New York (State)—New
York—Biography.   4. Widows—New York (State)—New York—Biography.
5. Terrorism victims' families—New York (State)—New York.   I. Title.
HV6432.7.F66   2005
974.7'1044'092—dc22   2005049935
[B]

ISBN-13: 978-0-7432-4624-8
ISBN-10:   0-7432-4624-1
ISBN-13: 978-0-7432-9824-7 (Pbk)
ISBN-10:   0-7432-9824-1 (Pbk)

To my husband, Dave;

for our son, Aidan

1

The Day

My eyes creak open and try to read the red numbers, blinking 8:15 A.M. A surge of panic rushes through me. I am late for my son's second full day of kindergarten. I should have laid out his clothes and packed his lunch the night before, but the organizational gene is recessive in my family. I scramble into his room to find him a clean shirt.

"Aidan! Wake up!" I yell. Aidan is sleeping in the middle room of our small floor-through apartment. When he was a baby, I would tiptoe through his room so carefully, it reminded me of scenes from the movie *Kung Fu,* trying to walk on rice paper without making an indent. Even at five years old, Aidan still looks like a baby, his mouth hanging wide, cheeks flushed red like tempera paint. I watch the soothing rhythm of his chest rise and fall and I stop to fill my own lungs with gratefulness.

"C'mon! We're late!"

Aidan stirs and I rush into the kitchen to make lunch and call Dave at the firehouse on Union Street, eight blocks away. Last night we tried to have our usual eleven o'clock phone call, but the Squad's PA system was broken. Everything was accompanied by a deafening sound resembling a bee caught in a microphone.

"I can't talk," he'd said. "This noise is driving me crazy."

"Ten more hours and you'll be on vacation for a *month,*" I reminded him before hanging up. Dave wasn't supposed to be at work, but I had insisted he switch shifts to have our anniversary off.

Dave was excited by our plans to go to the Whitney Museum today. Now that Aidan was in school, he could pursue his art again, maybe even apprentice with someone well known. He was also considering massage school or going back to college to get a master's in history. He had lists of projects and ideas scratched on paper all over the house, ways to supplement his meager income until he was promoted.

Aidan shuffles into the kitchen and sinks into a chair. "I'm tired," he complains, plopping his head into his folded arms. I kiss his hair, inhaling the scent of sweat and baby shampoo, and dial the firehouse.

"Squad One. Firefighter Fontana speaking."

"Hey. Happy anniversary," I say.

"You, too." He sounds exhausted. Ever since we returned from Cape Cod three weeks ago, Dave has been working extra shifts to pay back the firefighters who worked for him so he could go away. Smearing peanut butter on potato bread, I ask him when he will finish.

"I just have to shower," he answers. I picture him grimy and smelling of smoke. When he "caught a job" and worked at a fire, he came home smelling like the bottom of a fireplace. Sometimes the sooty smell could linger for days, Q-tips turning black when he cleaned his ears.

"Are you sure you're done?" I ask, prying the jelly jar from the refrigerator shelf. Firefighters work two twelve-hour and two nine-hour shifts a week. At the end of his shift, he cannot leave until a member of the new crew arrives and is prepared to take his place. Since Dave is the only firefighter who lives in the neighborhood, he is often the last to go. Despite my complaints, Dave stays late so the other firefighters can begin their lengthy commutes home to Long Island, Rockaway, upstate, and Staten Island. One firefighter travels as far as Harriman State Park.

"Yeah, I'm done," he answers. I can tell he is as excited as I am to be together today. My neck hurts from squeezing the phone, and Aidan is asking for a waffle.

"I'm late. Where do you want to meet?"

"Connecticut Muffin in ten minutes?" he suggests. I can hear the deep male voices in the kitchen, the coffee cups clanking into the sink. Some firefighters linger and talk to the incoming crew before they head home, to miss the rush hour and catch up with their friends. Usually they want to know about what kind of runs everyone went on the night before.

"Okay. I'll see you at Connecticut Muffin in ten minutes," I repeat, and hang up. That's it. No profound discussions. I can't even remember if I told him I loved him. We always did, but ingrained habits are forgotten sometimes, like leaving the coffeepot on or forgetting to lock the door.

8:36 A.M.

Outside the sky is so blue, it looks as if it has been ironed. Aidan is walking slowly, a squeeze yogurt hanging from his mouth. There was no time for waffles, and now I guiltily rush him the three blocks down 7th Avenue to his school.

At the corner near the school, local politicians are shaking voters' hands while fresh-faced college students hand out flyers. It's Election Day. I'd nearly forgotten. I try to get Aidan to walk faster, but he drags behind me like luggage.

"Can we get an Anakin Skywalker toy after school?" His little hand is warm and clammy. Even on busy days, I enjoy how it feels.

"Uncle Jason is picking you up."

"How come?"

"It's Daddy's and my anniversary today."

"Are you going to have a party?"

"No. We're going out in the big city."

"Can I come?"

"No. You have school."

"Can Jason buy me an Anakin?"

If Aidan were a dog, he would be a retriever. I convince myself that his obsessive single-mindedness will serve him well someday as we cross the playground to the school door.

The kindergarten room is noisy and stifling. Aidan bounces toward his seat, oblivious to the little girl next to him crying noisily and clutching her father's pants leg. I kiss Aidan good-bye on top of his head. His hair is so soft it feels like a new cotton pillow.

"I love you," I say.

"Love you, too," he answers distractedly.

Outside in the playground, I peek in the window. It is only the second full day of kindergarten, and I am nervous Aidan will miss me. A few other children are crying, but he is talking to a curly-headed boy next to him, his face expressive and sincere. His eyebrows bounce up and down like caterpillars dancing.

The air is warm and in it lingers the smell of summer. I spot my friend Kim, leaning on her blue Volvo and waving at me. Kim speaks crisply, filling her sentences with words I have to look up in a dictionary.

"I'm so glad I ran into you!" Her wide cheeks spread into a smile. "I'm leaving for the Congo on Friday and I wanted to have a chance to see you."

Kim is a former member of my weekly writing group; she wrote elegant travel essays, until she left last year. Everyone in the group writes from experience. While I spent my teens poured into Sassoon jeans and listening to Led Zeppelin at keg parties, Kim contemplated the evils of apartheid on the dirty back roads of South Africa.

I envy the exotic writing assignments Kim gets but know that I am not capable of such high adventure. Writing and performing one-woman shows about the curious urban characters I witness on the F train is about as intrepid as I want to be. We chat for a while until I suddenly realize that I am late to meet Dave.

Arriving at Connecticut Muffin breathless, I am surprised that Dave isn't already there. I spot Tommy behind the counter and smile. The soft-spoken black man in his late fifties hands me my coffee before I even ask for it. He chuckles and shakes his head when I tease him about smoking.

"Okay . . . okay. For you, I'll quit," he says.

On the benches outside, Park Slope mothers perch behind Maclaren strollers. I find a seat near the sidewalk and sit to wait for Dave. I remind myself to vote and smile in guilty pleasure at having the day alone with Dave. Unable to afford babysitters, we have struggled to balance the heavy tray of work, parenting, friends, writing, exercise, sex, and shopping. With Aidan in school, the possibilities seem endless.

I stir from my reverie to notice that the people around me are speaking animatedly. I hear the words "airplane" and "Twin Towers" when my friend Lori walks over. She is a short, blond ex-dancer with two wild boys and a face that's seen too much sun. She teaches aerobics at the Dance Studio where I worked as a gymnastics instructor for eight years.

"A plane just crashed into the Twin Towers," Lori says. People are pointing at a plume of smoke cutting across the sky like a black arrow. I picture a small biplane wedged into the top of the tower like a candle pushed into a cake. I wonder for an instant if Dave went. After all, he would never want to miss a fire, and I'm sure Squad 1 would go. Squad 1 is the first of seven squads that, along with five rescue companies and a Hazardous Materials Unit, constitute the highly trained division of the Fire Department known as Special Operation Command. SOC companies handle confined-space rescues, collapses, hazardous material spills, terrorist incidents, and more.

No, he's not there, I tell myself. *He said he was done. Someone came in for him and he was going to shower. It's our anniversary. He's probably at home waiting for me in bed, ready to fool around before we go to the city.*

I stand up.

"Where are you going?" Lori asks, concerned.

"I think Dave might be waiting for me at home." Dave hated that I was always late. Because I'd taught in the neighborhood, I could never make it down 7th Avenue without stopping to talk to parents, kids, and friends. Dave dubbed me "Pope of the Slope" and often insisted that we take the quieter 6th Avenue so we could get places on time.

More people are looking up over the horizon toward Manhattan at a second plume of smoke that is widening and bleeding into the blue sky.

"Let me come with you," Lori insists, following me down to 4th Street, to the ground-floor steps of our small brownstone apartment.

"Dave?" I yell down the hall, but everything is eerily quiet. In the living room, Lori turns on the television and I am stunned to see the top of one of the towers engulfed in flames, like a giant metal matchstick. My heart beats faster as I notice the second tower is also on fire. Footage of a plane crashing into the second tower plays and I am confused. Is this a stunt or some kind of camera trick? What is happening?

My breath catches in my throat as I watch people jump from windows, falling like ash. A man in a green shirt tucks his knees up, like a kid doing a cannonball into a pool, and is gone. The voices on the news sound confused, their cameras filming shakily as sirens blare in the background. Squad *must* be going. They're just a straight ride through the Brooklyn Battery Tunnel. Now I *am* worried. The cameras flash to the Pentagon, which is also engulfed in flames. The television cuts back to the towers as a man uses his shirt like a parachute and jumps. Lori is talking, but all I can hear is my heart pounding in my ears. The voices on the news report a crash near Philadelphia and planes grounded all over the country in case there are strangers in the cockpits.

It is the Apocalypse, I think. It is the end of the world.

"What's happening?" I ask the television. Everything sounds muffled, as if I'm underwater. My phone rings but sounds far away. Thank goodness. Dave is calling, he can explain what is happening. Lori answers in a hushed voice and hands me the phone.

It is Mila, my friend from college who lives in the neighborhood.

"Marian, are you watching TV? Please tell me Dave is with you," she says nervously.

"Yes. I don't know where Dave is . . . I think he might be there." Fear and doubt make my voice shaky.

"What would he be doing there?" Mila asks. Worry swells in my chest. Lori looks at me expectantly and then back at the television.

"He'd be running in, I guess . . . up the steps . . . to save people." I imagine him running, carrying a hundred pounds of equipment, the heat from the tower banking down like a heavy blanket.

Suddenly the television emits a low rumble. I can feel the vibrations through the set and into my stomach. Gray spires pour out like fireworks of dust, ash, and metal. I drop the phone and watch in disbelief as the South Tower falls. The ventricles of my heart start to pulse, popping and ripping, exploding in my chest. I clutch my heart, but it is as futile as trying to stop the ocean.

"Oh my God. He's dead. He's gone!" I scream, sinking onto the rug, trying to grasp one of the million thoughts speeding through my head like a movie on fast-forward.

"No. You don't know that," Lori says helplessly. "I'm sure he's fine. He's probably helping people." She tries to sound calm, but her hands are shaking when she takes the phone from me. I want to believe her, but I know he is gone.

I am scared to avert my eyes from the television, as if it is the only connection I have to Dave. Lori is talking to Mila and I am blinking to keep the tears from blurring the images on TV. Reporters are yelling into the cameras, shocked, their faces covered in ash. Images of Dave speed through my head like a highlight film: Jones Beach when we kissed under the green-striped umbrella, Dave massaging my feet while we watch TV, that argument on the R train, the snowball fight in front of the dorm, iced coffees in the backyard, rhubarb pie on the Irish coast, the crease in his shoulder, the way his fingers feel, his dimples, yoga, hands, legs. I stop the images, my face hot and wet from crying. I feel Lori squeeze my hand. I head over to the red phone in the kitchen, a call box that says "911" on the outside. Dave bought the novelty phone at a department store when he first became a firefighter. I pull open the door and frantically dial the firehouse and am not surprised when it's busy. I press redial and will Dave's voice to answer. I would do anything to hear it now, deep and quiet.

Answer. Answer, goddammit. Don't you dare be on that truck, Dave. I hang up and pace across the living room, staring at the television in confusion. My mind races with my feet, back and forth, back and forth, faster and faster. I pace as if my footsteps could turn back the clock, rewind what has happened. The phone rings and I dive for it.

"Hello?" I say expectantly.

"It's Jason," he says in his bass voice. He's my best friend from college and my neighbor. He has traveled with Dave, Aidan, and me on what we affectionately dubbed our gaycations.

"JASON!" I yell, noticing that I sound more like a hysterical, over-wrought woman than myself. "You have to help me! I can't . . ." I screech, out of breath as if I have run a long distance.

"Marian, calm down. He might not even be there. You just have to calm down. I'm coming over right now."

I hang up and pace again, covering my eyes with two curtains of fingers. I try to wipe away what I have seen. I run to the red phone again and dial the firehouse. Still busy. I contemplate walking there, but I feel as if someone is kicking my knees from behind.

"Do you think the school is safe?" Lori says, worry wrinkling her face. I realize I have not even thought about Aidan. "Maybe I should pick up the kids." I try to focus on what she is saying, but my mind feels like I have twelve radio stations playing at once, giving me different information. I press my hand to my head trying to recall who was working with Dave last night. *If he's with the experienced guys, he'll be safe,* I tell myself. Lieutenant Mike Esposito. What about Bobby West? He's as good as it gets—twenty-two years on the job in a busy house. They are talented firefighters who protect their men and would never put themselves in a situation that was too dangerous. Dave probably can't get to a phone, that's why he hasn't called, because he told me he would always call. He had promised me less than three months ago. On June 17, 2001.

It was 5:00 P.M. on Father's Day, and Dave still hadn't called. He always called at least once during his shift. Aidan was taking a nap, even though he had given them up almost a year before. I could hear him snoring on my bed as I hung up the sign we made that morning for Dave. It said "Happy Father's Day" in black marker.

I heard the report on the news first: There were firefighters missing. A wall collapsed after an explosion in a hardware store in Astoria, Queens. At least one firefighter was trapped inside the burning building. Two others were buried in the rubble. The reporter on NY 1 was standing in front of Rescue 3's rig when the cable TV cut out. I vaguely remembered Dave telling me he was going to work at another rescue company that day. My landlady heard me crying. She sent her daughter down to keep an eye on Aidan and helped me upstairs. She put a shot of whiskey in my shaking hands while her husband tried to fix my cable. We waited and waited until the phone finally rang.

"This is the worst day of my life." Dave's voice cracked; he was trying not to cry. I could barely talk I was so relieved. I thanked God. I told Dave I loved him. "I gotta go. I'm on this guy's cell and he hasn't called his wife yet. We found two guys . . . I gotta go."

"I'm so glad you're okay," I whimpered.

"Me, too. I'm sorry I scared you. I promise if anything like this happens again, I'll call. If you don't hear from me in twenty minutes, then you can worry. Okay?"

9:58 A.M.

It has been nine minutes since the South Tower collapsed. It turns out that I will have eleven more minutes to hope that Dave went to get me an anniversary present instead of jumping on the truck. I run to the phone again, press redial. Miraculously, someone answers.

"Who's this?"

"It's Jimmy Lopez, Marian." He is one of the new guys, short and stocky with hazelnut-colored skin. His eyebrows are probably furrowed, his usual expression.

"Is Dave there?" I ask. *Just say yes. Please, please say yes.*

"I think they're out on a run," he says reluctantly.

"Dave's dead," I tell Jimmy. "I think Dave's dead." I try hard not to get hysterical, not to cry.

"Naw. Naw. He's fine. I don't know what's going on, I just got in, but we'll go get him, okay?"

"It's our anniversary."

"Oh . . . listen, don't panic. He probably just couldn't get to a phone or something."

"A tower's collapsed!" I shriek. Jimmy is silent, and I wonder if he has hung up. "Hello?" I say.

"Yeah, I'm here," he says slowly, and I realize he has not seen the TV yet. "I gotta go."

"Maybe Dave's with Espo?"

"He's on the board."

"What about Bobby West?"

"His sister died yesterday. Matt Garvey is covering for him—I gotta go, Marian. I'll call you later."

He hangs up, and the silence echoes in my ears like a high-pitched buzz. I press the receiver and the dial tone staggers, telling me that there are messages. I curse myself for not having call waiting. My fingers shaking, I check the calls: two from my parents, one from my friend Theresa, one from my sister, Leah, who is vacationing in Maine—all in hushed and worried voices.

10:28 A.M.

The doorbell finally rings and Jason enters, his brown eyes wide with apprehension. I shake my head in disbelief and collapse into his arms, sobbing. He is one of only a few who know the thick onion layers that constitute my seventeen years with Dave.

"I know it looks bad, but you don't know yet," he says, and I turn my head back and forth, clutching my heart to keep it from breaking into smaller and smaller pieces. He guides me over to the couch and squeezes my hand as we watch TV.

"Did you call the firehouse?"

"Dave went," I cry.

"He might not have even gotten there yet. I'm sure there was a lot of traffic." And as if some terrible cue line, we watch in horror as the second tower falls, mimicking the first.

"OH MY GOD!" Lori screams. I am already on my knees on my thick purple carpet, praying. There is nothing else to do. After a few bewildered moments, Lori and Jason kneel with me, and we hold hands in a circle. The shrieks of panicked people echo from the TV as we bow our heads and pray silently.

"*Our Father who art in heaven, hallowed be thy name . . .*" I make pacts, treaties, promises, and vows to God in exchange for Dave's life.

On the TV, the giant puff of smoke rises like a wave to meet the first as the acrid smell of burning plastic begins to float through my window screen. The phone rings again.

"HELLO?"

"It's Joey." It is Mila's husband.

"I'm not sure, but I think I saw Dave on TV," he says calmly. "It's hard to tell, because they're all covered in dust, but it was this big guy who walked like him." Hope expands in my chest, separating my ribs with possibility. I hang up, sit on the edge of the couch, and stare at the TV, transfixed. Firefighters pass by the cameras, dazed, bloodied, and covered in dust. They are carrying people who are wailing and shaking their heads. The cameras film onlookers staring up at the devastation, hands clasped across their mouth, sobbing, and I am one of them, watching, in collective horror, the world change forever.

11:35 A.M.

The waiting is torturous. I begin pacing again while Jason answers the phone and I send Lori to the store to buy cigarettes. I have not smoked in thirteen years, but I need something to calm the nerves pressing hard against my skin. In the kitchen, I read the list of phone numbers from Squad 1 hung on the refrigerator with a magnet shaped like a fire truck that reads "No fire too difficult, no rescue too great!" I scan the thirty names and dial the first number. It rings and rings.

"Hello?" It is Kathleen Box, Gary's wife. Gary is relatively new to the company, but the guys like him; they've even nicknamed him "the barber" for the cropped military haircuts he gives them.

"It's Marian Fontana. Dave's wife, from the firehouse. Is Gary working today?"

"Yes! Have you heard something?" Kathleen's voice is shaky and nervous. I've met her only once, at the Christmas party. She stood next to Gary, looking as fragile as crystal.

"I know they're there. Jimmy Lopez said they'd call when they know something." I can tell her mind is racing as fast as mine.

She takes a deep breath. "You know, I think Gary's okay, 'cause he dreamed this whole thing." Goose bumps rise on my skin as she continues. "A few weeks ago, he had this nightmare. He never has nightmares, but he woke up sweatin' and shakin'. I was like, what's a matta? And he told me he had this dream that he saw a plane crash into a tall building and the rocks and stuff fell on him."

"Oh my God."

"So I'm thinkin' maybe he's okay 'cause he dreamed about it. I dunno. I gotta get off the phone in case he calls."

We promise to call each other if there is any news. I hang up, staring at the list. With a pink highlighter, I highlight Dave's name and Gary's and Mike Esposito's, but tears blur my vision and fall, smearing the ink.

"Oh, sweetie," Jason says, entering the kitchen. Without looking up, I can tell he is crying, too. I look at the wide black numbers on the wall clock. It is only 11:18 A.M., and it feels like it has been years.

12:00 P.M.

Jason and I sit in my small backyard where smoke lingers like humidity in the air. I wonder why no one from Dave's family has called. If I can feel the whole world vibrating, surely one of his six siblings on Long Island knows what happened. I stand up to call, but the doorbell rings. It is Lori, returning from Aidan's school, where she insists the children are unaware and safe, watching a movie in the auditorium.

I watch the thick white ash floating in the sunbeams and pour wine into two glasses for Lori and me. Jason, sober for many years, sips a Diet Coke. So early in the day, the wine tastes like bile. I drink it anyway and light a cigarette, hoping that something will slow down my body, stop the horrible images traveling through my imagination. "I can't take it," I say. I want to scream or kick something, fear and sadness and anger trapped like kinetic energy. Lori and Jason sit quietly while I cry and shake my head, refusing to believe.

"Why don't we play cards," Jason suggests, standing and clapping his hands like a fifties housewife.

"That's a good idea," Lori says. Before I can protest, Jason disappears into the house, the screen door slamming behind him. He reappears with a faded deck from Ireland, the corners white and bent. He deals us each seven cards on my rusty white table.

"Rummy? Does everyone know rummy?" he asks. I nod, slowly putting the cards in order, the familiar shapes and faces comforting me. *Two queens, one king, a four and five of clubs, an ace, a nine.* My leg is bouncing like a bored teenager's, but I force myself not to stand again, to focus on the cards. My hands are shaking like I have Parkinson's and I can't stop. *Put the ace with the king.* The doorbell rings, and I throw my cards down and run. Maybe Dave took a detour, went to the Clay Pot to get me an extra-special gift and bumped into Tara or some friends. . . . It is my friend Deirdre, a mom from the neighborhood, her belly bulging with her second child.

"Are you okay?" she asks. I shake my head no. She follows me down the hall. I am biting my lip so hard it hurts. It feels good to feel the teeth digging in.

Outside, Deirdre sees us playing cards and, as if the scene were completely normal, pulls up a chair. Jason deals her in. An image of Dave's father flashes through my head, and I stop and stare. Why am I thinking of him now? I have thought little of him since his death sixteen years ago, a year after I met Dave. Dave has his barrel chest, his nose, ruler-straight, his penetrating eyes . . . My chair scrapes loudly on the cement as I push it away from the table. I am crying and pacing again. I am a match poised on the fuse. I storm into the kitchen to find the Yellow Pages and begin calling hospitals. There are dozens of them. Jason, Deirdre, and Lori step carefully behind me, waiting for a signal of what to do. In a matter of minutes we are all dialing emergency rooms around the city. There are busy signals and confused ER nurses. They check their lists for names. Doctors and nurses near the towers are waiting, but the emergency rooms are virtually empty. I want to run to the hospitals myself, scouring the gurneys until I find Dave, and fling my grateful arms around his big shoulders the way I did on that Father's Day when he arrived home at 1 A.M.

I had been sitting on the couch listening for the sound of the door scraping in its frame. When he arrived, I ran down the hall and enveloped him like a net catching a fish. I kissed his face until he laughed.

"I didn't know you loved me so much," he said, and I stopped.

"I tell you all the time!"

"I know, I just . . . this is different . . . it's good to be home."

That night, in bed, I massaged the tired muscles on his broad, smooth back.

"I didn't stop," he groaned. "I just kept lifting brick after brick . . . oh, man." He moaned as I kneaded the knots, pressed into the braided muscles. "We found Harry Ford. He's got three kids, I think. Real nice guy. Lives in Long Beach." I worked my way down one of his large arms, landing in the palm of his square, callused hand.

"I hate your job," I said spitefully. I resented how dangerous it was, how it wore down Dave's spirit, for practically no money. It wasn't worth it.

"I always thought that the more I train, the more I drill, the less chance I have of getting hurt," Dave said, his voice muffled in the pillows. "But the guys that got killed today . . . they were just standing there and the wall just fell on them. It could have been any of us." Dave rolled over suddenly and looked at me, his rugged face lined with concern. "I don't want to worry about money anymore. I don't want to argue. I want to have another kid right away, and I just want us to enjoy ourselves."

I nodded, my throat burning as if I'd swallowed the lid of a tin can. I cupped my hands over my eyes to catch the tears. Through the cracks of my fingers I saw that Dave was crying, too. I had only seen him cry once before and there he was, his blue-green eyes filled, for the first time, with fear.

"Now will you switch to a slower company?" I asked. We'd had this argument many times before. I wanted him to go to a quiet firehouse, one in Staten Island, or a marine company. But that night, Dave smiled weakly, his dimples barely creased as he rubbed his hands through my hair.

"Between you and me, after I get my ten years in, I'll consider going to Marine Nine . . ." His voice trailed off, scratchy with fatigue. I rested my head on the soft pillow hair of his chest. Through one ear, I listened to his heart thumping in watery rhythms. He would celebrate his ten years on September 8, 2001, only a few months away. But when his heart reached the slow and steady beat of sleep, I knew he would never settle for the quiet of a slower house.

2:12 P.M.

We've called every ER in the tristate area. They are poised and waiting, but they tell us hardly anyone is coming in. The rooms are almost empty. I look at the garden, covered in a fine white dust that falls like rain. I try to imagine my life without Dave, but every time I do, my stomach drops as if I am at the very top of a Ferris wheel. Jason is on the phone in the kitchen, making arrangements for Aidan to go to my friend Caren's house.

"Caren says he can stay as long as he wants," Jason tells me, heading outside. Lori and Deirdre have left to get their kids. "She said he can sleep over there if you want." I nod, the tears falling again. I can't let Aidan see me falling apart, and a few hours of obliviousness is a beautiful gift. Jason reaches for me and I sob onto his bony shoulder, my muscles tightening. "What am I going to do?" How can I tell Aidan his father is gone? It just cannot be.

I pull away and head into the kitchen to call my friend Merri, who lives in Tribeca, a trendy neighborhood near the World Trade Center. We met in a writing class where I wrote my first one-woman show, which Merri later directed at Playwrights Horizons. Middle-aged and slumped, Merri has been like a Jewish Yoda dispensing humor and sage advice throughout our twelve-year friendship.

"What can I do?" she asks, trying not to sound as scared as she is.

"I need you to go find him, please!" I tell her tearfully.

She is silent on the other end.

"I'll go," she says. She saw the towers fall from her fire escape and was too frightened to call me.

5:16 P.M.

A steady stream of friends arrive, carrying food, bottles of wine, presents for Aidan. They tread carefully around me, trying to find something to say or do. A neighbor is heating up lasagna; Lori has returned with a salad and a case of energy drinks. Mila and Joey are sitting on my kitchen floor, organizing my cabinets. I can hear clanging pots and Tupperware falling. Why can't I throw anything away? Maybe I've always been afraid of losing something if I did.

"You should really eat something," Lori says. "You haven't eaten all day." But the thought of eating makes my stomach grip. I sit in the backyard answering the phone, my voice quivering as I tell friend after friend "I don't know anything yet. I have to get off the line." My sister,

Leah, keeps calling from Maine, where she is on vacation. She can't get over any of the New York bridges to get home. Her voice cracks and it is like hearing myself. People always mistake us for each other on the phone.

"Oh my God, Marian" is all she can muster. "I need to see you! I need to come home."

"Please . . ." I beg, suddenly desperate for my big sister. Eleven months apart, Leah and I grew up fiercely close, overlapping our thoughts and finishing each other's sentences. She was bossy, passionate, intense, and sensitive. Studying dance and flute, she was the elegant one, leaping easily across streams while I always managed to soak my shoes. I was the goofy one who studied bassoon, did pratfalls, and loved to make her laugh. She taught me how to read when I was four and protected me like a lioness. "I have to go," I tell Leah, worried that I will miss a call with news of Dave. Leah is crying so hard, she cannot even say good-bye.

I check the messages again. There are four of them from worried friends, one from my parents. They cannot come until tomorrow. They live in Staten Island, and the Verrazano Bridge between there and Brooklyn is still closed.

The bright sun dips down past the buildings, casting long shadows in the yard, when Merri finally calls. "I tried to get down there. There were hundreds of Army trucks lining Houston blockading streets. It's like a war zone. They seemed to just pop out of nowhere. I got past the first blockade and then there was another one on Canal Street. They only let me through because I showed them my driver's license, proving my residency. You couldn't see a thing, there was so much smoke, so I went back to the firehouse around the corner from me on North Moore. You know, the 'Ghostbusters House.' The firefighter who answered the door said he knew Dave, that they trained together, and so I gave him your number. He said he'd call you if he saw Dave. He was going to check the triage center they set up at Stuyvesant Town. Maybe he just couldn't call because none of the cell phones are working. They all stopped when the antenna on top of the towers fell."

I pretend to agree and hang up, defeated, remembering the pact that

Dave and I made. Twenty minutes and he would have found a phone. I know the truth. I can feel it in the center of my cells and the core of my heart. Dave is dead. He was about halfway up the South Tower when he heard a crack, and died as quickly as a glance. Of course, I cannot prove any of this, but I know it is true as surely as I know my name. But for now, knowing and believing are two different things.

6:00 P.M.

I am smoking my last cigarette when I realize once more that no one from Dave's family has called. Dave, the second youngest, grew up in a small, cluttered Levitt house in Long Island, where his mother and two of his brothers still live. I dial the number and the ringing makes my heart race. There is always someone home. After three rings, my mother-in-law, Toni, answers, her voice shaky with age and a lifetime of disappointments.

"Toni, it's Marian," I say. I imagine her small blue eyes staring at the faded white rug in the living room.

"Hello, dear," she says, and I swallow, trying hard not to cry.

"Have you been watching the TV?" I ask, unable to control the panic in my voice.

"Yes, but I thought you and Dave were going out for your anniversary today," she says warily.

"He's there."

"Oh, dear."

A long silence passes and I sob, gasping for breath. I have never cried in front of Toni in the seventeen years I have known her, and I can tell she is uncomfortable.

"Try not to excite yourself, dear," she says, sounding as if she could cry, too, but she stops herself.

"It's not good, Toni," I whimper. "It doesn't look good at all."

"No, dear. You don't know yet." My jaw tightens. I wonder if her small hands, freckled with age, are shaking the way mine are. She always had trouble hiding that Dave was her favorite, the one who pursued art, who played rugby, who told her he loved her. I wish I could tell her that I know he is gone, how I felt the exact second my heart fractured, sending thousands of tiny fissures through its red center, but I can't.

"I should keep the line free," I tell her. "Just in case."

"I wish there was something I could do," she says, sounding helpless. "Is there anything I can do?"

"No. I'll call you if I hear anything."

"Please do, dear." Her voice is shaking with fear now. "I'll pray." Like my mother, she is a devout Catholic, with a gold Celtic cross adorning her neck. Her faith is so strong, once she even considered becoming a nun. I wipe my nose on my sleeve and hang up slowly.

8:00 P.M.

As evening falls, I become increasingly numb with shock and grief. Friends try to coax me to eat, and like a stubborn infant, I refuse. I sit hunched on the couch, trying to focus on one of the millions of thoughts that fill my head, sharp grains of sand in my skull. Cliff, Dave's lifeguard friend from Jones Beach, calls to say he'll come as soon as he can get a flight from California. He tells me about Tommy Denard and Billy Burke, other lifeguards and firefighter friends who are missing. I call Aidan at Caren's.

"Hi, Mama," he says, his voice scratchy from play. "Can I sleep over?"

"Sure, if you want to." Forcing myself to sound cheerful.

"Yeah, yeah!" he screams, and I can hear Caren's son Emmet jumping up and down in the background.

"He's fine," Caren says.

"Do you think he knows? I don't want him to see the television or anything . . ."

"No . . . No . . . I completely understand. They know something happened, but I don't think they know what." I thank her and hang up.

10:39 P.M.

The phone is ringing constantly now and Jason takes over answering, his voice weary with whispered excuses.

"She's okay. She just can't talk right now. Thank you for calling. I'll let you know as soon as we hear." It feels like everyone I have ever known from every corner of my life is calling. My neighbor Susan arrives with a white pot of soup and her doctor husband, Ben. Dave and I always called them "the perfect family" because they met at Harvard, are incredibly good-looking, and have three sweet and beautiful children. I taught two of them gymnastics, and Susan always arrived at the studio smiling. Dave and I marveled at her spirit, how she could stroll down 7th Avenue with a baby on her back, a toddler in a stroller, another child walking alongside her, and a dog, and never look overwhelmed or flustered.

Ben reaches into his coat pocket and retrieves four brown plastic prescription bottles and lines them up on the coffee table.

"You're going to need something to sleep. This is Valium. You know what that is," he says, pointing to the first bottle. "This is Restoril. It knocks you out, but you'll feel drowsy in the morning. Lorezepam is great, but if you've been drinking I wouldn't suggest it. Then there's Ambien. This has no drowsiness, gives you a nice five hours, but some people experience nightmares."

I raise my eyebrows and snort sardonically, grabbing the bottle of Ambien. "I'm living one," I tell him. Ben nods and I bite my lip, watching him kiss Susan good-bye before he leaves.

11:24 P.M.

Firefighter Tony Edwards and Lieutenant Dennis Farrell from Squad 1 arrive, looking fatigued and uncharacteristically official. I have imagined this day like the films about war that I have seen, the soldiers arriving at the wife's door. I pictured myself perplexed as to why the fire company has arrived. A captain steps forward, and it suddenly dawns on me why they are here. I clap my hand over my mouth. The captain announces that Dave died trying to save a child from a roaring blaze. I could see myself in vivid detail, crying out. I could feel the pain when I collapsed in the hall. I reenacted the rush of adrenaline in my chest, and I simulated the drop in my stomach. None of it even comes close to the sonic blast I feel right now.

The couch sinks under Tony's weight as he lowers himself next to me. Next to Dave, Tony is the largest guy in Squad. He cannot look at me, his small brown eyes bloodshot, his bunker gear covered with white dust. Lieutenant Farrell sighs and silently sits on the edge of my blue wingback chair. In contrast to Tony, Dennis is small and compact. His blond hair and dark tan make him look much younger than his fifty-three years.

My friends sit expectantly on the rug in front of Tony, like nursery schoolers waiting for story time.

"We didn't find any of the guys," Tony begins, wringing his big hands, his jaw clenching. "The whole company is missing. The rig was parked on West Street, but we don't know where they went. It's just un-believable. Nobody knows where anyone is. It took us hours just to fig-ure out who was even there. The place looked like the moon." He stops for a moment and rubs his eyes. I can't tell if he is crying or if he is try-ing to get the dust out. He sits up taller and continues. "I thought Mike Stackpole was missing, and then I turn around and he's there." Tony takes a breath, biting his lower lip. He looks so sad and angry, I am tempted to comfort him, but I stare at his profile instead, playing with the skin on my lower lip. "It's hard to explain what it's like."

"They have the roster there, don't they?" I ask, staring hard at the side of his head.

"Yeah, but some guys came from home or stayed from a change of tours."

"How many?"

Tony tightens his mouth. "Eleven or twelve."

"But . . . I don't understand. Even with the other rig, it's eight at the most, right?" I say indignantly, sure they got their numbers wrong. How could almost half the company be gone? Twelve men? My mind is blurry with names: Matt Garvey was working, Mike Esposito . . . who else? I try to see the list in my head. There are thirty of them altogether. I think of the names I highlighted in pink: Tommy Butler, the captain . . . what's his name? Twelve out of thirty men? How can that be? I can't think be-cause anger is welling up in me for the first time. I start to think that maybe Tony was late and didn't relieve Dave in time and that's why he's missing and Tony isn't. I want to punch Tony's biceps until they are red and swollen and I am too weak to punch again.

"I know, but it was the change of tours, you know, like Dave wasn't even workin', and there are guys who came from home—Eddie D'Atri came all the way from Staten Island, and Stephen Siller was halfway home, heard it on his scanner, and turned around—ya know."

"How many firefighters in all are missing?" I ask.

Tony turns to me for the first time, his face riddled with loss. The enormity of it all hits me full force in the stomach. I have only been thinking of myself, but there are others. Countless others. There are probably firefighters like Tony and Dennis all over the tristate area arriving in wives' homes at this very moment.

"We don't know how many, but there's a lot of rigs," Dennis says in a soft monotone.

"Ladders all twisted up and crushed like toys," Tony says, shaking his head. "There's like ten stories of rubble."

"We're gonna keep lookin'," Dennis says. "They can be in a void or somethin'."

"He could be alive?" I ask.

"We don't know that," Tony says. "It doesn't look good."

Tony sighs and patiently answers my friends' questions while I stare blankly at Dennis. He sits in the wingback chair saying nothing, his blue eyes mapped with sadness. I wonder if he is counting on his hands, as I am, the roster of men who are alive and dead, like a teacher taking attendance. Sean Cummins: here. Brian Bilcher . . . no answer. Gregory Fagan: here. Freddy Lawrence: here. Huey Lynch: here. Eric Lynch: here. Eddie D'Atri . . . no answer. Tommy Butler . . . no answer. William Speiss: here. Phil Solimeo: here. Jerry Smythe: here. Mike Stackpole: here. Timmy Rogers: here. Paul Stallone: here. Bobby West: here. Or perhaps Dennis is realizing for the first time that he is the only surviving lieutenant of Squad 1.

1:26 A.M.

When the questions are over, Tony stands and hugs me good-bye, lingering in the hall as if he wants to say more, but they have to drive to Staten Island to tell Sally Siller the same news. I head back into my living room and collapse on the couch, shaking and crying. Lori offers me a Valium from a plastic bag and I take it without a word. I quickly regret it, though, as my head begins spinning. My friends look on helplessly as I try to speak, but my words sound slurred and senseless. I close my eyes and watch strange shapes floating behind my eyelids, like a slide in a microscope.

"You are wasted!" Jason says, covering me with a blanket. I can feel my neighbor Lynn sitting next to me, rubbing my head and whispering "Shhhh" softly in my ear, but all I can do is watch the film of amoeba shapes floating by. I strain to hear the hushed voices of my friends as they leave one by one. I can hear Jason pulling the mattress off the top bunk of Aidan's bed, and sliding it into the living room to sleep on. I hear myself moaning as Jason leans over me, talking to me as if I were deaf. "Do you want to sleep in your own bed?" he yells, and I shake my head vigorously no. I can't imagine lying in the bed Dave and I shared, smelling his scent on the pillows and the sheets. I cannot think, so I keep staring at the lava lamp shapes until I fall into a dreamless sleep.

2:45 A.M.

My eyes pop open and I am filled with a dread so intense I sit up wide-eyed in the darkness. I see the towers falling everywhere, in the corner by the TV cabinet, the window filled with blue glass. Bricks and steel are shattering the door, the bookshelf, the French doors leading into Aidan's room. I pull my knees up to my chest and balance my pillow there. How did I get this pillow? I am trying to remember things. I bury my face into the cotton, the cool pillow catching my tears and muffling my sobs. Jason sits up from Aidan's mattress on the floor, groggy, and rubs the back of my head until I am calmer, my breathing returning to normal. Since I am too scared to sleep, Jason turns on the television to MTV. I doze off in short naps, like a newborn rising and crying every few hours, my mind vainly searching for some reprieve from the pain that echoes like a scream throughout the night.

2

The Void

September 12

7:18 A.M.

We finally give up on sleeping. Jason fixes eggs in my yellow kitchen with its cracked linoleum floor. I sit at the table, staring into my cup of coffee as if it could tell me what to do.

"Try to eat something," Jason pleads, watching me poke the eggs with a fork. I take a bite, holding the gelatinous egg in my mouth. I am stunned by the depth of my sadness. It seems to reach deep into my body like a cancer. Suddenly nauseated, I run into the bathroom and hang over the toilet, my stomach churning and lurching like a dryer full of heavy clothes.

"You okay?" Jason asks, standing in the doorway. "I guess my cooking needs a little work." I smirk, clutching my stomach with one hand.

"I just can't eat," I say, moving to the sink to brush my teeth.

"Of course not," he says, watching me. "Can I do anything?"

I silently shake my head no. "Maybe I'll go lie down."

"Will you be okay if I go home and get a change of clothes?" he asks, following me into the living room as I collapse back onto the couch, nodding yes.

"Are you sure?"

"Go. I'm fine," I insist. He leaves reluctantly, backing out of the room.

23

With Jason gone, the house rings with silence. I follow the crack in the plaster that runs like a fault line across the ceiling. In the corner of my eye, I notice the light flicker slightly and turn my head to stare at the frosted light fixture in the ceiling's center. "Is that you, Dave?" I ask, but the flickering suddenly stops. I head into the bathroom and turn the shower on, amazed at my body's ability to perform these mundane tasks. My muscles ease as the hot water pounds my shoulders, releasing a fresh flood of weeping. With no one there, I am unabashed in my crying. I wail out loud, the sounds primal and raw against my throat. I feel as though I could cry forever, becoming a Greek myth of a widow whose tears fill oceans and lakes. And then somehow I am standing alone on the cold tile floor, weak and dripping, but I have stopped.

10:48 A.M.

By the time Jason returns, the house is filled with friends. He takes coats and arranges food, serving as host for this makeshift shiva. At around eleven, my parents finally arrive, their faces desperate and swollen. My mother runs down the hall, her arms outstretched. She pulls me to her, her distinctive scent of shampoo and vanilla filling my nose, her short curly hair brushing my face.

"We were up all night," she says, her face round and younger-looking than her sixty-one years. She unfurls an African-print scarf from around her neck. "Dad couldn't stop crying." Her amber eyes fill with concern. "I've never seen him like this." She sighs, blowing her already red nose with a tissue from her pocket. My father enters, slumped and exhausted. He catches my eye for a moment and drops his head, his rounded shoulders bouncing as he cries, his fingers pressed on his eyes, as if he is trying to plug a leak. I have only seen my father cry twice in my life, for reasons I can't remember now. When my grandmother died last June, Dave and I were surprised that my father dutifully fulfilled his funeral duties without ever shedding a tear. As I watch him now, his feathery gray hair falling forward, I am relieved to see him express the depth of his feeling for Dave. I know that, like me, he is replaying the slide show of memories with his son-in-law: the countless wrestling matches, the whispered conversations on the back deck in the summer, the wood they chopped for fires, the vacations, weddings, the fights.

"Did you hear anything?" he asks, wiping his heavy lids with a tissue.

"I've been calling. I don't know anything yet." My lip quivers and my mother puts her hand on her mouth, her face twisting with grief.

"Where's Aidan?" she asks, swiping her hand through her coarse black hair.

"He slept over at a friend's. I have to go get him . . ." I am suddenly ashamed at how little I have thought of Aidan these last twenty-four hours.

"I'll go with you," my mother offers. On any other day, I would have said yes. I would walk with her as she spoke animatedly about a new painting, bragged about my brother, Luke, sighed at the painful lives of her clients, giggled at a funny comic she read in *The New Yorker,* complained about her aches from Lyme disease. All I want today is the steady silence of my father, and even though I know it will hurt her, I say, "I want to go with Dad."

11:15 A.M.

The sun outside is blinding and I am shocked that people are walking around, buying coffee, going to work. How dare the world continue when so many people are suffering? My father puts his long arm around me, and then he starts to cry again, his head in his hands.

"I'm sorry." His voice is scratchy and higher than usual. "I can't stop."

"No. It's good," I say, handing him a tissue. "This is fucking sad."

"Yeah, but we need to think about Aidan. What are you going to say?" he asks, and I stop to light a cigarette. Mercifully my dad says nothing about my new habit and instead reaches for the pack.

"Give me one of those," he says, taking my matches. Though he doesn't smoke either, he lights the cigarette and inhales tentatively.

"I'm going to tell him the truth," I decide as we turn onto 7th Avenue. I drop my head, not wanting to see anyone I know, not ready for the uncomfortable sadness between acquaintances.

"Okay," my dad says cautiously, his large eyes raised in thought. We both know what we say to Aidan is critical. Ironically, my parents are therapists and recently were trained in trauma therapy.

"How about I'll practice and you tell me if it's okay," I suggest. I sigh, trying to stop my chin from quivering. "Aidan, Daddy was in a big fire at the Twin Towers, and while he was saving people, the building fell down on him and he's either really hurt or—" My throat constricts and the tears come. I bury my face in my father's shirt, trying not to notice that his chest feels older and smaller than Dave's.

We turn onto the wide slate slabs of 3rd Street, one of the nicest streets in Park Slope. The corner fish store has turned a small gated tree into a shrine with a few dozen candles burning around it. On its trunk, a sign written hastily in marker reads: "For all the Missing."

"Missing. Dave is missing," I say out loud, grateful for a word to explain the unexplainable.

"That's good. You just want to reassure Aidan that he is safe and we're all here. You know what to do," Dad says as we climb the steps to Caren's apartment.

Caren is new to Park Slope, a screenwriter who recently moved here from Los Angeles with her son and his father. "Sweetie," she says, hugging me. I squeeze gently back. "I can't believe this." I introduce my father and we follow her up the steep steps to her loft apartment. "Nice way to start the school year," she says, shaking her head. Her son is a year older than Aidan. With his olive skin and straight hair, he's a dead ringer for Mowgli from *The Jungle Book*. I am winded when we reach the top of the steps and Aidan leaps toward me.

"Mama!" he yells, jumping into my arms. He is tall for his five years—over four feet—and I wobble, trying to hoist his nearly sixty pounds.

"Look who's here!" I say with forced excitement.

"*Ira!*" Aidan yells, noticing my dad, who is struggling, as I am, to stay composed. He has never called my father Grandpa, but rather imitates my mother yelling up the stair "IRAA!"

Emmet leaps from the stair landing and screeches to a stop in front of us.

"We saw the towers fall down from the roof!" Emmet proclaims. I remember that Caren has a clear view of the skyline from her deck. Caren grimaces and shakes her head no at Emmet.

"I didn't let them up there," Caren assures me, rolling her eyes at her son.

"Your daddy is the—"

"Emmet! Enough!" Caren scolds. Thankfully, he stops.

"We better go," I say, fighting a strong urge to kick Emmet. How much has he told Aidan?

"If there's anything I can do . . ." Caren offers.

Out on the street, Aidan bounces like Tigger in front of us. Unable to wait any longer, I squat down in front of him.

"Aidan, I have to tell you something really terrible." His huge eyes are so brown they look like the stars and earth combined. "Do you know what happened to the Twin Towers?" I ask, tears sticking like chicken bones in my throat as I silently ask Dave, wherever he is, to make me strong.

"At school they said a plane crashed into the tower and there was a fire," Aidan says without looking up. He is kicking a raised piece of sidewalk with his shoe.

"That's right, and Daddy was there putting out the fire and saving people when the building fell down on him."

Aidan keeps staring at the sidewalk, kicking it harder and a little faster. "Well, he could just push the bricks off of him and get up." Aidan's small shoulders shrug as if it were as simple as tying a shoe.

"I don't think so," my father says, barely audible.

"Daddy's friends are looking for him, and when they find him," I say, gulping hard, "he will probably be dead or he will have really big boo-boos."

Aidan looks at me skeptically. "I think Daddy will push off the bricks and stand up," he says with certainty.

"Daddy won't be standing up." I am weakening with each word.

"But we're going to be okay. We're all going to take care of you and make sure you're safe," my dad says helpfully. I wish that I were still young and believed all the things my father told me. With red, swollen eyes, my father looks tired. He is handsome and fit for his sixty-five years, still taking on men half his age in full-court games of basketball, but in moments like these, I think about him dying, too. I had imagined Dave holding me at my father's funeral, the way he did at my grandmother's, and I shudder at the thought of suffering such profound losses alone.

11:43 A.M.

Aidan runs down the hall, stopping when he enters the living room, which is full of people. No one is crying, but he can sense grief everywhere. From the couch, my mother reaches out her arms, and Aidan gives her a hug while I sit wearily next to them.

"Why are you crying?" Aidan asks my mother.

"I'm sad about your daddy," she says simply. Aidan runs into his bedroom, reappearing with an armload of stuffed animals from his bed. He works his way around the room, carefully placing one in each person's lap. "It will make you happy," he says.

"You don't have to make us feel better, Aidan," I say, the tears involuntarily falling. "We're just sad."

"But they're going to find Daddy," he insists, climbing behind me on the couch and burying his face under a pillow. His feet, wide like his father's, stick out from under the pillow and I squeeze them in my hands. Everyone is crying and I can feel Aidan wedging himself deep into the couch as far as he can go. I wish I could join him in his escape, that we could flee together. I imagine driving the familiar highways to Jones Beach State Park, where Dave was a lifeguard for thirteen years, roaring through the Field 6 parking lot and across the sandy beach into the ocean. Blue-gray waves pressing on the windshield, tiny bubbles swirling up . . . I can hear the gurgling as the ocean's salty power bursts the glass, filling my lungs with water, and we float up, up and away.

3:22 P.M.

I sit on the front stoop alone. As I light my cigarette, the deafening sound of helicopters passes over. Army helicopters are heading toward Manhattan, their bellies like great whales swimming over us. Kevin, my landlord, opens his creaky red door and joins me on the stoop.

"How are you doing?" he asks, his voice a monotone and depressed. Dave and I nicknamed him Eeyore when we moved in ten years ago.

"I'm hoping he's okay," I say unconvincingly. We sit in silence until I wave the cigarette toward him. "I'm waiting for him to yell at me about the cigarettes."

Kevin forces a tired smile. "I saw the whole thing from my office," he says. I had forgotten he works in the city right next door to the towers. "We saw the first plane and I left, ran across the Brooklyn Bridge with all of these people," he mumbles.

The silence passes like seasons between us until, out of the corner of my eye, I spot Leah driving the van she borrowed to go to Maine. My heart leaps and I stand up, peering over the stairs.

"Well, let us know if you need anything," Kevin says, standing and walking back up the steps.

"Thanks," I say absently as I run to greet my sister. "Leah!" She flies out of the driver's seat toward me. We stand on the sidewalk hugging and crying, her arms like a lifeline around me.

"I'm so glad you're here!" I snivel. My big sister, my best friend, my Irish twin is here, and for the first time since the towers fell, I think I might be okay.

"Oh my God, Marian," Leah cries in disbelief. "I just wanted to be here so badly. I got a flat tire, they wouldn't let me over the bridge. My hands were gripping the steering wheel so hard, look at them!" She opens her hands; white bumps make an even pattern across her palm.

I help her with her bulky red suitcase. We head into the living room, where friends rise to greet her. Jason takes the keys to find a parking space for the van.

"Where's my boy?" my sister asks. I watch Leah squeeze Aidan, her chin wrinkling the same way mine does before I cry. I can tell she is overwhelmed by the number of people in my apartment, so I pull her into the kitchen and pour two tall glasses of whiskey, and we head outside. In the backyard, people are clustered in every corner. I watch Leah's elegant dancer neck stretching to kiss old friends. If Dave were here, this would be a wonderful party. I can see him sitting with one leg folded over his knee, sweat socks and hiking boots, his dimpled smile. I can see him so clearly that I delude myself into thinking nothing has happened, that this is a party after all. When Leah is finished greeting everyone, she finds a rickety plastic chair and faces me.

"Have you heard anything?" she asks.

"Nothing. It's been torturous." A fresh bout of sobbing begins, pressing against my ribs, the tears drenching my lap. Leah cries with me, her hand making circles on my back as we ride the wave together. When our eyes finally meet, I can't help but burst out laughing at the bizarre duet our crying makes. We sound exactly the same. Leah laughs, too, until we catch our breath, grateful for a reprieve, the eye in the storm.

5:15 P.M.

Dave's youngest brother, Ed, arrives. He has less hair than Dave and a rounder face, but his stature and mannerisms are eerily familiar. I hug him hard, savoring the feel of my head on strong, square shoulders. Ed is a science teacher at a high school in Huntington, Long Island, and I wonder then if he was teaching a class when the towers fell. I lift my head, apologizing for soaking his T-shirt, and squeeze the corners of my eyes until I see white spots. I greet Ed's wife, Romi, kissing her on a cheek that tastes salty from crying.

"I'm so sorry," she says, her tiny mouth frowning and her eyes filling with tears.

Dave had introduced Ed to Romi at the Bein' Neon shop where Dave worked after graduating college. Dave welded the boxes to display Romi's neon signs, which she made by bending hot tubes of glass. Dave got Ed a job installing the neon in the windows of local shops, and Ed soon fell in love and married Romi.

On Christmas Day in 1987, Dave covered my eyes and led me into the small bedroom at the back of the house where I grew up. I was home from college at Sarah Lawrence, where I had just transferred from C. W. Post. I heard a buzz and a hiss and could see a shining red light through Dave's long fingers. When he took his hands away, I saw the box Dave had welded. Romi had bent the glass tube to form my name, and surrounding my name was a bright crimson heart that glowed like the end of a fire.

"Hi, Aunt Marian," Martina says, jarring me from my memory. She is my ten-year-old niece, who inherited Ed's small lips and Romi's pointed chin. I spent most holidays on the floor with Martina dressing Barbies or teaching her cartwheels. Children and I have always gravitated toward each other in our mutual appreciation for silliness, and Martina has always been my favorite.

"I'm glad you're here," I say, tousling Martina's hair as she hugs me. Aidan squeals when he sees her, and she joins him in his room, carrying a glittery box of tattoos and nail polish.

"Have you heard anything?" Ed asks. I shake my head no. "I don't know," he says, looking grim. "I've been thinking about it all night, and I really think Dave could be okay."

"I don't know, Ed. I just don't think so." I bite my lip so I won't cry.

"Well, you do what you need to do, but I just have this feeling he's okay."

The stations in my head turn back on, and I am filled with doubt and confusion. What kind of wife am I? How could I give up on Dave so soon? A good wife would grab on to hope like a newborn to a finger and never, ever let go.

"I gotta get out of here." I'm overwhelmed once again by the people arriving, their whispered tones. "I'm going to the firehouse."

"Do you want to go alone?" he asks. I shake my head.

5:43 P.M.

My quaint neighborhood of Park Slope now looks alien and strange. Every shop window on 7th Avenue displays flags and signs for the injured and missing. All of the newsstands are covered with photos of the burning towers, and on Carroll Street, a heavyset woman in a folding chair is collecting money in a coffee can for Squad 1. Old First Church, whose mahogany doors remain closed except on Sundays, now has its doors flung open and covered in white paper where people are writing messages to the missing.

"I can't stop thinking of this one summer," Ed begins, and I picture Jones Beach. I used to lie on my stomach and, with one eye, watch Dave's silhouette in the high white lifeguard chair. While the other guards leaned back and chatted, Dave sat up, perched like an eagle, squinting at the water, waiting for something to happen.

"This asshole Charlie was our bosun that year," Ed continues. "Charlie didn't answer something Dave asked, and so Dave asked again. This guy was such a jerk, he turns around, sticks his finger in Dave's face, and yells, 'You know what your problem is, Fontana? You repeat yourself!' " Ed stops, smiling to himself. "For the rest of the day, for seven and a half hours, Dave chanted, 'Stop repeating yourself. Stop repeating yourself. Stop repeating yourself.' I couldn't believe how long he kept it up. Charlie was pulling his hair out." Ed's face suddenly turns somber. "I just can't stop thinking about that and how I know Dave wouldn't give up." He chokes back his tears until they sound like a hiccup. Ed is right. Dave is so strong he could be somewhere fighting to stay alive.

Ed struggles to keep up as I quicken my steps to the firehouse, hoping for some news. Turning onto Union Street, I stop in my tracks. "Oh my God."

A huge crowd is lingering in front of Squad 1, a narrow three-story brick building pressed between a Japanese restaurant and a food co-op. We approach slowly, gazing at hundreds of tall white vigil candles flickering on either side of the fire-engine-red door. From the ornate cornice on the second floor, purple and black bunting hangs, the markings of a firehouse that has lost its own. I spot two teenagers in tight skirts carrying bouquets of flowers. They squeeze them into the white Spackle buckets already teeming with bouquets in their clear plastic wrappers. A procession of solemn faces moves slowly, as if in a museum, reading signs, writing messages, stopping and straining to see something just inside the door. As we near the entrance, I recognize neighbors: the woman from the yoga studio, the parents of children I taught, the man who works at La Bagel Delight. I keep my head lowered and the crowd instinctively opens a path, letting Ed and me through. The wide engine door is up and the apparatus floor looks so empty, I feel as if I am standing at the bottom of a drained pool. There are no trucks, no bunker boots standing ready, no Technical Response Vehicle, no tools—only the cold cement floor cracked and stained with diesel fuel.

I scan the house watch, a small booth in front where firefighters take turns listening to the radio. No one is sitting at the desk or on the bench. The television mounted in the corner is tuned to CNN, where the death toll at the Trade Center scrolls at the bottom of the screen. Two red phones are ringing. I walk across the room, to the opposite wall, where a chalkboard lists the names of the men who were working: Esposito, Garvey, Bilcher, Butler, Carroll. Next to the board, an easel stands, with twelve eight-by-ten photos of the missing firefighters taped in neat rows onto white poster board. The head shots are from a group photograph taken at a fire that year. The men's names—Peter Carroll, Tommy Butler, Jim Amato, Robert Cordice, Brian Bilcher, Mike Esposito, Mike Russo, Eddie D'Atri, Stephen Siller, Matt Garvey, Gary Box, Dave Fontana—are written under each photo. Seeing Dave's name makes my stomach lurch, as if I am falling. *Dave Fontana. Dave, what are you doing up there? How can that be? You were supposed to come home. You said you would be careful. You* promised.

I can feel the crowd outside looking in, watching me, pitying me, imagining how they'd feel if their husband or son or father were gone. I can only hear muffled sniffles and muted cries because I have been dipped in Novocain. Ed puts his arm around me protectively and leads me past a folding table in front of the firehouse, where neighbors are dropping money and checks into a giant glass jar.

At the back of the firehouse, a door leads us into a modest living area where faded brown cushions rest on wooden platforms. Another TV sits on a high shelf in the corner, and there is an overstuffed recliner by a phone that is still ringing. About five firefighters whom I don't recognize stand when I enter, as if I am a visiting dignitary, and offer me drinks and coffee. They quickly explain that they are firefighters long retired who have returned to Squad to help man phones and collect donations. They offer their condolences, tell me the firefighters are sleeping upstairs; others are at the site taking turns and, like me, waiting for some news.

The living area opens up into a cramped kitchen where hundreds of boxes of pies, cookies, cooked food, and letters are strewn on a wooden table.

"Help yourself," a black man with a deep voice and basset-hound eyes tells me. "I'm George by the way. I worked here in the late seventies."

I imagine what it was like for him, probably the only black man in the company, civil rights still fresh in everyone's mind. Dave was always reading about history, and I remember him telling me about the riots in New York following Dr. Martin Luther King's assassination on April 4, 1968. Gangs of teenagers in Harlem and Brooklyn took to the streets, throwing rocks and bottles at responding firefighters. Arsonists set sixty fires, and firefighters were jeered and attacked as they responded to calls. The following year fire trucks were redesigned with crew cabs that allowed firefighters to ride safely inside.

"Someone was injured or died for every piece of equipment we have," Dave told me when, in 1994, he finally got the bunker gear they had been testing for months. It took thousands of burns, the deaths of three firefighters on March 14, 1994, and a lawsuit by one of the widows before Mayor Giuliani and Commissioner Safir finally issued protective bunker gear to the Fire Department.

I am relieved to see Joey O'Donnell, who enters looking weary, his eyes a fiery red. He just took a short nap and will head back to the site as soon as everyone else wakes up. He is a tall burly Irishman with a freckled face, a Santa Claus stomach, and cropped red hair.

"Is there any news?" I ask, watching him take a Scooter Pie from a shelf.

"We got a lot of our guys down there lookin'. As soon as we know anything, Marian, we'll let you know." He shoves the pie in his mouth and throws the wrapper in the garbage, taking another pie. "You want one?" he offers, the box in his hands.

"How can you eat that with all this homemade stuff here?" I gesture to cakes wrapped in tinfoil and cookies sitting everywhere on paper plates.

"They're my favorite," he says, and I notice how much his face changes when he smiles. He looks like his son Gerard, one of the three freckled-faced redheads he has at home. His wife, Deirdre, is expecting their fourth soon. "You sure you don't want anything?"

"No, thanks," I say, putting my hand on my stomach. "Unless you have Scotch."

"I don't drink, but somebody must have some," he says, pointing to the lockers outside. I nod, noticing my hands shaking again.

I sit on the edge of the brown cushions and sip a paper cup of whiskey that burns like hot soup, and light a cigarette. With each sip, I try to comprehend the loss. Twelve men. I go through the names again. I didn't know Matt Garvey and Robert Cordice. They must be new, or maybe on a detail. I think of the men I do know: Tommy Butler, Mike Russo, Eddie D'Atri, Peter Carroll, Mike Esposito especially. Out of all the men missing, I know him best. He and his wife, Denise, used to attend my comedy shows. I remember how eerie it was to call Denise yesterday, how she acted as if everything were fine, even though it had been almost six hours since the towers fell. "Marian! C'mon! It's Mike we're talking about. They're probably at a bar somewhere having a few beers." She laughed. I think of Peter Carroll, who was supposed to come over and paint our apartment in a few weeks, and Gary Box, who cut Dave's hair. Stephen Siller, whom I met at the picnic a few weeks ago with his five wide-eyed kids. Five kids? Oh my God. Could that be? What about Mike Russo? He just had a baby, too, didn't he? And Tommy just went to his son's christening. Dave had covered his shift. I gulp down the whiskey, staring at the photos lining the wall. The photos are mostly black-and-whites of fires Squad has been to. I have seen them many times, but there is one photograph that has always fascinated me. It is of a fireman climbing down a ladder, carrying a child who is limp and lifeless.

"Did that kid make it?" I ask George, pointing to the picture above Ed's head.

"I dunno," George answers, shrugging, and the other men shake their heads, unknowing.

"I always wanted to know," I say, taking a drag of my cigarette. In my peripheral vision I can see them all exchanging concerned looks, but I keep staring at the baby, limp and lifeless in the firefighter's arms.

7:10 P.M.

Joe, Ed, and I climb the steep steps to the top floor of the firehouse where the lockers are. Like so many city buildings, the room is dimly lit and the walls are painted an industrial green. Dark wood lockers line each wall, and gym equipment and weights sit at the far end.

"It's a mess. We just haven't been here," Joe says apologetically, picking up shirts along the way. Each locker door is decorated with postcards, pictures, porn, and bumper stickers. We stop at Dave's, in the middle on the right; it has nothing but a postcard of Jones Beach on the door. Joe reaches in and pulls a string. A bare bulb illuminates Dave's locker, which is the size of a walk-in closet. Pictures of Aidan and me line the door, and an Irish flag hangs under a mirror. A low bookshelf stands on the back wall with study books from his lieutenant's test lined neatly along them. On the top of each bookshelf are coffee cans full of change sorted by coin type. I smile, remembering how much Dave loved change and often rifled through my pockets to find some. What I viewed as the crumbs of disappearing dollars, Dave saw as college funds, possible vacations, and our dream house. I take his denim coat off the hanger and pull it around me, engulfing myself in his musky smell. It is large, like a blanket, with "Squad 1" embroidered in thick yellow letters on the back. Looking down, I notice Dave's shorts on the floor, the pair he wore on the last day I saw him, the morning he kissed me good-bye. They sit in a heap, an imprint of the moments before the call came in. It reminds me of our trip to Pompeii, where all the small moments in life are frozen in the ash. Inside one pocket, I find his old brown wallet, and my heart leaps when, in the other, I feel the chunky circle of his wedding ring. He never wore it at fires for fear it would get caught or melt in the heat. It is simple and solid, a thick shining band with THIS AND MY HEART etched deep into its silver.

7:48 P.M.

At home, I make a shrine to Dave on top of the entertainment cabinet using the ring and Irish flag from his locker, candles, rosary beads, and a black-and-white photo of Dave and me smiling in our backyard. We used the photo on our wedding invitation that read "At Last" in curly letters at the top. Dave and I dated for ten years, and "At Last" was a joke to my eighty-three-year-old Jewish grandmother, who constantly cried, "When is my boyfriend going to marry my gorgeous granddaughter?"

The house is packed with people, and Aidan is weaving through the crowd in a hyperactive tizzy. My friend Sal, whom I have not seen in over five years, arrives carrying ten trays of Italian food from a specialty shop on Long Island. A local restaurant where my friend is the manager sends over three more trays of lamb-stuffed ravioli, porcini risotto, and crab cakes. Ladder 122, the firehouse on nearby 11th Street, where Dave used to work, arrives with a glazed ham big enough for a small army. By seven o'clock, there is so much food, my father and Ed bring an extra table up from the basement. My friends and family *ooh* and *ah* at the spread, which makes my wedding banquet look like a snack, and I shake my head at the sad irony that I still cannot even eat. I have always loved food. After Dave and I traveled in Europe, he remembered the museums, churches, and architecture. I remembered the escargots in Brussels, that tiny café in Venice where they served the best gnocchi. I ate so much on that trip that by the time we landed in Capri, my thighs were scraping together. Now everything I force into my mouth tastes like stale bread. So, I sit in my backyard and smoke and drink and wait and wait and wait.

3

Awaiting

September 13

8:15 A.M.

I wake up early from an Ambien-induced coma. A secretary from Aidan's school calls, suggesting I continue to bring Aidan in "to give him a sense of normalcy." I chuckle bitterly at the thought. How can I make his life normal again? How can I leave him alone in a room full of strangers when I don't even know where his father is?

Aidan is hanging off his bed, snoring loudly. He hasn't been able to fall asleep until almost midnight the past two nights. People have to walk through his room to get their coats from my bed, and even with the French doors closed, he can hear everything through the one broken pane that Dave meant to fix. I am worried that someone will talk about the violence, the falling people, the ash. How will I protect him from it all?

Ed and Romi are sleeping in my room, Martina is on Aidan's top bunk, and I am sleeping on the couch. Leah has gone home to her apartment on the Upper East Side to drop off her luggage. She has been gone most of August, subletting her apartment to ballet dancers who train at the school where she teaches.

I feel as if I have bricks strapped to my eyelids as I try to rouse Aidan. I rub my hand across his sweaty head and stare at his ear, perfect small

38

paths of cartilage. I whisper "Time to get up" into it so softly that he only flutters his eyes and rolls over. I hate waking him and envy his vacation into the unconscious, where all is safe. The school had called again, urging me to bring Aidan in. "The longer you wait, the harder it will be," they said. Ed, who is already dressed and showered, shakes Aidan gently, saying "C'mon, buddy." I have asked him to help me take Aidan to school.

I lead Aidan into his warm classroom where the varnish is almost rubbed off his wooden seat by the door. I bring him his book bin, but Aidan is more interested in two classmates who are clinging to their parents' legs like barnacles.

"I'm going to do that when you leave," he announces.

"I have to go either way," I say, trying to sound stern, but I am unconvincing.

Aidan's teacher, a mousy woman with a gray bowl haircut, skitters over. "I am so sorry," she says, averting her eyes. "This is so terrible. I just saw your husband three days ago! I can't believe it! A little boy lost his mom in a car crash last year." She shakes her head, her eyes darting around the room. "I can't believe I have another one."

"Oh" is all I can muster with Aidan tugging at my jacket, wanting me to read to him.

I squat down beside Aidan and read a book about bats and how the mothers give birth to their babies upside down. They have to catch the babies quickly or the poor creatures fall, crashing to the earth below.

My thighs are burning when I finally stand up and kiss Aidan gently on the head. "I have to go now."

"You won't come back, like Daddy," he insists, his lower lip sticking out like a speed bump on his tiny face.

"I promise," I say softly, my voice unsteady. "I promise I will." Walking out of the classroom's back door, I feel tears knocking persistently on the back of my eyelids. I don't know if I am doing the right thing bringing him here, but I know he can't stay home with the endless stream of people arriving.

"NOOO!" Aidan screams, chasing me into the blinding sun of the playground.

"Aidan, you cannot leave the building!" I insist, and Ed heads over to help.

"Martina will be there when you get home, and we'll make some popcorn," Ed promises, coaxing Aidan back into the room. I find it as difficult as Aidan to walk away, his wet marble eyes looking back like magnets. I stare at the closed door until it is blurry and my tears fall with a blink.

Ed exits and shuts the door, his forehead beaded with sweat. I try to peek into the window, but the gates block my view. Cupping my hands around my eyes, I press against the window. Aidan spies me and lunges for the gate, climbing and squealing like a trapped animal.

"MOMMY!" he screams, tears spilling from his eyes. I feel Ed's hands on my shoulders as he guides me away from the window.

"I should take him home," I say, sobbing. "This isn't right."

"He'll be okay," Ed murmurs soothingly.

"I need to check on him." I march toward the front door where Mary, a large black security guard, sits. She is notoriously mean, with a watch-dog face set in a permanent scowl.

"My name is Marian." My voice quivers. "My husband is missing at the World—"

"Sign in," she snarls without looking up.

"I just have to check on my son. He just lost his fath—"

"You have to get a pass from the office," she says. I stand stunned and silent, anger rising like a tide in my chest. I look behind the desk, where the crossing guards avert their eyes. Mary is their friend and they spend their downtime gossiping together at the desk. I look over at Ed, who, like Dave, does not like confrontation. I sigh audibly, sign my name quickly, and start toward the office.

"You didn't put the time in," Mary calls after me.

I whip my head around. "Give me a fucking break!" I snap. The crossing guards shake their heads, clucking their tongues.

"Ooh! She cursed at you!" one of them says to Mary as Ed lumbers back to placate them. My face feels like I've stepped into a sauna when I emerge from the office with my pass.

"She's just upset. I'm sure you can understand . . ." I hear Ed say as I storm past them toward Aidan's classroom.

Looking into the rectangular glass window, I spot Aidan sitting on a rug. He has stopped crying now but is in constant motion, his legs and mouth moving like a silent film. A round-cheeked boy with loose blond curls giggles at Aidan, who collapses back, trying hard to make him laugh. Ed sidles up behind me. Without the energy to walk past the guard again, we slip out the back door into the warm sun.

We cross the street to Connecticut Muffin, where a long line twists out of the door. I notice Tommy is behind the counter, pouring coffee in his deliberate, steady rhythm. I have not seen him since the eleventh. When our eyes meet, he quickly turns away. Why is he avoiding me? In an unspoken challenge, I stare him down as he toasts bagels and takes money, carefully steering clear of my gaze. When it is finally my turn, he escapes into the back so I have to order my coffee from George, who smiles and tells me in his thick Spanish accent how sorry he is.

9:32 A.M.

Ed and I pass Old First Church again, where more white paper is stretched across the doors. As I pass, my eyes land on large red letters that read, "Five Rescue Workers Saved!" Why hadn't Squad told me that when I called? I reach for my cell to dial the Squad but stop suddenly. I squeeze Ed's hand and continue up the steps to pray that Dave is among them.

The church is less ornate than the Roman Catholic ones I am used to, but it is beautiful nonetheless, with long wooden pews and simple carvings. A low, melancholy hymn is playing, and I realize I have not heard music since the eleventh. We slide into a pew in the back, and Ed and I sit in silence. To escape the mayhem at home, Ed and I take walks, dropping to our knees in every church we pass, regardless of the faith or sect. Even though Ed claims to be agnostic, I know he is praying as hard as I am that Dave is okay. I drop my head.

I have always been grateful for all you have given me. I've thanked you many times for sending me Dave and then Aidan. I have always been blessed by you and I have thanked you often, haven't I? Doesn't that count for something? Maybe I have been selfish. Maybe I have not given back enough. I don't know why this is happening, but I am begging you to spare Dave. I will do anything to have him back. I will pray every day, go to mass again. I will stop cursing. I will be generous and won't lie, send thank-you notes on time. I will try not to get annoyed at my mother. I'll give all my clothes away and I will apologize more often, be more patient and take nothing for granted. I'll drink less and pay bills on time. I will volunteer, be less vain, not talk about people, and I will never worry about money again. I will do this and more, whatever you ask, just please . . . PLEASE . . . make Dave among the five who were rescued today. I can't live without him. I can't live with my heart like this. . . . Please. Thank you for listening. I know you are busy. People begin to stand and say their prayers out loud. In our pew, a young woman with thick brown hair tied in a loose braid stands.

"I pray that my sister's boyfriend from Cantor is okay."

There is silence and a man stands. "I work at Euro Brokers and was home sick on Tuesday. I pray for all my friends."

Another silence. A businessman stands up. His face is ragged and his voice shaky. "I am one of the engineers of the Twin Towers. When I saw the damage, I knew it could collapse. I tried to call but I couldn't get through." He sits back down, and Ed and I watch as he drops his head, weeping into his hands.

After each person, I consider standing up. If there is strength in numbers, then I want everything Dave can get, but a tall woman with a flat, wrinkled face and large gray curls stands instead. "I pray for all the pets who are waiting for their owners to return."

10:00 A.M.

An old rig is backing into the firehouse when we arrive, and Lieutenant Farrell is the first one to jump off the truck.

"It wasn't anybody," Dennis says glumly when I ask about the saved rescue workers. He looks even more tired than that first night at my house. "There were a couple of guys that were searchin' and some stuff fell on 'em, and they were trapped for a couple of hours. The press is fucked up for getting your hopes up like dat. I dunno what to tell ya. I don't know what to tell any of my guys," he adds miserably. "I gotta go home. I haven't been home at all." Dennis Farrell lives in Rockaway and makes surfboards on the side.

Sean Cummins, a cross-eyed Irishman with a sharp wit and a body like a pit bull's, avoids me when he jumps off the truck. Squad has just returned from a twelve-hour shift at Ground Zero, and I can smell the pungent smoke from the fires that continue to burn like the earth turning itself inside out. I watch the men silently remove their thick Carhartt pants, the color of butterscotch, and toss them into a Hazardous Materials bag.

"Any news?" I ask Sean, whose grizzled face is set in an uncharacteristic grimace.

"We found Petey Carroll today," he says softly, and I know from the silence it is bad. I picture Peter's handsome face covered in ash and blood.

"Where was he?" I ask, hopeful and terrified.

"He was near the rig," he answers in a lilting brogue. "He didn't get far, about twenty feet. He was the chauffeur, so he was probably the last one off the truck." I imagine Peter driving the truck through the tunnel, the lights blaring, the horn honking.

Sean reaches up on top of a shelf and retrieves a half-empty bottle of Jim Beam. "Have you met my good friend Jim?" he asks, taking a swig.

"Actually, I borrowed some yesterday. . . . Does Toni-Ann know?" I ask, referring to Peter Carroll's new wife.

He shrugs. "I know Connor O'Brian was trying to find all his kids. I think he was married three times. Said it was like a treasure hunt tracking them down." I shake my head. "Two of the guys went out to tell her. I know I can't do it. I can't even look at you girls." I know seeing me squeezes his heart, reminding him of his own family.

"Do you think they'll find more guys?" Ed asks.

For a moment Sean's eyes stop and he looks as if he could cry. "I don't know what to tell ya. There are these big voids. I was down in this huge hole, and I was digging and looking, and if the bastards just let me stay down there another minute—maybe . . ."

"You got to be careful," I say, but secretly I am glad Sean is working so hard. A former Navy SEAL, he is indefatigable and determined.

"I just keep thinking we're going to find them all down there in one of those restaurants, you know, eating and drinking, and they'll just be like 'Hey, guys, what took you so long?' " This time tears fill his eyes and he excuses himself, saying he has to take a shower.

I meet Lee Amato, a handsome, short man with eyes so large they look like they have makeup on them. He has been at the site with the Squad guys, looking for his brother, Jim, the captain from Squad who is missing. Dave had mentioned the captain a few times, how he was a Jehovah's Witness and had a bunch of beautiful kids. Ed talks to Lee and I head into the back room, where Billy Spiess is on the phone rolling his eyes and dragging on a cigarette. Perpetually cranky, Billy was dubbed "Misera-Bill" by the firemen of Squad. He has become the unofficial firehouse manager, handling phone calls, donations, and the influx of food and gifts. He slams the phone down, his forearms thick and muscular.

"Aw, Jesus. I can't take this shit," he says, smashing out his cigarette. "That was Princess." "Princess" is the fiancée of Lieutenant Eddie D'Atri, one of the missing firefighters. Eddie resembles GI Joe with a wide Cheshire smile. He was long separated from his wife and planning a divorce. On September 11, Eddie heard about the towers and drove in from Staten Island to help, despite Princess's pleas to stay with her in bed.

Billy lights another cigarette and runs a hand across what is left of his hair. "I got Lynda, the wife, calling me, and I'm like, 'I don't know nothing.' "

"Wait," I say, confused. "Isn't Princess named Linda, too?"

"Yeah, that's why Eddie called his fiancée Princess." I raise my eyebrow as the phone rings again.

Billy rolls his eyes and picks it up. "Yeah. He's here. HUEY! Outside, phone!" he yells out of the door.

"So anyway," Billy continues, dragging hard on his cigarette. "Lynda, the wife, is going over there to take Eddie's van and his wallet and shit like that. Princess is upset. She wants us to come help her." The phone rings again and Billy looks as if he is going to scream.

"Hey, Princess," he says, trying not to sound annoyed. I signal Billy to let me talk to her. He hands me the phone gratefully.

"Hey, Linda," I say softly. "You okay?"

"No! She's on her way over here to take his stuff!" Her voice is squeaky and tired. "I don't want his money, but all of a sudden she's interested? I mean, they have been separated for over seven years! She's got a boyfriend. What do I have?"

"Give me her number," I say. "I'll see what I can do." I signal Billy to give me a pen and I write the wife's number on a memo pad.

"I don't know what the hell I'm doing," I announce to Billy as I dial. The phone rings and a voice with a thick Staten Island accent answers.

"Lynda?" I ask.

"Who's this?"

"It's Marian Fontana. Dave's wife."

"How are you?" This question stumps me. I stare as if she has just asked me to explain quantum physics.

"Shitty," I answer finally. "This waiting is really hard." A long silence ensues. "Listen, I've been talking to the other wives, and we've decided to just sit tight right now, you know, not do anything until we hear something."

"Okay," she answers slowly.

"So I was thinking that maybe you can hold off on getting Eddie's stuff for now 'cause it's just too soon?" This silence is longer than the first one.

Finally, she says, "Fine." Billy sighs as I say my good-byes and hang up.

"Thanks, Marian. What the hell am I supposed to do? It's been nuts. This place is crazy. I mean, look at this shit!" Every corner of the small back room is piled high with drawings and notes from kids. The shelf that divides the kitchen and sitting area is jammed with cookies, fruit baskets, and cakes. On the reclining chair, a clear Hefty bag full of teddy bears sits.

"I got something for ya." Billy disappears upstairs as Paul Stallone enters and hugs me hard. He is a born-again Christian with a face so sincere his eyebrows look like two sides of an isosceles triangle.

"Keep the faith," he tells me.

I shake my head. "I think it's stupid to have hope," I confess.

"No. You have to. There are big voids down there," he says confidently. The other men in the kitchen roll their eyes and shake their heads as Paul hugs me again, even harder.

"Jesus Christ. Enough with the freakin' hugs," Billy snaps, entering again. The men are always teasing Paul, who was raised on a tiny island in Italy where hugging was as common as pasta.

"I can't help it," he says, smiling shyly.

Billy hands me a cell phone. "Verizon donated these so we can get in touch with you easily if we hear anything."

"I have one already," I say.

"I know, but they need to have everyone's numbers in case we have to get you right away," he says, pushing up his sleeves. He has dark skin and thick hair covering his body. "We're making up a list of everybody's numbers, but I haven't gotten to it yet."

"A bat phone," I joke, sliding the cell into my pocket as Mike Stackpole enters, his face puffy and sad. His brother, Tim, a captain in 103, is one of the missing firefighters. Tim had fought hard to get back on the job after he was severely burned in a fire in 1998. I can still recall Tim in his wheelchair, posing with Mayor Giuliani after countless painful skin grafts and physical therapy. Tim made it back to the job in June 2001 and was promoted to captain on September 9. Before I can offer Mike my condolences, I am intercepted by Chief Hayde, coming down the stairs to greet me. Since so many chiefs are missing at Ground Zero he has been promoted to chief. Chief is one of the highest ranks you can achieve in the department. Each promotion requires a grueling written test. When Dave was studying for the Lieutenants' test, he had thick binders scattered all over the house. Most of the guys study for years, purchasing expensive study guides and paying for classes to prepare for the test.

Tall and grizzled, Don Hayde was once the captain at Squad. Now, as chief, he will work for numerous houses at the same time directing fires the way a conductor leads an orchestra. He is thin with small squinting eyes and distinct chiseled features.

"Hey, Marian! Where the hell's Dave been?" he asks curiously, and my face freezes. There is a long, awkward silence.

"He's on the list, Chief," Mike Stackpole whispers, leaning in to the chief's ear.

"No way. I checked the list a hundred times," he insists.

"He's on there, Chief," Stack tells him again. Chief Hayde looks back at me, dazed, his mouth slightly open.

"There's so many—it's hard to remember," I say, trying to help.

"I'm so sorry," he says, bewildered. "I checked the list—"

"Forget about formalities. This is—" Before I can finish, he turns, climbs the steps two at a time, and slams the office door behind him. I follow him up the twisting steps, where old photos of retired firefighters line the walls. On the left is a small bathroom, and I stop abruptly because Jerry Smythe is exiting the shower.

"Oh, God, sorry!" I yelp, covering my eyes and skulking back down the stairs.

Mike Stackpole is putting on his jacket and gathering up his things.

"I feel so bad for the chief! It was a simple mistake. Can you tell Don I want to talk to him?" I ask Mike.

"I can't. I've gotta go home. I want to see my kids. I haven't even seen my dad yet."

"I'm so sorry about your brother," I say.

"Yeah, well, you— I don't know what to say— I mean—" Mike stops, practically holding his breath. "Unbelievable."

"Go." I force a smile.

"I'll talk to yas later," he says, leaving. The buzzer sounds as the front door opens and slams shut.

I am thinking about Mike returning home, his kids gathered around, when I hear Jerry gallop down the stairs two at a time. I turn to see him take the last four steps with a jump.

"What are you doin', tryin' to see me naked?" he asks, his raspy voice belying his healthy lifestyle. His hair is still wet from the shower and he smirks when he sees me. He zips up his uniform shorts and smiles. One of the youngest men in the house, at thirty-one, Jerry has the restless energy of a hyperactive six-year-old.

"Yeah . . . I saw everything," I tease.

"You loved it, right?" Jerry continues.

"You must have taken a cold shower," I joke. "Is Chief Hayde still up there?"

"Yeah, go ahead. We're all decent, I think."

"Yeah, right." I climb the dark stairway again, knock softly on the office door. Hearing no answer, I crack the door open and spy Chief Hayde blowing his nose. Like a teenager caught smoking, he sits up in his chair and signals me to enter.

"I just wanted to tell you not to worry about that," I say gently. "It was an honest mistake."

"I just—I had no idea Dave was on the list. Dave was the best . . ." He stares at an empty chair for a long minute and then continues. "He'd sit there and ramble off all this stuff about Brooklyn and history and we'd shoot the shit. He was such a smart guy. He was . . . the best."

Hearing Dave spoken of in the past tense makes my scalp tingle.

"He is," I say finally.

4

Flicker

September 14

6:30 A.M.

I hear an unfamiliar ring and, for a minute, I have forgotten where I am. Leah is sleeping on the futon on the floor and I am on the couch and the bat phone is ringing. The bat phone is ringing. The bat phone they gave me for emergencies! *This is it. This is it.* I dive for the phone, my heart clanging against my ribs.

"Hello?" I am breathing fast and my voice sounds panicked.

"Taisha?" a woman's voice says.

"Wrong number," I whisper, unbelieving.

"Sorry," she says, hanging up. I stare at my blue glass collection in the window. There is the vase from our wedding, its bottom looking like the inside of a shell. There are the salt and pepper shakers Grandma gave me, the one time she didn't fold money into my hands. There's the demitasse cup I bought in that antique shop in New Paltz that smelled like a basement. *Dave is still missing.*

"Was that a wrong number?" Leah asks groggily, slowly sitting up.

"I can't do this anymore!" I scream, smashing the phone into my pillow. My sister sits next to me on the couch, gingerly removing the phone from my hand. I collapse, howling, into the pillow. I scream at the top of my lungs. Physically, it feels the same as vomiting. My stomach clenches, my eyes feel as if they are bulging, and all sound stops as my voice, muffled but full of rage, releases into the pillow. I stay this way for a long time, until my face is hot and my stomach is sore and slowly, very slowly, my sobs peter out, like a train pulling into the station, and finally, after what feels like a lifetime, I stop. I hear Aidan stir and pad into the room.

"How's my boy?" my sister says, squeezing him as he jumps into her lap. He looks at me skeptically. I wipe the tears off of my face, sit up taller, and try to smile. I feel like I have never used the muscles before.

"Why are you always crying?" Aidan asks me cautiously.

"I'm sad about Daddy," I say. I know my tears are like another wall crumbling in his once-sturdy home. "It's what people do when they're sad."

"I don't get sad," Aidan decides, jumping onto the futon. "I'm a chipmunk," he says, sticking his bottom up in the air and digging his head underneath my pillow. "Pretend you find me," he directs. I look at my sister and sigh.

"What's in this hole?" I ask with forced animation. "Who's in there?" I peek under the pillow. Aidan smiles and bursts out of the pillow, pretending to eat a nut. He pulls up the bottom of the futon, revealing a coffee stain underneath, from when this ratty mattress was the couch in our first apartment.

Dave had wanted another futon couch when we first moved to Brooklyn, but I insisted on a sleeper sofa, asserting that a futon felt too much like college. When he left the onus on me to decide, buying a couch became imbued with monumental significance, an archetypal symbol of our relationship. To me, the couch was as much of a commitment as marriage, so I searched for something sturdy, comfortable, and cheap.

I spent innumerable hours in Jennifer Convertibles, scouring styles and fabric swatches, and tentatively settled on a Victorian reproduction with small curled arms. I brought my mother for her approval.

"It looks like an old-lady couch," she said finally. After two more hours, my mother chose a modern couch with wide arms and a textured white fabric. A few weeks later, the couch arrived, hauled by two burly men wearing tank tops and ill-fitting shorts. They tried for thirty minutes to wedge the couch through the narrow brownstone basement door until one of the men approached me with a clipboard.

"It don't fit," he said, breathless and sweaty. "We got to disassemble it in the factory and then put it together inside your apartment. Two hundred fifty dollars. Sign here."

Two hundred fifty dollars? That was more than half of Dave's salary for a week, and the couch only cost eight hundred dollars. Clutching the clipboard, I excused myself and called Dave at Ladder 122.

"Just tell them to put it in our landlord's apartment," Dave said, acting frustratingly calm.

"But Sally is going to be home in less than an hour!" I had become friendly with Sally, the woman who owned the house with her husband and two kids, but I certainly didn't feel comfortable leaving a large piece of furniture in her house without asking.

"Just put it in their living room," he insisted, and in less than five minutes, the fire truck pulled up with a gaggle of booted men. The couch, wrapped in pink plastic, sat conspicuously in the center of the landlord's living room rug on the parlor floor. Three firefighters grabbed the couch and followed Dave to the back of the house, through the kitchen, onto the deck outside. Two others had already passed through with a giant ladder that they hoisted over the railing of the back deck, propping it against the flower boxes in the garden below. Kevin and Gonzo stood laughing in their bunker gear, making jokes as they removed the screen door leading into our apartment.

Richie heaved the couch onto the railing, and it teetered there, like the climax of some silent movie, until Owen tipped it up and gently eased it onto Vinnie's head. Slowly, he backed down the ladder.

"Hey, that's using your head!" Richie joked, bracing the ladder from above.

"Hey, couch potato! Watch your step," another one said.

"Stop making me laugh, you dicks," Vinnie said, breathless.

All the while, I was whispering in my head, "Please don't get a run." If they were called to a fire, they would have to drop the couch and go.

Ten minutes later the firemen watched as Dave and I eagerly pulled off the plastic and pushed the couch against the living room wall.

"I like it," Dave said, standing back.

"You better," Richie joked as a muffled voice reported a car fire and the firemen ran out, leaving me with a new couch and the lingering smell of smoky turnout gear. I was disappointed when Dave transferred to Squad 1. I had grown attached to the men at 122 and their wives. I had called 122 on the eleventh and they told me everyone was okay. They had arrived after the first tower collapsed and had seen the Squad 1 rig. When the second tower was falling, they ran under a walkway. Miraculously, it didn't collapse on them.

Now a colorful throw is draped over the cushions of the couch in a vain attempt to cover up nine years' worth of baby throw-up, cat hair, and soda. Aidan and Dave have made so many forts with the cushions that yellow foam pokes through the corners. As Dave predicted, the pull-out couch is painfully uncomfortable, so whenever guests come to stay, we drag out our old green futon from college, which we keep tucked behind the bed.

10:10 A.M.

Leah takes Aidan to school while Jason shuffles around the kitchen toasting bagels, making sarcastic jokes, and pouring me coffee. I want to tell him how he feels like a lifeline, how his presence gives me hope that I will survive this, but all I can muster is a feeble "Thanks." He sits across from me, his long legs crossed. He is impeccably dressed in a gray Armani shirt and crisp blue jeans, his hair worked into short spikes.

"You okay?" he asks, sensing the storm coming.

"I just want to know where he is. I can't take this limbo," I say. I am crying again. I sob softly into my hands in short, shallow breaths. My coffee is tepid and I am staring blankly into my cup, exhausted. Jason hands me a tissue and then takes one for himself.

"I can't take another day of sitting and waiting."

"We can make up drag names!" he offers feebly, and I smile despite myself. Jason and I used to play this game while we waited backstage for our shows to begin. We performed together often, first doing comedy in college and then performing sketches in venues around the city. Most recently we combined two one-person shows. I remembered how nervous I always was backstage, practically nauseated with fear. To calm ourselves, we would pace the small musty dressing room and make up names for drag queens.

"Miss Dee Meanor," he says, standing and refreshing the coffee in my cup.

"Ummm . . . Miss Jenny Talia."

"Oh, that's bad." He giggles. "Miss Anita Mann."

"You've done that one before."

"Okay . . . Miss Anna Conda."

"Good one," I say. Jason drops back into his chair and stares at me, his lashes wet fans over his eyes. "What?" I ask as he sits up, placing his long hands gently on the table.

"Dave told me something this summer," Jason starts, his voice turning uncharacteristically serious.

"So he *is* gay!" I joke, but Jason is intent on telling me something important.

"He told me he wanted me to take care of you if anything happened to him."

I am not surprised by this remark. After the Father's Day fire, Dave talked about dying more than he ever had. "I can't hear this," I would tell him, covering my ears like a child, refusing to imagine my life without him. Dave spoke of Jason, too, mentioning often that it comforted him to know I had a friend like him, who cared about me the way Dave did.

"That's a huge mess to dump on someone," I tell Jason, waving my hand over his head. "I hereby absolve you of that burden."

"I want to," he says. "I love you guys. I told Dave it was an honor." I bite the bottom of my lip hard to try to keep the tears back, but they come anyway, softer now. "Oh, please. I bet you always wanted a gay nanny," he says, and I am laughing and crying at the same time, trying not to make Jason feel the full weight of my relief, the gratitude I feel having him here. Jason looks at me, his large brown eyes watering. "I know you wanted a woman from the Dominican Republic," he whispers, "but I'll have to do." I smile weakly as the phone rings. Jason jumps up to get it. "Just don't expect me to have sex with you." He crinkles his long nose in disgust. "Girls are gross!"

11:03 A.M.

Elvis rubs against my leg and slowly folds himself onto the floor. Dave never liked the cat the way I did, nicknaming him "Smellvis" for his odorous trips to the litter box. On September 10, I returned home from dropping Aidan off from school to find Elvis in the middle of a seizure, convulsing and twitching on the floor. I yelped and clapped my hand over my mouth, but there really was nothing to do except watch helplessly as he suddenly stood up, hobbled into the kitchen, and collapsed. I ran into the basement and searched the dusty shelves for the pet carrier that had brought him to my apartment six years before. I slid a can of tuna to the back of the carrier and coaxed Elvis in. He was still breathless from his seizure but managed to eat a little bit before lying on his side. I ran out the door and made it only two blocks before I was panting and sweating. Elvis was a corpulent cat and was sliding around in the box, making him impossible to carry the nine blocks to Animal Kind clinic.

It was a minute later that Squad 1 passed, the last time I would see Dave. They honked and laughed at the sight of me rolling Aidan's Radio Flyer wagon with Elvis's pet carrier parked inside. When I finally had Elvis examined, they wanted to charge me more than eight hundred dollars to keep Elvis overnight, run a battery of tests, and clean his teeth. *Clean his teeth? Why? So he can look better in the box?* I thought, but politely explained to the bored secretary that I could not afford the fee. Dave and I were barely scraping by. I was forced to go bargain shopping. I rolled Elvis throughout the neighborhood until I found an old-fashioned place that was willing to charge me one test at a time. It didn't take long to determine that Elvis's heart had enlarged to twice its normal size and would soon burst. The best thing to do was to take him home and make him comfortable. It was my last conversation with Dave. I was crying about Elvis and he told me I was a good person for loving a cat like him. On the morning of the eleventh, I looked at Elvis, willing him to live. So far, he was listening.

I brush my teeth and catch a glimpse of myself in the mirror. I am shocked at how I look. My eyes are red and swollen from crying and lack of sleep, and my face looks as devastated as I feel. I lean in closer and notice my eyebrows need tweezing, and a thick stripe of gray seems to have appeared in my hair overnight.

"Knock, knock," I hear my mother say to the bathroom door.

"I'll be right out." I try to yell back but my voice sounds weak and tired.

"I just wanted to tell you your brother's on his way home. He should be here by tonight."

"You can come in."

She enters as if there were never a door. "He couldn't get a bus. There's no buses running to Port Authority so a friend is driving him home. Isn't that sweet? I feel bad for him up there all by himself." She stands behind me, talking to my reflection in the mirror. "I'm so worried about him."

I sigh audibly, thinking about my brother, who started college only a few weeks ago. When I was sixteen, I asked for a dog for Christmas. On Christmas Eve, my parents held hands while they announced a new baby was coming. My mom was forty-two years old, and unless she was giving birth to a black Labrador, I wanted nothing to do with it. I can still picture that hot summer, my mother, nine months' pregnant, floating in the pool, her stomach poking up like a smooth rock. "This is the only place I am not miserable." A week later, I watched in horror as my baby brother wriggled into the world. My parents had assigned me the job of documenting the birth with photos. I planned on taking photography at college in the fall, so I imagined myself the Diane Arbus of birthing rooms. My sister was in Martha's Vineyard, grateful to be missing the drama. Watching my mother give birth was bizarre, like spying on a piece of your past that you're not supposed to see. She screamed and sweated and grabbed my father's hand while I took thirty-six pictures of her vagina. When the baby finally made his grand entrance, I was out of film but madly in love with my new brother, Luke.

My mother stares at my sad reflection in the mirror. "My beautiful girl," she says. "I wish I could take this away." She puts her fingers over her mouth and cries hard, her shoulders rising up and down in little shrugs. My mother has always cried openly in front of me, and it always leaves me feeling like an actor with no lines. She takes some toilet paper and blows her nose while I lean against the sink, parting my hair.

"Look what Dave's done to me." I show her the gray stripe lining the top of my head.

"Why don't we dye it?" she says. I nod and she kisses me.

Sally from upstairs graciously offers me the use of her house while her family is at school and work all day. It has been years since I have seen the upper floors of the brownstone. I remember envying the sunshine that poured into the long, narrow windows and the intricate wood carvings from an era when people had the time and money to care about such things.

Jason takes over, greeting the stream of guests, taking their Tupperware dishes full of food, and answering the phone while my sister, mother, and I sneak out of the apartment, tiptoeing up the creaky wooden stairs to the bathroom on the top floor. Sun fills the room and the stained-glass flower on the window casts prisms of color on the white-tiled floor.

"I love this bathroom," my mom says. She has always appreciated beautiful things. When my sister and I were young, our mom would let us have a special day alone with her, and we would take the ferry to Manhattan and go to a museum. I remember the magical mobiles of Calder and how Picasso made a bull from a bicycle seat. I remember eating lunch at MoMA, where we sat in front of the windows, our mother sighing at the beauty of snow falling on Giacometti sculptures.

My mother looks like a Mary Cassatt painting, sitting on the side of the claw-foot tub. In the warm water, my clenched muscles ease, and I watch the pea-green leaves on the trees outside bend in the slight breeze, the sky still an unchanging blue. My mom mixes the hair dye, talking continuously, grateful to be given a task, to have her daughters to herself. Leah leans on the sink, tweezing her eyebrows, her long, fine features outlined by the sun.

"You have to try this," Leah says, handing me a magnifying mirror and a small pink tweezer.

"Oh, man," I mutter, startled by the hair under my eyebrows and my features reflected back huge and intense. I tweeze my eyebrows into a smooth, clean arch, remembering how much Dave hated when I did this.

"Leave 'em alone. They're beautiful," he'd say, but I tweezed them anyway, insisting that I'd look like Eddie Munster if I didn't. "They were like that when I met you," he reminded me. I kissed him on the cheek for loving me the way I am.

My mom applies the dye in thick gooey clumps. "Isn't this for men's beards?" my sister asks, sneaking a sideways glance at me.

"Yes, but it's great for touch-ups," my mom insists, "and it's a lot cheaper than hair dye."

"I'm going to look like a man," I say, staring at the box where a guy in a black beard smiles back at me. My mom laughs too hard at my joke, relieved that my humor is one of the few things that has not yet been broken.

5:30 P.M.

Squad 1 calls to tell me the neighborhood has organized a peace vigil that will start at 6 P.M. at Aidan's school and end at the firehouse. I put on makeup for the first time in days. The gray in my hair is gone, but the Grecian Formula has made my curls feel stiff and strange, as if they have been spackled. I pick out two photos of Dave to replace the more official-looking ones hanging in the firehouse.

The strong smell that has been lingering over Park Slope like a fog has finally dissipated and a moist, earthy smell of fall scents the evening air. The streets are filled with people, and the mood is almost festive, with local shops handing out candles stuck into cardboard circles to people passing by. Jason, Ed, Romi, Martina, Mom, Leah, and I quickly

Marian Fontana

make our way to the firehouse. I keep my head down to avoid my friends and hang on to my brother-in-law like a crutch.

At the firehouse, the poster of the twelve missing firefighters has been placed outside and even more candles burn in giant patches on either side of the door. There are so many flowers, people have given up placing them in buckets and leave them on the ground or balanced against the wall of the firehouse. Some of the wives have already replaced their husbands' photos with pictures of their own, and I gently reach into my bag to do the same. I hang up a small photo of Dave holding Aidan in front of the fire truck, a heavy helmet teetering on our son's small head. Aidan is about four years old in the photo, and I remember being surprised that he could keep the heavy helmet on. Next to the helmet photo, I tack up Dave's favorite photo of himself. He is dangling from a rope high above the ground in rescue training drill on Randall's Island, known as the Rock. He is smiling a satisfied grin that is as familiar to me as my own.

"He is so handsome," a shaky voice says, and I turn to see Theresa Russo. Her eyes are watery and red and she is staring, not at Dave, but at the photo of her own husband, Mike.

"He is," I say, remembering their wedding. She has tacked up a photo of Mike standing in a pool that matches his eyes. He is smiling wide as he holds their baby, Mike Jr., in his arms.

"I just got that picture back from the store. It's from a month ago," she says. Tears slide across her freckles and land in her small mouth. "I can't . . ." she says, shaking her coarse chestnut hair and crying in short, high-pitched gasps. I rub her back in circles, the way my sister does, and we cry together. I imagine other wives, everywhere, doing the exact same thing at this very moment, like an alternate universe of grief.

"This is too much," Theresa says, handing me a tissue and waving her hand in front of her face.

Aidan runs up and presses his head into my stomach. "Can I have a candle?"

Theresa follows us to the vigil candles in front of the firehouse door. It seems like the whole neighborhood is out tonight. I am amazed at the

58

outpouring of love that has begun all over the city and the world, as if the sky has become a giant roof, sheltering us all together.

I pick out two candles and carefully hand one to Aidan, who stares into the glass, hypnotized by the flame, curious about its heat. "Can I touch it?" he asks, his eyes flickering.

"No! You have to be very careful with fire," I answer, righting the candle in his hands and sweeping the hair from his face. "He's just like his father," I murmur to Theresa.

Dave was fascinated with fire. After a "good job," he'd describe in artistic detail how the smoke banked down so thick and black you couldn't see a hand in front of your face except for a thin line of oxygen where the smoke never touched the floor. In this line, you could see clear across an apartment, and it reminded Dave of Milton Avery paintings or the horizon on the ocean at night. He loved the inside of the fire, too, with flames that swirled and twisted, bright in the middle, like the inside of a star. Most of all Dave loved that there was a science to fire, a sense of order to the chaos: The hose must circle clockwise or the fire will pull toward you. Firefighters on the outside of a fire must vent the windows so the fire has a place to go. Deprived of oxygen for too long, a fire could explode into a fireball or create a backdraft.

"Oh my God! I picked St. Michael!" Theresa stares at her white vigil candle adorned with St. Michael, archangel to God, patron saint of soldiers. "Of all the candles I could have picked!" She sounds almost hysterical. "That is just too weird. He has been sending me so many signs!"

I smile weakly in her direction, nodding uncomfortably. I am still unable to give over to that feeling that Dave is around me, showing me the way. "We need to get going," I announce.

"But Luke and Dad aren't back yet," my mother says. "Dad went to pick him up."

"We're already late." I try not to sound annoyed. We squeeze our way through the crowd toward Aidan's school, where the vigil will begin. By the time we get close enough, a speech has just ended and the people are applauding, hugging each other, and crying. Then the crowd begins the somber march to the firehouse. The sheer size of the crowd makes it impossible for us to go against the tide, so we turn around to join them.

"This is incredible." Theresa is awed by the mass of people, their candles flickering like a swarm of fireflies.

I spot my father walking with Luke and wave. My mother waves frantically to them, too, relieved that they have found us. Luke looks dazed and sad, his hands dug deep into his oversize jeans, his shoulders hunched in a hooded sweatshirt. He has surpassed our father's height by at least two inches but still walks with the same loping gait. How strange for him to leave his quiet college campus in Cortland, New York, and enter into this scene.

"Hey, Luke," I whisper as he encircles me in a hug, dropping his shoulder onto mine. It is difficult to walk this way so I guide him forward.

"I thought we'd missed you guys." Dad tousles Aidan's hair and grabs a candle from my mom.

"I was so worried you wouldn't make it!" Mom hugs Luke so long and hard that they fall back in the crowd. When they catch up to us again, my brother is blowing his nose and wiping his eyes.

"This is weird," Luke says, looking around the crowd. He hoists Aidan onto his shoulders so he can see the wide ribbon of candles stretching three blocks in either direction.

"Is this a parade for Daddy?" Aidan asks curiously.

"It's for Daddy and all the people missing," I reply, my throat tight.

Aidan collapses forward until his chin rests in Luke's mop of shiny curls. "Daddy's not dead, you know," Aidan says. "He's going to get out of the rocks at the Twin Towers."

The people walking in front of us turn and look up at Aidan, their eyes full of pity. Aidan continues, unaware that he has triggered a wave of tears.

"This is a sad parade," he announces, sitting up tall again to see the ocean of lights floating toward Union Street.

Luke cries softly, his tears shimmering in the light of his candle.

Farther back in the crowd, people have begun to sing "America." *"For amber waves of grain"* echoes behind me, and I realize for the first time that my personal loss is just one stone in the huge mosaic of what has happened to this country. *"America! America! God shed His grace on thee."* The current of sound, the flags, and the soft candlelight overwhelm me.

"And crown thy good with brotherhood from sea to shining sea," the crowd sings. Thousands of American flags wave across the country in a collective act of patriotism.

The crowd turns onto Union Street and gathers in front of the fire-house, where a microphone and speaker are set up. I am surprised to see Toni-Ann, Peter Carroll's wife; Pete's wake is tomorrow afternoon. When Huey went to Toni-Ann's house to tell her Pete's body had been found, she'd thrown him out of the house in a rage. "You're a liar!" she screamed, slamming the door in his face.

Now I watch her staring blankly past me, her eyes fixed and dilated. "Hey, Toni-Ann," I say, kissing her on her cheek, which is painted thick with makeup. She doesn't say anything, but stands swaying slightly, her platinum hair clipped on top of her head like the pom-padour of a Pekingese. She is in her mid-forties, with a small straight nose and bronzed skin. "Ohhhhh," she moans, until her parents gently lead her to a chair and sit her down. Theresa, a nurse for fifteen years, studies Toni-Ann, who groans softly, sinking into her chair.

"They're giving her too much medication," Theresa whispers into my ear.

Bernie Graham, a lawyer and one of the fathers from the neighbor-hood, has begun a speech. I stare at the glowing faces in the crowd, the candles stretching so far back, it looks like a distant city.

"We pray for the twelve firefighters lost from Squad One and their families . . ."

Theresa reaches for my hand; it feels like the world is watching us cry. In my peripheral vision, I notice Toni-Ann standing with us now, wavering like a drunk. My attention is torn between my own emotions and Toni-Ann, whose body leans suddenly to the side. I turn back to the firemen who are standing behind us. I spot Huey Lynch, nicknamed "Baby Huey" for his young-looking face. Dave loved working the night shift with Huey because he would play his guitar and sing, his velvety voice echoing through the firehouse late into the night.

"I think she's fainting," I say to Huey, who scoops up Toni-Ann and sits in a folding chair.

"I wanna die! I just wanna die," Toni-Ann wails into his shoulder, and he rocks her like a father trying to get his child to sleep.

5

The First Wake

September 15

The morning of September 15, for Peter Carroll's wake, Ed, Leah, Aidan, and I drive out to Staten Island. Since the funeral parlor is only a few blocks away from where I grew up, my parents have offered to take care of Aidan. The dust in the sky has cleared and the brilliant blue is back, obstructed only by soft, powdery clouds that float over the giant arches of the Verrazano-Narrows Bridge, which connects Brooklyn to Staten Island.

"The traffic's so light for a Saturday," I say, trying not to look toward the Manhattan skyline on the right.

"That's probably because the bridge is a terrorist target," Ed says flatly, drumming his fingers on the steering wheel. Ed has become an ambassador, keeping Dave's family informed, but at a distance. It is too painful to have them over each day, like a surprise party where the main guest never shows.

My eyes can't help but drift toward the water, usually bustling with ferries and giant tankers being pushed by tugs. Now the harbor sits empty, except for a few Coast Guard boats hovering near the Statue of Liberty. I close my eyes, remembering how, when I was young, I used to sit up extra tall in the back of our Dodge station wagon to see the Emerald City of Manhattan across the bay, its millions of lights winking at me.

"God, the city looks weird," my sister mumbles, and I can't help but turn to see Manhattan, the Mona Lisa with the missing smile. The spot now known as Ground Zero is encased in a yellow smoky fog, and the skyline looks like that of any other big city, a line of dull gray block buildings.

When I was in high school, many of my classmates in Manhattan did not know where Staten Island was. "We actually have indoor plumbing," I used to joke. I was embarrassed to live in a place known for Fresh Kills, the world's largest garbage dump, visible from space (along with the Great Wall of China). I usually did not have the energy to explain that Fresh Kills was the South Shore, and that where I grew up, on the North Shore, was actually quite beautiful. I loved our yard, with its wide expanse of green grass, bordered by chestnut trees and a giant ancient oak that held our tire swing. I loved the yew tree in the front with its low straight branches that made a perfect barre for Leah and me to do our gymnastics. I loved our old 1870 farmhouse. I treasured the maids' quarters, with their cozy rooms and angled ceilings and odd corners. More than anything, I loved the quiet, the absence of sound that does not exist in the other boroughs.

Vanilla, my parents' dog, hangs on the fence as if she has been expecting us. Cosmos and African daisies linger in my mother's garden, which seems perpetually lush with bright flowers and vegetables. I spot Mom watering plants on the back deck, which Dave built with his eldest brother, Hank, ten years ago.

My mother beckons us into the pale green kitchen, where she scurries around, taking out snacks and cutting up fruit. Like my dad, she is a psychotherapist; I often joke that having shrinks for parents has made me either really healthy or really screwed up. Sometimes it's difficult to know.

Half an hour later, Ed and I cut through the courtyard of St. Mary's Church, a route Leah and I used to take on our way to grammar school. A wide slate path winds through the rose garden. One December when I was nine, Leah and I walked through, kicking clumps of icy snow from a storm a few days before. As we passed the churchyard sculpture of the Crucifixion, Leah and I stopped to stare at the large brass cross that hung in a fenced-off section of the rose garden. The cross had long since weathered to a mossy green. Poking through the snow, near Jesus' nailed right foot, stood a solitary pink rose in full bloom, as bright and comfortable as if it were the middle of May.

"Jesus did that," my sister said casually. I followed her out of the church gate, believing that miracles existed.

Now we climb up the hill to the Harmon Funeral Home on Forest Avenue. The funeral parlor, originally a colonial home, is one of the few surviving houses on the busy strip now filled with Irish bars and small businesses that change as quickly as the seasons. The wake is being held in the largest room in front, where the dark carpeting and floral wingback chairs have not changed since I attended the wakes of two grandmothers, one grandfather, and a friend from junior high who drowned in Silver Lake.

The smell of lilies and gladiola overpowers the dimly lit room where Peter's casket stands against the far wall, a photo and helmet balanced on top. Jimmy Lopez and Sean Cummins stand stiffly in front of the coffin, their class A uniforms starched, their gloved hands clasped behind their backs, their feet slightly apart.

"Hey, guys," I say, greeting Jimmy, who stands motionless, his eyes staring forward. I kiss Sean on the cheek, but he, too, doesn't move.

"I think they're standing honor guard," Ed whispers as my sister stifles a laugh.

"Shut up," I whisper, embarrassed, following Leah to the back of the room, where we sink into a worn blue couch.

"Where is everybody?" Leah asks, scanning the room. Only a few firefighters mill in the corner.

Ed pushes up his sleeve to read his watch, a gesture so much like Dave's, it catches my breath. "It's after two."

I stand up, pinning my Squad 1 patch onto my jacket. "Well, I'm going to pay my respects before it gets crowded." Sean and Jimmy steal sideways glances at me as I kneel down in front of the coffin. I consider praying but my mind feels as blank as a dreamless sleep. I stare at Pete's photo instead. He is standing in front of the firehouse, his helmet salty—the term the guys use for gear that's seen a lot of fire. The brim of his helmet casts a shadow across his eyes, which have lashes so long, it seems unfair to waste them on a man.

Hey, Pete. It's me, Marian. You were supposed to paint my apartment in three weeks. Remember? I keep thinking of all the times you yelled my name over the speaker on the fire truck until everyone on 7th Avenue was staring at me. You would sing "Vigilante Plumbing" (the jingle to the plumbing commercial I was in years ago) at the top of your lungs whenever you passed me in the neighborhood. Dave told me you took out a piece of the engine door when you pulled the truck out too fast. I guess the door couldn't open fast enough for a firefighter who could never miss being the first to arrive—"first due," as you say. The guys told me yesterday they are leaving it that way as a tribute to you.

People keep telling me Dave could still be alive in the rubble somewhere, but I know in my heart . . . So, maybe, if it's not too much trouble, you could ask him to send me a sign. Not a flicker of light or a song that we love on the radio. These can easily be misconstrued, right? I need something clear and obvious—as bright as the neon signs Dave used to make. I want something huge, overstated, Hollywoodesque, with a Vaseline-smeared lens bathing Dave in a soft, ethereal light, his beautiful dimples splayed. I want him to hover above me and whisper "I love you," and touch my cheek with his big square hands, and then I want you to make him hold me one last time. That's all I want, really.

I begin to cry, but I stop when Toni-Ann enters, leaning so heavily on her teenage daughter that I wonder how much medication she is on today.

"Marian—" Her voice sounds slurred. "I can't believe you're here."

"Of course," I tell her as she hugs me hard.

"I don't know how you're so strong."

"I'm not really—"

"I wanna die, Marian. I wanna go with him." I watch her daughter, looking helpless, reach for a pack of cigarettes and head outside.

"I know, but we're going to be okay," I say.

She shakes her head, looking past me at the coffin. Her voice is like syrup dripping. "He was my rock. He took care of me. I'm sick, you know. Did you know he took care of me?" I nod and she teeters slightly, her jacket falling open. "I don't wanna live no more," she says without inflection.

"I know this feels unbearable—" But she is not listening. She is walking right past me and heading for the coffin.

She stands looking at it for a moment and then flings herself on top of it. "PETEEEEEY," she wails, the helmet and photo sliding to the floor.

"Shhh." I gently try to pull her off.

"I wanna see him. I want to *see my baby!*"

"C'mon, let's go sit down." I rub her back gently, as I do when comforting Aidan after a nightmare, and lead her to a seat, but she yanks her arm away, lunging for the thick brass handles on the front of the casket. Without thinking, I swat her hand away and clamp my own hand around the cold metal. Frantic, Toni-Ann tries to pry my fingers off, moaning and crying.

"*Guys!*" I call to the firefighters. "You wanna help me here?" Toni-Ann starts for the handles on the other end of the casket. Jimmy breaks honor guard and pulls her from the waist.

"C'mon, Toni-Ann," he says. "Don't do this."

"*Let go of me! Let me go with my baby!*" she screams, pulling so hard on the other handle, my grip loosens. I hear my heart pounding fast in my ears as the coffin lifts slightly and I realize that I *want* to let go. I want to see what Peter looks like. Maybe it would make this all seem real. But for the last few days I have sat in the firehouse kitchen, hearing whispered conversations about body parts and fingers and skin hanging on jagged steel like windless flags, so I tighten my grip. Other firefighters rush over to help, but Toni-Ann's emotions have made her strong, and she manages to lift the coffin lid another inch before it slams down with a bang.

Huey carries her to a seat, propping her up, her mascara smearing under her eyes. "Leave me alone!" Toni-Ann wails, swatting away the pills her parents press to her mouth.

Huey's wife, Kathleen, offers Toni-Ann tissues, and soon her wails diminish to a low, pitiful moan. Sean and Jimmy resume their honor guard as other guests enter, oblivious to the scene that has just taken place. I join Ed and Leah in the back, biting my lip hard, the tears burning my cheeks as I plop onto the couch.

"You okay?" my sister asks, handing me a tissue. I nod and shrug at the same time. "That was like a *Sopranos* episode." Leah watches Toni-Ann, catatonic now, her green eyes never leaving the casket, even when she swallows the sedatives her parents have finally convinced her to take.

"That was crazy," I say, blowing my nose, but secretly I am envious of Toni-Ann. I wish I could let my feelings fly raw and uncensored, letting everyone see my pain. I want to kick and scream and cry until my throat hurts and the endless reservoir of sadness, anger, and shock empties.

We walk home in silence, fatigue making my steps slow and laborious. The sun drops low, making the windows look like they are on fire. I cannot wait to climb into my parents' soft bed before the firefighters come over for a late lunch in between viewings.

"Oh, God," Leah moans as we approach the worn wooden gate surrounding our yard. Dozens of our parents' friends are clustered like crows across the lawn, sitting in lounge chairs and eating from paper plates. I wearily accept hugs and mumble "thank you" to my parents' friends who danced at my wedding eight years ago.

Leah brings me a plastic cup of red wine and I slump into a lawn chair, staring at the spot in the front yard where the white tents of our wedding stood on September 11, 1993. I can still picture the smooth white cake with fresh-cut wildflowers, the wild hoop earrings that the lead singer of the Cajun band wore, smiling with Dave at the motley mix of firefighters, dancers, hippies, gay actors, lifeguards, and my grandmother as she danced the two-step. Most of all, I can see Dave pressed against me, my friends and family smiling in a swirling blur of color as we danced to Etta James singing, *"At last, my love has come along. My lonely days are over . . ."*

When the firefighters and wives arrive, I am surprised to see Toni-Ann among them. Huey and Jimmy flank her, helping her down the sloping green lawn into a folding chair next to me.

"This is a beautiful yard—you grow up here?" Her voice is tired. I nod, following her gaze to the garden in the back where basil stands in overgrown stalks of white stems and the last of the tomatoes hang heavy on thick vines. "You're lucky."

Jimmy returns with a glass of wine and joins his pregnant wife, Karen, on the other side of the lawn.

Toni-Ann's lip liner curves into a perfect O as she takes a long sip. "Did you know Pete and I had sex five times a day?" she says nonchalantly.

"I heard something like that," I answer, remembering how defensive I became when Dave reported what Pete had told him at the firehouse. "Who the hell has time for that?" I argued, guilty that sometimes sex felt like one more item on an endless list of things to do: *buy diapers, mail bills, xerox scripts, have sex.*

"It's true," she says, smiling slightly. "Marian," she continues, grabbing my arm and leaning in. "When this is all over, you and me are going to the West Village and buying dildos this big." She stretches her arms out as wide as a table. "They come in colors, ya know." I giggle, imagining Toni-Ann and me perusing the aisles of sex shops, trying to find the perfect-colored toy.

"Did you really have sex five times a day?" Toni-Ann nods. "How did you have time for that?" I ask.

"When you want something, you make time," Toni-Ann answers, her eyes glazing over again.

6

Ripple of Grief

September 18

It has been a week. One whole week and I am looking for Dave's DNA in my house. I find an old hairbrush with Dave's short salt-and-pepper strands still visible in the teeth and place it in a plastic bag. I search for a second toothbrush, since I used his last night in a desperate attempt to taste him and secretly pretended I was being kissed. I sift through cluttered drawers looking for combs or something with Dave's unique cells. Surely he couldn't have disappeared without a trace. I can hear Ed pacing the living room. We are supposed to be driving in with the other families from Squad to a meeting at the Hilton Hotel, and his siblings Dennis and Vicki are almost an hour late. They are coming to have their mouths swabbed with giant Q-tips and matched to Dave's DNA if he is found. I am nervous to see Dave's sisters and brothers. Along with Ed, they are adamant that Dave is alive. Their devotion to this idea is so complete, I wonder if I am a bad wife for believing otherwise, for knowing in my heart that he is gone. I have had moments of hope, clichéd in their melodrama with Dave trapped in the rubble, weak and waiting, calling out for help as if Lassie would somehow hear him, but ultimately I know. I can read the faces of the firefighters returning hopeless from the site each night. I have heard the whispered conversations that there are no survivors and that tonight's meeting will announce the transition from search and rescue to search and recovery.

It is almost six-thirty by the time Dennis lumbers down the hall. I can tell he is agitated, his mouth tight under a thick mustache that hangs over his lips like a scraggly curtain. He has not changed at all since I met him seventeen years ago; he wears the same haircut, same large eyeglasses, faded blue jeans, plaid shirt.

"Hello." He stands awkwardly in front of me. I try to hug him but he stiffens, leaning forward like he is being tilted onto a dolly. "Vicky's coming eventually. You know how she is."

I can hear the door open and Vicky, the eldest sister, hurries in. She smiles weakly, small dimples appearing in her chubby cheeks.

"The traffic was awful," she says, brushing the gray hair from her face. Although Vicky has said little to me since Dave died, I can tell from her shaking hands and her sad blue eyes that she is rattled with grief. Most of the pictures I have of Dave as an infant show Vicky, almost ten years older, lovingly holding him in her arms.

When we arrive at Squad, the other family members are already sitting in a dark green Parks Department van. I climb into the first seat and am thrilled to see Denise Esposito, whose husband, Mike, is among the missing. We hug each other hard. In her arms, I tear up again.

"Don't get me started," she says as I kiss her on the cheek. It is soft and smooth, belying her age.

"It's about freakin' time," Tony Edwards teases. He is driving tonight.

"I'm sorry," I tell everyone as Vicki and Dennis slide into the seat behind me.

"Wow. Look at you!" Denise is staring at Ed, who sits on her other side. "He looks like Dave," she whispers to me.

"Tell me about it."

"This freakin' sucks, huh?" she says, squeezing my thigh. More than anyone else in the firehouse, it was Mike I was saddest about. For weeks after she and Mike saw my shows, he would call, leaving suggestions on my answering machine about how to improve some of my jokes. He wanted me to write a Squad 1 musical, and he sang excerpts from made-up songs when he called.

I turn around and wave to Lynda and Princess Linda, who sit in the back looking annoyed. I introduce myself to Robert Cordice's mother, who flashes me a warm, earthy smile. When I turn back, Denise is leaning her head on Ed's large arm.

"Do you mind?" she says to Ed. "This is what I miss. A big arm to squeeze." I laugh at her as Ed turns a crimson red. Denise is a pretty woman with small, refined features and straight brown hair.

"Hey, watch it back there," Tony says, starting the truck, and Denise giggles.

Phil Solimeo from Squad 1 climbs into the front passenger seat with a smile, greeting everyone. Phil reminds me of a young Dave: sincere and shy, a tiny dimple on each cheek. As Phil was one of the newer guys, Dave had taken him under his wing when he first arrived at Squad. Most firefighters initiated the new guys with relentless hazing and teasing, but Dave was always kind, showing them around the firehouse and teaching them what to do.

"Ed, you better watch out for Denise," Tony teases.

"Oh, please. I'm a harmless old lady," she jokes.

"Go for it," I tease. "We should put the firefighters on a mutual chart at the firehouse to take care of us girls." I elbow Denise and she winks.

"I'll take care of both of ya," Tony retorts, speeding down Union Street.

"Oh, baby." Denise laughs and then stops, staring up at the ceiling of the van. I know she is remembering Mike because she squeezes my thigh, trying not to cry.

"Do you remember this past Halloween?" I ask Tony, and he squints trying to recall.

"Those costumes Dave made were the best," Phil says.

"This past Halloween," I say, "Dave made a huge spaceship covered in tinfoil and wore it with suspenders. Aidan was dressed as Buzz Lightyear on his shoulders, and I was an alien."

"I remember that," Tony says. "That spaceship was big!"

Tony's raspy laugh is infectious and prompts me to keep going. "It was huge! And phallic! We're walking down Seventh Avenue in the parade, and mothers are pointing and giggling at Dave. He has a bucket covered with tinfoil on his head and he's smiling and waving at everyone."

"Awww." Denise smiles.

"Until we get to Union Street, where Squad always parks on the corner, and Mike takes one look at Dave and screams across the street, 'Hey, Dave! You look like a freakin' penis!' " Everyone laughs hard this time and Denise grabs my thigh, giggling.

After a moment she exhales loudly. "Oh, it feels good to laugh. Mike always made me laugh."

There are five policemen standing at the entrance to the Brooklyn Bridge, sending cars away. Tony rolls down the window, flashes his badge, and the policemen usher us through, peering into the windows as we pass a lone van on the once-busiest bridge in New York City. The van grows quiet and I stare out the window, taking in the gothic arches. I remember Dave told me it had taken sixteen years to build the bridge, required six hundred workers, and claimed more than twenty lives.

I instinctively search for the familiar beacon, the Twin Towers. I can feel everyone in the van looking at the empty spot where they used to be. Floodlights used by the rescue workers create an eerie yellow glow in the skyline. Smoke from the still-burning wreckage rolls across the beams of light, giving downtown a strange, ethereal fluorescence. We curve around an empty ramp of the FDR Drive, speeding past the spinning blue lights of police cars that block every entrance and exit on our trip uptown.

At the 42nd Street exit, Tony shows his ID again and the policeman moves the barricade to let us through. The United Nations Building stands like a giant deck of cards as we head toward the Hilton.

The hotel is crowded with firefighters and families riding escalators up to the Grand Ballroom. Ornate chandeliers hang over wide round tables packed with victims' families. Since we are late and there are no tables left, we climb to the second-floor balcony and find a row of padded seats. The stage is set with chairs and a giant screen that depicts a fuzzy aerial photo of Ground Zero.

Governor Pataki stands at the microphone and tells us that we will be

taken care of, that the city will never forget, that our children will receive an education, and that the firefighters were heroes. The crowd
shifts uncomfortably. We are not ready for the future. We want information about our loved ones, and we want them still referred to in the
present tense. The governor gushes about Mayor Giuliani, how strong
he has been in the face of tragedy, and the mayor gets to the podium, his
wide forehead wrinkled in solemn thanks. The two men embrace and
vigorously shake hands until the mayor finally gets to the microphone.
With his familiar lisp, he tells the story of what happened to him that
day, how he saw Chief Ganci—MISSING—Chief Downey, a Special
Operations chief—MISSING—Chief Barbara—MISSING—Chief
Gaeraghty—MISSING—Terrence Hatton—MISSING. And finally, he
mentions how it could have been him. He talks about being there just
moments before the collapse and how he cried from the helicopter that
flew over the wreckage.

"We are doing everything that is humanly possible to bring your
loved ones home, but it is difficult to know from this picture the mag-
nitude of the event," he continues, pointing to the blurry photo that
looks like it was taken from a satellite. My stomach tightens, and like
that of the teacher in the Peanuts gang, Giuliani's voice fades to a cacophony of sound where words are no longer distinguishable. I squint
at the photo that encompasses almost sixteen acres of land and wonder
which tiny speck Dave could be. From the balcony, I watch hundreds of
faces stretched with sadness, the ripple of grief spreading out farther
than I can possibly see.

The fire commissioner, Tom Von Essen, stands up to speak next.
With his blond hair swept to the side, he resembles a general from the
Third Reich, save for his posture, which is slumped and defeated. He
speaks about losing countless friends and how he, too, just missed
being killed on that day. He talks about the rescue operation, his voice a
depressed monotone.

"You have to understand, there is an issue of compression. The buildings were designed to pancake so they wouldn't cause collateral damage,
and because of that, we have one hundred and six floors compressed to
less than nine stories, so the likelihood of people being found—"

The families begin to mumble and bubble like pots of water.

"How can you tell us that! My friend's husband was found yesterday!" one woman yells out.

"I'm not saying they won't," Von Essen says wearily. "I just want you to know the reality of the situation." But the crowd is seething and squirming in their seats, ready to pounce. Lynn Tierney, the deputy commissioner, heads to the microphone to save her friend. Her soft voice belies her hardened face. "We're not saying they won't be found. It's just that there is an issue with compression," she says gently. I imagine bones smashed and shattered like toothpicks under the falling cement. Denise stands up like a fish flipped from its bowl as she tries to gasp for air, crying. Vicky quietly hands me a tissue as Denise's tears flow like an electrical current from her eyes to mine. The room becomes heavy as other people begin to rise, demanding responses to unanswerable questions, and a heaviness hangs above us like a toxic cloud. I excuse myself and head downstairs, where I spot other families from Squad 1 sitting at a table by the exit.

"Where are you going?" Princess Linda asks. She sounds desperate to escape the stifling room.

"I need a cigarette," I whisper.

"Me, too." She follows me through the double doors to the lobby bar, which is crowded with men in dark suits. I order two cosmopolitans and absently pick at a bowl of peanuts.

"This is totally useless," Linda says, lighting a menthol cigarette. "I don't think they're going to find Eddie." Linda is the kind of pretty men love, with long, dyed platinum hair, tight jeans, and blue eyes.

"Don't say that," I say.

"Have you gotten any signs?" she asks sincerely, and I shake my head no, almost embarrassed. Leah insists the lights are flickering and that doors have been slammed, but these are too easily explained by old wiring and the wind.

"I've been gettin' tons of them, and it's weird," she says, lighting my cigarette with a lighter in the shape of a fish. "I was talkin' to Eddie up in heaven, right? . . . and I tell him, I don't want pennies from heaven. I want dimes, and then dimes are showin' up everywhere in weird places.

Even the bottom of my toilet! Places ya wouldn't find dimes." The men in the bar watch her as she flicks her hair and continues. "But that's not good enough for me. I want more. So the other day I'm cryin' hard and I want a sign. You know how Eddie just moved in with me a couple a months ago. Right? Well, right after he moves in, I can't find my jewelry, but I didn't want to say nuthin' to him 'cause I didn't want him thinkin' I was thinkin' it was him, so I says while I'm cryin', 'If you're up there,' I says, 'when I open this drawer, my jewelry box will be there.' So I open up the drawer, and there it is!" Linda raises her eyebrows and stamps out her cigarette. "Weird, right?"

"So he did steal it!" I joke. Linda smiles while I berate myself for being cynical, teetering between intellect and giving over.

Linda and I stare into our drinks.

"We should get together more. I feel alone," Linda says into her glass.

I, too, am craving the solidarity of other grieving wives. "I'll plan a dinner," I say, when I spot my brother-in-law riding down the escalator.

"There you are!" Ed walks over to the bar. "I didn't know where you went."

"I had to get out of there," I say, signaling the bartender for the check.

"I don't blame you. They collected our DNA samples. I think everyone wants to go."

Back upstairs, Theresa Russo is standing next to her in-laws, and when we hug hello I can tell she has been crying hard. I watch families file out looking grim, others pressing toward the stage to ask more questions.

"That was a killer," Theresa says, and I nod.

"Our husbands have been *compressed*," I say sarcastically.

"I had a dream last night that he was lying in a pile of debris with a big slab of cement crushing his legs, but from the waist up he was perfect. Not a scratch on him."

"Maybe he is," I say, trying to be optimistic.

Phil Solimeo gently grabs my hand. "There's someone here I want you to see," he says, pulling me through the crowd toward the stage at the other end of the ballroom.

I spot Susan Cullen at a table in the far corner. Susan lives two doors down from a mutual friend on Staten Island. At countless dinner parties and birthdays, Susan, Lori, and I told funny anecdotes about our kids while Dave and Susan's husband, Tom, talked about being firefighters. My stomach drops when I realize that Tommy must be dead, too. He had just started on the job. Their little boy is not even two yet.

"I've been meaning to call you," Susan says, her face drawn but her large eyes still bright.

"Oh my God, Susan. I didn't know." We stare at each other, not believing that the degrees of separation can be so small.

"Tommy and I were good friends," Phil offers.

"What a small world," I say, knowing my trite phrase is inadequate. "How's little Tommy?" The boy is a miniature version of his father, with straight spiked hair and apple-shaped cheeks. Susan shrugs and tears up, and we hug good-bye, promising to keep in touch.

It is past eleven when we finally head home. The conversation turns to Pier 94, the place where families go to get assistance.

"You haven't gone yet?" Denise asks incredulously. "It takes all day."

"Timmy Rogers will take you on Monday," Jimmy says. Theresa, Martha, and Kathleen are the only ones who haven't gone yet. "You have to bring social security numbers, your marriage certificate, birth certificates, bills, bank statements, passports . . . I think that's it."

"Is that all?" I ask sarcastically.

I think of all the papers filed loosely in my cabinet at home, the only proof of our seventeen years together. The van is quiet again as we automatically turn our heads to the luminescent patch of sky. I can picture the smoldering rubble and the black skeleton of steel that is shown on TV, but most of all I imagine the thousands of tiny bits of paper, burned and floating like confetti above Ground Zero, the detritus of almost three thousand lives.

*   *   *

I wake at 3 A.M. to a pounding, terrifying rain that feels like the end of the world. Thunder cracks and booms, rattling the windows and my frayed nerves. I stare into the darkness, my heart racing as the rain teems outside the living room window. I imagine Dave in a dark void among the ruins at the World Trade Center. He sits there, shaking, injured, and cold, the water rising higher and higher. He thinks only of Aidan and me, and he cries miserably knowing he will never see us again. The pain becomes more intense as the water rises and rises, covering Dave's handsome face until his breath stops and he drowns, his salt-and-pepper hair floating above him, as if swept up by a breeze.

* * *

"I heard about people surviving for three weeks after a mudslide," my sister says, trying to cheer me up as we rifle through dozens of packages and letters arriving daily in the mail.

"I dunno. They haven't found anyone alive."

"Yeah, but . . . I saw a show about this guy who was trapped and he lived for three weeks and if Dave is in one of the voids like the firefighters said they might be . . ."

"Leah. Everyone they find is not only dead but . . . *compressed*." I shake my head. The movement has become my tic of grief.

"They'll find him. I know they will." Leah's words sound as shallow as a line from a soap opera. She squeezes my neck and I yelp at how much it hurts. My grief has made my head feel like overripe fruit hanging heavy from my neck.

"Sorry." The doorbell is ringing again, and I sigh. I am starting to doubt myself again. Wouldn't it be wonderful if it were true, that Dave is alive?

Neighbors and friends arrive with more lasagna, soup, and wine. We can't even fit any more food in the refrigerator. I stand to greet my friends, wondering how long this endless shiva will last.

* * *

It's almost 9 P.M. and I can't get Aidan to sleep. It is so noisy, it's like trying to take a nap in the middle of Times Square. People are walking through his room—the only path to my bedroom—and my small living room is filled with people. I lie in bed rubbing his smooth head and sing, *"Hush-a-bye, don't you cry, go to sleep, little baby. When you wake you shall have all the pretty little horses."* Dave and I have been singing this song to him every night since he was six months old. I can hear Dave's voice humming until Aidan's eyes would become heavy, his lashes fluttering like palm fronds. The weight of raising Aidan alone overtakes me, sits on my chest like a rock, making it difficult to breathe.

I slowly get up from Aidan's bed, checking one last time to see if he is still asleep. In the kitchen, I take a plate of sushi that a friend from college had sent over. I am about to head outside to the backyard when someone announces that Sara from Maine has just arrived. Free-spirited, eccentric, and devilishly funny, Sara is the first person I met when I transferred to Sarah Lawrence. We have been close ever since.

"Oh, honey." She runs toward me for an embrace. She is wearing a velvet hat from the 1920s with a huge flower in the front, and her face is already streaked with tears. I put my plate down on the television stand before she pulls me into the bathroom, the only room that is empty. She hugs me again and I cry into her hair, which smells like rosewater, her favorite scent. Dave and I had just visited Sara at her old storefront in Portland, Maine, where she sells her pottery painted whimsically in cheery, colorful glazes. Only five weeks earlier, Dave and I were sitting on her bright purple porch drinking wine and gazing at a sky speckled with stars. Huge pink flowers burst from vines that crawled up a trellis. Sara talked loudly while she chain-smoked and grilled tuna and told us that Portland is probably the only city where you can see stars at night.

"I just can't believe it," Sara says, sitting on the edge of the tub, holding my hand. "I can't believe he can be gone!" I pull toilet paper from the roll and hand some to her. She digs her hand into a large velvet patchwork bag and retrieves a pack of Marlboros. Even though I have not told her about my new habit, she lights two cigarettes and hands one to me. Her white skin is blotchy from crying and the remnants of red lipstick outline her bow lips. "This is so fucking horrible." She inhales deeply, squinting from the smoke. Despite her added weight, Sara still reminds me of a flapper, her black hair cut in a 1920s bob. "My friends in Maine just don't get it at all. They couldn't understand why I haven't stopped crying since I heard. Even my dad cried." Sara sniffles hard.

Dave's favorite part of our trips to Maine were when Sara would close the shop and take us all up to her parents' house, less than an hour north. With a cigarette dangling from her lips, she would drive the twisted roads past ancient pine forests and honey-colored marshes until we reached what felt like the end of the world. A large gray house with a wraparound porch and a widow's walk stood on a rolling expanse of green that stretched to the ocean. Sara's father, Peter, who founded the Maine *Times* newspaper and loved to tell us dirty jokes after a few cocktails, was always in the garden or sitting on his mower. On our last trip, Pete came up to Dave and asked if he liked striped bass.

"Yeah, sure," Dave replied, and Pete procured a fishing pole and they disappeared onto the jagged rocks where the Atlantic's deep-green waves smashed against them. Less than twenty minutes later, they returned, a large, gleaming bass in Peter's hand.

"Now, that's how to live," Dave said with excitement.

That night Pete grilled the fish he had caught and served it with fingerling potatoes and leeks from his garden and a dry, crisp chardonnay. Sated, Dave and I walked in the wet grass swatting mosquitoes and staring at the star-filled sky. "I wish I could live like this." Dave sighed, and I braced myself for the recurring wish list of things he wanted to have someday, but instead he inhaled, his square jaw pointing toward the stars. "It's great to have everything you need right in front of you."

7

Widow's Walk

September 23

Sara and I sit at the firehouse drinking wine from plastic cups, smoking and waiting for them to return from what they have dubbed "the Pile" and what the news calls Ground Zero. Even though women are rarely in the firehouse, my shock and despair have made me unselfconscious about being here. When I sit on the soft foam couches in the common room, I can imagine Dave practicing his knots while he watched TV or chopping vegetables in the kitchen for the meal that they all chipped in for. I used to see Squad shopping at Key Food for their dinner when I was coming home from teaching gymnastics at the Dance Studio. I liked the way the men joked as they filled their shopping baskets and talked to each other in different aisles over their radios. "You guys want peas or broccoli?"

Once, when I was shopping for Dave's surprise thirtieth-birthday party, I was shocked to see him sauntering into the market in his bunker gear. His first company, Ladder 122, was coming in to buy dinner. I was panicked, knowing that if Dave saw my cart filled with soda, chips, and cake mix, he would know I was up to something. I had ducked down an aisle when Kevin McCabe, a firefighter, saw me. I signaled him to come over. After I explained my predicament, he offered to solicit the other men to get me out of the store without Dave seeing me. First, they "borrowed Dave's radio," and with the precision of Green Berets on a secret mission, they notified each other of Dave's whereabouts until I was safely out of the store.

At seven o'clock the truck still hasn't returned from the site. Only a few firefighters mill around, answering phones and collecting the endless offerings of food. Billy Redden, one of the newer guys, sits on the couch across from me, staring at his thumbs.

"What's taking them so long to get back?" I ask.

"They found Captain Amato," he says.

"Oh." Jim Amato is only the second firefighter from Squad 1 to be found in two long weeks.

"Where was he?" Sara asks.

"On top of a pile. He was in real good shape. He must have gotten blown up into the air, and he landed right on top of this big pile. They didn't have to uncover him or anything. Pretty amazing."

"Did anyone call Debbie?" I ask.

"Bobby West and Joe O'Donnell are going out there to tell her."

We grow quiet; Sara stares up at the muted TV. On CNN Ground Zero footage seems as permanent as the Yule log at Christmas. I have grown used to seeing the piles of debris and the yellow smoldering fires, the firefighters crawling through the wreckage.

"How are you doing?" I ask Billy, who has not stopped staring at his thumbs.

He looks up, his small eyes the color of lapis lazuli against pale, freckled skin. He shrugs, looking as if he could cry. "I liked Dave a lot, you know. He welcomed me to the firehouse, showed me around. . . ." I've heard this often from the newer guys. When Dave first arrived at Squad, there was one firefighter who was relentless in his hazing rituals, hurling an endless barrage of insults as soon as Dave entered the door.

"If the guy is such a great firefighter," Dave would snap when he arrived home angry and upset, "then why doesn't he teach me something instead of just being an asshole?" His jaw would tighten. "The older guys should be teaching the younger ones. That's how it's supposed to be." And so he did this for all the new men who joined Squad.

"Dave really liked you, too," I tell Billy.

"He talked about going to dinner one night . . . with my wife . . . you know, all of us," Billy says slowly.

"Yeah, it's too bad we never did." I find out Billy went to the High School of Performing Arts like I did, but dropped out after only one year.

"I was a dancer. I'm straight. You do the math," he said when I asked why he left. I couldn't help but laugh at this muscular man leaping through the third-floor dance studios of Performing Arts. It turns out we know many of the same people from there, and I smile and shake my head.

"It's a small world," I say.

"Too small," Billy says as we hear the engine door open and the loud beeping of the truck backing in.

*   *   *

On the evening of September 24, the bat phone rings. I brace myself for more bad news. Tony Edwards from the firehouse is on the other end.

"What's a matter? You can't get enough of me?" I joke, trying to disguise how scared I am.

"Listen," he says in a voice so serious it makes me gulp. "I'm sorry to bother you with this, but I know you're in the neighborhood and every-thing."

"What?"

"A chief came by and told us they're closing Squad."

"WHAT?!" I scream, anger boiling like lava in my stomach. *"Why?"*

"I dunno. Special Operations lost so many guys, they're sayin' they don't have enough trained men to fill the spots. They're gonna send us to firehouses around Manhattan."

"They can't do that!" I yell, the lava rising higher.

"That's the department for ya. Kick us when we're down."

"I haven't even cleaned out his locker!"

"Nobody has. It's only been two freakin' weeks!"

"Who told you this?" I ask, my mind racing.

"Chief Norman." I write "Norman" down on a pad as I try to catch my breath. "He came by last night and told Huey and me and a bunch of the guys that they're closing Squad. We're goin' over to Lynn Tierney's house now." I can see the deputy commissioner's blue eyes widening when she opens the door to see eight angry firefighters standing in the doorway of her apartment on 12th Street, in Brooklyn.

"Do you have Chief Norman's number?" I ask him, and I write this down, too.

"I just didn't want you to hear it from somewhere else," he says.

"Are you kidding? This is bullshit. I'm gonna call a couple of friends. See what I can do." I am pacing now, fast and furious across the cracking linoleum floor. "I think we should have a protest tomorrow."

"We're all going to Tim Stackpole's funeral."

"They found Timmy?" Again I think of Timmy and his struggle to return to the job he loved, only to die a month later.

"Yeah, the other day. I thought you knew. It was in the papers."

"No, I didn't. Where's the funeral? I want to go." Though Tim wasn't at Squad 1, I want to support his brother Mike.

"You don't have to."

"I want to. Is Mike okay?"

"Hangin' in, I guess. Who the fuck knows."

"Where was he found?"

"South Tower, I think." My mind does a sharp turn to the left and I think about Dave. I know he is in the South Tower. They are finally finding bodies there.

"Hey, what about Chief Hayde?" I ask. "Can't he help us?"

"Naw. He's one of them now. In fact, Chief Norman is his friend," Tony says bitterly.

I hang up, my rage refueling me, giving me purpose. I call Dede, my friend on 3rd Street. We decide to start a phone chain in the neighborhood. "We'll have two rallies," I decide right then. "One at three-thirty, so the kids can come. One at six-thirty, so the press will have time to hear about it." Adrenaline rushes through me.

I rant to Leah, Jason, and Sara, who are sitting on the couch eating leftovers. They shake their heads at the right spots, noting my outrage with polite surprise, watching me pace back and forth as if watching a tennis match. I finally take a deep breath and exhale, surprised at the energy I suddenly have. I excuse myself and storm into my room to e-mail friends and acquaintances I have acquired over the last four years—946 of them—Chief Norman's number.

I'm still hammering on the keyboard, working on a flyer to plaster around the neighborhood when my sister sits up.

"It's two in the morning," Leah complains. She is sleeping on my bed.

"Am I keeping you up?" I respond, distracted, surprised at how late it is.

"Yes, and you should go to sleep," she says, groggy. I listen to her breathe until she drifts back to sleep, and then sit back to read my flyer.

A Widow's Plea

My husband, Dave Fontana, is a firefighter from Squad 1 missing from September 11's attack. Last night, the firefighters of Squad 1 informed me that the firehouse doors will close tomorrow. The firehouse is not only a place of refuge for me in my grief, but is an integral part of the Park Slope community.

The firefighters of Squad 1 are working tirelessly to retrieve their fallen brothers and are heartbroken to be displaced from their home. Please don't let my husband die in vain by letting the firehouse he loved and served close.

The firefighters and I have been touched and strengthened by the outpouring of support shown to us by the community, but we really need your help now. Please call Chief Norman at SOC command at (212) 570-9440 and make your voice heard! THANK YOU!

I print forty-five copies and find a thick roll of tape to use in the morning. Still wired, I take two Ambien and lie on the couch, staring at the cracks in the ceiling, until I fall into a deep, blank sleep.

I wake up the next morning to the sound of Aidan's deep and hopeful giggles as Leah wrestles with him in my bed. I put on the teakettle, noting what a wonderful sister Leah has been. I had always imagined us getting married around the same time, having children together. After I moved to Brooklyn with Dave, Leah stayed single on the Upper East Side, teaching ballet and performing theater and music on the side. Leah stumbles into the kitchen dramatically with Aidan latched on to her leg.

"Your son's crazy!" she says breathlessly, tickling Aidan, who collapses to the floor. I try to smile, but I feel as if my face is frozen, my mouth incapable of turning up at the ends. Leah looks at me cautiously and drags Aidan into the living room.

"I'm thirsty!" he yells.

"How do you ask?" I say robotically.

"Please?"

I pour orange juice into a *Star Wars* cup and hand it to Aidan, kissing his head. "How are you doing, sweetie?" I ask, running my hands through his hair.

"Fine." But I can tell he is not fine at all. "I don't want to go to school today," he says miserably, gulping down his juice.

"I know, but that's your job."

"What are you going to do?" he asks, launching himself into my lap.

"I have to go help the firefighters today," I tell him.

"Can I come?" he asks, climbing up again.

"Not now, maybe after school."

Aidan stands up and stomps into his bedroom. I follow him to his bed, where he buries his face in the pillows. In his short five years, I have nursed Aidan through jaundice, inguinal surgery, the croup, splinters, countless flus, and strep throats. For every trial, there was always a cure and Dave standing next to me, his face as twisted in worry as mine. Now I feel helpless, rubbing Aidan's back, telling him I love him and that someday we will feel better. I feel like a liar.

"When you get home we can make Goops," Sara says groggily from the top bunk.

Aidan pops his head up from under the pillow and we laugh at Sara's voice coming from nowhere. The Goops are from a 1920s book that Sara showed Aidan in Maine. They are old-fashioned cautionary tales about the importance of manners, and Aidan was intrigued by the round-headed cartoons depicting countless varieties of bad behavior. *"The Goops they lick their fingers. The Goops they lick their knives. They spill their broth on the table cloth. They lead disgusting lives."*

With Aidan's pinky in one hand and my flyers in the other, I walk the path to school, shocked that a number of telephone poles are already plastered with flyers announcing rallies at Squad 1. In front of school, mothers stand with petitions to "Help Keep Squad 1 Open." I smile at them, gulping back tears. I spot Dede and give her a hug.

"I made one phone call," she says. "The neighborhood did the rest."

I walk Aidan into his classroom. The children are already seated at their desks, reading, when Aidan's teacher scurries over, her eyes darting to and fro.

"You really need to bring Aidan on time," she says softly, and I am dumbfounded.

"There's crowds of people in my house every night until midnight," I say nervously. "His bedroom is right next to the living room so it's hard for him to fall asleep, and I try not to wake him up." My face grows hot with shame.

"It's okay to bring him tired," she says, looking over at a table. "Excuse me, Amanda!" Her voice is shrill and nasal. "I don't see you reading!" She looks at Amanda and then turns to me. "He really needs to be on time so he has a routine. You know, for some normalcy."

"I can barely get my shoes on," I mumble, trying hard not to cry.

I head over to Aidan to give him a kiss. He squeezes my arm hard, not wanting me to leave. I don't react, my heart thumping hard against my chest. I want to scoop Aidan up and run away. What is *normalcy,* anyway? Life stopped being normal for us over two weeks ago. *Two weeks.* Aidan finally lets go of my arm and I kiss him on the cheek, tiptoeing out of the classroom into the fall sun.

9:15 A.M.

When I return home from putting up posters, Sara is on the phone. I hand her one of the two coffees the size of ice cream shakes that I am carrying.

"Jesus Christ! These are huge!" she says, hanging up.

"I wanted a small, but I couldn't remember the stupid name for it."

I haven't gone back to Connecticut Muffin, since Tommy won't even look up when I order.

The phone rings. By the time I'm finished with the call my lip is trembling.

"What's wrong?" Sara asks.

"It's Squad. They saw the poster. They think it's too early to use the word 'widow.'" My jaw shifts to press the tears away and I whisper, "They are not ready for me to be a widow yet."

When I return from ripping down my posters, I am sweating and the phone is, as usual, ringing.

"Marian. It's Don," Chief Hayde's voice bellows through the phone. "You're going to Timmy's funeral today, right?"

"Yes," I say cautiously. How does he know this?

"Can I pick you up?" he asks. I deduce that he has been told by the fire department to placate me.

"Sure," I say tersely, and a long silence follows.

Half an hour later, I climb the high steps and hoist myself into the wide leather seats of Chief Hayde's SUV. I remember Dave telling me how chiefs made six figures a year, standing outside of fires directing the other firefighters. The top chiefs in the department were at the towers that day at a Command Center inside the lobby. When things starting getting worse, the chiefs, including an expert in collapse, moved the Command Center across the street, where, it is rumored, they could tell the top floors were in danger of collapsing, and radioed a Mayday to the firefighters inside—a Mayday that probably wasn't heard.

"How are you doing?" Don asks.

"I'm pissed," I say, staring straight ahead, and Don sighs, obviously uncomfortable with the topic.

"Listen, Marian," he starts quietly. "I've known Chief Norman my whole life and he's a good guy. You can't shoot the messenger."

"The messenger should have read the message before he sent it," I say curtly. His driving is nervous and erratic as we head toward Marine Park.

"Look, you don't need to make a big deal about this. The guys told me you're having a rally—"

"Two, actually," I say, checking my lipstick in the mirror on the back of the visor.

"You really don't have to do that," he says more cautiously, his eye twitching.

"Then why don't you tell the Special Operations chiefs to leave Squad alone?"

"Shit!" Chief Hayde slams on his brakes behind a delivery truck. "Sorry," he mumbles, shifting uncomfortably, scrambling for something to say. I stare out of the window and watch a Hasidic man walk hurriedly down the avenue, his long side curls bouncing like springs. He holds his small daughter's hand as she runs to keep up with him, her other hand hiking up her long black skirt.

"Dave was a great guy . . ." Chief Hayde offers after a long silence.

"The best," I say, looking at my distorted reflection in the window.

"We used to talk for hours about history and books. I could talk to him about anything."

I say nothing and watch the magnified drip of a tear glide down my cheek in the window.

"I really loved that guy," Don says softly, the traffic moving again.

"If you really loved him," I say, sitting up and facing forward, "then you wouldn't let them close Squad."

Don sighs audibly, shifting again. We drive in silence for the rest of the trip until we spot fire trucks blocking the road ahead. Circling, we find a spot on a wide street with low brick houses and faded green lawns.

Don parks and runs ahead of me, sliding on the white gloves of his uniform, promising to find me later. Firefighters are stretched for blocks, outlining the street in a wide band of blue.

I press myself past a row of firefighters to where neighbors and friends are squeezed in. I inch my way toward the church. The crowd's so thick, I try to turn back, but I am being pushed forward, as in a whirlpool. The haunting roll of snare drums begin in the distance, and I watch a sea of gloved hands rise in a salute. A cacophony of bagpipers begin marching past me with puffed red cheeks. Dave loved the bagpipes, their reedy drone forever connected to the lush green hills of Ireland. He was the first of his family to meet his Irish relatives with whom his mother had corresponded for many years. I can still remember watching Dave's head from the backseat of the tiny Renault his aunt Alice was driving. She was talking in a fast brogue, pointing out churches and schools dotting the hills and Dave's head flopped forward, as he lost his battle with jet lag.

The tears drip into my mouth as I summon up Dave sipping Guinness in the tiny pub with the wobbly stools, a mustache of foam framing his contented smile. My memories both comfort and torture me as I recall walking back to the B&B from the pub, holding hands in the black Irish night, inhaling the earthy smell of peat. The clean air filled our noses as we watched the stars, a thousand pinholes of light above us.

Ladder 103 passes us, covered in wreaths and a flag-draped coffin followed by a limousine, black and slow like a cat. The limo stops in front of me, and Tara Stackpole and their five freckled children exit. Timmy, the youngest, named for his dad, clutches his father's heavy black helmet like a pillow. I spot Huey arriving with his wife, Kathleen, and Sally Siller, one of the other widows, and realize I forgot to call him and tell him not to pick me up for the funeral. "What happened to you?" Huey says, gesturing like a mafia don.

"I went with Chief Hayde. I'm so sorry." Huey is probably late because of me.

"What'd you go with him for?" he asks, pulling on his white gloves.

"I dunno. I thought it would help things."

"Did it start already?" Sally asks, jittery and tense. Her husband, Stephen, was on his way home to play golf when he heard about the towers on his scanner and ran through the tunnel to his death.

"They're all in the church. I saw the family," I tell Sally.

"I can't watch the kids. It kills me," she says, walking toward the church. A microphone squeaks through giant speakers outside.

"Me neither." I think of Tara Stackpole, Timmy's widow, and all she's been through.

"Oh my God," Sally exclaims, noticing how big the funeral is. "I feel bad we're so late. It's all your fault!" she jokes.

"I'm sorry. I'm just a little caught up with the Squad closing thing."

"Don't even get me started on that!" Her voice is rising. "If I didn't have five kids at home, I'd be right there with you." She stops suddenly and turns, her face drooping with sadness. "I can't believe we're going to have to do this. I told my sister, 'He's coming home. Don't even tell me Stephen's not coming home.' " She starts walking again and I struggle to keep up, her strides fast and short like those of a sandpiper running from the sea.

3:30 P.M.

By the time I get back to Squad 1, friends and neighbors have already arrived and news vans are parked along the street. A stooped woman stands at a table by the curb, collecting signatures, and Sara, Leah, and Jason are in the firehouse with Aidan. I head to the back, where the firemen are hiding, unused to all of the fuss. A few reporters stand around, pads in hand. The firefighters look self-conscious and wary.

"Hey, guys," I say, breathless, plopping my bag on the couch in the back room. "What a freakin' day."

"I heard you talked to Donny this morning," Tony says sarcastically.

"Yeah, he was definitely nervous," I start.

"I wouldn't fuck with ya," Misera-Bill teases.

"Don't. I'm an angry widow." The word catches me off guard. I *am* a widow. I picture myself standing on the roof of an elegant Victorian home, looking out at the vast expanse of ocean, a wrought-iron fence making a square around me. I stand on the widow's walk waiting in a long black dress, my shawl fluttering behind me like crows' wings. Then, suddenly angry, I imagine myself hiking up my dress and kicking the fence until it falls to the yard below.

"I wouldn't mess with you, either," one of the reporters says in a tired voice. "I'm Michael Daly from the *Daily News*. I live in the neighborhood over on Garfield." He is hunched, with a long raincoat that makes him look more like a detective than a reporter. Although his hair is gray, his furrowed brow and surprised blue eyes remind me of a young boy. "Do you mind if I ask you a couple of questions?" he asks, flipping over a page in his notebook.

"I have a rally in a few minutes. Maybe after, okay?" He nods and I head out onto the apparatus floor. More people have arrived and are waiting expectantly in the street.

"You're gonna talk to these people, right?" Eric says, setting up a microphone in the front. Eric Lynch plugs the amp into the wall. The guys in the firehouse nicknamed him "the pig farmer" since he commutes from Harriman State Park, over a two-hour drive upstate.

"No. You guys should," I reply.

"We can't. We can get into trouble," he says, his hair flopping over his eyes. "C'mon. You're an actress."

"This is different," I say, looking at the crowd that has swelled past where I can see.

A bunch of the firefighters recently attended my one-woman comedy show at a small theater in Chelsea. I remember seeing them all silhouetted in the blinding lights, hearing Theresa Russo's distinctive giggle from where she sat with Mike. Dave was in the back row. I couldn't see him or hear him laugh, but I knew he was there, beaming proudly.

Bernie, the tall Irishman who spoke at the vigil last week, arrives, gives a short speech about the neighborhood, then turns to me, his red eyebrows raised. "Do you want to say anything?" My sister stares at me anxiously from the audience, holding Aidan's hand.

"Why not," I say, stepping up to the microphone, pulling Dave's denim jacket tightly around me. My mouth feels like I've swallowed dirt. I jam my hands into my pockets to keep them from shaking, and I look out at the sea of people standing quietly.

"My name is Marian Fontana. My husband, Dave, is one of the twelve men missing at Ground Zero," I begin.

"We can't hear you!" someone shouts from the back, and I move the microphone closer to my mouth. "My husband loved this neighborhood and he loved this firehouse," I continue hesitantly. "This place was his second home, and now it has become mine." I see reporters writing furiously, people taking pictures, and my former students holding signs that read SAVE SQUAD 1.

"Closing the Squad is a slap in the face not only to the men missing, but to their surviving brothers who have been searching for them." I stop abruptly, my voice cracking, and I squeeze my lips closed, trying not to cry. I feel Bernie's hand on my back as I try to breathe, but my chest feels like a tight belt is around it. I can feel Dave around me, inside me, with me, and the tears come quiet and strong, dripping onto the sleeve of Dave's denim jacket.

I look up again and see that my neighbors are crying, too. I see my friends from the Dance Studio, Ashley from preschool—they are all crying. I step back up to the microphone and continue. "The firehouse has become my second family, and this neighborhood that has been so amazing needs this family here. It is a vital part of this special community. Thank you all so much."

"We love you!" someone yells from the audience as applause crescendos into a solid, deafening sound. Voices in the crowd begin chanting "Squad One . . . Squad One . . . Squad One." The energy is overpowering, like the force of a blast. I can do nothing but stare dumbstruck and overwhelmed into the crowd. Finally, someone leads me away as Alan Hevesi and local politicians take the mike. The actor John Turturro hands me his number. He tells me he lives in the neighborhood and if there's anything he can do to help, he will.

My sister grabs my shaking hand and pulls me toward the sitting room at the back of the firehouse, but we are intercepted by a woman with platinum hair and teeth like Chiclets gum.

"Hi, I'm Linda with ABC, can I talk to you for just a sec?" I signal Leah to go ahead, and stand awkwardly. "I just want to say how sorry I am. This has been such a hard time, and my prayers are with you."

"Thank you," I mumble, staring at the station's logo adorning her microphone.

"Can I ask you to spell your name, please?" she says, stepping closer to me, the cameraman peeking behind her like a shy child. I notice other reporters inching toward me, some with microphones, others with long memo pads.

"M-A—"

"Don't look at the camera. Look at me," she warns, and I turn toward her again, trying hard not to glance at the wide black lens pointed in my face.

"Why is it so important that Squad stays open?" she asks, her head tilting to the side.

"Well, we have—there are twelve men missing," I stutter angrily. "If my husband knew that Squad One was closing, he would roll over in his grave, if he had one."

The reporter nods vigorously. "How old was he?"

"He'd be thirty-eight in three weeks."

"Thirty-seven," she says into her microphone. "Is it possible to get a shot of your husband's locker?" the reporter asks brazenly, her orange foundation glowing in the bright light of the camera.

"No . . . I don't know . . ."

"Is there anyone I can ask?" she says, insistent, before another reporter steps in, wielding a tiny voice recorder.

Five interviews later, Eric leads me into the back room, where eight of the guys sit.

"What?" I say defensively, eyeing Tony, who sports a wry smile.

"Nothing. Dave would be proud of you."

I bite my lip to keep the tears from coming again.

"You shouldn't even have to be doing this," Huey says.

"But we appreciate it . . . We can't say nothin' or the job will come back at us," Dennis says.

"Well," I say, wiping my eyes, "I know this would kill Dave if he were here."

Eric enters with a fax in his hand. "Von Essen's saying that it was only a rumor. They never planned to close Squad."

"A rumor!" I say, snatching the paper from his hand and reading.

"A rumor named Chief Norman," Huey retorts angrily. "Assholes!"

"Why the hell would we make something up like that?" Tony snorts. "Like we wanted it."

"If it were a rumor," Jimmy Lopez starts, "then why would we all go to Lynn Tierney's house last night at midnight!"

"We were all sitting there. We all heard the same thing. They said they were going to close Squad. We wouldn't just make it up."

"They're backpedaling," I say, thinking of Dave. Dave, like most firefighters, had an inherent mistrust of "headquarters" and the chiefs and commissioners who worked there. Dave felt that they were out of touch with what firefighters were really doing in the field and did not keep their best interests in mind. The men felt this way particularly about Tom Von Essen, who became a commissioner after being union president, an unusual career move that most firefighters considered traitorous.

"Are you gonna have the next rally?" Eric asks.

"Yeah," I say slowly, still reading, "because this doesn't say that you won't be dispersed all over the city."

Dodging reporters, I head to Lentos, a dark pizzeria across the street from the firehouse.

"What took you so long?" my sister asks, sipping Jack Daniel's and ginger ale. Jason sits next to me, drinking a Diet Coke. I order a cosmopolitan from the bartender, who recognizes me. My friend Peggy and I used to come here on Thursday nights after we taught at the Dance Studio on the corner. Sipping merlot and cursing like sailors, we would tell funny anecdotes from our classes and wave to Dave if he passed in the fire truck.

"How's Aidan doing?" I ask Leah.

"He's fine. He went home with Mom and Dad. They're going to tuck him in." I take a deep breath and pull a cigarette from Sara's pack.

"You were amazing, honey," Jason says sincerely. "I don't know how you're doing this."

My sister leans in and grabs the cigarette from my hand and lights it. "Man, I was like—who is this person?" She takes a long drag and hands it back to me. On the TV perched in the corner of the bar, the same blond newscaster magically appears, standing in front of Squad.

"Ooh! Can you turn this up, please?" Sara asks the bartender. I watch in disbelief as my image appears on the television. I look different from how I picture myself, the lines of grief evident under my eyes, my flaws raw and exposed.

"Oh my God. I look like shit," I say, rubbing my fingers through my hair, embarrassed.

"Shut up. You look beautiful," Jason says, and I love him for saying this.

* * *

I peer out the window, where another crowd has begun to gather for the second rally. It is larger than the first, filled with Slopers returning from work. Men in suits and backpacks stand next to wives with strollers. I pay the check and wearily cross the street to begin.

"You sure you want to have another rally?" Eric says. "Von Essen sent another fax saying it's open."

"Yeah, but what about you guys being put all over the city?"

"They didn't say anything about that."

"Then we should have it to make sure we keep the guys together." Eric shrugs and heads to the back.

The words come more easily this time. I feel like a lion protecting her cubs, fierce and determined. I speak more freely with reporters. I talk to Michael Daly in his London Fog coat. I like the easy way he asks questions, his thick Brooklyn accent, his little-boy laugh, his tired Irish eyes. He tells me he knows a lot of the firefighters, that he was close friends with Father Mychal Judge, the first firefighter casualty of September 11.

"I wouldn't mess with you," he tells me again, an eyebrow raised. "These guys better watch out."

I meet Charlie LeDuff, a reporter from the *New York Times*. He wants to do a series on Squad, but firefighters are suspicious of reporters lurking around the firehouse like dogs waiting for a restaurant to close, and Charlie does not look like the other reporters. He drives a giant orange Studebaker with a broken muffler, and his long brown hair is tossed haphazardly into a braid that travels halfway down his back. He is half Puerto Rican and half American Indian, with dark mocha skin; his brown eyes flash as he chews on a straw. He gives me his card and asks if he can come over the next day. He will profile me instead of Squad.

At 10 P.M. I plop onto a couch at the back of the firehouse, my pockets full of tissues and business cards. Chief Hayde arrives, looking serious and gathers the men where I am sitting. We squeeze together and I make jokes. Looking worn and haggard, Chief Hayde clears his throat, his eyes staring at mine. "Marian, if you wouldn't mind waiting outside, I gotta talk to the guys."

"Sorry, Chief, but she *is* one of the guys," Tony says.

Phil grins and adds, "An honorary firefighter."

"I don't know if that's a compliment or an insult," I say.

Giving up, Chief Hayde begins. "I talked to Special Operations Command, and the house is gonna stay open." His eye with the tic is twitching like crazy.

"What about the guys?" I ask.

"They're not going anywhere."

"For how long?"

"We can't guarantee anything now, because we have a lot of problems. SOC lost a lotta guys, and we don't have enough trained guys to fill the houses."

"You know we can run this place on an AB schedule," Dennis says. This means dividing the limited manpower in half, switching back and forth, from group to group.

"I know that, we just can't promise anything," the chief says.

"Well, I can," I continue, poker-faced. "I promise that if SOC tries anything with Squad again, this is just a small example of what I will do." There is a long silence, and I keep my eyes on the chief, who shifts on the arm of the sofa. In my peripheral vision, I can see the firefighters smirking. The chief breaks our stare, smacking his hands on his thighs and standing. "Well," he says, his face slowly relaxing, "it's my birthday today so I'd appreciate it, Marian, if you'd let me buy you a drink." I stand to wish the chief a happy birthday, feeling guilty and relieved. The guys smile, clap Chief Hayde on the back, and I make my way once again to Lentos for a drink.

* * *

The next morning, Aidan clings to my leg as we walk down the long hallway to his classroom. I peel him off and guide him to his seat.

"Don't go," he whines faintly into my thigh.

"I have to, honey."

"Noooo!"

"I'll stay one minute," I say sternly, and open a book to read to him. In between pages, I search for Aidan's teacher, who sits at a table, her straight bowl cut flopping into her face. When the book is finished, I kiss his head and start for the door, pushing it open as guilt churns the bile in my stomach. I hear Aidan crying on the other side of the door and I lean in to listen. Some moms from the class who are chatting in the schoolyard cluster around me, offering me tissues as I stare at the door, crying.

"As soon as you're gone he'll be fine," Nicholas's mom, Nadia, says in her thick Russian accent.

"He's fine," Amisa's mom, Lisa, says, peeking in the window. "He's playing with Charlie."

"He's having a hard time, huh?" Gina reaches in her pocket and retrieves some crumpled tissues.

"I just don't think he's getting what he needs. The teacher seems distracted. I mean, she told me I've been late too many times. Can you believe that?"

"That's crazy," Lisa says.

"Does she know what's going on?" Gina adds.

I nod. "They keep telling me to bring him for consistency! How am I supposed to leave him here if I don't feel like he's— I'm going to talk to them," I announce suddenly. I march pass the pit bull security guard toward the principal's office. Roy Ann, the early-childhood social worker, spots me and heads over, smiling. She met Dave and me last year when Aidan started preschool.

"Are you okay?" she asks, her head tilting to the side.

"Not really."

"Do you have a couple of minutes? We can talk about it." I nod, following her into the lunchroom that smells of sour milk. I recall my own lunchroom smelling the exact same way and wonder how they could sustain that odor throughout the years. I force myself to focus again, clumsily climbing into one of the white Formica picnic tables.

"Tell me what's happening," Roy Ann says.

"Aidan is scared when I leave in the morning, and I need someone in the class with him," I begin slowly, my chin involuntarily contracting into the cry position. There is an ESL class going on, and some Spanish and Chinese women are reciting the names of animals in thick accents.

"Was there a counselor in there yesterday?" she asks, running her fingers through wavy hair the color of black ink.

"I don't know, maybe. There is often no one, and if there is someone, she's always different," I complain.

"Well, I can come in on Thursday mornings and we'll get the same person for the other days. That's no problem."

"Good."

She tilts her head to the side again. "How are *you* doing?" Her sympathy suddenly annoys me, makes me feel small.

"I'm fine," I say, but it is too late. I am gone. I cup my hands over my eyes so she will not see me crying, so she will not know that I am, in fact, falling apart.

"This is very hard," she says. "I know it's not the same, but I lost my sister. She was very young when she died." I say nothing but stare instead at the peeling nail polish on my toes. "There are quite a few of us who really love Aidan and who are watching out for him and making sure he's okay. You're doing the right thing, bringing him here every day." I want to tell her how guilty I am, how I resent having to parent alone, how I can't even be alone with Aidan because I feel lopsided with a corner of our triangle missing, but I say nothing and listen to the voices echo "*Caballo,* horse, *gato,* cat, *perro,* dog."

* * *

Friends and family begin to arrive again in the evening, eating donated lasagna and drinking wine. I sit in the backyard watching long shadows fall across the garden. It's getting darker earlier now, and I shudder at the thought of winter. Fall was Dave's favorite time of year. He wore shorts and hiking boots and loved the smell of wet leaves and apples. To me, fall always meant endings, something shifting inside. It was the end of summer, the end of warmth, the end of green, languorous heat.

"I need a wake-ation," I say to the group seated at the table. Everyone laughs too hard, especially my friend Caren, whose giggle U-turns sharply into crying, and we all grow hushed again. "I want to go somewhere with no memories. Somewhere I've never been with Dave. I need someplace quiet . . . to collect myself and plan Dave's funeral." The silence that ensues feels as permanent as the words I have just uttered for the first time.

8

The Wake-ation

September 27

7:00 A.M.

I am sleeping on the couch again when I spot Dave's silhouette in the doorway. He's home! He's finally home!

"Dave?" I say eagerly.

"It's Ed." Ed is standing in the foyer, a towel wrapped around his waist. "I'm sorry. I didn't mean to scare you."

"I thought you—" I am crying already, sore and tired from sleeping on my lumpy couch for almost three weeks. Ed sits next to me, the couch groaning under his weight.

"I keep seeing him everywhere," I say, shaking my head. "I just . . . you look like . . ."

"I know. Every guy I pass on the street that's built like Dave . . ."

I nod, and after I am done crying, every muscle hurts like I have run a marathon. "Grieving is exhausting," I say out loud.

"I was thinking that after I take you to the wake today, I should go home." Ed's words are suspended like a feather floating in front of us. I say nothing even though I know he is right. As much of a solace it has been for him to be here, the familiarity of his gestures haunts me. "I have to get back to school anyway. I'm surprised the principal hasn't fired me yet." Ed forces a chuckle, his shoulders bouncing. I can't imagine teaching again, the joy I showed to my students seems so long ago. Ed clears his throat and puts a hand on my thigh. "It's hard to go."

"I know," I tell him. "You've been . . . well, I'll call you right away if I hear anything."

"Hey, buddy." Aidan has just tiptoed into the living room. He climbs up on my lap rubbing his eyes. All these comings and goings will be hard for him.

"Are you crying again?" he asks me, lifting his head.

"I scared your mommy before," Ed says lightly, "but she's fine now."

Ed gets Aidan dressed while Sara and I sneak into the garden, smoking cigarettes in our pajamas. I can't believe I am smoking almost a pack a day. I stare at the wilting impatiens, their delicate pink faces drooping from the cold and still coated in a light Ground Zero dust. Has Dave turned into ash as fine as baby powder? Is he willing himself to float across the harbor and land in our tiny garden? The news last night said that the fires have been burning for over two weeks and no one has been found alive.

"I'll water them today," Sara says. I shrug, sadness and smoke sticking in my throat.

"Sweetie," Sara says softly, but I am too tired to cry again. I stand to make coffee inside.

Leah and her boyfriend, Neil, are finally up. Neil arrived on the thirteenth, and they have been sleeping at Lynn's apartment across the street. I spy Aidan in the living room, leading Neil by the hand to a pile of knights on the floor. A tall and soft-spoken man who writes descriptions of movies for a video database, Neil has been a calming presence, quietly doling out tissues, washing dishes, and being infinitely patient and kind to Aidan. Leah kisses me good morning and fills the teapot with water.

Neil's wide mouth is turned up in a crooked smile as he plays. He has thick, messy black hair and glacier-clear green eyes. Leah watches Neil thoughtfully. She only started dating him a few months before September 11 and has been reluctant to commit.

"He's been unbelievable," I say to Leah, reaching for the coffee cup Dave bought me in Disneyland two years ago. It has a cartoon of Belle from *Beauty and the Beast* with a thought bubble above her that reads: "Why are men always such Beasts?"

Leah sighs, taking a cup, too. "I'm just so screwed up right now, how can I tell anything?" she whispers, her chin wrinkling in possible tears. "It's hard to know how I feel."

"Just don't question it." I take the coffeepot off its stand and pour a cup. Over the years, Dave and I watched Leah step on countless land mines in the dating field. She always chose model-perfect men whose sculptured features were a convincing decoy to their damaged insides. "All I know," I tell her, "is if Neil sees you through this, he'll see you through anything."

"I know. I just . . ." She stares dreamily into the living room again.

"Dave liked him." We met Neil at my thirty-fifth birthday party. Neil was a wild dancer, throwing his body around with uninhibited glee. He grabbed me to dance, spun me around, and dipped me so low, he dropped me on the carpet. Dave laughed so hard, his dimples formed two vertical lines on his cheeks. "You didn't look that heavy!" Neil exclaimed as he laughed, too, pulling me up from the floor.

"Well, Dave had good taste," my sister says, bringing me back from my reverie.

"He definitely did." I can't help sighing at the irony that my sister may have finally found love at the moment I have lost it.

*   *   *

On the two-hour drive to Jim Amato's wake in Ronkonkama, Long Island, I play with the radio, trying to find a station. It seems like every DJ in the city is conspiring against me, playing songs about finding love, losing love, how wonderful love is. I finally click it off and close my eyes, imagining that Dave, not Ed, is in the driver's seat, reaching to squeeze my thigh, cursing bad drivers, sighing at traffic, and humming along to the songs he liked.

"I heard they're Jehovah's Witnesses," I say, breaking the silence.

"The Amatos? Really?"

"Yeah. I remember Dave telling me they didn't come to the Christmas parties because they don't celebrate holidays."

"Weird."

"Sounds good to me right now," I say, thinking of all the holidays I will now have to celebrate alone.

We arrive early and pull into a supermarket parking lot for sandwiches. Ed is quiet, so I talk incessantly to fill up the silences.

"Remember that toboggan ride?" I ask. Ed had come to our dorm at C. W. Post College to visit one winter evening with a toboggan and a thermos full of rum toddies. Giggling and dizzy, a group followed Ed and Dave up a steep snowy hill by the horse fields behind our dorm. One lone streetlight shone on the snow, making it sparkle like a Vegas stage as eight of us squeezed onto a toboggan meant for four. We made our descent, screaming into the night. Dave squeezed my thigh as we picked up speed, my hair flying into his face. "Turn *left!*" Ed yelled, but we all leaned in different directions like an open Swiss army knife and ended up cutting a hole through a hedge, where we finally skidded to a stop. I laughed so hard my stomach cramped and I could feel Dave staring at me, his cheeks streaked red from the cold.

The funeral parlor is sparse, with no crosses, a dictum from the Jehovah's Witness church. Joe O'Donnell and Jimmy are standing honor guard in front of a flagless coffin. In ten minutes, two firefighters will replace them; ten minutes later, two more will take their turn. It will go on like this for hours, until the wake is over and they convene at the firehouse or go out for drinks. The men will talk about the Yankees or how dirty their uniforms are, because with so many funerals, there is no time to clean them. And when they realize the time, they will drive home to their wives in Staten Island, Long Island, or Rockaway Beach, and they will collapse in their beds, their wives long asleep, exhausted from tucking in the children alone.

I wave to other widows and wives who talk in hushed clusters throughout the room. Ed and I join a long line of people waiting on the far wall to offer condolences. I spot Debbie Amato, Jim's wife, sitting in a large chair across from the coffin. She is a strikingly beautiful woman with smooth Spanish skin and the high round cheekbones of an Egyptian sphinx. Her brown eyes look empty; she stares straight ahead as if watching TV, her four children flanking her. Her two teenage girls lean on the chair protectively. They are a striking combination of their parents, with exotic green eyes and hair as thick and black as horses' tails.

Ed and I pass a collage of photographs: Jim and his family on vacations, standing in pools, or in a crowd at a party, his eyes a Coke-bottle green. Debbie's own eyes light up when she spots me, a fellow traveler on the road of loss.

"How you doin', baby?"

I shrug helplessly and smile at her daughter. "You must be exhausted," I say, noticing the line getting longer, twisting out of the room and into the hall.

"I can't even stand up." Debbie groans. "I know you're supposed to, but I can't."

"Whatever gets you through." I can identify with the weary fatigue in her voice.

"I wish these people would just go away," she says miserably, staring ahead again.

"I know. Maybe you can have a button on your shirt with a recording: 'Thank you for coming. Thank you so much. Yes he was. Thank you for coming,' " I say.

"I know, right?" She laughs weakly. I kiss her on the cheek and continue on to Jim's brother, Lee, a firefighter from Miami whom I had met at the firehouse a few days after the eleventh. He had found his brother at Ground Zero.

"I wish I could do what he did," Ed whispers as we sit in chairs in the center of the room. "I should take Dave's gear and look for him."

"Dave wouldn't want that," I say absently, remembering that Ed was once almost a firefighter, too.

*　　*　　*

The following day I'm in my car, watching the sun lower like a curtain, casting the Tappan Zee Bridge in a coppery light. Quaint white houses dot the low cliffs flanking the Hudson River and I note that the leaves have already begun their slow metamorphosis to yellow. Neighbors I have met only once have generously offered Leah, Sara, Aidan, and me their home in the country for the weekend.

"I'm hungry!" Aidan announces halfway across the bridge. We pull into the giant Palisades Mall in Nyack, New York. We visited the mall once before on the way home from a hike in New Paltz. I remember how disappointed Dave felt that day; he had envisioned a family adventure exploring the marvels of nature, explaining to his eager son how hawks glide on wind currents, but Aidan complained, periodically collapsing on the hiking trail, his plastic Viking helmet sliding off his head as he whined.

"C'mon, you're a hiking Viking!" I cajoled Aidan, trying to ease the tension that made Dave clench his teeth. "He's just a kid," I reminded Dave, annoyed.

"I know. I just—I just—I want him to remember doing this stuff with me," Dave said, hoisting Aidan onto his shoulders. "He's just too young, I guess."

Aidan and I sit in the food court eating Burger King while Leah and Sara go upstairs to "take a quick look" in the H&M store.

"Daddy and I went on that before," Aidan says, pointing to the giant Ferris wheel that turns like a mill in front of us.

"That's right. After we went hiking last year." I am thrilled he remembers this, and it gives me hope that he will retain many more memories of his father. I take a bite of my Whopper. The food court sounds like an indoor pool, with voices echoing, bouncing off the walls.

"Is Daddy dead?" Aidan asks unexpectedly, biting into a chicken nugget. I stop chewing and stare at him. It is time to tell him what is going on. I had planned on telling him when we were safe at the country house on a walk somewhere quiet. Not here, not now. There is a lady next to me, with dyed jet-black hair and a jogging suit. I can tell she is eavesdropping because she suddenly stops moving, straining to hear.

"Yes," I say in a raspy whisper, "Daddy's dead. The towers were too big and heavy, and when they find Daddy, he'll be dead." The tears fill my eyes, making Aidan's face go out of focus.

"You're a liar," he says without malice, as simply as if he is stating that the sky is blue. "They're going to find him."

"If they find him, sweetie, he won't be alive."

"You're lying."

"I've never lied to you."

"It's not nice to lie."

"I'm not, honey. I wish I were. I do. This is so sad and I wish I could make it not be true, but tha—"

"Look at my new toy!" Aidan says, pulling a plastic Disney character out of his paper bag. I can feel the lady next to me staring, and I try to stuff my tears back, like I'm trying to close a drawer filled with too many clothes. She is drinking a shake now, staring ahead, wondering, I'm sure, what kind of mother tells her son his father is dead in a food court in Nyack. She doesn't know, the way I do, that nothing really goes exactly as we plan.

*   *   *

"Holy shit. It's dark," Sara says as I pull into a long dirt driveway.

"C'mon, Maine is darker," I tease.

"Ooh, she said the sh- word," Aidan says. Sara has always loved to be naughty and eccentric. I dubbed her shop in Portland "the Land of the Misfit Toys" based on the numerous local characters who frequent it.

I squint until I can see the house, silhouetted like a black shadow against the night sky.

"I can't see anything," my sister says. I dig around in the side door of the car. Dave was always prepared for anything. I find his flashlight, his glasses for driving at night, a mask for doing mouth-to-mouth (just in case we saw an accident on the road), and a multipurpose tool I gave him two birthdays ago.

"Thank you, Dave," I whisper as I turn on the flashlight and lead everyone to a creaky screen door of the house.

"I'm scared," Aidan says, his voice tiny and faraway: Mickey Mouse on an old album.

"I'm right here." I reach for his hand.

"Shit. It's cold." Sara stomps in her army boots.

"Ooooh. Sarah said 'shit' again!" Aidan tattles.

"Saraaaa," I scold.

"I'm trying!" She giggles.

"Ooh, look at the stars," Leah says. I can just make out her chin jutting toward the sky flecked with tiny white stars.

"They're better in Maine," Sara decides.

I try the key again, pushing hard on the door until it swings open, smashing into the wall. I search for a switch where a bare bulb illuminates a mudroom filled with rubber boots, sand toys, and sleds. A wall of windows shows a frost, sparkling like spilled glitter on the long grass outside. We take off our shoes and I make my way into a large, drafty kitchen. Wooden cabinets filled with Fiestaware plates line the walls. The speckled linoleum floor creaks. My grandmother had the same floor in her tiny apartment in Queens. A wide wooden table sits in the center of the room scattered with papers and bills. On the right wall stands a giant old-fashioned refrigerator.

We plop our bags down and Aidan runs into a large living room, where he discovers a box of toys in the corner. Sara claims a large bedroom in the front while Leah and I wander back to a narrow staircase leading upstairs. I choose the smallest room on the right, a little girl's room with walls the color of cotton candy. Two single beds covered with cozy flowered throws sit across from each other. Tiny shoes poke out from underneath like shy mice.

"Are you going to fit on that bed?" my sister asks, leaning into the room.

"At least we're in separate beds," I say. I have never been able to sleep with Aidan, who flips like a fish throughout the night.

I bathe Aidan in a fancy tub the size of a small pool and smile as he swishes himself back and forth, his small round bottom poking through the bubbles. I take out his *Star Wars* figures, and we pretend the bubbles are a planet full of snow.

"Luke, you don't know the power of the Dark Side." I am Darth Vader, breathing heavy into a hand cupped over my mouth.

"You don't do the voice as good as Daddy does," Aidan says.

"I do a lot of things different than Daddy," I say, trying not to get annoyed.

"You can be C-3PO," he directs, and I dutifully adopt a staccato English accent. Last year I was C-3PO for a solid month while Aidan pretended to be Anakin showing me around his planet. "These are called bagels," Aidan would say when we left the bagel shop with a warm dozen.

"I do say, Master Anakin, how on earth can you eat a hole?" I would answer, to Aidan's delight.

Dave was so charmed by our game that he bought me a giant C-3PO mask for Mother's Day. I loved it and walked around the house, moving my arms like a robot, saying, "I do say, Master Anakin, your father is quite strange. What kind of flowers are these?"

After his bath, I tuck Aidan into one of the tiny beds, holding his damp hand and waiting impatiently for his breathing to slow into the deep rhythm of sleep.

"Mommy," he murmurs softly.

"What, honey?"

"I want to see Daddy."

"I know, honey, but he's up in heaven."

"When can I see him again?"

"Not until you die."

"I want to die," Aidan says.

"It's not time to. You have a lot of life left."

"I don't want to be here without Daddy," he says, and I glide my hand across his wet hair.

"Shhh. There are so many wonderful things you haven't done yet," I tell him, my voice a slow, quiet monotone. I will make this his meditation, his bedtime story for tonight. "You haven't seen a volcano, or made a marionette, or skied off the top of a high snowy mountain, or played an instrument in an orchestra. You haven't learned how to read or write or swim alone in an ocean. You have stories to make up and sunsets to watch. You've never been to beaches in sunny places far away. . . . You haven't eaten ice cream made from scratch or drunk coconut milk . . ." I go on and on, my voice slow and soft, until Aidan's breath whistles lightly in sleep.

I tiptoe out of the room and climb the steep steps down to the kitchen, where Leah and Sara sit drinking wine. Sara pours me a glass and lights a cigarette for me. I smoke, staring at the high ceiling covered in white square tiles.

"I can't do this anymore," I say as if I can wake myself up. I shake my head back and forth. Sara is playing nervously with an Etch-a-Sketch Aidan left on the table. My crying makes her uncomfortable. Leah slides off her stool and wraps her arms tightly around me. Emotions fly through my body like comets as I cry so hard, my body hurts. When I finally stop, we are silent for a long time. I can hear a distant train. The curtain billows slightly in the window. After a long silence, Leah says, "I've lost the feeling in my left thigh." Her words strike me so funny, I begin to laugh. She's been crouching in an awkward position to hold me and now we are all laughing.

Later we sit in rocking chairs on the enclosed porch that runs the length of the house. We are wrapped in blankets, sipping wine, staring at the dim stars.

"I think I should have Dave's funeral on his birthday," I announce.

"Okay," Leah says cautiously.

I rub the soft fringe of my blanket through my fingers. "That gives the firefighters almost three weeks to find him." The flash of a match illuminates Sara's face as she lights another cigarette. "I don't want a funeral parlor. I hate funeral parlors, and I don't want a catering hall. It feels too much like a wedding."

"I should write this down." Leah stands and disappears into the living room.

"I think his birthday is perfect," Sara says, the orange circle at the end of her cigarette glowing stronger as she inhales.

Leah returns with a blank book and takes notes. Planning large events comes naturally to her. She has produced numerous plays, including one that I wrote.

"I think the park would be nice," I say.

"It might be cold," Leah replies. I can tell she feels better doing this. It makes her feel less like she is staring at a wounded deer, twitching and writhing on the side of the road.

"How about the Picnic House then?" I suggest, recalling the big glass room in the middle of Prospect Park that overlooks the field. On warm days, we would pull Aidan in a red Radio Flyer wagon to the big field and watch the teenagers playing Hacky Sack and Jamaican men flying colorful kites that buzzed and whirled above us like a horde of beautiful bees. Aidan would pounce on Dave to wrestle and I would often join in, Dave swatting us off as easily as flies.

"We could get Matthew to cater it," Leah suggests.

"Maybe a place in the neighborhood," Sara says. The lights in the living room flicker in short sporadic surges and we grow quiet.

"That's weird," Sara says.

"It's Dave," Leah says. When the lights in my apartment do this, she insists that it is him.

"Stop it," I snap, pulling the blanket closer around me, my intellect overriding the deep desire to know that Dave is with me.

"No, really, Marian. You said it's the old wiring in your apartment that makes the lights do that, but what about here?" Leah persists.

"It's an old house, too." My voice doesn't sound as sure as I would like it to.

"I think it's him," Sara says. I shrug and head into the kitchen to open another bottle of wine.

Later, after I collapse onto the small creaky bed across from Aidan and stare at the ceiling trying to sleep, I think, *If you really are here, Dave, make the light flicker now.* I stare so hard at the bulb on the ceiling, I can see the fiery filament inside. *Dave, are you there?* I stare so long, my eyes begin to water.

"*Fuck you,*" I say, flipping the light off and staring at the dark ceiling as teardrops drip past my temples, tickling my ears.

*   *   *

"Get up, Mommy," Aidan says, kissing me awake. My eyes are not convinced it is morning and struggle to open.

We tiptoe down to the kitchen, where it's so cold, I can see my breath. While searching the cabinets for a coffee filter, I notice a lush mountain framed in the window above the sink. Hay-colored grass glistens as the sun casts the front of the mountain in a bright, encouraging light. I fashion a filter from a paper towel, listening to Aidan talk to two tiny Cabbage Patch babies, cradling them and cooing in their ears.

"These are my cousins." He holds up the dolls, their faces painted with perfect brown circles for freckles. "They have no Mommy or Daddy."

"That's so sad," I say, scooping coffee.

"No, it's not, because she has a brother," he says. I freeze: There will be no brother or sister for Aidan. No second baby. I am suddenly angry at Dave for promising Aidan we would give him a brother or sister soon.

"Let's go for an explore," I say quoting from our many evenings reading *Winnie-the-Pooh*.

As we sit in the mudroom sliding on our boots, Leah makes her way downstairs, her slippers squeaking on the linoleum, her eyes flaming red.

"Where are you going?" she asks, watching us zip our coats.

"We're going on an adventure," Aidan announces. "I'm a dinosaur scientist. I'm going to find some fossils."

"Can I come?" Leah says.

"You can be my assistant!" Aidan says, excited. Leah wraps herself in a down coat and slips on her boots.

The air smells like new sheets as we make our way through the wet grass. Aidan has found a backpack to carry his orphaned babies and whispers to them conspiratorially. The steep hill makes us lean forward as we climb; a valley of green and yellow trees appears in the distance. Fog hovers above the trees and we climb through the wet mist to the top.

"Wow," Leah pants. I look at her face. Her eyes are big like mine, but a forest green. She reaches for my hand and we stare out at the vista, quiet and hopeful. The sun spotlights the small hole left by chicken pox on her forehead and the thin scar on her upper lip where our dog, Muffin, bit her one Christmas Eve. I wonder if hearts heal like that, in holes and tiny lines, where the fissures fuse together, hardening into a scar.

"Let's pretend you're an archaeologist and you find some dinosaur bones," Aidan tells Leah as he squats in a patch of broken clay rocks.

"That's called a paleontologist," Leah tells him. "Dr. Aidan, I think I found a *Tyrannosaurus rex* tooth!" she exclaims, picking up a triangular rock.

"No, let's pretend we're the people that look for rocks and we're look-ing for gold," he directs.

"What is that called?" my sister asks me.

"A geologist, I think."

"I'm so tired," Leah says, watching Aidan climb on top of a boulder pretending to look for precious stones. "I had this horrible dream. I dreamed your arm was ripped off. Your left one. It was bloody and dis-gusting."

"Eww."

"It was scary." She picks up a rock and hurls it. We listen to it thud into the grass below and I like the sound. I pick one up for myself. The rock is oddly shaped, gray, with white lines running through it, and I throw it with all my might. It snaps off the branch of a bush below be-fore it bounces to a stop.

"That felt good," I say, picking up another one, rounder and heavier than the last, and heave it into the valley. The small drop of anger I felt earlier in the morning turns into a blinding rage as I begin hurling rocks faster and faster, furious at Dave for leaving me alone, for having to be a hero, for promising me he'd be safe. I am grunting now, hoisting one stone after another, listening to them hit the earth and roll. Leah and Aidan watch me like I'm some crazed Neanderthal. I want to fill my lungs and scream, letting my anguish echo across the mountain and fall into the gurgling streams below me.

"I want to do it, too!" Aidan jumps down from the boulder. Together we lob clay-red rocks over and over until I am sweating and my shoul-der aches. It takes a long time for me to catch my breath, bending over the steam puffing from my mouth.

"Feel better?" Leah asks. I nod, my hands pressed on my knees, and slowly stand up to return to the house.

Later, when we run errands in town, I stop short. "Oh my God. I know this place. This is Callicoon." Dave and I visited here last year when our friends from Brooklyn bought a B&B on the Delaware River, across the street from where we are staying now. "I can't believe it," I say, wondering if this is a sign or if it is simply impossible to avoid seventeen years' worth of memories.

9

Butterflies

I drive under the gray arches of the Verrazano Bridge on my way to Stephen Siller's wake. It is the first one I will attend alone; it is also the first wake I will attend where there is no body in the casket. The firefighters are frustrated, hopeless, and guilty for not returning our husbands to us, as if somehow, if they worked harder, they could do so. But as the days pass, I find my goal shifting from Dave being found, to hoping he will be found in one piece.

"Welcome to Staten Island, the Borough of Parks" the sign reads as I pass the tollbooth and exit on Clove Road to go, once again, to Harmon Funeral Home.

There's plenty of parking. I find a spot toward the back of the lot and pin my Squad 1 patch to the lapel of my black suit jacket. I turn off my cell phone, which reads "13 missed calls." It is only 2:00 P.M. Mike Daly wrote a lengthy piece about Dave in the *Daily News,* and Charlie LeDuff wrote a piece about Squad in the *New York Times.* My phone has been ringing off the hook with interview requests. Last night, instead of returning the dozens of media calls, I impulsively dialed Sally, Stephen's wife, to see how she was doing. We commiserated about the overwhelming influx of people, how the press won't take no for an answer. Sally told me the press had been relentless since they heard that her eighteen-month-old, the youngest of five, has four penny-size holes in his heart.

"*Dateline* called and wanted to do a story, but I just didn't know if it was right. So I told Stephen I want a sign. Something with butterflies. That has always been my thing. Butterflies." Her voice trailed off. "So I said, 'I need to see three butterflies tomorrow if you want me to do it.' " I can hear two of the girls screaming in the background. "Where was I?"

"Three butterflies," I say.

"So yesterday I get a package, and it's from my friend who sent butterfly pins for Katie." Katie is her oldest daughter, tall and pensive, with Stephen's wide eyes. "I'm watching TV and the Microsoft commercial comes on, that's two; and then my mother arrives to babysit, and she has a butterfly pin. But then that's not good enough. I want more. So I say to Stephen, 'I need more,' and so, Marian, I swear to God, I look out my window this morning and there's butterflies all over the place."

"So you're going to do the show?"

"I dunno. Maybe. The thing is, Marian, I shared Stephen with everyone when he was alive. He was so friendly and he would do anything for anybody. Part of me feels like I don't want to share him in death." I nod, knowing that as much as she wants to keep her husband to herself, she will never be able to. What happened to our husbands and so many others has made privacy impossible. Dave and Stephen have become a thick strand woven into history, and there is nothing we can do to extract their threads and keep them for our own.

The wake room is filled with pictures of Stephen playing with his kids, on vacations with friends and family. He is usually smiling, his eyes as big as quarters. For me, the photographs are the hardest to bear, the faces smiling unwittingly into the camera. Then there are, of course, the children. Five beautiful children with eyes as large as Stephen's and as blue as Sally's. After a long cry, I sit in the back. Theresa Russo is there, and I can tell she has been crying, too. She sits with other widows and wives from the firehouse. The sadness is so thick, I start to make jokes. I can't help myself. Ever since I was a young girl, I used humor to shovel through anything uncomfortable. I could make my mother laugh, no matter how furious she was at me, and I made friends at school by doing imitations of the teachers. The widows and wives crack relieved smiles as I whisper in a mock Vegas voice, "Thank you very much, folks. I'll be playing here at the Harmon Funeral Home every night at two and seven P.M." They cover their mouths like geishas trying not to laugh too hard. "Boy, what a dead crowd tonight!" I say.

"Amazing Grace" is being piped in on the speaker above us. I shift my voice into a DJ announcer, soft and demure. "And here, now in the number one slot this week once again at Wake 101 . . . 'Amazing Grace.' " I notice Theresa tearing up and recall her wedding a year ago. The bagpipes from the Fire Department had marched in playing "Amazing Grace," and Theresa's face shifted from a smile to panic. No one knew why. She is standing now and I follow her as she heads out the back door.

"I hate that song," Theresa says, stepping into the bright heat outside. "Remember how Bronco's friend played it at my wedding?" She pats her eyes with a tissue.

I smile, remembering Bronco, a firefighter who used to work with Dave. His real name was Durrell Pearsall, but everyone called him Bronco because he was built like the truck. He transferred to Rescue 4 and is among those missing. "Remember?" Theresa asks and I nod, recalling the catering hall with the red marble floors. It was the happiest she had ever been.

"Yeah, but why did you freak out?" I ask her. "I never knew why you got so upset."

"I dunno. I knew it was a bad omen. I could feel it. I was so in love with Mike, it just felt like something was going to happen, like it was too good to be true. I got the video yesterday and you can see my face, you can hear me telling the piper to stop, that it's a bad omen. Isn't that weird, Marian? I knew something was going to happen. I will never be able to hear that song without thinking about that."

10

October

It takes a few minutes for me to realize that I am sleeping in my childhood bedroom. Everything in it is exactly as I left it. The ceramic pencil holder I made in Mr. Hasandras's class, the Rolling Stones sticker on the casement window, the itchy crocheted blanket on the bed. The bed itself is from my sister's room, an old full-size with a creaky frame and mushy mattress. Dave and I slept on it the night of our wedding. He tossed and turned, too excited to sleep, our flight to Hawaii leaving in only a few hours. "Dave," I moaned, trying to get some sleep. "You're like an elephant on a canoe. Every time you move, it wakes me up."

"I'm sorry," he said, turning to face me. I could feel him staring at my face. "My *wife*," he said, tasting the words, and I smiled, never opening my eyes.

I walk to the window across from the bed to let the unseasonably warm air fill the room. I put on a short-sleeved black dress for Stephen's funeral and quietly climb the narrow stairway down to the kitchen, trying not to wake Aidan, who is sleeping next door.

"Good morning, sweetie," my mom says, hugging me hard. She is making French toast and strong tea.

"Mariooch," my dad says, entering from the dining room, his gray shirt half tucked in. "How's my daugh-taaa?" I try to smile, but my mouth twists into a strange half smile. He kisses my mom on the cheek and I feel my heart stop. *That's supposed to be me. I am supposed to be getting old with Dave, too.* I sit in one of the rickety chairs and sip my tea, poking at my French toast with a fork.

"What time's the funeral?" Dad asks, sitting down.

"Connor's picking me up in a minute," I say to my plate.

"You didn't eat anything, though," Mom says, disappointed. She heads over to the cabinet and begins rummaging through it. I hear a beep outside and stand, the chair scraping so loudly, my mom flinches.

"This is great for a snack," she says, stuffing a Zone Bar into my purse. "In case you get hungry later." I kiss her on the cheek. "I love you," she says softly.

"Have a good day," my dad says, hugging me. "Well, you know what I mean."

Connor O'Brian's red sports car feels like a toy as I slide awkwardly inside. "Nice car," I say.

"I just got it," he says. "You want some coffee?" He gestures to a hot cup of coffee in a pop-out holder.

"Thanks . . . Is this a midlife crisis mobile or what?" I joke. He sighs through his nose, the sides of his mouth wrinkling. Connor retired on three-quarters pay two years ago when a staircase collapsed on his shoulder during a fire. The guys at the firehouse sarcastically refer to him as "the sexiest man alive," because he loves to dance and wear tight shirts.

The sun is hot and shining onto the uniformed men lined up in thick rows in front of the church. The widows and wives are already on the steps when I arrive, and I quickly squeeze myself into the group, simultaneously kissing them on the cheeks, pinning my patch on, and waving to the firefighters. The familiar sound of bagpipes begins and I am surprised by how routine this already feels.

Sally exits the limo looking angelic, her white face like porcelain in the sun. Stephen Jr. sits on her hip, and she gingerly guides the other four ahead of her. I can hear Theresa's high-pitched moan and reach for her hand, squeezing it. The surviving wives hand us tissues as sniffles and tears intermittently pass through the crowd. I hear a clicking sound and turn to notice Nancy, the photographer from the *New York Times* who has been hanging around Squad, trying to get photographs for Charlie's articles. The camera feels like a gun aimed at my wet face, so I reach for my sunglasses and turn away. The sun is relentless, turning my chest a splotchy red as Theresa nudges me, signaling me to notice Toni, my mother-in-law, and my brother-in-law Dennis making their way up the steps of the church. Toni straightens the Squad 1 pin on her lapel, her small body stooped and slow, and gives me a small wave as she passes. Her chin is always quivering now, and I wonder if it is age or her effort to hold back tears. I try to imagine what it would feel like to lose a son, if Aidan were gone, too, and I decide that the funerals must offer her a safe place to let go and cry.

The church is mercifully cool inside, and we slide into a reserved pew near the front. I watch the firefighters take off their blue caps, which leave rings around their heads like halos. They dab their fore-heads with handkerchiefs, their necks rolling slightly over the collars of their class A uniforms. From my pew, I can see Sally slumped in the front row, her children wriggling and twisting in their seats during a long, solemn homily. Sally and Stephen Siller live around the corner from my parents in an old Queen Anne with a wide front porch. Dave and I often drove past the house and noticed the work Stephen had done, the etched glass door, the new shingles, the rebuilt porch.

An Indian priest speaks in a thick, hypnotic accent about Stephen's life and God and the goodness of people. Lynn Tierney, the deputy commissioner, tells how Stephen abandoned his car and ran through the Brooklyn Battery Tunnel on foot.

Libby Pataki, the governor's wife, speaks about heroism, bravery, and freedom, of the war in Afghanistan, and I grow restless in my seat. This is not a place for politics. Stephen's brother Russell reads a poem he wrote and recalls raising Stephen after their parents were killed in a car crash when Stephen was only two. He talks about Stephen's gregarious personality, his kind spirit, and of course his love for Sally and their children. During the eulogy, Theresa elbows me and I turn my head to catch a glimpse of a lone, dull brown butterfly flitting across the church. A murmur passes through the crowd as the butterfly continues its er-ratic flight to the front of the church, finally landing on Sally's shoulder.

Covering her trembling lips with her hand, Sally turns to watch in stunned awe as the butterfly flutters over our head and flies out the church doors.

* * *

Ever since we returned from our weekend upstate, Leah is constantly on the phone, planning for a funeral with what she surmises will be a thousand guests. She is in full producer mode, organizing a website with directions for the guests, programs, flowers, lists of people who will need sleeping arrangements. I ask Huey to sing a song he wrote about being a firefighter, and I call my friend Mila from college as well. Dave loved her singing voice, how it could sound both ethereal and strong at the same time, and we always attended her gigs when she played at smoky clubs on the Lower East Side.

"I'm scared I'll cry," Mila tells me.

"I totally understand if you can't," I say gently.

"I want to," she says slowly. "It's just . . . I sang at your wedding." I gulp hard at the irony.

Only a year ago, Dave, Aidan, and I flew to Wisconsin to attend Mila's wedding on one of the hottest days in June. It was held in a Great Gatsby–style mansion with deep green lawns that rolled toward Lake Geneva. Aidan, dressed in a seersucker suit, was Joey and Mila's ring bearer, and I played bassoon in a classical trio made up of Mila's musician friends. During the reception, Dave and I smiled proudly at Aidan, who toddled up to each table showing off his suit, announcing "I'm a gentleman like my daddy."

"What do you want me to sing?" Mila asks softly.

"I dunno. Dave sang Aidan 'Danny Boy' every night, but changed the words to 'Aidan Boy,' " I tell her. "Aidan actually gets offended when he hears the original song."

Mila tries to laugh. "How many songs should I do?"

"I don't know. Two, I guess. I dunno. I've never done this before."

"God, Marian, I never in my wildest dreams . . . Joey and I were looking at pictures of Dave and Danielle from our wedding . . ." I imagine the black-and-white photos of Dave and Mila's younger sister,

Danielle, who just a few months ago was diagnosed with a tumor the size of a baseball on her brain.

"Of course I'll do it," Mila whispers.

I decide to have the wake last one day as opposed to the usual two. Everyone is exhausted from attending memorials, and the thought of making the firefighters stand honor guard for an extra day is too much. Of course the firefighters say "anything you want" when I talk to them, but I can tell from the bags under their eyes, the dirt on their class A uniforms, that they are relieved. I think they like that the funeral will be in the neighborhood, too, so they can go back to the firehouse in between viewings. I find myself wondering what Dave would be doing had he survived. I know he would be searching at Ground Zero, yet in his ten years on the job, Dave never missed a firefighter's funeral; he even took Aidan to Harry Ford's funeral in June after the Father's Day fire. What would our relationship be like now? Would he be shut down and quiet from losing all of his friends, or would he cry openly in my arms at night? The only thing I know for certain is that he would hold Aidan and me tighter than ever before, if that was possible.

I remember one morning when Dave came home from work after being up all night at a fire. The fire was out by the time Squad arrived, but Dave was doing a secondary search of the building. In the kitchen he saw the outline of a woman's body squatting in the corner. The soot had settled around her shape. Intrigued, Dave went closer until he noticed her hair had melted to the wall.

When he got home, he climbed into bed, where I was sleeping, spooning me from behind. He told me how a woman had died, clutching her ten-month-old baby in her arms. His warm breath tickled the back of my neck, but I just closed my eyes, imagining the wide eyes of the frightened mother in the dark. When he finished the story, he squeezed me hard, pressing his head in between my shoulder blades, his grip desperate. I said nothing, even though it hurt, staring instead at the sun beginning to shine through the gated window, making circular shadows on the floor.

Every morning, for seventeen years, I rolled over in bed to lie with Dave, two parentheses, recounting our dreams, lingering in our half sleep, easing into the day. Even after Aidan was born and he slept between us like a tiny hyphen, Dave would return from his morning pee and slide his body against mine. After a while, he'd lift himself up on his elbow and peer over my shoulder and, together, we would watch Aidan sleep as if we were lying on the beach, marveling at the ocean. As Aidan got older, he would burst into our bedroom, where Dave and I groggily joined him under the covers as knights and pirates, bears in a cave, or Indians huddled in a tepee. Amid the dark and giggly play, Dave would find me, drawn like a magnet, and we would steal our secret spoon.

The next morning, as I leave the comfort of sleep, I still reach across, waking to find myself contracted into a half-moon shape, a pathetic puzzle lying without its last piece. I am in my own bed for the first time in over three weeks, and it feels as big as eternity without Dave next to me.

I turn onto my back and stare at the ceiling. I imagine Dave staring at me from space somewhere, an aerial view of my tired, lonely body. I sigh and sit up. I am determined to sort through the piles of paperwork I need to go to Pier 94 today, to begin the lengthy process of making his death official.

When I return from dropping Aidan off at school, Leah, Jason, and I begin the daunting task of gathering all the documents I need. Jason makes jokes about my filing cabinet, which is overstuffed with theater playbills, credit card statements, and articles I have saved in the hope of someday reading them.

"Don't throw anything away," I tell them almost hysterically. I feel insane with grief as we dump out dozens of folders, searching for birth certificates, passports, bills, car statements, and our marriage license.

"Here it is," Jason says, finding my marriage license, waving the pink paper in his hand. I stare at its gilded stamp and the thick, official-looking lettering on the front. I remember how, in May 1993, Dave and I stood in line at the Brooklyn courthouse behind a pregnant Spanish girl who wore a tight white wedding dress and carried a drooping bouquet of daisies. Dave and I held hands and joked about the woman behind the desk who moved as if her shoes were stuck to the ground, ignoring ringing phones and shuffling to her own slow rhythm. Finally, when it was our turn, the woman asked how I would like my last name to appear, and as at so many other times in my life, I felt completely unprepared. I looked at Dave, who shrugged innocently. I had grown up a Goldstein, a common Jewish name, and while I was proud my father was from a Jewish tradition, I was raised a Catholic. I resented having a last name that implied a religion, and yet I had become attached to it.

"Why don't you hyphenate?" Dave suggested, and I thought about the implications of both names. Goldstein-Fontana seemed too long to write on checks each month.

"How about I make Goldstein my middle name?" I decided, and with sixteen letters and a stamp, I became Marian Goldstein Fontana. We admired the certificate as we walked down Pierrepont Street in Brooklyn Heights, its elegant cobblestones leading us to the Promenade overlooking Manhattan. We sat on a bench and went over details of the wedding. Firefighters would sit at one table, my gay musical theater friends at another. We laughed at our mixture of friends, the odd circumstance of our meeting, about how many kids we might have. I remember we sat there for a long time, pink cherry blossoms swaying in the breeze and the lights of the Twin Towers flickering like stars in the fading dusk.

My papers secured in a backpack, I throw on a dirty T-shirt and run to the firehouse. I can't seem to do laundry and makeup seems as pointless as putting Christmas lights on a condemned building. Theresa called twice from the firehouse, teasing me that she can make it from Long Island in less time than it takes me to walk the eight blocks to Squad. Even though I know Squad's future is secure, I am gripped with fear when I see a large media van parked outside the firehouse, thick black wires stretching under the engine door like tree roots. I try to walk to the side door, but a young man with a baseball cap and a goatee lights a cigarette and absently says "Walk around, please" without looking up.

"I'm one of the widows," I announce brusquely, the anger in my voice surprising me. The young man stands up suddenly. "I'm sorry. Can you just wait one second?" He quickly retrieves a walkie-talkie and whispers into it. The flowers in the buckets have begun to wilt and most of the candles have melted away, leaving thick black soot inside the glasses.

The boy looks at me, his eyes wide. "If you can just wait one sec. They'll be just a minute."

"What are they doing in there?"

"It's *Third Watch*," he says, leaning back on the van. "It's a documentary we're doing for the show."

Inside, the firehouse is lit like a baseball stadium, with giant squares of light in every corner. Huey sits on a stool, a camera pointed toward him, his eyes full of tears. I am furious. My heart beats faster as I walk toward the back room, angry that they are exploiting our loss, profiting from our tears. A member of the crew in black jeans and a Def Leppard T-shirt steps in front of me to stop me from entering the back room. I glare at him.

"If you could wait, please," he whispers, a giant headset perched on his head like earmuffs.

"I'm late and people are waiting in the back for me," I snap.

A tall thin woman with a white blouse and freckled cheeks approaches, smiling. She stoops down to me. "Hi. I'm Heather," she says sweetly. "Are you one of the . . . ?"

"Yes," I say.

"I'm so sorry. We're almost done. It'll just be another minute."

I turn to see Huey. As he talks he twists his mouth to the side, trying hard not to cry. I stand listening, watching the lights reflect in his eyes as his head drops down; he's embarrassed to show his grief. The filming stops and Huey heads over and gives me a kiss. A man in a baseball cap and a wiry beard comes up to Heather.

"Marian," Heather says, smiling, "this is John Wells." I nod and say hello.

"I'm so sorry about your husband," he says. "I just wanted to tell you a little bit about what we're doing here today. We've been to a couple of firehouses and have just basically been letting the cameras roll. We're going to do a *Third Watch* episode in a documentary style. We know a lot of the guys that are missing, and we all were really affected by what happened. So this will really be a historical document that you can have for your kids."

"Oh," I say, feeling embarrassed now for getting angry.

"It's been amazing, the interviews we've gotten. I mean, the guys have just been spilling their guts, and I think it's been really incredible, and we're so grateful that these guys are letting us film them being so vulnerable." I nod, not knowing what to say. "If you and the wives would like to do that . . . we'd love to have you, too," he says.

"Well, I dunno," I say slowly. "I'll talk to them."

"Great. I heard you're a screenwriter," he says, and I nod. My creative mind has always fueled me; now I find that it's left me. It's disappeared. I have spent the better part of my life writing plays and scripts, performing my own shows, and now I cannot even think about writing. I do not even remember how it felt to care about those things.

"We'd love to take a look at your script, if you want to send it to Heather," he says, and I shake my head, amazed. Only three weeks ago I would have loved that. Heather gives me her number and I stick it in my pocket, knowing that I will toss the yellow paper into a drawer and never send a script. These things just don't matter anymore.

I disappear into the back room where Timmy Rogers, Bobby West, Theresa, Gary Box's wife, Kathleen, and Tommy Butler's wife, Martha, sit at the table drinking coffee.

"TIMMAYY!" I say, mimicking Cartman from *South Park*. Dave had done this to Timmy so many times that everyone in the firehouse began doing it every time Tim entered a room.

"Hey, Marian," Timmy says with a smirk as he pours coffee. Timmy is the firehouse leprechaun, with short gray hair and a round Irish face. Theresa greets me, kissing me on the cheek. She has driven in with Bobby and Martha from the very end of Long Island, over two hours away.

Dennis Farrell enters and writes the information for another funeral on the board. "That's John Wells out there, you know," Dennis says, impressed. "He's the one who did *ER* and all them shows. Nice guy."

"Yeah, he wants us to be in his documentary," I say, looking at the girls.

Theresa looks at me and shrugs. "I'll do it if you do it."

"I don't want to do it," Kathleen Box says, her voice shaky as she chain-smokes quietly. Gary's wife is small, with mouselike eyes, long wavy brown hair, and bangs that she flicks nervously from her face.

"I'll do it if you do it," Martha Butler says, surprising me. Soft-spoken and petite, Martha could be mistaken for a teenager were it not for her mouth hardened into a stony frown. She has three children at home, one only a few months old, and I have trouble imagining three children coming out of such a tiny woman.

"Look at me!" Theresa says, staring down at her clothes. "I can't go on TV like this!"

"Sure you can. Look at me." I am wearing a dirty T-shirt, baggy jeans, and no makeup.

"All right, I'll do it," Kathleen says, and we all laugh nervously.

Out under the lights, we sit on four stools holding hands, interlaced like a rope. John Wells sits in a canvas director's chair across from us and asks us to describe our husbands. I watch Theresa smile as she remembers Mike. "He was the moon," she says.

The next question makes my stomach drop. "Have you had any signs?" he asks.

Theresa smiles at this, too. She is filled with stories of Mike's messages from beyond. I scramble to think of something, to see if perhaps it is true, and then I remember my vacation with Dave, only a few weeks before the eleventh. We had left late in the day for the seven-hour drive up to Wellfleet, Cape Cod. I had cracked the window and let the car fill with the balmy summer air and the excitement of our first vacation alone without in-laws or any family. I made Aidan a mixed tape with Beatles songs, Motown, the Beach Boys, and *Star Wars*, and we laughed when Aidan sang along.

"If you had a million dollars and could do anything, what would you do?" Dave asked playfully.

"Oh, man—" I sighed. "I would go to graduate school for writing, I think."

"Where?

"I dunno—Columbia, maybe."

"You should go for it," he said.

"I thought we were going to have another baby," I said, sounding more defensive than I meant to. "I can't do it all. I can barely handle everything as it is."

"It's just a game," he said, putting his hand on my thigh and squeezing. I smiled weakly and turned to face him.

"Okay, I'm sorry. What about you?" I asked, staring at his profile.

He didn't think long before he said, "I would buy a cabin in Maine with a big sculpture studio and I would kayak every morning and sculpt all day, maybe go to massage school."

"Ooh. You can practice on me."

"Yeah, baby," Dave said, doing his best Austin Powers imitation. He looked in the rearview mirror at Aidan whose head was bopping in rhythm to the music. "Love you, buddy," Dave said into the mirror.

"What?" Aidan asked, lifting one headphone.

"I said I love you, buddy."

"Love you, too," Aidan yelled back.

I tell John Wells about our million-dollar game and he listens intently, stroking a light brown goatee. I tell him how my sign came a few days after the eleventh, when among the piles of sympathy cards, donations, bills, and letters, a dark green catalog from Columbia arrived.

"I don't want to do this," Kathleen says suddenly, standing and walking with her head down toward the kitchen.

"Let's stop," John says to the camera crew. Martha, Theresa, and I follow Kathleen.

"You okay?" I ask, but Kathleen doesn't answer. She sits at the long wooden table in the kitchen. The table was a gift from Theresa's husband when he was promoted to lieutenant only a month before the eleventh. A red ribbon with the names of the firefighters painted in black calligraphy curls its way around the edge. My eyes immediately land on Dave's name.

"I'm not like you guys," Kathleen begins, lighting a cigarette uneasily. "I just don't want to talk about it."

"That's okay," Martha says. "I don't know what the hell I'm saying, but at least we're together."

"I don't want to," Kathleen insists, staring into the corner. Theresa and Martha and I look at each other and give up, heading back to our seats outside.

The chairs are spaced wider apart now but we still hold hands like cords plugged together. I go on and on, as if these are my last words. I know what I am saying is political, too controversial for prime-time TV, but I say it anyway, knowing it will end up on the editing floor. It feels good to say the things I have always felt about the job as I listened to Dave talk late into the night. I hated seeing his love for firefighting squelched by an ancient bureaucracy that put nepotism and politics before the men on the front lines. Most of all, I hated how we struggled financially, despite the fact that Dave risked his life every day.

"I want to use this time to promote the firefighters. They don't get paid a lot of money. I think they need to make more money," I begin. "We struggled in our lives and they shouldn't have to. I think people are now aware that these guys are the bravest guys in the world. They would do anything for anybody, and it's time for the country to support that financially. It's always bothered me that someone on Wall Street can make a million dollars in ten minutes, but I doubt any of those people would run into a burning building."

After the taping, we pile into a Parks Department van with Timmy and Bobby West and make our way uptown to Pier 94.

"I hope we get everything done," Timmy says. It's after eleven, later than we would have liked. "It takes a ridiculous amount of time."

Timmy shows his firefighter ID to enter the West Side Highway, where the streets are caked with Ground Zero mud and rescue workers walk in their heavy boots, wearing masks and helmets. Theresa turns away, her eyes already red from crying, but I want to look, for the first time, at the place where Dave lies. I see the bridge connecting the towers to the Winter Garden, hanging like a pirate's plank over the highway. I see the shell of the building first, peeking up like an ancient cathedral from the debris. The debris. The amount of material is staggering, rising like a mountain from the ground. The unmistakable smell of flesh and fire lingers, and smoke rises in separate plumes as if there were dozens of smokestacks. Theresa's whimper is so painful to hear, I crack jokes to clear the gloom that has filled the car. I stop staring at the pile because it will make me imagine Dave's death, the scenario that has been plaguing my thoughts, playing the reel of the unthinkable again and again. My heart beats faster as Timmy swerves to avoid a cab veering ominously in our direction.

"Asshole," Timmy mutters under his breath, regaining control of the car.

"Why couldn't the towers fall on cabdrivers?" I say flatly, trying to get my heart to slow down. Timmy chuckles and reaches for his glasses case. Theresa's wail has quieted to a whimper.

"So that's where you keep the penis pump," I tease. Timmy's Irish face turns deep crimson. Theresa finally laughs. Thank God.

"Whoa!" Bobby says, chuckling. "You made him blush with that one!"

"You're bad," Theresa says, smiling, as we pull into a parking lot that floats on the Hudson River.

The pier is so massive, I am immediately overwhelmed. The numbing fluorescent lighting illuminates dozens upon dozens of booths that have been set up by organizations to help the victims' families. On the far right wall, family members have tacked up missing posters or photos of the dead. Teddy bears and flowers are propped against the wall that stretches for two blocks along the length of the pier. There is a giant cafeteria in front with donated food and volunteers who are serving lunch to exhausted family members. In the left corner, there is a door marked CHILD CARE. A woman is sitting in front, rocking a crying infant from side to side.

We are ushered into a tent marked FDNY, where a Captain Joyce, with a worn but friendly face, leads us to some plastic seats. Timmy and Bobby collect our papers and give them to the captain to make copies.

"This is unbelievable," Theresa says, her brow furrowing. She begins to cry again, fanning her face as if she were hot. "I just don't want to be here. It's too much!" I nod and hand her tissues, waiting for her to catch her breath.

"I got her," Bobby says, pulling Theresa up and walking her outside.

Bobby and Mike were close friends, and photos of them decorate Theresa's refrigerator: Bobby and Mike at the ski races, Bobby and Mike golfing, Bobby and Mike scuba diving, their faces tanned and happy.

The captain returns with dozens of copies of our documents and a list of all the tents we need to visit. Our first stop is an order of Buddhist monks from Sri Lanka. They do not speak English but gesture for us to sit in the plastic chairs. The tent is tiny, with barely enough room for all of us, but a monk in long pink robes calmly takes our papers and sits at a desk. He seems oblivious to the sounds and bustle surrounding the tent as he patiently fills out forms, rarely raising his shaved head from his work. In less than twenty minutes, a small Asian woman in a black skirt approaches and hands us each a check for $1,000. In broken English she tells us that it is an honor to serve us now and that they are sorry for our loss. Then, as we stand, the three monks in the tent and the Asian woman begin bowing to us over and over again. And then I am crying, not from sadness, but because I am deeply moved by these serene people who have chosen to spend each day here doing this generous act thousands of times. I want to tell them how touched I am, that it is more than a generous act; for me it is an affirmation that our humanity as a people is intact.

Four hours and five tents later, we finally stop to eat. Friendly volunteers dole out rice and beans on paper plates, and we sit exhausted at a round table. I shovel the food in without tasting it, just wanting something in my stomach so I can take an aspirin for the headache that started at the Salvation Army tent an hour ago. We have already visited FEMA, Crime Victims Bureau, Red Cross, Safe Horizons, and Social Security. At each booth, we hand over our papers, answering the same questions, filling out the forms over and over. It is difficult to write Dave's name again and again, as if each time I do, I feel like I am making his death more permanent, nailing his empty coffin into the ground. I have his social security number committed to memory.

When we are finished, we get in a long line to wait for our checks. Timmy and Bobby pull us to the front, past Mexican men with round brown faces.

"I don't want to cut them," Theresa says flatly.

Bobby turns back and whispers. "Look, the firemen are here volunteering to usher you through the process quickly."

"I know, but they lost somebody, too, and I don't like that. I'll wait in the back," she says, walking to the end of a line that has remained motionless since we arrived. The volunteers behind a big folding table seem as confused and overwhelmed as we are. We hold our piles of papers, shifting from one foot to the next, as Timmy and Bobby disappear and return, smiling, a few minutes later with a pile of checks in their hands.

"Let's get outta here," Timmy says gently, grabbing Theresa by the arm.

"This is not right," Theresa says.

"You see, Theresa, you have to understand. The Fire Department is a city agency that already has a system in place for all of you. The fact that the rest of the civilians don't have that is not your fault."

Outside, the sky is tie-dyed dark blue and white, with only a sliver of pink sun left on the horizon. I am so tired that I have to heave myself into the van seat, plopping my knapsack onto my lap. I try to arrange the papers in my bag, but it is stuffed with checks for over $10,000 and there is more money on the way. Dave and I always struggled. Why money now? I stare out the window as we pass the giant meat markets of Chelsea, where men in white aprons covered in blood haul their shipments from trucks onto dollies. "This is blood money," I tell the girls, who stare out the window.

"That's how I feel," Kathleen says. She has said little all day.

"I know. This is weird. Tommy and I had nothing . . . *nothing*," Martha says. "This is too much," and I wonder if she is talking about the money or all of it.

"Don't feel bad about it," Bobby says. "You guys deserve it. Your husbands worked hard so you would be taken care of." Theresa starts crying again, and we all grow quiet. Bobby is squeezing her shoulders as Timmy turns onto Canal Street, mumbling about the rush-hour traffic. I stare out the window, watching people hurrying home from work. Our van feels like a spaceship, separate from the rest of the world, as we work our way east toward Chinatown. Women with black hair bargain with fishmongers, pointing and yelling in Chinese. The car stays silent as we crawl past a McDonald's with signs written in Chinese characters, the front arches like a temple. The silence lingers as Theresa finally stops crying, the sky now dark as we roll under the elegant arch of the Manhattan Bridge, leading us back toward Brooklyn.

11

Dust to Dust

Aidan is still asleep and the house is quiet. I notice how time has taken on a strange dimension as I drag myself to the bathroom, my fatigue making me feel as if I am filled with pocket change. In the shower, I stare at the lines of grout so long that they start to move in speedy lines like racing tracks. I feel as if I am in someone else's body, somebody else's life. Everything is altered, and yet the aching reality is there like a tumor. I marvel at how, when I picture Dave there, it can still make my stomach drop the way it did almost a month ago. How can that be? I wrap myself in my bright blue robe covered in sunflowers, a gift from my wedding shower, and head into the living room. Leah is curled up on the couch, sitting with Sara.

"Hey," Leah says cautiously.

"What time is it?" I ask, confused. I didn't even look at the clock.

"Almost ten," my sister says, sipping tea, while Sara stares straight ahead, her eyes puffy with sleep and her hair in two greasy pony-tails.

"I can't believe Aidan's still sleeping." I squeeze onto the couch.

"He rolled around a lot last night," Sara says in scratchy voice.

"I didn't want to wake him," Leah says. "Is it okay if he's late?"

"Well, too late now . . ." I feel cranky, like telling everyone I hate them. Leah is silent. "It's fine," I say, softening. I try to remember the faint images of my dream. I vaguely remember coffins and candles, but I can't quite see it, as if looking through binoculars from the wrong end. I wonder if it is the Ambien that makes me wake up feeling confused, unsure of where I am.

"You were snoring like crazy last night," Leah tells me.

"You never used to snore," Sara says.

"Maybe you're channeling Dave," Leah jokes, and Sara laughs, remembering the countless nights I nudged and poked Dave, willing him to roll over, his exhausted body lying like stone, an earth-shattering snore vibrating through the room. I don't feel like talking, so I take the remote and turn on the news. There have been no recoveries in the last two days. No news. Nothing. *Where are you, Dave?*

The French doors shake as Aidan struggles to open them. I quickly snap the television off. As far as I know, Aidan has yet to see the site, and I want to keep it that way. I know I will not be able to do this forever, and I wonder how odd it will be for Aidan and all the children of 9/11 to have the site where their parents were murdered the most popular image in modern history. Aidan pulls back the curtain and stares at us all sitting on the couch, his face soft from sleeping.

"Good morning, sweetie," I say, feeling lighter when I see his face. Aidan dives headfirst next to me, his priceless blanket clenched in his hand. I rub his back, his spine like smooth stones under his pajama shirt.

"I don't *want* to go to school," he says. I look to my sister, who shrugs and mouths, "Let him stay home."

"We're already late . . ." I begin. Aidan picks his head up hopefully.

"Okay . . . just for today," I say, and he smiles widely.

*   *   *

I arrange a dinner for the widows at the restaurant across the street from the firehouse. Too upset to drive by themselves, they arrive with friends and relatives until the table is so long, it feels like the Last Supper. Joanne Modaferri from Rescue 5, whose husband worked at Squad for many years, arrives. Theresa Russo, Martha Butler, Toni-Ann Carroll, Kathleen Box, Denise Esposito, Eddie's fiancée Linda Mari, and Debbie Amato are all here, and even though everyone put on extra makeup, we still look like vases that have been glued back together. We order a round of cosmopolitans, and when the pink glasses arrive, Toni-Ann says, "We look like *Sex and the City* girls." She seems less medicated tonight, wearing skin-tight jeans and a cropped white shirt.

"Without the sex," I say.

"Don't even go there," Denise replies, sipping her drink.

Joanne smiles weakly. She looks particularly vulnerable, her brown eyes watering as she watches a table full of teenagers give their friend sweet-sixteen presents. We order pizza and salads and talk about the awesome onslaught of friends, family, money, funerals, cards, and goodwill.

"It's all too much," Martha says. "Our life was so quiet before this."

"I know, right?" Debbie says. "I'm not used to it. And the press keeps calling and they want to get in your business. It's like we're famous."

"Famous for *this*?" Theresa says.

"I can't take it. I know Mike is shaking his head at it all," Denise says.

"To the guys," I say, raising my glass. We toast to our husbands and lovers, what could have been.

The bartender sends over another round of drinks and everything begins to soften around the edges. Toni-Ann pulls down her pants to expose her lower back, where a large tattoo spells "Pete" in wide looping letters with flowers and vines underneath.

"That's huge!" Martha giggles.

"I like that," Kathleen says softly.

"We should all get tattoos," I suggest, and most of us agree to get a small Squad insignia on our backs or ankles. "I'd get it on my butt," I joke. "But if I bent over, everyone would think Dave was from Squad 10."

"You are crazy," Denise says. "You're as crazy as Mike." We all laugh, some guiltily, until a woman with long curly hair pulled back in a macramé clip comes over carrying a light blue gift bag.

"I don't mean to interrupt," she says. "But the firefighters across the street told me you were all here, and I just wanted to give you these earrings I made. They are all different stones that have different qualities." She hands everyone a box and explains the stone's spiritual essence.

Some of the women raise an eyebrow, reluctant to take a gift from an eccentric stranger.

"Thank you," I say, and the women at the table nod and thank her, opening their boxes of earrings, some even putting them on. In my box is a small pair of amethyst earrings, a purple stone that Dave always gave me on holidays. The woman tells me amethyst is used for psychic empowerment, that it radiates energy and healing. I put mine on, fingering the smooth stones, as the woman smiles and leaves.

We talk loudly, competing with the party going on next to us. When they sing "Happy Birthday," we all stop talking, choking up. I know we are all thinking about the countless birthdays and celebrations we will have without our husbands there to enjoy them.

"It's October eleventh today, you know," Toni-Ann says. "It's been a month."

"Can you believe that?" Debbie asks. She has been uncharacteristically quiet tonight.

"We should do this every month," Theresa says.

"The Merry Widows' club," I suggest.

"I hate that word!" Martha exclaims. "I really do. Can we have something else?"

"The crazy bitches who lost their husbands?" I offer this time.

"I like that," Denise says.

"I just like being around everybody. I don't feel so alone," Theresa says, her voice cracking. "No, really. I can't imagine doing this alone. I wish it weren't this way, but I'm glad we're in good company." She raises her glass and we all toast awkwardly, the pink liquid spilling a bit as we lean down to drink to the sad event that brought us together.

*　　*　　*

The next afternoon Dave's cousin Kat arrives from London for the funeral. She wears a pink suit and gives Aidan a gift. Even though she now speaks in an English accent, she looks the same as I remember from twelve years ago, pale skin setting off eyes like water on a coral reef.

"Did you know Dad called Toni?" she says, scooping up the wrapping paper Aidan tossed on the floor. Kat's father, Toni's brother, has not spoken to my mother-in-law for over a decade, since he and Dave's father had a business dispute. "I was quite surprised," she says.

"I heard." I watch her straighten her suit and disappear into the kitchen to look for the garbage, and I marvel at the thousands of tiny shifts taking place since Dave died.

Leah offers to babysit so Kat and I can have dinner at the firehouse. I am supposed to bring mashed potatoes, so I stop at Key Food to buy the ingredients. When we finally arrive, Paul Stallone is cutting up carrots and Phil is setting the table with chipped white plates.

"Sorry I'm late," I say, plopping down my groceries. I introduce Kat to everyone. She smiles stiffly and shakes their hands. She seems more formal than I remember, but I've only seen her once since Dave and I visited her in Belgium almost twenty years earlier, when she was working as a journalist for Reuters. She now runs a Reuters office in London. Her husband is English and they have two boys, Henry and Benedict.

Tony and Huey enter. They have just returned from Gary Box's wake.

"*Marian!*" Tony yells, entering and stumbling toward me like the Abominable Snowman. He squeezes me hard and looks down at me, suddenly serious. "You doin' okay?"

"I should be asking you that," I say, turning toward Tony's wife, Donna, who rolls her eyes at him. "Hey, sweetie." I give her a kiss. "This is Kat. Dave's cousin from London."

"London!" Tony growls. "I didn't know Dave had a cousin in London. Lovely to meet you." Tony attempts a British accent and kisses her hand. Huey drops onto the couch in the living room and begins playing his guitar. "She's fuckin' snooty," Tony whispers to me as he watches Kat make gravy.

"Shh!" I say, punching his arm.

"She's got a hot little body though."

"Shut up!" I say, punching him on the arm again.

"Ow!"

Freddy Lawrence enters and removes a roast from the oven, filling the kitchen with the smell of garlic and cooked meat. He is the most senior man in the house now, with over twenty years on the job.

"What a piece of meat!" I exclaim, setting Fred up for a joke, but he only smiles weakly. Since the eleventh, he has said little to me. The other guys make excuses that he is shy and old-fashioned, maybe uncomfortable with having women around the firehouse, but I can tell it's more than that.

The room grows quiet as we listen to Huey sing. Finally, the potatoes ready, I pour water and we all sit down to roast pork, salad, Italian bread, potatoes, and candied carrots. Tony can barely keep his eyes open as Huey tells us about planning Eddie D'Atri's funeral.

"We got this monsignor who's a dick," he says, slamming potatoes onto his plate. "You know, he's telling Princess Linda she can't even speak at Eddie's service because they weren't married, and now he's saying he's not gonna let the coffin into the church."

"Why?" I ask, astounded.

"A mandate from the Catholic Church says that a coffin can't enter a church without a body," Paul Stallone says, pouring gravy onto his potatoes.

"But none of the priests are following that since the eleventh . . ." Huey says, annoyed. "But then this asshole says he doesn't want no coffin in the church . . ."

"I'd like to see this jerk go down to Ground Zero and see what's really going on," Tony says.

A consummate reporter, Kat asks the firefighters a million questions; they eye her suspiciously.

"The roast's delicious," I tell Fred, who's seated next to me.

"Thanks," he mumbles, staring at his plate.

Smaller conversations begin around the table and I sit listening, trying to choose one to join in, when Fred says, without looking up, "I used to sit right across from Dave on the rig, you know."

"I didn't know that." I push the meat around with my fork.

"We were in the same group." I think of the calendar I kept in my wallet that marked the group chart. Every firefighter is assigned a group that rotates days and nights. Dave was in Group 18, and I've been following his schedule, even though he has been gone for over a month.

"Yeah, every tour he sat right across from me," Fred says ruminatively. He looks up at me for the first time, his blue eyes vivid and fierce.

"Oh" is all I can muster. Now I am the one staring at my plate, not knowing the right thing to say.

*   *   *

I pick up Aidan from school, and he bounds toward me, running full speed like a puppy, smashing me hard in the stomach.

"Ow!" I say.

"Can I have a playdate with Charlie?" he asks. I notice a father walk past us, holding his son's hands.

"We can't, honey."

"Why not?"

"Because we have to go talk to Mary."

"Who is she?"

"She's a therapist. She helps kids."

"I don't want to talk to Mary."

"You don't have to. We're just going to meet her." Aidan's bottom lip sticks out and his eyebrows purse in anger. He walks behind me, stomping his feet as the parents pass, smiling at us. A surge of pain shoots up my back as I realize Aidan has run full force into me, again practically knocking me down.

"OW! AIDAN, THAT HURT!" I scream, turning angrily toward him. He looks suddenly guilty now, his head dropped and his giant eyes staring. I notice parents turning to look. "That really hurt!" I seethe, lowering my voice and squatting down in front of him. "It is okay to be angry, but you *cannot hit me!*" I hold back my left hand, which I realize is shaking with anger. I have never hit Aidan in my life, but my anger feels bigger now. Half of me wants to hit him for letting everything out on me, and the other half wants to hug him and take it all away. Instead, I grab his hand and we walk home.

Aidan insists on donning a skeleton mask, a fire helmet, and a toy gun when we go to therapy, and I am too tired to protest. People stare and point on our short trip around the corner to Mary's office on 5th Street.

"My, my, my. What do we have here?" Mary says softly, opening the ground-floor gate to her brownstone. She is stern-looking, with round Mrs. Claus glasses and shoulder-length blond-gray hair combed close to her head. She smiles at me as Aidan enters.

"He's really subtle," I say sarcastically, following her into a small office. Aidan follows her to a closet filled with toys and chooses a box of soldiers, dumping them onto an Oriental rug. I sink into the warm folds of the couch and watch Aidan play. "Pshew, pshew," he says, blasting the soldiers in battle. The white-noise machine, dim lighting, and cavelike quality of the office make me sleepy, and I struggle to stay awake, watching Aidan arrange his soldiers in two straight lines to kill each other.

"Oh, which ones are the good guys and which ones are the bad?" Mary asks.

Aidan points to the line of soldiers on the left. "Those are the bad ones."

"How can you tell which is which?"

"You can't," Aidan says, running over to the closet and pulling out some blocks. He takes the blocks and puts them on the couch next to me and makes them crash on top of the soldiers, covering them.

"Oh, dear," Mary says to Aidan. "What's happening?"

"Everything's falling on them."

"Are they okay?"

"The firefighters are going to dig them out. My daddy's in the Twin Towers, you know." I feel the familiar ache as my jaw tightens.

"I know," Mary says, her voice exactly the same as before. "That's a very sad thing that happened to your daddy, but you know that is not what happens to most daddies."

"AAAAhhhhh," Aidan says as another block falls onto a soldier.

"Oh, boy. These poor soldiers." Mary pushes up her glasses on her nose, but Aidan is concentrating on the soldiers, now buried in a pile of blocks.

* * *

That night I drive out with Timmy Rogers to Gary Box's wake. It is held in a funeral parlor with a blinking green neon sign in front. Kathleen looks diminutive in a black dress, her two kids circling her legs. Classic rock blares from a boom box next to the coffin and an endless line snakes its way through the parlor and out the back door. I recognize the stooped form of my mother-in-law waiting on line with Dennis. The parlor is so crowded, I lose Timmy after waiting for hours, and end up catching a ride home with Tony, Huey, and Connor. The parking lot of the funeral parlor is almost empty now, and Tony rubs his eyes, which seem to be permanently red since the eleventh.

"Man, it's late!" Tony exclaims, starting the car and eyeing the digital clock. They'd arrived at Gary Box's funeral almost five hours ago. "We gotta be back here eight A.M. tomorrow."

"That sucks. I haven't fucking seen my kids in weeks," Huey says, shaking his head and pulling out a bottle of Jack Daniel's.

"I'll take some of that," I say. My nerves are rattled from hours in the funeral parlor, with crowds of people pressed into the small, hot room.

Huey passes a bottle to the back of the truck where I am sitting next to Connor. "That's the serious stuff." I have never liked whiskey straight, but I take a swig that is warm and smooth, like stepping into a hot tub. Led Zeppelin's "Whole Lotta Love" blares from the car's speakers, and Huey sings. I watch the back of his head bopping back and forth to the music as we speed down the Long Island Expressway. I feel like I am in junior high school, the world spinning by so fast, I can barely see the people in the cars we pass. I see the blur of a Madonna hanging from a rearview mirror, a flash of a bald man talking on his cell phone, a glimpse of a man talking with his hands to his wife. "You all right back there?" Tony asks, jarring me from my thoughts. "You're awfully quiet."

"I was thinking about the Lieutenants' test, I tell him."

"Man, Dave was obsessed with that thing," Tony says. Dave started studying for the Lieutenants' test in 1996, right after Aidan was born. While the Police Department studies one thick book for promotion, the Fire Department requires dozens of thick binders that must be updated and memorized. The test seemed to wake up Dave's deepest demons of insecurity and doubt about his own intelligence, regardless of how much he studied.

"I heard that test was the hardest they've ever had," Connor says.

"It was," Huey adds. "But Dave tortured himself over that thing. I'd be like 'Dude, relax, there's nothing you can do about it,' but he wanted it bad."

I chuckle, remembering sadly how it was the most painful time in our relationship. With a brand-new baby and Dave studying, we were always vying for time. I resented Dave for always being at work and having to study when he was at home. In the end, Dave passed with a 79, but since half of the test was based on seniority, and Dave was one of the younger guys, his position on the Lieutenants' list was disappointingly low.

"You okay?" Connor asks as I stare out the window.

"I'm fine." I'm trying not to cry.

"I got the pictures back," Tony tells Huey.

"What pictures?" I ask, grateful to be distracted.

"It's the rig at the site. Right after we found it."

"What did it look like?" I ask, and see Tony flash Huey a look. "I want to know." Maybe it will make some sense, like clues a detective puts together. I never read mysteries or watched detective shows, thinking it didn't really matter what happened because even if they solve the crime, the person is still dead, the family still heartbroken, the spouse still ruined. Now I see it could give solace, make sense of something as illogical as sudden death.

"Well, the rig wasn't in too bad shape. We found it right away. The wheels were on it and everything," Tony says. I assume this is an anomaly. I have heard about the trucks, twisted and mangled, smashed like soda cans under the falling debris. "It was kind of parked farther away from everything on West Street."

"I guess it couldn't get that close," Huey adds, looking out the window.

"The roof had caved in, shit was all over the place," Tony continues. I watch the side of Tony's closely shaved head, the veins rippling across his temples like rivers on a globe.

"It was quiet," Huey says softly.

"Yeah, it was freaky how quiet everything was," Tony continues. "Huey and I are just staring at the back of the trucks thinking of all the guys—so many fucking guys . . . Then, out of nowhere, I start to write the names in the dust."

"We were tryin' to figure out who was workin'." Huey's voice is so low, I have to lean forward to hear it.

"We just started writin' and it just felt natural . . . you know, to do that." Tony turns his head to see me crying now. I feel blindsided by emotions I can't seem to control.

"I'm sorry," I say, not wanting them to stop talking. I am moved by this improvised memorial from Dave's friends.

"Go ahead and cry," Tony says. "There's nothing wrong with cryin'!"

"Yeah, this is too fucking sad not to cry," Huey adds.

"I loved Dave. You know that, Marian," Tony says. After a long, somber silence I watch his huge arm reach for the volume. "I love this song." It is "Good Times Bad Times," another Led Zeppelin song. Connor lights a cigarette, lowering the window a crack. The wind whips my hair across my face. He hands the cigarette to me and I take a drag, listening to everyone sing. *"I know what it means to be alone, I sure do wish I was at home. I don't care what the neighbors say, I'm gonna love you each and every day."*

* * *

The Victorian entrance of Green-Wood Cemetery, with its delicate brownstone steeples, reminds me of a sandcastle or one of those Gaudi buildings that I have always wanted to visit in Spain. Inside the bottom of each gate are offices of dark wood with thick rugs and small leaded-glass windows. Jason and I enter an office on the left. I asked him to help me pick out a gravesite for Dave, "just in case they find him," the funeral director advised. A friendly secretary directs us to a man in a bland polyester suit. He has a thick head of black hair, a handsome round face, and seems too young to be in the business of death.

"I'm very sorry for your loss," he says, gesturing toward two dark mahogany chairs.

"Thank you." I stare at my feet. I still don't know how to respond to this simple offer of condolence. I have spent my whole life saying "It's okay" when people apologize for something they've done. "I'm sorry I broke the vase." "It's okay." "I'm sorry I hurt your feelings." "It's okay." "I'm sorry for your loss. . . ." It's *not* okay, and so you say thank you. How odd.

The man takes out some papers and hands them to me. "The total fee for a gravesite is five thousand dollars. Under the circumstances, we can hold the site for as long as necessary, but we do require a forty percent nonrefundable deposit."

"And if I wanted to have him cremated?"

"Well, we do have a repository next door. That is only two thousand dollars, if you should decide—"

"No, I don't want that," I tell Jason. "I want a site to visit and sit."

"Well, we have just cleared an area for police and firefighters, so that's a really nice option." He opens up a map with green ink demarcating hundreds of winding paths and roads with names like "Winter's Walk" and "Magnolia Path."

He leads us to the back of a station wagon and drives us past hundreds of tombs, monuments with stone seraphs, giant mausoleums adorned with angels, saints, and elaborately carved crosses. We pass a children's section with tiny lambs sitting like tired cats on top of small, low stones. I squint to read the dates, unfathomable in their briefness.

"It's so pretty here," Jason remarks. I tell him how Dave and I used to walk around here when he was researching firefighters who had been killed during World War II.

"This was built in 1838," the man says. "So you can really see what the Brooklyn landscape looked like originally." I had read somewhere that the beauty of Green-Wood Cemetery inspired Calvert Vaux and Frederick Law Olmstead to create "Greenslaw," which later became Central Park. I loved when Dave brought me here in the spring. The gentle rolling hills, reflecting pools, weeping willows, dogwoods, magnolias, and giant ancient elms make it feel more like a botanic garden than a graveyard. Dave knew where the monument to the soldiers of the Civil War was and where famous New Yorkers were buried. He told me about Boss Tweed and Tammany Hall, Louis Comfort Tiffany and New York mobsters Joey Gallo and Albert Anastasia. We didn't have time to see where Margaret Sanger's grave was or that of the composer Leonard Bernstein.

The cemetery man parks the car across from a dull, flat road, empty of trees. Red dusty earth sits in a giant pile next to the newly created gravesites.

"Horace Greeley is buried there," he says, pointing to a bust of an unattractive man.

"I don't think I want Dave staring at him for all eternity," I mumble to Jason. "Can we look at the other one?" The man drives us up a steep incline where a lake covered in lily pads blooms in the valley below and stops. He opens the door for us and we follow him halfway up one of the hills that is still covered in green grass. A cool breeze causes a few copper leaves to trickle down from a tree with lovers' initials carved in its trunk. He points to four unmarked graves underneath the giant birch.

"This one is available, and this one." I spot a low pine, Dave's favorite tree, a few feet away, and a new breeze blows the faint smell of old Christmas wreaths into my nose.

"I'll take this one," I tell the man, pointing to the site closest to the pine tree.

"There's room for five here if you cremate," he says, and I nod. Perhaps I will offer this to Toni, my mother-in-law, who I know will not be able to afford a grave herself and I'm sure will want to be buried with Dave. I stand wondering how long it will be before I join Dave here. I am even jealous of my mother-in-law for being able to see Dave before me. Suddenly, I am crying, tears dripping on the knotted roots that lay like rope near my feet, and I wonder if the trees grow so tall here because they are watered by thousands of moments like these.

"This is perfect." Jason squeezes my shoulders and hands me a tissue. I nod, licking the tears off my upper lip, and hold his hand to climb back down the hill.

A Widow's Walk

That night I drive Kat out to the Columns Funeral Home on the South Shore of Long Island to attend Eddie D'Atri's wake. The funeral home was named for its attempt to look like a Georgian plantation house, but the overdone lighting in front merely highlights its faux appearance. We squeeze past hundreds of firefighters milling around out front and enter a large marble foyer. We slowly walk toward the back of the building, finally finding Squad and their wives sitting on overstuffed couches in front of a fake fireplace. I spot Bobby West in the corner, sliding on his gloves, his small, squinting eyes looking more tired than ever.

"Hello," he bellows, heading over to kiss me on the cheek. I introduce him to Kat and we stand staring at each other.

"Alison's pregnant," he tells me, trying to smile.

"Congratulations!" I say, kissing him. Dave and I just attended his wedding in Montauk last year.

"Yeah. It's good. That's why she hasn't been coming to anything," he says, spinning his hat in his gloved hands.

"Yeah, she's the only wife from Squad One I haven't seen."

"She's tired. You know she's working. It's a lot." Bobby looks around nervously. "Did you go in yet?" I shake my head.

"We can just wait," I whisper, embarrassed, as Bobby brings us up to the front of the line.

"No. You're one of the girls," he says, looking straight ahead.

Lynda, dark-featured, with tanned skin, brown eyes, and raven-colored hair, looks nothing like Princess. Her two large sons, looking restless, flank her, their hair spiked with gel, their necks laden with giant gold chains.

"I'm so sorry for your loss," I tell her, kissing a cheek already filled with lipstick marks.

"You, too," she says, trying to smile.

I take a mass card on the way out of the room. A photo of Eddie's characteristic Cheshire smile dons the front. I put it in my suit pocket, which is quickly filling up with cards.

Out in the lobby, I see Vinnie D'Angeles and Kevin McCabe, fire-fighters from Dave's first firehouse, Ladder 122.

"Hey, guys." I kiss their cheeks. "I didn't know you knew Eddie."

"We don't. We're here for Stevie Harrell's wake," Kevin says, and I look up, confused. When I called 122 on September 12, they told me everyone from the firehouse was okay.

"Stevie got promoted a couple of years ago," Vinnie says. I recall Stevie at the company dinner, singing loudly and playing the piano. "His brother Harvey was killed, too."

"Oh my God." I shake my head, trying to understand it, wondering how deep the well of grief can go.

"I thought you knew." Vinnie looks past me to greet his wife, Christina, who arrives carrying their new baby boy in a car seat.

Kevin and Vinnie lead me to the front of the line at Stevie's wake, across the hall from Eddie's.

"Two wakes in one night," Kevin says to no one in particular.

"Life doesn't get any weirder," I say.

I excuse myself from the swelling crowd and find a small bathroom downstairs, relishing the privacy of the stall, where I can cry freely. Leaving the bathroom, I stop at a wake room where an old man lies in a casket lined with white satin. It is startling to see a nearly empty wake room and even stranger to see a casket with a body. I have grown accustomed to seeing coffins that are not only closed but empty.

The following morning I speed down Hylan Boulevard, looking for the church. "It's a beautiful day," Kat says, looking out the window at the endless strip malls and fast-food restaurants. At a red light, I take my sunglasses out of the brown leather case in my bag.

"All the funerals have been on days like this," I tell her, finally spotting fire trucks double-parked outside of a modern brick church. "I bet the weather will be crappy for Dave's. He always loved dramatic weather." I quickly pin on my Squad 1 patch. "Fuck. We're really late." Everyone is already inside.

The church is smaller than I expected, with simple, curved wooden pews. It's also half empty. "There must have been a lot of funerals today," I whisper to Kat, grabbing a program and looking around. On the other side of the church, I spot the familiar pained expressions of my mother-in-law and Dennis. The ominous chords of an organ shatter the silence and a voice begins to sing. It is so loud and out of tune, I bite my lip to stifle a giggle.

"THE LORD IS MY SHEPHERD," the man bellows in a thick Staten Island accent, his voice crescendoing. He sounds like the air being squeezed out of a balloon. I am laughing so hard now, my shoulders begin to shake uncontrollably. I look to Kat, but she sits staring somberly forward. I can see the widows, my comrades in arms, sitting a few rows ahead of me, and I wish I had arrived on time so they could laugh with me. Princess is with them, too. I am relieved to see her. There was a rumor she would not be allowed to attend.

When the song ends, the monsignor Huey told me about stands up and slowly makes his way to the pulpit. He is stooped and short, with thinning gray hair and a pointed nose, making him look more like Scrooge than a beneficent priest. He shuffles slowly past the coffin, draped in a white blanket embroidered with a Celtic cross. The monsignor refused to let a coffin in the church without a body, so Huey told him that Eddie had been found. The mean monsignor had no choice but to bless the coffin, sprinkling holy water with a flick of his wrist. "We are gathered here to remember Edward Dyeatry," the monsignor says in a bored monotone that sounds like that of a teacher a day away from retirement. The firefighters turn to each other, shaking their heads in disgust at the mispronunciation of Eddie's name. The congregation seems desperate for encouragement and words of hope, but receive platitudes. I drift in and out, watching an overweight altar boy teeter slightly, struggling to hold the heavy Bible. The monsignor reads the blessing of the Sacrament like a cue card, holding up a giant round host.

" . . . took the bread and said, . . . 'Take this and eat. This is my body.' " Even I, a lapsed Catholic, half Jew, know this is wrong. "Jesus took the bread and said unto his disciples, 'Take this, all of you, and eat *from* it.' " I've heard it a thousand times, and it is as comforting as a bedtime story. " 'This is my body which shall be given up for you.' "

Libby Pataki, the governor's wife, makes a speech I have heard and Mayor Giuliani's representative reads the eulogy that has been recited at every funeral so far. The politicians always read their speeches first so they can make a hasty exit before the most difficult part of the mass begins—the eulogy written and read by the deceased's friend or family member. It is the ultimate testament of love, a ritual of mourning, a safe-deposit box of memories for us all to keep and remember.

Jimmy Lopez from Squad 1 stands up first, and his stocky body looks small standing behind the large podium. He talks about Eddie the lieutenant: fearless, stubborn, and strong with arms as big as those of an action figure. He was an aggressive firefighter, serious about his work, passionate about the team of firefighters he led. When Jimmy finishes we applaud heartily, then wait for the next speaker. Women cross and uncross their legs, firefighters finger the plastic brim of their hats, a woman behind me coughs. Who is speaking next? we are all wondering. I look at the modern stained-glass windows, Cubist renditions of the stations of the cross: Jesus Falls, Jesus Falls Again. It sounds like a sequel to a movie or part of a trilogy. *Jesus Returns: Part 3,* or *Jesus Rises: The Final Chapter.* I admonish myself for thinking these things. I should be focused on Eddie. The silence has lasted so long, heads are craning around, trying to figure out what is wrong. I start to think about Princess Linda, Eddie's fiancée, who was told she could not read a eulogy for him today.

One of Eddie's friends stands up and tentatively makes his way to the altar. Clearly he did not plan to speak today. He tells an anecdote about working out in the gym with Eddie and then sits down. A silence longer than the first one hovers like smoke above us. I look through the congregation to see Eddie's wife, staring, motionless, her sons on either side. The monsignor cranes his head around the congregation, but no one stirs. Finally, he stands, looking relieved that the mass will end so early. He signals the organist to play the closing hymn and the chords from "Eagle's Wings" begin.

"You are the people who come unto the Lord," sings an out-of-tune voice. I stare at the dark blue jackets of the Squad 1 firefighters in front of me. Two of them rise. Huey and Tony are moving quickly to the front of the church. I see them head over to the monsignor, who shakes his head no. I see Tony puff out his chest, his teeth clenched, and Huey adjusting the microphone at the altar. "Excuse me, excuse me," he says, and the organist stops; the church grows quiet.

"I have something I'd like to read about Eddie," Huey announces, and the monsignor, whose whole head has flushed a deep red, reluctantly sits down. "If you'll bear with me a minute." Huey retrieves a piece of paper from his pocket. "I have a note from Linda, or Princess, as Eddie liked to call her. She has a few words she would like me to read."

12

Sitting on an Angel

"It's Carolyn Leary, Marian. How are you?" Her words are overenunci-
ated. I scan the Rolodex of my memory, trying to remember her name.
Is she a distant relative? Is she someone professional? Carolyn Leary.
Carolyn Leary. "I'm okay," I say carefully, hoping a lightbulb will illumi-
nate the answer.

"If this is uncomfortable at all, please let me know, but I was hoping
I could read a eulogy for Dave at his memorial." Finally I am able to picture her. She was in her mid-fifties, wearing a tailored plaid suit with a
white ruffled shirt. Her hair was blond and brushed away from her face.
She had met Dave tentatively. After all, who was this stranger who had
entered her life?

Dave made it his mission to dedicate plaques to the thirty-three
Brooklyn firefighters who died serving in World War II. He started his
research at his first firehouse, Ladder 122 on 11th Street, where he discovered that two firefighters had died serving in the war. Dave began
sending dozens of letters to libraries and military organizations, sifting
through archives, trying to piece together accounts of John Leary and
Eugene Steffans. Insecure about his writing skills, Dave often asked me
to help construct his letters. I did so grudgingly, confused as to why he
would choose to spend so much of his time, energy, and money on
strangers who had died so long ago.

"Why not work out, or sculpt, or fix that door that's been squeaking for over two years?"

"Because they deserve it" was all Dave would say.

With the help of his former captain, Mike Feminella, Dave organized a ceremony and built a wooden box to hold photos of the men, with patches and badges he had collected from their bomb groups and airborne divisions tucked inside. Finally, when everything was in place, he contacted the families to attend the plaque unveiling on March 30, 2001.

I was shocked by what a large event Dave had organized. More than a hundred firefighters, veterans, family members, and neighbors attended. The Emerald Society Pipe and Drum band played, and there was a twenty-one-gun salute by veterans. Dave, my shy husband, with quavering voice, read a speech he had spent hours writing. He spoke of the bravery of these men and how he felt indebted to them for the freedom he enjoyed today. I was awed, surprised by Dave's resolve and proud of what he had accomplished. The sad irony overwhelms me as the words of Dave's speech echo his own fate: *"His courageous gesture of self-sacrifice undoubtedly saved many lives."*

A few months later, a package arrived containing a crystal Waterford clock and a letter. I watched Dave read it by the kitchen window. He said nothing for some time, and I could tell he was moved. He didn't cry, but his head was pressed in his hands in his distinctive way that let me know he was overcome. Finally, without saying anything, he handed me the letter.

Dear Dave:

The day of my father's celebration is still prominent in my mind and heart. I made an album to commemorate the wonderful dedication ceremony, and your photo clearly marks that you were the spirit behind the day. I was overwhelmed with your tenacity in planning and researching the event. I wondered what inner voice drove you to accomplish such a feat. However, you did accomplish a miracle.

Dave, I was a baby when my father was killed and never mourned his loss. My brother and I never knew him. Of course there were times I wept because I did not have a father. Making Father's Day cards was never part of my experience and in high school the father-daughter dance was very painful. One of my uncles came with me, but it was never the same. You gave me a chance to mourn the loss of a great man and for this I am eternally grateful. You gave my brother and me the opportunity to rejoice in the memory of a hero. We learned things about his death that we never knew, and you gave us a chance to get to know him through his heroism. There is a special place reserved for you in heaven and that will be in the heroes' wing for your goodness and good deeds are truly heroic. Thank you, Dave, for providing a day which will go down in our family's history. God bless you and your family.

Sincerely yours,
Carolyn F. Leary

"I know I didn't know him that well," Carolyn says to me. "I would just read something short . . ."

"Of course. It's perfect," I say without hesitation. I notice there is a sense of clarity in my remark, as if the decision is not being made by me at all.

"Who was that?" Leah asks when I hang up. I tell her the story. Leah writes Carolyn's name in a book and asks me for her number. With Dave's funeral less than a week away, she is running on full throttle. Leah is on the phone as much as I am, attending to all the details of the service: programs, wake cards, music, flowers, food, drinks, and accommodations for visitors from out of town. It feels good having her at the helm. The casket will be borrowed, my friend Heather will do the flowers, Dizzy's restaurant will cater the reception. My cousin Matthew, a caterer, will supply the dessert, my friend Dave, who owns Fred's in Manhattan, will do the appetizers. The Budweiser company is donating beer. My high school friend Henry, who owns a restaurant in Manhattan, donates cases of whiskey. Romi's father from Oregon is bringing cases of wine. My friend Wendy is blowing up pictures of Dave, and neighbors and friends are making copies of keys for visiting relatives to use their guest rooms. The phone rings again.

"Hello?" I say cautiously.

"This is the mayor's office. Please hold for the mayor."

"This is Mayor Giuliani," the voice on the other end says. At first I think it is a recording, one of those ads that sound robotic and inhuman. "I want to tell you how sorry I am for your loss."

"Thank you."

"I was hoping to speak at Dave's service on Wednesday, but I was told you don't want any politicians there."

"Right," I say.

"Can I ask you why?"

"My husband didn't like politicians," I say, and then add quickly, "Nothing personal. I just want people who knew Dave to speak."

"I understand. Would it be all right to just say a few words at the wake then?" he asks. "Only if you want me to," he adds. And I look up as if the ceiling has the answer written on it.

"I guess that would be okay."

"The commissioner said he knew Dave. Would you be opposed to Tom speaking at the service?" he asks, his familiar lisp evident. I stop to think. Decisions. More decisions. Why is everyone asking me to make choices? What would Dave want? What would he tell me? I am deciding my fate while traveling full speed on a wave of grief that feels completely out of my control.

"Yes," I say finally. "That's fine."

The phone rings all day. Friends with tentative "Hellos." Journalists want to know if they can come to the service. I answer with a brusque "No way." The most difficult call comes from Dave's eldest brother, Hank, who hadn't spoken to Dave in over four years.

"I would like to come to the wake, if it's okay with you," he says. My mind is a spin art of emotion, anger spraying into sadness into pity. I want to berate him for cutting Dave out of his life when Dave had been nothing but kind to him, but Hank stopped speaking to everyone in the family for reasons that were never clear.

"Hello?" he says. "Are you there?" Part of me wants to tell him how hurt Dave was by Hank severing their friendship when Dave had worked hard to be close to him. Dave tried a dozen times to call Hank and find out what he had done, but Hank refused to even come to the phone.

"Of course you can come," I whisper. "You have to live with your-self." I want to say more, but I know that no matter what I say to Hank now, it will make no difference, will never change the sad reality that he missed out on an amazing man like Dave.

In the evening I watch Aidan jump into his bed, his skin still shining from his bath. He has always loved the water, from the moment I laid him on top of me in the bathtub when he was just three weeks old.

"I want bankie," Aidan says in his newfound baby voice. This whiney sound thoroughly annoys me, but Mary, his therapist, assures me that it is normal for grieving children to want to go back to a time that was safe and secure.

I slide into the bunk next to Aidan, and he nuzzles me, his hair wet and cold against my neck. He pulls his small cotton blanket around him.

"I love my bankie," he tells me.

"I know, sweetie. It's very special."

"The hearts on it mean I love you." He points to light pink hearts in large squares.

"Aww," I say, kissing him on his nose.

"And the cars mean I want to run you over," he says with no malice, and I smile, knowing this sentiment perfectly synthesizes the polar ex-tremes of feelings that seesaw Aidan and me from one moment to the next. I begin reading the *Star Wars* book I have read a hundred times. Uncomfortable with stuffed teddy bears and monkeys poking me in the back, I stop, grabbing a handful of animals to make more room. I hurl them onto the top bunk bed. "No!" he yells. "They are part of my king-dom!"

"Well, I can't fit!" I stand up and Aidan tries to make more room, pil-ing animals at the bottom of the bed. I squeeze back down, keeping one leg on the floor to keep from falling off.

"You sure you don't want to read something else?" I ask wearily. But as usual, Aidan is insistent. He is a beautiful boy, with a bridge of freck-les on his nose and full, expressive lips. He wriggles as I read, putting his feet on the top bunk and bouncing stuffed animals off his chest.

"I'm not going to read if you don't pay attention," I say. I try to skip parts, but since he has memorized it, I have to go back and reread them. When his foot lands hard on my shin, I slam the book closed.

"*That's it!*" I yell.

"*No!* I'll stop!"

"I'm sitting over here," I say, pulling up the old Kennedy rocker I bought in Maine for twenty-five dollars the summer I was pregnant.

"Don't sit there!" Aidan whines, but my patience is waning.

"I can't fit in your bed," I tell him.

"There's someone sitting there already," he says sincerely.

I feel my brow furrow. "Who?"

"It's a firefighter angel."

A chill trickles down my back like cold water. "Is it Daddy?" I ask.

"No. He has firefighter clothes on and wings."

"Oh, like the picture we have?" I say, deflating.

"No, his clothes aren't dirty and he's not sad. It's one of Daddy's friends."

"Who?" I ask, trying not to sound desperate, but it is too late. Aidan is finished with this conversation.

"Keep reading," he insists, and so I slide back into bed with him, not wanting to sit on an angel.

*   *   *

It is another balmy morning when Kat and I arrive at my mother's priest's house on Staten Island. Since I only attend church on the holidays when I am visiting, Father Bartley is the only priest I know, and the only one I have liked since my childhood. My parents were members of a hippie church nearby called St. Garage, named after the small garage on the Notre Dame High School campus they used for services on Sunday. We sang Crosby, Stills & Nash songs instead of hymns and baked brown bread instead of hosts, and my first confession consisted of me sitting across from a young, bearded missionary priest who was later killed in Africa.

Father Bartley answers the door looking tired, but he manages an exuberant hello. He is balding, in his mid-seventies, with skin like a strawberry shake and an easy smile.

I introduce him to Kat and we follow him through his rectory next door to St. Paul's church, a low brick building built in the sixties. It was originally built as a school, and so Father Bartley preaches to a small congregation in a large basketball gym. Wooden sculptures of the crucifixion hang next to basketball hoops and the altar sits on the three-point line. When Dave and I went to weddings with Aidan, he would look for a hoop among the stained-glass windows, and we had to explain to Aidan that Jesus did not in fact play basketball.

In the small sitting room, Father Bartley lowers himself into an antique chair. Kat and my mom flank me on the couch across from him. He talks about the order of Dave's mass, the homily he will give. I find myself drifting off, staring at the thick wooden crucifixes lining the wall behind him. Next to the crosses, a series of framed color photos shows Father Bartley when he, too, served as a missionary in Africa. He is standing next to high-cheeked African women with tentative smiles and skin as dark as used motor oil. Other photographs show him standing among his nine siblings in Ireland.

"How is Aidan doing?" Father Bartley asks in his thick brogue. I want to tell him the angel story, but say "up and down" instead.

"It's very hard. I've been meeting with so many families, and it's not easy." Father Bartley shakes his head. "Only God can give us those answers. He is with you now." I want to believe him with all my heart, to imagine a serene bearded man watching over me, but something has shifted, and even my limited spirituality seems to have been squashed among the debris.

"Thank you for doing Dave's service," I say.

"I'm honored to do it. It's my birthday that day," he says, and my eyes widen.

"Wow. It's Dave's, too." I squeeze my lips together, trying not to cry, and I make a mental note to buy the father a cake.

Kat takes rigorous notes while I rifle through psalms and readings. My mother, the only religious one in the family, decides to read the prayer of St. Francis.

"My mother-in-law wants to do a reading in Gaelic," I tell him.

"Oh, lovely," he says.

I hand him an elaborately decorated Bible that Toni wants me to use. "She was hoping you'd pick one out," I tell him.

He begins flipping through the pages. "Who will be doing the eulogy?" he asks, not looking up from the book.

"Well, my father will be reading a poem, my mother-in-law, Carolyn Leary, a friend of Dave's . . . and then me."

Father Bartley stops and looks up. "Are you sure you want to do that?" he asks cautiously. "Because I see a lot of people during a service . . . you know, that can't make it through . . . It's hard."

"I want to do it."

*   *   *

I am lying on the Oriental rug in my parents' living room, inhaling the odor that reminds me of security and calm, when life was wide-eyed. I have its patterns memorized. I know where all the white swirls are and where each blue circle repeats itself. I inhale the wool. It smells of animal fur, smoke from the fireplace, and sweat from endless wrestling matches.

"You need to pick out a card for Dave's wake, or they won't be able to make them on time," my sister says, handing me a gray plastic binder. More decisions. More choices. My sister sighs. She looks as exhausted as I am.

"I hate this," I say. I skim through the pages of saints, crosses, prayers, and popes. I think of the collection in the pocket of my black suit, the morbid party favors of these events, a small photo of the lost pressed between plastic, a prayer typed underneath. Some are bookmarks with tassels, others are cards. Fatigue and grief make me feel silly, and I begin to giggle.

"Uh-oh. She gets like this every night," Leah warns Neil and his brother as she giggles with me. "It's the funeral hour."

"How about this one?" I point to a picture of black hands folded together in prayer. "Or this?" Jesus' thorns leave bloody trickles on his forehead, his blue eyes rolled back in his head. Leah covers her mouth but laughs anyway, and Neil joins in, too. All of a sudden I am mad. Not angry mad, but crazy mad, like the Mad Hatter. I am laughing and crying at the same time now, and I can't seem to stop myself. I feel insane, straitjacket crazy, but I can't hold back anymore. Even though everyone is staring at me, I keep going. I am deranged from grief. It is so easy to do, really, to split at the seams, to step off the cliff of sanity because the pain inside is so intense. And so I am teetering there, wanting to jump, but my sister's hand on my back keeps me from falling off.

*   *   *

The next day Aidan's teacher asks me to make Aidan leave his blanket at home. He had been swinging it around the classroom, and on Friday it hit someone in the face.

"Can I just tell him he can't swing it around, that it's just for snuggling when he feels bad?" I ask.

"I'd really rather he keep it at home," she tells me.

"But I think he needs something to help him get through right now, some sense of security."

"It's dangerous for the other kids. I don't understand why he is so wild!"

I bite my lip. What does she expect him to do? But instead, I squat down in front of Aidan and tell him I have to take his blanket home. Aidan shakes his head vehemently, his bottom lip quivering, and I am trying not to lose it when Roy Ann, the social worker, enters.

"I'll take care of it," she tells me when I explain why Aidan is so upset. I leave the blanket and head home to write Dave's eulogy. The memorial is two days away.

I remember the anticipation of writing, the scary and exciting beginning of a new screenplay, article, or show. Sometimes I loved taking the creative ride, the ideas bouncing around the labyrinth of my mind, gelling into perfect sentences. Other times it was pure torture, the computer my judge and enemy. *What do you have to say that's worthwhile?* it would taunt, the white screen glaring at me. *Why are you even bothering?* Dave would listen patiently as I confessed my insecurities, questioned my talent, labored over deadlines.

"Why take the ride, if you're not going to enjoy the trip?" he'd say. He encouraged me to quit my job and write full-time even when we had barely enough to live on. My articles for magazines were infrequent, and we were relying on Dave's paycheck, which, without overtime, netted us only about four hundred fifty dollars a week. Dave tried to work as much overtime as he could, but without it we often had trouble making ends meet. For years, a weak and often corrupt union has made New York City firefighters some of the lowest-paid workers in the country. In fact, less than twenty miles away, in Suffolk, Long Island, police officers make 50 percent more than New York City firefighters and police. Dave was anticipating his 3 percent raise at the time of his death.

I wipe off the dust from the computer screen and try to think of where to begin. I write comedy, screenplays, and articles about children. How am I going to sum up seventeen years with my best friend, my husband? How can simple words express how huge my love is? Maybe Father Bartley was right, and it is not appropriate for me to attempt a eulogy. I pace the kitchen, staring at the celery-colored walls Dave and I had painted last fall. I lean on the sink staring out of the narrow window at the evergreen in a clay pot outside. Dave had planted it when we first moved in and it never really thrived. Every time I tried to throw it out, Dave would point to the tiny patch of green on its left side and say, "It's not gone yet."

I sit back down and make a list of the things Dave loved. The list goes on and on. There is so much more, but this feels like enough. I crack my knuckles and stretch my back, the muscles pulling taut and sore. The phone is ringing, but I don't answer. I am shaping the list into sentences and paragraphs talking about how we met, his family, his sincerity, the way he loved Aidan. I feel my breath quickening, but I don't cry. I don't want to lose the thoughts that are piling in one on top of the other, getting ahead of my typing. A snowstorm of memories and thoughts and feelings is coming quicker. They are a tide rising up under my fingers. Click. Click. Click. I can feel Dave's presence in the kitchen and I inhale him in deeply, like hot steam. It is after three. I have been writing for three hours but I am finished, and it is done.

*   *   *

Wake boards. I never knew what they were until I began attending dozens of firefighter funerals. They are the poster boards filled with photos of half a life lived, and I am dreading making Dave's. Boxes of photos were shoved into the basement years ago, and since Dave died, the basement is even messier than before. For weeks we have been tossing packages and letters and bags of Dave's things into the basement to make room for guests. Now I push past a box marked ART SUPPLIES and a musty-smelling puzzle and pull down a giant plastic box of photographs.

"Oh my God," Jason mutters as he grabs the box from me. "How many freakin' photos do you have in here?"

"I like to take pictures," I say, hauling out another box marked WEDDING AND BABY PICTURES and we head upstairs. Leah's friend Maureen and her boyfriend, Richard, have arrived to help. We begin to divide the photos into piles: Dave's childhood, Lifeguard Dave, Firefighter Dave, Artist Dave, Dave with Friends, Dave with Family, Dave and me, holiday photos, wedding photos, vacation photos.

My mother-in-law has sent over color xeroxes of photos from when Dave was young. I love the pastel palette of old color photos, the faded red of Dave's shoes when he was two. There are numerous family shots, too, everyone standing awkwardly in front of the small house. Dave's father had moved out by then and I try to imagine how hard it must have been for my mother-in-law, raising seven children on her own while working full-time as a teacher. Hank, the eldest, is always in the back, looking angry even then, his arms folded across his chest. Vicky, the oldest girl, stands beside him, her face hidden behind thick glasses and bangs. She is holding Ed, an infant. Dennis starts the second row, his hair combed into a middle part, exactly the way he wears it now. Then there is Brian, the one no one talks about; his eyes stare off, far away. Brain damage caused it, but no one knows why. The story Dave knew was that Brian fell down the stairs when he was two, but Ed told me that Brian was born that way, his speech delayed, his mind unfocused. No one in Dave's family ever named what was wrong with Brian, and since he was never treated, he stayed the same, piling up papers in his room and binge drinking. On holidays everyone sat in uncomfortable silence as Brian made loud, racist jokes in a pathetic attempt to connect with someone. Romi, Ed's wife, was the only one who confronted him, who told him the jokes were insulting, who treated him like the adult he was. Next to Brian is Ellen. Her face looks the most like Dave's, the perfectly straight nose, the small hazel eyes. Her blond hair falls past her shoulders, making her look like a Renaissance princess. Dave always near Vicki, leaning on her legs or holding her hand, his red shoes polished and his dimples splayed.

"Dave was such a *hunk!*" Maureen exclaims, staring at the pile of lifeguard photos. Dave in a lifeboat, his muscles flexed as he rows in through the waves, his body tan and young.

"I took this one," Leah says, pointing to one of my favorite photos of Dave hugging me, his large arms clutching my shirt.

"That was in Ireland." I point to a picture of Dave and Aidan and me, standing in front of the bed and breakfast on the Dingle Peninsula, the rolling green hills looking like a movie set in the background.

"This one's funny," Jason says, pointing to a photo of firemen posing on the roof of a building. There are five of them: Sean Cummins, George Ebert, Captain Hayde, Bronco. Their eyes are red, and their faces are smeared with black soot, a fire blazing behind them. "Do they know the building is on fire?" Jason jokes. Maureen finds the black-and-white photos I took in Chinatown when I fancied myself an art photographer. There are close-ups of dried fish and Peking ducks in the windows and a picture of Dave grabbing his crotch in front of a restaurant called Mei Dick. We laugh at the pile of Halloween photos in which I documented Dave's infamous costumes for the parade. There was a dragon that Dave sculpted when Aidan was nine months old, and a fire truck Dave made from Pampers boxes and flashing lights. Dave wore it around his waist and put Aidan on his shoulders, dressed as a firefighter. I was a burning building, standing next to them, a crown of fire around my head. My favorite was a train, complete with smoke and lights, carefully constructed on top of Aidan's tricycle. Aidan pedaled inside, dressed as an engineer, and Dave and I were railroad crossings. Dave made fun of me for all the pictures I took, the viewfinder always pressed to my eye, but tonight with thousands of photographs piled up like years around me, I am glad that I did.

Five hours and seven photo boards later, we are finally done. Maureen heads home and Leah goes into my bedroom to sleep. I am wired, too sad and exhausted to rest. Jason is wired, too, swearing it is the coffee he drank and not his worry for me that is keeping him here. We begin to sort through the mail stacked in piles on top of the television console.

"Jesus," Jason remarks, marveling at the endless notes and packages arriving from around the country. We sit on the couch and look at a stack of drawings from a first-grade class in Indiana. Crude pictures of the towers burning and planes are in every picture and barely legible notes reading "Dave was a hero." A man from Montana sent an idea on what to build at the site, a church in Wisconsin sent a teddy bear in turnout gear for Aidan. There is an angel pin from a woman in Texas, a check from a firehouse in California, and sympathy cards, countless sympathy cards, all with long notes. I read them all, touched by the outpouring of emotion, awed by how many lives Dave touched in his few short years.

Dear Marian,

I don't know if you remember me, but my sons Ben and Dave were in your gymnastics class. There was one afternoon that Ben was playing with his new soccer ball in the playground. He kicked it too high and it landed on the roof of the school. Ben was inconsolable. Dave was there playing with Aidan and he came over to help. We tried everything to get the ball down, but the roof was too high. Dave promised Ben he would get it back and the next day, Ben found his ball in his cubby at school. Dave had come with the fire truck and gone up on the roof to get it. It is a rare person that would be so kind, and the world is less bright with Dave gone. Our hearts are with you at this time.

Regards,
Nancy

Jason is sorting the notes into separate piles.

"You just can't stop sorting into piles, can you," I tease.

"Ooh, a CD," Jason says.

"I already have a CD pile," I tell him, pointing to a pile of CDs next to the television.

"Oh my God," Jason says, laughing. "Can we listen to them?" he asks devilishly.

"We shouldn't," I say, feeling guilty, but after years of performing with Jason, nothing is immune to our humor and so I line up five CDs in the player and press spiral. There are religious songs about heaven and angels, patriotic songs about flags and America. There are political songs about terrorists and presidents and refugees, folksongs about dying and running from the towers. Jason and I giggle at someone who signed his CD simply "A guy from New Jersey." Because the sound quality is so poor, we imagine he is a teenager with a four-track in the basement of his mom's house. "And the eagles flew when the towers fell and the people died," he sings passionately, and slightly out of tune, and when the guitar hits the wrong note, the singer stops, says "oops" and begins to play again. Blended with my laughter is my continued awe at how far-reaching this tragedy has become, from the burkaed women in Afghanistan to the teenager in New Jersey who wrote a song for a widow in Brooklyn.

The next morning, my sister-in-law Ellen, her daughter, Christina, Leah, Martina, and I go for manicures before the wake. It feels good to get out of the crowded apartment and sit in this sunny room. The nail techs are cackling back and forth in Korean as Ellen and I await our turn.

"I hope this doesn't make us late," she says. She's the only Fontana with a thick Long Island accent. I have always loved Ellen, the way she mutters jokes under her breath and laughs easily when we exchange waitress stories. "I can't believe how many friends you and Dave have," Ellen says as she chooses a bright red polish.

"Yeah . . . we were blessed," I say almost sarcastically.

"I don't know. I just can't believe it, really. I mean, I know logically he is gone, but I keep thinkin', maybe he bumped his head and he has amnesia and is stumbling around downtown somewhere. And every time I feel sorry for myself, I think of you two and how in love you were—" She is crying now, the only one in Dave's family who will do this in front of me. She is the only one who cried at her father's funeral in 1986, a year after I met Dave. Christina, her four-year-old, climbs into her lap and pats her back.

"I'm sorry. You don't need to hear this," Ellen apologizes.

"It's okay," I tell her. "I cry all the time."

When it is my turn, I sit in a squeaky vinyl chair and soak my fingers in warm soap. The young Korean tech has acne and a thick black ponytail. She looks up shyly and smiles. After filing, soaking, trimming, and buffing my nails, she takes strong-smelling pink hand cream and begins to massage my hands. I close my eyes. I have always loved to have my hands rubbed. It is what Dave did during my labor to ease the pain. When she stops, I am thirsty for more, but it is time to go. The wake begins in fifteen minutes.

The Montauk Club is a beautiful Victorian mansion on 8th Avenue in Park Slope. Leah has filled long tables in the elegant front foyer with wake cards and blank books for guests to sign. The wake itself is in the Grand Room on the right, where the empty coffin, draped with an American flag, sits under elaborate stained-glass windows. Dave's helmet—the one he didn't use much—is perched on top of the coffin. Instead of the garish wreaths found at most funerals, Heather has adorned the room with graceful arrangements of fall flowers. A photo board stands on each antique wooden table, a sprig of Irish heather in front of it. Next to the coffin, a large easel holds a giant framed photo of Dave from his first year on the job. An orange Proby placard adorns his helmet. The photo was taken a week before the placard would be replaced with his official red-and-black one. He is smiling so wide his eyes are squinting. The photo is transposed on top of another of the fire truck after the towers fell. Dave's name is barely visible, written crudely in the dust on the side of the truck. It is the photo Huey and Tony took on that day.

Jimmy Lopez and Sean Cummins stand honor guard in front of the casket. The other firefighters are clustered nearby, preparing the list of rotations. Dave's mother and siblings seem like an island unto themselves, standing awkwardly as if they are at a party of someone they don't know. Groups of friends and relatives begin arriving. I decide not to stand in one place receiving people and move about instead, greeting people as if I am the hostess at a depressing affair. Aidan runs through the room like a pinball, bouncing off of legs and walls. Mourners walk quietly around the room, looking at the photo boards, praying at the casket, and then kissing me somberly, searching for something to say.

"That's so sweet the way they put a plaque for Dave outside the room," one of them says, and I nod, confused.

Leah brings me a glass of water and a tissue.

"Fucking Nancy was in here taking photos for the *Times*. I just threw her out," she whispers. She has been arguing with Nancy, a *New York Times* photographer, for weeks, as she always seems to appear behind us, poised with her camera.

"I told her I didn't want any photographs in here! And she kept snapping photos even after I asked her to stop!"

I shake my head, disgusted.

"I gotta go. Some lady is out front freaking out. She can't stop crying," Leah says, but before she can leave, I point to a group of men in black suits who have just entered, wearing curly wires behind their ears. They scan the room, checking every corner. I watch my sister greet them, speak to them for a while, and then finally head back over to me.

"Mayor Giuliani's here," she says. "I have to get the family together." Leah rushes around corraling the Fontanas while Jason goes to find Aidan.

The mayor walks in looking stooped and tired, his small mouth pressed into an expression of friendly concern. He kisses my sister hello as if he has known her for a long time, and she offers him water, which he gratefully accepts. He looks bigger than he does on television and that night at the Hilton, his prominent forehead giving way to small intense eyes hung with two dark curtains of fatigue. He kisses my cheek while shaking my hand.

"I am so sorry about your husband," he says. "Is this your son?" he asks, and I pick up Aidan who is focused on a twenty-five-cent toy that is green and gooey and looks like snot.

"This is Aidan," I tell him. "Aidan, this is Mayor Giuliani." But Aidan is not looking up from his toy.

"He's a little distracted," I say, embarrassed. "Aidan, someone is talking to you."

"What is that?" the mayor asks Aidan.

"It's Goop!" Aidan says, holding it up to the mayor's face.

"Oh, Aidan, no!" I scold, but it is too late, and a piece of green goo lodges itself on the lapel of the mayor's suit.

"I am so sorry." I try to wipe it away, but the mayor shrugs, smiling slightly.

"It's okay."

The bodyguards hover around the mayor like buzzards, their arms behind their backs as he stands in front of the coffin and makes a brief, improvised speech. He is a natural orator, as comfortable speaking as any actor I've seen, and his words seem unrehearsed. "The sacrifice Dave made with his fellow firefighters saved twenty-five thousand people. Without their efforts, who knows how many people would have died, and we cannot underestimate this sacrifice."

I scan the crowd. Everyone is listening intently, heads cocked and tissues ready. I am struggling to hold Aidan, who feels like a giant sack of feed in my arms, his legs wrapped loosely around my waist.

"I want to go home," Aidan whines. I ignore him, trying to concentrate on the mayor.

"Dave, knowing the risks, knowing that his life was at stake, chose to go into that building and save strangers, because he cherished human life and dedicated his life to protect others. I cannot say enough about how proud I am to be a New Yorker, to be the mayor of the best city in the world, and to oversee the best Fire Department in the world."

Everyone is applauding when I notice Dave's oldest brother, Hank, staring at Aidan. He has not seen Aidan in years. I barely recognize Hank, his face covered in a thick beard, his belly round and low. He is with Joe, his youngest son, who at sixteen has already acquired his father's stony face.

By the time the evening wake begins, I cannot avoid a receiving line that stretches out the door, into the hall, down the steps, and around the block. Firefighters from all over the country line up, hugging me heartily, telling me the brotherhood of firefighters is there for me. They arrive in droves from Colorado, Ontario, Virginia, Chicago, Hawaii, Massachusetts, California, and more to support their fallen brothers and fill the empty spaces at funerals. Traditionally, firefighter funerals are huge events, with thousands of firefighters attending. Now, with as many as six or seven funerals in one day and firefighters working at the site, there are not enough of them to go around. As a result, firefighters from across the country have traveled here, using their own vacation time and money, to fill the empty lines at funerals, bring money to the families of fallen firefighters, and line up among their New York brothers to pay their respects.

A firefighter in his late forties with large freckles and a thick mustache leans in for a hug. His voice is rough and Southern, but his eyes are wrinkled with sincerity. "Some of the guys from Miami have come up, and we just want to tell you how sorry we are for your loss."

"You're so sweet for coming. Thank you."

"No, thank *you*. We saw you last night, and we appreciate what you're doin' for us."

"No problem," I say, confused, and he continues past me to greet my mother.

A handsome firefighter from California is next and kisses me gently on the cheek. "I love what you said on TV," he says, hugging me. "You're an amazing woman, and I'm deeply sorry for your loss."

My mother leans in as he walks toward my mother-in-law. "What did you say?" she asks curiously.

"I have no idea."

By eight-thirty, my back is so sore from being hugged, I can barely stand. The owner of the club brings me tissues and sherry, and my mom tries to get me to sit, but it feels rude making people stoop down to kiss me and so I stand, the line never appearing to have an end.

"Some people have really bad breath," my mother whispers.

"I know. Maybe we should hand out mints instead of wake cards."

"Stress produces bad breath."

"No kidding." Mom hits me on the arm, and we giggle while trying to keep our faces stern.

A firefighter from Hawaii approaches. He is short and dark, with high cheekbones and a warm smile. "You are something, standing up for us like this in your time of pain. Thank you."

"What did I do?" I ask, pulling him back by his elbow.

"You were on *Third Watch* last night and you said that we should get more money and something about stockbrokers making a million dollars but they wouldn't run into a burning building."

I toss my head back, recalling the taping of *Third Watch* almost three weeks before. "I can't believe they kept that in!"

"They did," he answers, walking over to my mother. I shake my head, grateful that I said what I did for Dave and all these men, this amazing brotherhood that does so much for others.

Mike Leddy, a firefighter friend of Dave's, saunters up, his eyes red and full of tears. He looks like an aging football star with strong broad shoulders and a mop of white hair. Mike was on the Disaster Assistance Relief Team with Dave, a Red Cross volunteer group from the Fire Department. In 1994, they traveled together to Los Angeles to help with the earthquakes and to Texas to help the victims of the floods. The guys at Squad told me that Mike is at the site every day, taking pictures or helping with the recovery.

"Thank you for coming," I tell him. He tries to speak but can only shake his head. It is impossible to see such a big man weep and not cry with him. I remember meeting Mike at a Red Cross function years ago. He had become a peer counselor after working at the Happy Land fire on March 25, 1990. He had crawled into the dance club to do a search. The ground was soft and rubbery beneath him. He didn't know then that they were the bodies of the people he had come to save.

"I put some great pictures of you up," I say finally, gesturing to the wake boards, and he nods.

"Those were good times," he says quietly, walking over to my mother-in-law.

The wake is supposed to end at nine, but a long line still twists out the door at half past ten. I can't believe all the people who have come out from the tiniest crevices of our past to pay their respects. There are teachers, students, neighbors, organizations, distant cousins, politicians, old friends, strangers. My feet ache from standing, and I shift from one to the other, remembering one of the many running jokes Dave and I shared. He would wake up in the morning, exhausted and sore. "Hey, did you get the number?" he'd say.

"What number?" I'd retort.

"The number of the truck that hit me."

Tonight, as the room finally empties, I know what he meant. Leah looks exhausted, too, but finishes her duties by arranging for Aidan to be tucked in, and the photos and bouquets of flowers to be brought to the church in the morning. Dave's family helps carry the boxes of mass cards and books and presents that people have brought, and we load them into the Fire Department van. I am so glad I asked people not to give wreaths and flowers, but to donate their money instead to the Elsasser Fund, a charity for widows of non-line-of-duty deaths.

I take a sprig of Irish heather and hold it to my nose. It smells of peat and Ireland and Dave. In the front foyer, I am about to grab my purse when something catches my eye. It is a small bronze plaque hanging on the wall outside the wake room. It reads THE FONTANA ROOM in large metal letters. I am surprised I had not seen the plaque before. I have attended other events here, weddings and meetings. I look closer, wondering if maybe someone had put it up for the night, but its detail suggests something much older. I lean in even closer to read the florid lettering and the small print: "The Fontana Room. To honor the memory of Alexander V. Fontana, elected to membership on January 16, 1945. He was a resident of Brooklyn for most of his life and generously supported the borough's humanitarian activities. Windows restored in memory of Pauline V. Fontana and Clementina Mary Fontana."

*   *   *

"Marian. We don't have much time. Let's go," Leah says. It's after eight, the morning of Dave's memorial service.

"I'm so tired." My body feels like it is filled with sand. I roll over in bed to see the shade billow slightly, the wind making an eerie whistle between the windows. I slide on my glasses and sit up, the floor cold under my feet.

"It's chilly," Leah says, "and really windy."

I sigh, rolling up the shade to see a sapling tree bend in a strong gust of wind. It is blustery, the type of day Dave loved.

On the Ides of March 1996, a nor'easter dumped over a foot of snow on New York, bringing the city to a standstill. A benefit that I was supposed to perform in was canceled, so Dave and I cuddled on the white couch we had just bought and watched hailstones bouncing off our window gate.

"This is so crazy," I said, mesmerized by the balls of ice.

"Let's go for a walk." Dave stood.

"Are you nuts?" I asked, but Dave was already pulling me up.

"It's beautiful out."

"It's thundering!"

"Don't be such a wimp."

Bundled in thick down coats, we headed outside, where a cement-colored sky stretched low above us.

"Ouch! Dave! This is dangerous!" I whined as hail bounced off my hood.

"C'mon. It's fun." I could barely feel his hand when he grabbed mine to walk up the hill. We stopped on 8th Avenue to help a car stuck in deep snow. "Push!" Dave yelled as we hoisted the bumper, its back end swinging like a woman's hips until it finally rolled away.

Usually bustling, Prospect Park was empty except for a cross-country skier gliding like a ghost across the wide field. Dave wrapped a big arm around me. All sound was muted in a mattress of snow.

"I don't think this is safe," I said, as lightning flashed and low thunder rumbled like a subway passing beneath us.

"Just a tiny bit farther," he insisted. I pretended we were Arctic explorers or wayward hikers caught in an unsuspecting storm until we arrived at the other end of the field. I followed Dave into a tent of pine trees where the thick green boughs sheltered us from the wind.

"It's so quiet in here," Dave said, sniffing hard, his cheeks striped red.

"Okay. You're right. This *is* beautiful."

"It's a good place to ask someone to marry them," Dave said. I checked his face to see if he was joking. "Very funny." Dave was already down on one knee. "Stop joking!" I pushed him until he fell back into the snow. I jumped on top of him, giggling and kissing him, his tongue soft and warm.

"I'm not," he said finally, holding a velvet box between our mouths.

I jumped up, and Dave resumed his position on one knee.

"I'm not good at this stuff, but . . . um . . . I know you don't believe in love at first sight, but I do." His eyes were green that day. They had changed color to match his coat. I laughed nervously, a giggle I didn't recognize. "From the moment I met you, you've made me a better man." The ring was water sapphire flanked by two green tourmalines. I had seen it at a friend's craft shop on 7th Avenue and admired the color, an unusual, incandescent purple. "Will you marry me?" he asked as a clap of thunder snapped and boomed.

"I better say yes," I said, still giggling as he slid the ring onto my finger.

*　　*　　*

Dave's family arrives and I slink into the bathroom to get dressed.

"Why are they here so early?" I whisper to my sister, annoyed, as I yank on my black panty hose.

"I dunno. I told them there were bagels and coffee upstairs," she says, fixing her dress in the full-length mirror behind the door. I brush my teeth hard and sigh at the dark puffs under my eyes, a by-product of so much crying.

"We should create a line of grief makeup," I announce, smearing foundation under my eyes.

"We'd be rich."

"Skin-colored patches for under the eyes," I continue, "like the football players wear."

"Waterproof everything," Leah adds.

"Definitely—and perfume—Eternity—no. That's been done." Leah and I laugh alike, loud and nasal. I stop so it will not turn into tears.

"I look so ugly," I say, missing the way Dave told me I was beautiful even on days I didn't believe him.

"You look great," Leah says, opening the door a crack. "Hurry up. The limo will be here soon."

I sit on the closed toilet lid, listening to the floorboards creak above me. I hear Aidan in his room, dumping out toys. I don't want to face my son spinning in an anxious whirlwind around the small apartment. I don't want to see the anguished faces of my in-laws sitting awkwardly in my living room. I want to stay in the sanctuary of this bathroom, its windowless walls cool and empty. I want to sit on this toilet, its cold black seat holding me up, until this day is over. I don't know how long I have been crying when my sister walks back into the bathroom. She dresses me like a five-year-old, while I stare forward catatonic, shaking my head no over and over again.

By the time I head upstairs, the limos have arrived and it's time to go. My stomach gurgles as I step out onto the stoop, pulling my wrap around me. A strong wind blows my hair in front of my face. Dave's family is piling into the cars and my brother, Luke, is behind me, arguing with my mother.

"I don't want to bring a whole box of tissues," he says. "I'll just put some in my pocket."

"That's not going to be enough. Just bring the box," my mother says.

"Ma, leave me alone! I don't wan—"

"Why can't you just—"

"Ma, stop!" Luke says.

"DON'T FUCKING DO THIS TO ME TODAY!" I scream, whipping my head around. For the first time in my life, they stop and quietly follow me down the steps. I slide into the cold black leather seat next to Leah, who automatically puts her hand on my thigh. Dave's brother Brian sits on the other side of her, staring out the window, his expression blank and unusually quiet.

"We'll have to wait here for a bit," the driver says after only two blocks. My mother-in-law, Vicki, and her husband, Eric, are in the backseat, silent. There are police barricades and a line of traffic. I look out the window at dozens of friends and neighbors walking in clusters toward the church for the memorial.

"Oh, God," I say, my breath making circles of steam on the window. Anguish and grief detonate inside of me, obliterating hope and everything I used to be. *This is happening. This is really happening.* This memorial today makes Dave's death official and permanent. It is the end of possibility, the final good-bye, and the pain makes my stomach clench like a labor contraction. "I think I'm going to throw up." I open the door and spit bile onto the curb. I get out of the car wailing and shaking my head, pacing back and forth—a tiger in too small a cage. My sister gets out, too, the wind whipping her curls across her face. She hands me a tissue, and I spit into it. I am hysterical now, talking fast and crying at the same time.

"I've made a huge mistake!" I sob. The wind makes my hair stick to my lips. "I should have waited until they found him! What am I doing? This is all wrong!"

Leah is crying, too. "No. This is the right thing. Aidan can't wait anymore. It's cruel," she says. I nod, knowing this is true, but my stomach is lurching, and I bend over from the pain.

"I can't do this!" I blubber, spitting onto the sidewalk. I can feel my family getting out of the limo behind us to help, but they stand back as if there is an invisible circle around me. I stare at the rocks embedded in the cement until my vision blurs. *You have to pull yourself together . . .* and like the prelude to some tragic opera, the bagpipes begin.

"Oh, God," I moan as Leah gently guides me back to the car. My mother-in-law hands me a tissue, and the limo rolls slowly forward past an ocean of firefighters lined up in rows ten deep. I know Dave would be moved by the sheer number of firefighters, standing, in gloved salute, their eyes forward as if looking at something on the horizon. The car is silent except for my crying, a low moan that comes from a sadness deeper than I have ever known. The Squad 1 engine is in front of us with Lieutenant Dennis Farrell and Billy Redden marching alongside it. Jerry Smythe and Fred Lawrence stand on the back, their faces frozen. I can see the coffin sitting on top of the hose bed, draped with a flag and wreaths, an empty symbol.

The crowd stretches for blocks and blocks, and the volume of people makes me feel dwarfed by the crowd's presence, a tiny cell under a microscope. There are people pressed against the gates of the church and hanging from the windows of the brownstones we pass. The limo finally stops, and the drums and bagpipes echo through the wind vibrating in my ear. I try to gather myself up as the driver opens the door, but I am lost on an island of grief. I can't look up when I hear the news cameras clicking, the hushed whispers, a million sets of eyes watching me. The funeral director takes me by the elbow and I slowly climb the steps, never lifting my head except to see the other widows lined up on the steps like a string of black pearls.

Dave, what is happening? Why are you making me do this? The cold, cavernous church calms me as I listen to my footsteps echo off the high vaulted ceilings and thick marble columns. I slide into a wooden pew in the front. High stained-glass windows cast prisms of rainbows into the aisles. I spot Mila sitting to the side of the altar with Joey, her husband, and Lyris, the violin player from her band. My senses feel raw and exposed, every nerve on the surface. Leah slides in next to me, and Aidan climbs in between us. Kat is at the end of the pew, reciting my eulogy softly to herself. She and Leah will be my understudies if my nerves fail. Four priests sit to the side of the elaborate altar, their hands folded into their crisp embroidered robes. There is Father Duran and another priest I do not know. Father Chris, a chaplain from the Fire Department in his friar robes, and of course Father Bartley. I meet eyes with Gregory, a young redheaded boy I taught gymnastics to. His father told me that Gregory requested to serve as altar boy for Dave's mass today.

The church is filling up behind me, and I listen to heels clicking across the marble floor, programs rustling, an organ playing a melancholy hymn. I have not been inside this church since Aidan was baptized four and a half years ago. I look up to a stained-glass window depicting Jesus standing on a cloud, a gilded halo floating above him, serenely welcoming all into heaven. I wonder if Dave was received into Jesus' arms, or perhaps this is all a pathetic attempt to make us feel better about losing the people we love. I want to believe that Dave was saturated in that golden light, experiencing love and peace, though I cannot help but think that perhaps he turned away, craning his neck, desperate to glance back one last time, to see Aidan and me.

Everyone watches as Father Bartley blesses the casket. I think of the Vatican law, how he is not supposed to perform this ritual without a body, and I am grateful that he does it anyway, that he lives the life of God rather than being crushed by the Church's doctrines. He walks slowly around the coffin, splashing it with holy water, shaking frankincense, and muttering prayers. He is slow and methodical, his large body covered in a gilded white robe.

"Is Daddy in there?" Aidan asks, wriggling in his seat, and I panic, trying to figure out what to say. I had planned on saying "Daddy's spirit is in there," but now that seems too obtuse and so I simply say, "Yes."

"Is Daddy's skeleton in there?" I feel my whole body tighten. I have never lied to Aidan.

"Yes," I lie, sliding him closer to me.

When everyone settles down, Father Bartley climbs the steps to the pulpit, clears his throat, and pulls the thin microphone to his face. He begins a homily, an entreaty to God to remember Dave and his life. He talks about the towers and all who died. He talks about seeing Dave at church, how he sponsored my brother for his confirmation, what he remembered most about him. I can feel Dave as deeply as if I were standing next to him, his warm flesh pressed against me. I stand and sit and kneel and cry, feeling dazed and numb, as if time were stopped and life frozen in the church. I try to keep Aidan as quiet as I can as he slides his Matchbox cars across the pews, kneeling on the floor in front of me. When the homily is over, the priest stops and bows his head. Out of the silence, a lonely and sad violin echoes through the church, and Mila begins to sing. *"Oh, Danny Boy, the pipes, the pipes are calling . . ."* If emotion had a sound, Mila's voice would embody the sadness everyone was feeling that day.

Glancing across the aisle, I notice that all the firefighters, even the most stone-faced, are crying. My mind floods with memories of the countless nights Dave tucked Aidan in, his big body pressed against Aidan's as he sang soft and low, changing the words as he went.

"Oh, Aidan Boy. Oh, Aidan Boy, I love you so."

My mother stands and climbs the steps to the pulpit next. She looks small in the ivory-carved box as she recites the prayer of St. Francis, her favorite psalm about transformation. I am exhausted from trying to keep Aidan still. He keeps climbing under the pew, and Leah keeps pulling him out by his belt buckle back into our aisle.

"Ow!" he wails, his brown eyes glaring at me.

"Shhh!" I hiss. He is quiet, and now I am mad. I press my mouth tightly closed, as if someone were trying to pry it open.

"I want to go home!" Aidan whines, and I try to breathe. I want Aidan to remember this day, to have it imprinted into his brain to find over and over again.

"Shh!" I say, pointing to the pulpit. "Listen to Nonna." I pull him onto my lap and wrap him in his blanket, but he cannot stay still. The more upset he is, the more he spins to evade the pain that he is too young to understand.

Finally, Leah takes Aidan, and Kat brings my nieces, Aidan's cousins, Martina and Christina to the back of the church to bring up the offering. Dave's siblings Dennis, Ed, and Ellen recite the Prayer of the Faithful. Father Bartley blesses the host and the communion begins. People file into the aisles, making their way to the front of the church. Huey sings a song about being a firefighter that he wrote ten years ago, the muscles in his neck clenching as he sings, *"I reach out my hand and give all I can so that one might live tomorrow."* His voice rings through the church as people make their way slowly up the aisles mumbling "Amen."

After communion, Commissioner Von Essen begins the eulogies, walking slowly and steadily up to the pulpit. He wears the same weary expression he wore at the Hilton. Despite what I have heard about this man, the eulogy is actually nice. He calls Dave a Renaissance man, extolling his virtues as a firefighter, an artist, and a historian, and then at the end, without much fanfare, he looks me in the eyes and announces that Dave will be posthumously promoted to lieutenant. The applause starts like a rumbling thunder, spreading across the church, its impact making me cry. *You did it, honey. You made it.* Tom walks over and kisses me on the cheek, and I wonder what Dave would think of it all, if I am a traitor accepting all of this: the hypocrisy, the irony, the empty promises, the promotion he will never live to enjoy. But I smile at the commissioner, say "Thank you," and squeeze his hand. What else is there to do?

Leah reaches for my hand as we watch our father walk slowly to the front of the congregation. She knows we will both cry, as we always have done when our father reads a poem. He has written them for us every Christmas since we were young.

A Widow's Walk

> He didn't leave floating
> an angel, heliumlike
> on wide white wings
> A blink of the eye,
> a golden light
> and he was welcomed by the spirits
> of his mourned history . . .

My father stops, takes off his glasses, and squeezes his eyes. "I'm sorry," he says. My sister clenches my hand to let me know she is crying, too. My father drops his head, his white hair shining, and I stare disbelieving. There is my father, strong and invulnerable, standing in front of thousands, his small shoulders drooped, and he is crying for my husband, whom he considered a son.

Carolyn Leary climbs the stairs next. She looks poised in a smart, dark suit, coiffed hair, and pearls. She must have been quite beautiful as a young woman. Standing erect in front of the microphone, she reads a letter addressed to me.

Dear Marian,

Both my brother and I were heartbroken with the news that Dave was among the missing at the World Trade Center. . . . When Dave contacted my brother about the dedication ceremony, neither of us had any idea what he had planned or accomplished. On the day of the ceremony last March, when I actually had a chance to meet Dave, I felt as though I had met a long-lost brother. My feelings were such because Dave had pursued honoring a man with the zeal of a son. Dave was overwhelmed that day, and on several occasions, I saw the tears in his eyes.

I am convinced that as the thousands of souls approached the gates of heaven on September 11, a side door was opened and a young soldier who had been a New York City fireman, my father, moved through the crowd until he saw Dave. My father embraced him and said, "I have a place of honor for you in the heroes' wing. . . ."

Happy Birthday, Dave

I am exhausted from crying but can't seem to stop my emotions being stirred from every direction.

"This is so intense," my sister says, shaking her head and showing me her empty pack of tissues. I reach into my purse and give her another pack. I have brought three. Aidan climbs under his blanket and lies on my lap.

Toni, my mother-in-law, stands up next, looking weary as she walks. I smile, thinking of my grandmother; if she were here, she'd whisper, "You couldn't make an eleven with two of her, she's so thin!" Toni's chin quivers as she pulls the microphone toward her, clearing her throat. She quotes a sculpture teacher of Dave's, praising his talent. She thanks Aidan and me for making Dave happy and says "I love you" and "Life is great" in the strange, guttural sounds of Gaelic. When she steps down, I kiss her softly on her cheek, which feels like chenille. And now it is my turn.

I become aware of the wooden pews creaking and the expectant whispers of friends who are nervous and worried, and I realize that I am as unsure of my strength as they are. My legs feel like they are someone else's as I stand and walk cautiously up the narrow steps, smiling weakly in Father Bartley's direction. From the pulpit, I can see thousands of faces looking up at me expectant and sad. The pews have stopped creaking and I wonder if my neighbors, family, and friends can hear my heart beating as loudly as I can. I draw a deep breath and pull the microphone to my mouth, biting my lip to keep from crying.

"*It is difficult to distill an extraordinary life into a few short minutes,*" I begin. "*September eleventh was our eighth wedding anniversary. Dave chose the date because he liked to tell people our anniversary was nine-one-one.*" The congregation gives a grateful chuckle. "*It has been difficult to grasp how the happiest day of my life could also be my saddest. Even though I am a firefighter's wife, I never really imagined losing Dave. He seemed impossible to bring down, as solid, strong, and indomitable as the towers themselves. More painful to bear is that Dave, like so many of his fallen brothers, wanted so much to live. Dave had sculptures to carve, children to father, places to travel, waves to surf, fires to extinguish, ropes to tie, and innumerable memories to share with his family and friends. I want this day to be a celebration* of David's life. He would have been thirty-eight today, and I know he would be deeply moved to see how many people love him.

"I met Dave when I was eighteen years old and in the wildest of my college days. He was twenty—shy, introspective, charming, and absolutely gorgeous. We both lived in the arts dorm at college at C. W. Post. On our first date, Dave told me it was love at first sight and that he wanted to be with me forever. So on our second date, I cooked him an elaborate steak dinner and broke up with him."

The congregation laughs hard, thankful for a respite from the pain.

"It was when he got down on the ground, lay still, and did his impression of a speed bump that I knew he might be the one.

Falling in love with Dave was like taking a long, reflective walk on the beach and then finding that perfect shell or stone. His gentle nature, genuine sweetness, outrageous humor, loving soul, and creative spirit won me over. The more I got to know Dave, the more walks we took, the more deeply I fell in love with him, and in our seventeen years together, I fell in love with him over and over again.

"Dave was an amazing person who loved so many different things: rugby and Ireland, the ocean and history. He loved tying knots and fighting fires, kayaks and hiking. He loved pine trees and hawks, reading and yoga. He loved playing practical jokes, climbing mountains, and helping people. He loved children and camping, fresh salmon, a cold pint of Guinness, and a warm fire. He loved to laugh hard and work hard, riding waves and rowing boats. He loved welding steel, the smell of wood burning, and starry skies. He loved his brothers and sisters, his mother and father, his nieces and nephews more than they'll ever know, and most of all he loved being a father.

"Dave proposed to me during a nor'easter in Prospect Park. With hail-stones falling and lightning clapping, he professed his love, as he had ten years before. But it was two years later, when Dave became a father, that I learned how limitless Dave's love is. I knew he would be a good dad, but Dave embraced fatherhood with a zeal that surpassed my wildest expectations. He did laundry, changed diapers, and he loved toys more than any child. Aidan was his pride and joy, and he loved his son from the top of his head to the bottom of his big, flat feet.

"I remember one night when Aidan was tiny and refused to fall asleep.

After hours he finally nodded off, and I tiptoed out of the room. A few minutes later I caught Dave sneaking into Aidan's room to make sure he was covered up with his blanket. I scolded Dave, fearful that he would wake him up. A little while later, I heard Dave in Aidan's room again. I was furious. I threw open the door to find Dave leaning over the crib whispering 'I love you' gently in Aidan's ear over and over. He stood up, dimples folded in a wide smile. 'I just want Aidan to know, deep in his consciousness, how much I really love him.' "

The memory gets snagged in my throat and I stop. I can hear people crying, sniffling echoing in the silence. I turn my face toward Aidan, who looks so small in the large wooden pew. He is staring up at me, his wide brown eyes flickering like candle flames; he is still and listening for the first time today.

"Aidan, love is the only thing that lasts forever, and even though Daddy's gone, I hope you will remember how much your daddy loved you and keep that in your heart for the rest of your life.

"I have tried hard to find the good to come out of losing the love of my life. This summer Dave insisted on buying a hat that he saw his friend Jerry at the firehouse wearing. It read 'Life is good,' and for Dave it truly was, especially in his last months. Dave strove to live his life fully, to love his family and friends, to feel his feelings and be an honest and good man. I think he accomplished that. I hope everyone here will use Dave's life as an example. I know I will. So tell the people around you that you love them, mend grudges, don't stay angry with people, and be kind. Dave did these things. His heart was as large as his frame, and I feel privileged to have called myself Dave's wife."

"Dave's wife" echoes in my head as I swallow hard, trying to imagine myself as anything else, but before my mind can wander, everyone is standing, their applause surging forward. Even though my knees are weak, I feel Dave supporting me, escorting me back to my seat. The applause lasts a long time, filling the church with a din so loud, I am certain Dave can hear it.

It takes almost eight stanzas of "America the Beautiful" to get everyone out of the church. When it is finally empty, the funeral director takes my elbow and escorts me down the aisle.

"Oh, Marian," my mother-in-law says, practically running to catch up. "You sent him out like a warrior!" I picture Dave on a Viking boat, floating away. This seems to make more sense to me. The simplicity of it.

Outside, the crowd is waiting. There are fire trucks, firefighters, and giant lenses from the photographers pointing toward me. I wonder how our small, simple lives could turn into such a spectacle, how my sadness has become a show. I look up as helicopters fly in formation, their rotors roaring overhead. I worry about Aidan, knowing the sound will scare him, and pull him to me. I realize I am shaking, tears falling of their own volition.

"Company, salute!" someone yells, and thousands of firefighters snap their gloved hands to their foreheads. The guys from Squad look as ravaged as I do, standing stiff and straight, their eyes red and worn. A lone bagpiper begins to play "Carrick Fergus," a haunting song that Dave loved to hear played at an Irish pub uptown. It is not a popular song, the bagpipers didn't know it, but one of the best players made it his business to learn it for Dave's funeral.

A highly decorated chief heads over and hands me a helmet. It has a white lieutenant's placard on the front with a gleaming new yellow number 1 pressed into the leather. I pull it close to me, wishing it were Dave's real helmet, the salty one, the one he actually wore to work. All the wives want their husbands' helmets. They are the most valued possession of every firefighter. I imagine the metal beams falling on Dave, cracking the helmet, melting the tin eagle in front, its talons trying in vain to keep his placard in place, but the helmet had no choice but to crumble and melt into the debris at Ground Zero.

The firefighters pull the flag off of Dave's coffin and fold it into tight, neat triangles. Aidan watches intently, leaning his weight on my leg. I press tissues to my eyes, but it is like trying to stop the blood from a giant wound. My sister squeezes my elbow. A twenty-one-gun salute startles me with an ear-piercing blast. Aidan jumps and grabs my leg harder.

"Why do they do that?" he asks, his eyes widening.

"I-i-it's for Daddy," I manage to say as the pipe and drum band begins again and we are led back to the limousine. Aidan slides in first to look out of the window. I sit next to him, watching my friends in front of the church, looking dazed and exhausted.

"I see Daddy," Aidan says suddenly, pointing at the now-empty church steps. My sister and I exchange glances.

"Where is he?" I ask.

"Right there. He's giving the thumbs-up," he says, the secret code that Dave had taught him.

The limo moves slowly past the rows of firefighters standing in a firm salute. I roll down the window a bit to see their faces, to acknowledge their overwhelming support. As we pass, I see their chins trembling, their tears passing like a ripple through the crowd. It takes me a moment to realize that they are not looking at me at all, but at Aidan, who is leaning out the window wearing Dave's class A hat, his tiny hand saluting them back.

The car turns onto Union Street and the procession heads toward Prospect Park. We roll past the firehouse, its purple bunting flapping fiercely in the wind. We climb the hill of brownstones up to Grand Army Plaza, where I watch mothers stop their strollers and point at the procession of fire trucks and limousines.

The Soldier's Monument stands majestically in the center of a busy rotary, its giant arches reminiscent of the Arc de Triomphe in Paris. Dave loved the weathered brass sculpture on top depicting soldiers on horseback in the heat of a dramatic and bloody battle. On warm days, you can climb to the top of the arch and stare out at the manicured lawns of Prospect Park and watch hawks gliding on the wind.

The rotary circles onto Prospect Park West, where we pass limestone mansions and formidable Victorian homes built by prosperous citizens long ago. Dave would tease me, diagnosing me with "brownstone envy" as I peered into the grand living rooms with plushly upholstered couches, antique stained-glass lamps, and rugs from exotic places I've never been. As we watched prices skyrocket, I knew we would never be able to afford even a small apartment here on our salaries.

Like the gateway to Valhalla, two fire trucks flank the entrance to Prospect Park, their long tower ladders stretched five stories into the sky, a giant American flag draped between them, waving in the wind.

"Is that for Daddy?" Aidan asks, stretching his neck to see.

We pass under the ladders and turn in to the circular driveway of the Picnic House. The house is simple and elegant, one cavernous room with arched windows on every wall and wood floors. Buffet tables have been set up in the center of the room and there is a bar stocked with cases of donated wine, Jack Daniel's, and plastic cups. Tall French doors are flung open to reveal a cement porch already filled with firefighters drinking beer from kegs parked outside. The room fills quickly, until it's impossible to cross the room without stopping to speak to friends, family, neighbors, strangers, cousins, and acquaintances.

Finally, I escape onto the back porch steps, which hide me from the swelling crowd, and light a cigarette. At the bottom of the steps, my sister, the widows, and firefighters are huddled together, drinking and laughing. Nancy, the photographer from the *New York Times,* clicks away. I want to tell her to leave but I am too tired. I walk over to Theresa, who hugs me and squeezes my arm.

"Oh my God," she says. "I don't know how you got up there in front of all those people. You killed me."

"Me, too," Martha says.

"I know. God." Denise Esposito joins us. She shakes her head, pushing her large glasses up her tiny nose. "That was somethin'. You made me want to do that for Mike."

"You should," I tell her, watching her stare dreamily into her wine.

Long striped shadows from the trees begin to stretch across the lawn as leaves reluctantly fall in the windy gusts. I hand out bouquets of roses to the widows who linger as the crowd thins, not wanting to return to their empty homes. Shivering, we head back into the Picnic House, where stragglers are getting drunk. I remind my sister to bring out the birthday cake, and we sing "Happy Birthday" to Father Bartley and of course to Dave. My friend Lori from Staten Island reads a story she wrote about our last summer vacation together, just two weeks before Dave died. She talks about "the art of a well-packed cooler," alluding to Dave's finesse at organizing and planning the daily beach lunches. I suddenly feel panicked about taking care of myself for the rest of my life. Dave did so much. I've felt like an unpacked suitcase since he died, clothes strewn all over the house, laundry piled up for days.

Everyone laughs and drinks and toasts Dave. Friends and firefighters begin to go up to the microphone and tell their stories. Kevin McCabe from Dave's first firehouse steps up first, smiling impishly, his thick red hair shining. Dave used to call him Howdy Doody and sing the theme song when "Red" entered the firehouse.

"I remember one day when Dave was at the firehouse. We all thought he was a nice quiet guy. He was shy and didn't say much." The other guys from 122, cups of beer in hand, laugh knowingly. "After a while, we notice Dave has been gone for a while, so we call him down 'cause dinner was ready. We're all sittin' there eatin' when Dave jumps from the stairs. He's wearing a giant refrigerator box that he painted to look exactly like a brick, and he's got this cape."

"BRICKMAN!" one of the firemen yells from the back, and Kevin laughs.

"Dave's got this cape tied around him." Kevin puts his hands on his hips posturing like a superhero. "And he says, 'I am Brickman. I've come to save the day!' and then he would run full force into the door, which of course he couldn't get through because of this big box, so he'd fall back. It was hysterical." Kevin's laughing. *I am Brickman! I need to get laid!* Everyone is laughing and I smile, remembering how funny Dave could be. To most people, he was reserved, but to a select few he would reveal the outrageous little-boy humor that I loved.

I stand in the background, sipping wine, listening to dozens of stories about Dave from his friends. I have heard them all, but they make me smile anyway. I think about Dave in college, how he sat in my dorm room while I played backgammon and drank gin and tonics with my girlfriends. He was always in the corner, smiling, with his chair tilted back, just watching us sing along to Joan Armatrading or the Rolling Stones. He laughed at my Mick Jagger impression as I strutted around my room, my lips sticking out in an exaggerated pout.

"Dave, what did you do?" one of my girlfriends asked one night as we sat smoking Marlboros by the window. My friends and I had been in the room for hours, dancing and laughing, when we suddenly noticed it.

The Fontana Family
From left: Brian, Hank with hands on Dave's shoulders, Victoria carrying Ed, Ellen, Dennis

Ellen's Communion
From left: Victoria holding Dave's hand, Ellen with arms around Ed, Hank in back row, Dennis, Brian

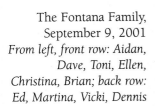

Dave at the beach

The Fontana Family, September 9, 2001
From left, front row: Aidan, Dave, Toni, Ellen, Christina, Brian; back row: Ed, Martina, Vicki, Dennis

Leah and me
1971

My family at Jones Beach, 1988
*From left, front row: Mom, Dad; back row: me, Leah,
Luke, Dave*

With my parents in Martha's Vineyard,
1986
From left: Mom, Dad, me, Dave

Me, Leah, and Luke
(Photo by Robin Locke Monda)

Dave on C. W. Post rugby team, 1985

Dave and me, Martha's Vineyard, 1986

On my twenty-fifth birthday

Dave and me

Jones Beach Field 6 lifeguard crew
and Dave's sculpture

(right) Dave at Field
6 lifeguard races

(below) Dave and fel-
low lifeguard Steve
Levy

Dave with surfboard, Jones Beach

Dave's graduation from the fire academy, September 8, 1991

St. Patrick's Day Parade, Commissioner Safir
and members of Ladder 122

With members of the D.A.R.T. team
after Los Angeles earthquakes, 1994
*From left: FF Mike Leddy, FF Kevin
Burns, and Dave*

At fire with members of Squad 1
*From left: Dave, Capt. Donald Hayde, FF Matt
Garvey, FF Stephen Siller, FF Sean Cummins*

Our wedding day, September 11, 1993

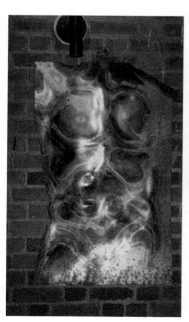

Our honeymoon in Hawaii

Dave's Torso, steel sculpture, in art show

Dave in Class A uniform

Squad 1
Dave, sitting on rig

Squad 1 in dress blues,
Christmas 2000

At Squad 1
*From left: Durrell Pearsall
(Bronco), Dennis Farrell,
Mike Russo, Fred Lawrence,
Dave, and John Flatley*

Members of Squad 288
Top row, from left: Jonathan Ielpi, William Quick, Dave Fontana, Lt. Tony Belisari; bottom row, from left: Kevin Kubler, Pete Brennan

(below)
Firefighters from Ladder 122

Members of Squad 1

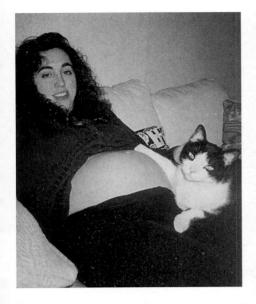

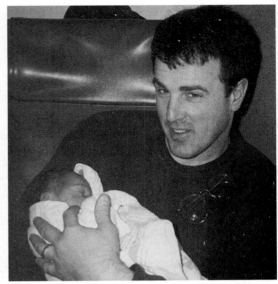

(*above left*) Me, pregnant, with Elvis the cat

(*above right*) Dave with Aidan at hospital, February 19, 1996

Aidan, at 5 months

Squad 1 Christmas party, December 2000
Dave, me, and Aidan with fire dog

Aidan, at 2 weeks

(*top left*) Dave and Aidan, Cape Cod, 1996. (*top right*) The family, Cape Cod, 1997

(*above*) The family, Cape Cod, 1999. (*bottom left*)
At the Prospect Park carousel. (*bottom right*) Dave
and me at a dinner party, June 1999

(*above left*) Pirates

(*above right*) Aidan, age 3, on Dave's shoulders

(*left*) Aidan in fire truck made by Dave

(*below left*) Aidan and Dave in Maine, summer 1998

(*below right*) The family in Dingle, Ireland, 2000

(*top left*) Dave

(*top right*) At a wedding in Ireland, 2000

(*above left*) Halloween Parade, Park Slope, October 2000
Aidan atop Dave, who is dressed as a spaceship and talking to Mike Esposito

(*above right*) At a wedding in Chicago, June 1999

Aidan and Dave on a fire truck, December 1999

(top) Candlelight vigil, September 14, 2001, Park Slope. (left) Squad 1 after 9/11

Arriving at the memorial service for Dave, October 17, 2001

(left) At the memorial reception in Prospect Park

Memorial at Jones Beach, Field 6, October 21, 2001

From left, bottom to top—Row 1: Marian Fontana, Mr. Potatohead, Paul Butler, Don Turner Row 2: Katie Konop, Jim Rooney, Kristin Mund Fried, Jay Lieberfarb, Robert Cornacchia, Diane Slevin Boyle with daughter Meghan, Roy Lester Row 3: John McCarthy, Marv Levenson, Tim Graham, Paul Franco, Jack Levenson, Bill Hosek, Dave Bluvol, Steve Levy, Steve Shtab Row 4: Joe Lisa, Bob Berkely, Al Uris, Scott Riegel, Dave Turkheimer, Matt Lindbolm (behind), Chris Cimaszewski, Bill Hroch, Sean Dowling, Gene Gorman, Carolyn Rooney Konop Row 5: Tony Battisti, Jim Figlioulo, Scott Fried

At bill signing with Senator Clinton, Washington, D.C., November 2001

At meeting with Mayor Giuliani

Dinner with the widows from Squad 1
(from left) Theresa Russo, Debbie Amato, me, Martha Butler

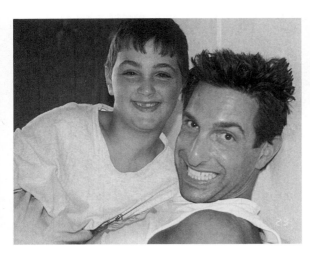

Me with Theresa Russo in Hawaii, December 6, 2001

Aidan and Jason, August 2002

Rope rescue drill at Randalls Island, 1998

Paper sculptures hung all over the ceiling, one more beautiful than the next. Long blue spirals, pink origami stars, aqua geometric collages hung down like colorful vines from every corner. We all stared at the ceiling and *oohed* and *aahed* as if we were watching a starry sky. And that's how it was with Dave, his beauty surprising and subtle—something to be spied, like a gold ring under the sand.

*   *   *

The next morning, it takes a long time for me to get home from Aidan's school. Neighbors and friends want to talk about the funeral and the impact it had on them, how they were so moved by it. I nod. I was up most of the night, replaying the day, trying to impress its poignancy into my memory. There is no doubt something incredible happened. My friend Louise tells me her Jewish friend who attended the mass is converting to Catholicism, and I can't help but laugh.

When I finally turn down my block, I notice a parking ticket on the windshield of my car. I forgot to move it this morning for alternate side of the street parking. I am struck by how my emotions seesaw so quickly, from calm to rage in less than a minute when I have to face these hundreds of small details. Dave used to move the car at midnight when the nurses left the hospital. I head back into my house, holding the ticket, and sink into the couch.

"Libby and Michael offered to take care of us this weekend in Sag Harbor." Leah comes in from the kitchen, a giant cup of tea in her hand.

"I can't. The widows are all going to the Heroes' Concert at Madison Square Garden on Saturday night, and that memorial service for Dave at Jones Beach on Sunday."

"I know, but you've been going nonstop. Let's get away from everything for a little while."

I shake my head and shrug. "I can't make any more decisions," I say as the phone rings again.

Leah answers it, rolling her eyes. She gets the pad next to the phone. "Yeah . . . uh-huh. Well, I'll have her call you back. Okay. Go ahead." Leah copies down a number, then hangs up and says, annoyed, "That was the *Oprah* show. They want you as a guest."

"What? Why?"

"Cooking tips? What do you think?"

"Oh my God. I—I—No . . . I—I dunno. What do you think?"

"Just talk to the lady and find out what they want." I call the production assistant. She sounds young and talks fast and staccato.

I call the producer and before I know it she's arranging for a crew to come to Dave's service on Long Island on Sunday. I hang up and notice my stomach shift slightly. Something doesn't feel right. My stomach always tells me so.

"You don't have to do it if you don't want to," my sister says, reading my mind the way sisters do.

"They think I'm doing it."

I tell Leah how it feels good to talk about being a firefighter's wife. People don't know how little money they make, that they have to work second jobs to keep up. "I dunno," I say. "I want to raise awareness."

"Fine. Then let that be your boundary. You'll only go on TV if you can talk about the firefighter salaries."

I nod. This feels right, and my stomach settles a bit. Sara enters with a large coffee and the *Daily News*. "Guess who's in all the papers?" She plops a pile on the kitchen table. We flip through the *News* and find a full-page photo of me exiting the church, my head down and crying, Toni's head pressed against me. It is strange to see myself, my devastation, captured on film. My family and friends surround me, their faces equally distorted, wrinkled with grief.

"Look, Sara. There you are," I say. She has never looked so joyless.

"I look scary," she says.

"You look sad," Leah replies. "We all look sad."

In my dank basement the next morning, I search for the videotapes of my wedding. In the long hours I spent with Aidan as a baby, I videotaped him constantly, as if to prove to myself that he actually came out of my body. I have tapes marked *First Three Weeks, Two to Six Months, Six to Nine Months,* and so on. Dave teased me about going overboard, but I am glad I did. I know a lot of them have Dave playing with Aidan.

"Marian, forget about the *Oprah* people. They aren't meant to have them then!" Leah calls from the top of the stairs. She is getting impatient. We were supposed to leave for Sag Harbor two hours ago.

"I know I put them down here!" Is it the coffee or my panic that is making my heart race and a cold, clammy sweat form on my forehead? The tapes feel like Dave himself as I accelerate into a frenzied dumping of boxes, looking behind crates, wondering how everything seems to be disappearing. I overturn boxes of photos, rifle through half a lifetime of broken blenders and picture frames. I spot Aidan's baby quilt covered in mold and his baby carrier crusted in mildew. I have saved all these things for the second baby we just started to try for. Then I stop suddenly, wiping the sweat off my brow with the end of my shirt, realizing, for the first time, I have lost my chance at a second child, too. We had begun trying for a little girl. We even had a name picked out. We chose the name Aidan immediately from a book of Irish names. It was one of the few we hadn't heard a hundred times and that I didn't associate with my former students. Aidan was perfect. We liked the story of St. Aidan, and the actor Aidan Quinn, but most of all we loved that the name meant "little fire" in Gaelic. It was perfect. A girl's name was harder to find, but we settled on one after a long discussion on the way home from vacation this summer.

"I like Fiona," Dave said, driving.

"Francesca." I imagined a little curly-haired girl in pigtails. I would call her Franny for short, and she would have a raspy giggle like Aidan's.

"Grace. She was a queen. A powerful woman in Ireland," Dave said.

"I like that as a middle name," I offered. I was torn about having a second child. I had hoped to be further along in my career, to be in a house, but Dave and I already realized that life never falls into place exactly the way we imagine it to. It was time to have another.

"Maeve," Dave suggested.

"What does it mean?" I asked.

"I dunno. She was an Irish queen, too, I think." Dave put his hand on my thigh. I loved this gesture more than any other. It was small, but it made me feel bound together, safe and reassured.

"I like it. You know why?" I said, smiling smugly.

"Why?"

"It combines Marian and Dave."

"Yeah," Dave said, grinning. "I like that . . . Maeve."

"Marian!" Leah yells. "We seriously need to go. You gave them the number out there! They'll just have to do without them!" I don't want to leave the cool dampness of the basement, the quiet place where I can sit with my memories and indulge in my grief alone.

"Coming!" I call, sliding the crates back and stacking a few boxes.

It is almost dark when we pull into the long, bumpy driveway leading to Libby and Michael's summer home. The sun flashes like headlights through the thin pine trees as we round the circular driveway to the front of the house, where Libby stands on a brick porch waving madly, a crooked smile forming.

"Yay! You're here!" Libby rasps. She resembles a young, skinny Jessica Lange, with shoulder-length blond hair, small blue eyes, and freckled porcelain skin. "Let me help y'all with your stuff. Hi, Aidan!" Libby still has a North Carolina drawl, even though she has lived in New York for almost fifteen years. "I was just putting the grill on for some appetizers. Do you like pizza, Aidan?"

"Yup," he says without looking up, holding his blanket around his shoulders. We follow Libby up the steps to an open white kitchen with low ceilings and an island in the center of the room. Libby's husband, Michael, is leaning on the counter, a phone squeezed to his ear. He waves at us, holding up a finger to indicate he will be off in a minute. A carpenter when we met him, Michael surprised everyone by becoming a successful director and producer in Hollywood.

"Tell him he's got to do another rewrite. I gave the freakin' guy—" Michael forces a hard laugh as we pass through the small living room with white wicker furniture and pale blue walls. The house is old, a former boarding home for wives whose husbands were off fighting in World Wars I and II. The women who lived here were self-sufficient, growing vegetables, taking care of each other's children, raising chickens, and patiently waiting for their husbands to return home.

We follow Libby up a narrow stairway to a room at the top of the stairs where Dave and I have stayed before. Putting my bags down, I notice that Libby has written my name in calligraphy and hung it on the door. Aidan is thrilled to recognize his own name on the adjoining bedroom.

"Red or white?" Libby says as I climb downstairs with a bag of army men for Aidan. Aidan takes them, dumps them onto the living room floor, and a war immediately ensues.

"White," I say.

Libby grills pizza outside and shows Aidan where Cal the chipmunk will appear in the morning. Michael answers the phone on the first ring.

"It's the *Oprah* show," he says, handing me the phone and rolling his eyes. I take the phone reluctantly.

"We're sending a crew for the memorial on Sunday," the production assistant says tersely.

"Oh," I say hesitantly.

"Do you have the videos?"

"I actually couldn't find them. . . . When are you guys coming?"

"During the memorial. It won't take long. We just need to get a shot of you and Aidan walking down the beach holding hands."

My stomach shifts again and I am silent. "I don't know about that," I say finally. "I feel uncomfortable."

The producer sighs audibly. "Let me call you back." She hangs up quickly, clearly annoyed. A few minutes later they call to tell me the shoot is canceled. My stomach immediately eases.

"Oh, good! Now you can relax!" Libby says, lighting a silver candelabra in the dining room. "Dinner's ready!" In the dining room, Tiffany plates are set with succulent grilled steaks, rosemary mashed potatoes, and green beans sautéed with sea salt and almonds. I eat and drink slowly, noticing how my taste buds are slowly coming back alive, yet a part of me feels guilty for taking pleasure in a meal without Dave.

After I tuck Aidan in, Michael and I sit on the front porch with after-dinner drinks. A few die-hard crickets are chirping in the yard and large white moths flutter dangerously close to the dusty outside light. Michael leans back in his chair and lights a cigar.

"That eulogy, Marian," he says, exhaling. "That was your finest moment."

"Thanks." I'm uncomfortable and shift in my chair.

"It totally changed my life. I called Richie, you know. The next day. That part about forgiving people. It got to me." Richie was Michael's cinematographer and childhood friend whom he had stopped speaking to after an argument about a film.

I want to tell Michael how it actually was the worst moment of my life, saying good-bye to such a man, but instead I say, "I'm glad," leaning forward to peek at the sky.

The next morning Aidan's bed is empty and his door is open. I climb down the creaking stairs into the kitchen, where he is sitting on a high stool decorating Halloween cookies.

Aidan looks up, his face excited. "Look at my skeleton!" He smears orange icing onto a skull-shaped sugar cookie.

I kiss the top of his head. "Great job, buddy." Libby pours me coffee as I watch chickadees swoop in and out of the bird feeder on her window.

"Good morning, Martha," I tease as she cuts me a thick slice of home-made banana bread.

"Stop it!" She giggles and turns back to the stove, where she pours batter into a pancake mold shaped like a pumpkin. "I hate Martha Stewart."

"Please. I am the anti-Martha," I say, thinking how ironic it was that I wrote articles for her *Kids* magazine only a few months ago. "I think I'm domestically challenged."

"No!" she says, chuckling and watching the pancake brown. "Actually, Michael and I have been thinking, and we wanted to know, and don't feel like you have to, if we could fix up your apartment for you."

I look up from my coffee, surprised.

"When we were there last week, we just thought . . . maybe some fresh paint and new furniture would make you feel better. Here. Just look." Holding the spatula in one hand, she slides a stack of papers toward me and returns to the stove. There are furniture catalogs and paint swatches and magazines about design. "Michael can fix the floor in the kitchen, and my parents have a furniture store in North Carolina, so you just need to tell me what you like."

"Libby . . . I just . . . I dunno," I say, my voice cracking.

She turns to see me crying. "Oh, honey! I didn't mean to upset you! You don't have to decide anything now. I just brought some things for you to peek at." She slides the pancake onto Aidan's plate.

"She's crying again!" Aidan says, annoyed.

"I'm not sad, honey, I'm . . . Libby is the best," I say, watching Aidan pour too much syrup onto his perfect pancake.

After breakfast, I head upstairs to my room to take a shower.

"I want to take a shower, too," Aidan whines, watching me gather my things for the bathroom.

"No. I need privacy," I tell him.

"I want to play soap monster," he says. I think of all the self-help books, the advice columns, the Shakespeare plays that advise against showering with your kids at this age, but with everything that has happened, all bets are off.

I growl at Aidan with a soapy sponge in my hand. His giggle is deep and infectious, happiness distilled and rising from his bubbled white belly.

"No, I'm alive again!" he squeals. "See?" The bubbles slide off like wet snow.

Then, like a left hook, I am struck with missing Dave again. I turn my body away from Aidan and put my hands on the tiles to hold myself up.

"Are you crying *again*?" I imagine how scary this is for him, his father gone and his mother falling apart before his eyes, but the harder I try to stop, the more the tears come. Aidan moans and stomps his foot on the bathtub floor and I turn back to him.

"You know what?" I struggle to speak. "I'm going to be okay. People cry when they're sad, and then they get better."

Aidan ignores me and begins drawing sad faces with his finger on the steamy shower door. I watch in silence, rinsing my tears in the shower as he draws a circle around the faces with a line through the middle like a no-smoking sign.

"No crying!" He points to a face with a line slashed across it.

"I'll try." I make a smiley face on the door next to his. "I can't promise, but I'll try."

---

* * *

As a surprise, Libby has hired a limousine to drive us into Manhattan for the Concert for New York—a benefit for the Robin Hood Foundation tonight.

"Libby! This is too much!" I exclaim as the limo struggles to turn in the circular driveway.

"It's really so I can drink." She giggles, filling the limo with bottles of chardonnay and grilled vegetable sandwiches. We climb into the sleek black interior and I feel like a kid, staring at the strip of disco lights lining the top, changing from green to red to blue, marveling at the bar that lines the side, the white napkins standing up like flowers in each glass. I have never been in a limousine in my life, and I wish Aidan were here to see it. My sister-in-law Ellen, who lives in the next town, took him for a sleepover tonight.

Libby maneuvers easily through the limousine serving drinks, her blond curls bouncing when we hit the bumps on the Long Island Expressway.

"You look great!" Libby hands me a sandwich. She and Leah convinced me to take off my fire department sweatshirt and wear my green leather pants. I have not worn them since my thirty-fifth birthday party last March. Dave invited some friends over and Jason brought a cake with a photo of me performing as one of my characters in a show. Dave stood in the corner and chuckled as I stuffed our furniture into the basement to make a dance floor in the center of our living room. "You would do anything to dance," he said, as I stood sweating in our empty living room and smiled because it was true. I love to dance and always have. It is what I imagine seagulls feel, floating above a beach. Later that night, the firefighters from Squad showed up to the party, turning my girlfriends into giggly teenagers, making the room smell of smoke. They let my friends try on their helmets and then dance awkwardly in their boots. I laughed and clicked away with my camera, kissing Dave as I passed.

I sigh out loud, thinking that most of the men there that night were killed with Dave when the towers fell.

"You okay?" Leah asks. She seems far away on the wide black seat.

"I'm fine," I lie, forcing a smile and biting into my sandwich.

On 8th Avenue, traffic is at a standstill. I look out of the tinted window to see hundreds of mustached firefighters entering the stadium wearing sweatshirts from their firehouses. I recognize some of the widows, their husband's faces printed on T-shirts.

"I knew I should have worn my sweatshirt," I mutter, feeling guilty. The Rolling Stones, the Who, Paul McCartney, David Bowie, and Elton John are supposed to play tonight, but I am most excited about U2, who are rumored to be making a surprise appearance.

The cavernous stadium is packed with victims' families, firefighters, Port Authority police, emergency service workers, and police officers. Squad 1 takes up three rows toward the back of the middle section. I smile when I see that almost everyone is here. Sally Siller is with her sister in the front, wearing a T-shirt that reads "Some were saviors, others were saved" in red, white, and blue letters. Jimmy Lopez, known as J-Lo at the firehouse, is here with his wife. Bobby West and his wife; Alison; Stack and Lynn; Huey and Kathleen; Tony Edwards and Donna. Theresa runs over and squeezes me in a powerful hug. We have become close lately, spending hours on the phone each night, sharing our grief with the intensity of two teenagers.

"I'm so glad you made it!" she says, a cocktail in her hand.

"Vodka and cranberry?" I ask, pointing to her drink.

"Of course! You want one?" I take drink orders for Libby and Leah and follow Theresa to a smoky bar packed with firefighters drinking beer from plastic cups. Theresa is like a puppy, waving and smiling at everyone she passes.

"Are you drunk?" I ask her.

"No! I am just so happy to be out. The baby has been driving me nuts! He got up five times last night. I thought I would die." We press our way toward the bar and order drinks. "Did you see that Bobby's wife is here?" she asks me. I have not seen Alison since their wedding last summer. "I don't think it's right that she's here," Theresa says as we squeeze our way out of the bar, holding our drinks over our heads. "I mean, where has she been? She hasn't been to one wake or funeral. All the other wives are goin' to funerals." I remember thinking how out of character Alison looked at her wedding, a biker chick in a Cinderella dress, her five-year-old daughter overdone in makeup and lace. "She doesn't show up to any of the funerals, but she can show up for a free concert?" Theresa is indignant. "I don't think that's right."

David Bowie sits onstage singing softly about America, a small Casio in his lap.

"Bobby told me that she can't take off from work," I tell Theresa, trying to calm her down. Theresa stares at Alison a few rows ahead.

"Not for nothing, but I think that's bullshit. The wakes are at night, and she's a teacher. They don't have kids . . ." Theresa takes a sip of her drink and we listen to David Bowie's distinctive voice echo through the hall. "She's been doing nothing but giving Bobby a hard time, and the poor guy is at the site every day, his sister just died, and all of his friends . . . She's a piece of work." I nod, listening to the music.

"I'm going to say something," Theresa says suddenly, walking away.

"Theresa, don't—" But she is already in Alison's row, sliding her way toward her. I watch Alison's smile fade as Theresa leans in, yelling over the music, her eyebrows pursed.

"What is Theresa doing?" Leah asks as I take my seat next to Libby and hand them their drinks.

"She's telling Alison off because she hasn't come to any funerals," I say as David Bowie heads offstage.

"Oh, man." Leah sips from her drink, watching Theresa and smiling. "I like her."

"*Hey! There's the girl from* Third Watch!" I hear a man's voice scream. "*Hey, you! Over here!*" I crane my neck to the side balcony, trying to match a face to the voice I hear, but the lights from the stage make the audience look like a giant Rorschach test. "*Over here!*" the voice says again, and I shield my eyes with my hand and squint into the balcony again. "*Thanks for sticking up for the firefighters!*" he screams, and I smile and wave in the darkness.

Libby, Leah, and I dance to the Goo Goo Dolls and laugh hard at Adam Sandler's Operaman. The crowd goes wild when Mayor Giuliani walks onto the stage. He speaks earnestly about the firefighters and rescue workers being heroes and how incredible New Yorkers are. I feel my emotions rise and fall, changing from anger toward the mayor and the Fire Department for not protecting Dave, to pride for what Dave did that day.

The widows begin taking their wake cards to the front of the stage and giving them to a bewildered technician, who projects the images onto a giant screen. I berate myself for not bringing Dave's picture. Most of the bands are playing sad ballads, and the audience grows restless, walking through the aisles drinking and talking. We are tired of sad songs and having our emotions stirred by music. We want a vacation from sorrow, a reprieve from the grief. Leah, Libby, and I have found empty seats closer to the front, and as we move, Mick Jagger is sliding across the stage. A drunk woman steps over me to take her seat. Her eyes are bloodshot and swollen. She tries to sit, but she misses the chair, falling to the floor. I help her up, smiling.

"Whoa! Sorry," she yells to the people behind her, who roll their eyes in disgust. "Hey!" she says to me, wavering slightly. "I saw you on *Third Watch*!" I smile weakly in her direction. "I lost my brother . . . He was a firefighter," she slurs.

"I'm sorry," I say, watching Mick shake his head, his lips puffing out like a kiss as he finishes "Miss You."

"My other brother Mike's on the job, too," she continues. "Where is he anyway?" Michael J. Fox is walking on stage, his Parkinson's noticeable as he stands at a microphone, shaking, trying to introduce Commissioner Von Essen, but the firefighters have begun to boo. "C'mon guys . . . please," Michael says, his face filled with confusion. The booing becomes deafening as Tom steps onto the stage. He stands at the podium waiting, his face red and angry, but the booing never stops, and he has no choice but to leave.

The drunk woman next to me is wavering, laughing. *Oh, shit!*" I see a commotion up front as security attempts to pull a firefighter off the steps. I watch him dodge the security guards, leaping like a cat and landing near the microphone, which he grabs from Michael J. Fox. He begins to make a speech about the men we lost—his brother, John, and twelve members from Ladder 3. He talks about Rockaway Beach, which lost so many. "They are gone, but not forgotten," he says. "And one more thing." He screams into the microphone, "OSAMA BIN LADEN, YOU CAN

KISS MY ROYAL IRISH ASS!" Everyone screams as he moons the crowd before he is escorted offstage by security guards. The crowd is chanting and cheering "U-S-A! U-S-A!" The woman next to me laughs and points. "That was Mike Moran!" she says, laughing. "That's my brother!"

The bar closes, a wise move on Madison Square Garden's part, since the crowd is getting drunker, louder, and rowdier than when we arrived. They boo Hillary Clinton so loudly, I have to cover my ears.

"What are they booing her for?" my sister asks.

I shrug. "I don't know, but I wish they'd stop. It's embarrassing. I like her."

The stage grows dark and I walk over to Mike Stackpole and his wife, Lynn. While I am talking to Lynn, I suddenly imagine a plane crashing through the metal roof, a ball of fire rolling toward us as we explode like firecrackers in an anthill, shattering into a million pieces. I want to tell Lynn how scared I am all the time, how I have bad dreams and think about the surviving guys at the site, but the lights brighten and I see for the first time the sheer number of people filling the Garden. Their voices form a loud hum in the background, then the dramatic opening chords of "Baba O'Riley" by the Who begins. Suddenly everyone stops. People who have been milling around and talking through other performances are now silent. The audience stands, singing along. I drape my arms around Mike and Lynn and we join in, yelling the lyrics at the top of our lungs, fury and emotion catching me in my throat. Music has always had that effect on me, but nothing can compare to the feelings pulsing through the crowd and me at this moment. We are like charged atoms, one energy united, as we sing in a collective voice, "DON'T CRY, DON'T RAISE YOUR EYE! IT'S ONLY TEENAGE WASTELAND!" The feeling seems to last forever, everyone one heartbeat as the Who begins "Won't Get Fooled Again." We are riveted by Pete Townshend as he screams *"YEAHHHHHHHHHH!"* with the anger and energy we all feel at that moment. His voice vibrates in my stomach as the bass enters, the guitars wailing, and everyone is jumping up and down and screaming. I look around, smiling, marveling that everyone is moved by this anthem from our youth when the white sheet of our future lay before us clean and untouched.

13

Adrift

The highway to Jones Beach is empty and I stare out the window at the tall dunes lining the side of the road. Dave drove this highway every day for the thirteen summers he was a lifeguard, and when I joined him, I would look for rabbits on the trip home as they came out to feed in dry patches of grass. I roll down the window and inhale the smell of summer that lingers like a sated guest. Clouds float like stretched cotton against the perfect blue that I will now forever link to the day Dave died.

The windows in the fee booths at Field 6 have been boarded up for weeks and the giant parking lot is dotted with only a few cars. I pull into a spot near the lifeguard shack, where some of Dave's happiest memories were formed. A fraternity of lifeguard friends will be here today to honor him. The smell of pine trees and decaying dune roses wafts through the window as I gather photos of the lifeguards that Dave kept in hand-carved frames.

A crowd has already gathered on a deck in the front of the small wooden lifeguard shack at Field 6. Steve Levy, Dave's rowing partner and lifeguard friend, strides over to greet us. He has arranged this day for Dave, e-mailing a tight network of lifeguards who work here, the eldest celebrating almost half a century on the beach. Except for his shaved head, Steve looks just as I remember him, his mischievous amber eyes wide, his body tanned and strong, a slight stutter when he speaks.

"I'm glad you made it! It's unbelievable how many guards are here from the old days," he says proudly as I follow him to the front, the ocean revealing itself in a perfect blue line at the shore. The wide stretch of beach is empty except for a beer-bellied man with a metal detector and a woman flying a kite in the distance.

I greet Dave's friends, many of whom I haven't seen in over fifteen years. They tell me stories about Dave and I listen intently, letting the memories linger like a mouthful of expensive wine. They laugh at the photos I brought. We joke about the hot tub parties, food fights, life-guard races, practical jokes and the Big Kahuna, a giant sculpture Dave carved from a driftwood log. The sculpture became a mainstay at Field 6 even after Dave left.

Even though Aidan looks tired, he runs through the sand with the energy of a puppy, ricocheting through the crowd and bounding to-ward the ocean. "He's definitely his father's son," everyone remarks, watching Aidan leapfrog over the waves, his jeans soaked.

Steve hops up onto a box on the side of the shack and whistles loudly to get everyone's attention. He tells the story of how Dave came to the beach, how he fell in love "with this chick from Staten Island in a cro-cheted bikini." I blush, recognizing myself in his story. Billy Hosek stands up next, his white-blond hair flopping into his face. He has driven up from Baltimore, taking time away from a busy schedule as an emergency room doctor. He holds up a frayed rope looped in a circle around a shriveled potato.

"I have carried this necklace all over the country to apartments in al-most every city," Billy announces proudly. There are a few sniggers in the crowd. "I know many of you recognize it. Dave carved this potato on a rainy day in the shack, into a very convincing likeness of Jay Lieberfarb." The lifeguards laugh knowingly and look toward Jay, a short, thin man who recently celebrated forty-five years as a lifeguard at Jones Beach. The potato does bear a remarkable resemblance to Jay, with wrinkled skin the color of cherrywood, long angular features, and wiry black rope hair.

"Marian, I am giving you this treasure to keep for Aidan when he works at the beach, and Jay is still here." I am hoisted onto the storage box to receive my gift. I put the necklace around my neck. The rope scratches my neck, but I hold it up and kiss Billy on the cheek. I make a short speech thanking the lifeguards. I swallow back tears, recalling how Dave loved the beach and his friends here, how touched he would be to see them today. We toast the other lifeguards killed on September 11, Billy Burke and Chris Maulpi.

With the sun setting red and low, we reluctantly begin to gather our things. The lifeguards pass around wallet-size Sears portraits of their kids, we exchange phone numbers, promising to keep in touch, and I kiss everyone good-bye.

"Pick me up!" Aidan whines as we walk toward the car, our shadows like long Giacometti sculptures.

"I can't." I tell Aidan I'm feeling weary from the weekend.

Aidan drops his head dramatically, moping next to me. "Daddy used to put me on his shoulders," he says pathetically. I can feel the strings around my heart tighten. Grabbing Aidan under his arms, I hoist him over my head onto my shoulders. Like an Olympic weight lifter, I bobble a bit, trying to steady him. I hold him tight around the ankles and struggle through the sand to the parking lot. My brother-in-law Dennis offers to carry him, but I want to prove to Aidan that I am strong, that I can be both mother and father to him. Perhaps by completing this task, I can convince myself that it is true.

The traffic on the Belt Parkway rolls slowly forward as angry drivers force themselves into small spaces between cars, weaving like slalom skiers through the traffic. Aidan is wiggling in the back of the car, pressing his feet into the back of my seat.

"Stop kicking," I snap, feeling my nerves taut under my skin, ready to pop and fray.

"You okay?" my sister asks, and I shrug, staring ahead, my jaw clamped shut. Like the cars, my emotions seem to be coming out of nowhere. An SUV cuts hard in front of me and I have to slam on the brakes. Leah reaches for the dashboard, trying hard not to say anything.

"Fucking asshole," I snarl through my teeth.

"Mommy!" Aidan scolds, and I squeeze my jaw tighter. *I hate you, Dave, for making me do this.* I am suddenly filled with resentment that I have to drive at all. *This is Dave's fucking job,* I tell myself. I make a mental list of all the things I will have to do alone now: laundry, bills, take out the garbage, parent/teacher conferences, car inspection, dental appointments, haircuts, pediatrician appointments, illnesses, painting, baseball games, fixing, sweeping, oil changes, class trips, parking, cleaners, after-school classes, shopping, cleaning, homework, making lunches, Cub Scout meetings, driving. All of it alone. It is too much. It is more than I can take. I exit the highway, convincing myself that if I just keep moving, everything will be fine. Within minutes I am lost in the bowels of Brooklyn, in neighborhoods where once-beautiful buildings stand neglected and empty. I stare at the road ahead of me, everything dark and unsafe. *You've left me here to do everything by myself. You promised me you would take care of me. You promised me we would grow old together. I am lost.*

"Are we lost?" Leah asks.

"I don't know." Anger fills me, heating up my body.

"I'm scared," Aidan says in a small voice.

"We're fine," I snap.

"Daddy never got los—"

"Well, Daddy's not here. So I have to find it myself."

I turn left on Atlantic, where the yellow lights of bodegas flash on and off. By the time I find 4th Street, Aidan is fast asleep and anger is howling in my head.

I double-park and carry Aidan into the house, his body heavy on my shoulder. He moans slightly when I cover him with one of the quilts that someone sent us. It is made of American flags and has a teddy bear in the middle. "Robert Concardo—2nd grade," it reads on the bottom. I stand up quickly, knowing that if I watch Aidan's fluttering eyes or linger on the rhythm of his breath, I will be lost. Leah looks carefully at me as she unpacks her suitcase and I head out to find a parking space.

It seems as if the whole neighborhood is returning from family weekends away. On every block, Volvos and minivans are double-parked as daddies hoist their sleeping children onto their shoulders to carry them inside. Every hazard light that blinks taunts me, *"You're alone, you're alone, you're alone."* I can feel the muscles in my back where I strained to hold Aidan on my shoulders. I squeeze the car into a too-small spot three blocks away from the apartment. Smashing against the bumpers of the other cars is oddly satisfying. I walk quickly toward my house, feeling like a dam about to burst, straining to keep the tears back, the anger from bursting through.

Leah is sitting on the couch, looking at me like a dog that just peed on the floor.

"What?" I ask brusquely.

"Nothing." She's read my mood like a map and decided not to speak.

"WHAT!"

"The cat . . . I guess he jumped up and he broke some of your blue glass." I look over at the window where my collection of blue glass lines the windowsill. The vase from my wedding is gone, the cups from the weekend in Delaware, the salt and pepper shakers from Grandma . . . gone. The bricks of the dam pop as I run into the bathroom, slamming the door behind me. My breath quickens, my fists clench, and despite all my efforts to stop it, the volcano erupts. I grab a towel from the rack and scream into the folds until my throat hurts. My sister bangs on the door, her voice frightened.

"Marian. Let me in," she whispers, sounding like a little girl.

"LEAVE ME ALONE!!!!!!!!!!" I scream, my chest rising and falling. I resist the urge to smash my head on the tile, to kick the wall with my foot, to crash the full-length mirror. I pace back and forth, sobbing and screaming.

"Marian, please . . . you're scaring me," she says.

"GO AWAY!!!!! I wail so loudly, it echoes through my head. I can hear Leah whimpering on the other side of the door, but I am too far gone, my pain blasting on full volume, making me deaf to anything but my own cries.

"Marian, please . . . what can I do?"

"I WANT . . . DAVE!!!!!!!!!!!!!!!!!!!!!!!!!! I WANT MY HUSBAND TO COME HOME!!!" I scream in an all-out tantrum, growling like a mad dog, throwing bottles of shampoo at the wall until the thick soap drips like syrup down the wall, its sickly sweet smell filling the room. I hear Aidan, crying but I am too far away to care. I want to rip my own skin off, pull the hair from my scalp. I pull at my clothes, kicking the door, as Aidan's cries increase. "WHY DID YOU GOOOOOOOO! HOW COULD YOU LEAVE MEEEEEEEEEEEEEEEEEE!!!!!!!!!!!!!!!"

"You're scaring him!" Leah calls out, and now Aidan is crying as loudly as I am. I collapse onto the toilet seat, crying more softly now. I am sweating and out of breath. The tears burn as they roll down, the snot pouring out. I don't care about anything. Nothing at all. I just stare at the stained grout, numb, my ears ringing. My eyes land on a razor and I fixate on it, my heart clanking and thumping inside the cage of my ribs. I wonder how it would feel to die. I try to imagine this pain stopping, ceasing to exist; what it would feel like to have my heart fused back together like a video of a breaking glass on rewind. Most of all, I imagine seeing Dave. Would he be there greeting me with that warm yellow light? Or would I just be as alone as I feel now—in the darkness with nothing all around, absolute nothingness?

"Marian, let me in," Leah says more insistently. I am tired now, too weak to answer or even look away from the razor that sits provocatively on the edge of the tub. "Just let me in," she sobs. "I'm calling the firehouse." I can hear her footsteps fade, the creak of the floor, and the familiar combination of tones on the phone pad.

I stand up and slowly open the door. Eyes forward, I walk past Leah into the kitchen and collapse into a chair. I light a cigarette, staring fixedly at the spot on the floor where the linoleum has curled up like a cold flower, away from the plywood underneath. Leah returns the phone to its charger. I concentrate on the smoke filling my lungs, burning my sore throat. It feels good to think of nothing. The perfect red circle at the end of the cigarette makes the paper burn a little, and an ash the color of slate falls in my lap. I don't move or try to wipe it away.

"You scared the shit out of me," Leah says softly, sliding an ashtray toward me. I can feel her staring at me, wanting me to say something, but I don't look up. She stands up quickly and the breeze makes some of the ash fall away. I see her feet in my peripheral vision as she walks around the kitchen, her toes making cracking noises from being broken too many times in toe shoes. Glasses clink, drawers open, cabinets close, and she sits back down and pours me a glass of red wine.

"You really scared me," she says softly again, breaking the long silence. I pick my glass up and nod slowly, saying nothing, just smoking my cigarette down to the cottony filter.

*　　*　　*

If it is possible to have an emotional hangover, I have one. My head feels swollen from crying and my back is out. I never knew what that term meant until now. It is "out" as in "out of order." It just won't move freely. Whenever I walk, a highway of pain shoots down my left leg.

"That's from lifting Aidan yesterday," my sister reminds me, and I think of how heavy he felt on my shoulders, pressing on my neck. Leah is sipping tea, the light from the window casting dramatic shadows across her face. She has just returned from taking Aidan to school again and will be leaving soon to rehearse at her friend Marianne's house for Two Chicks and a Casio. I have appeared with them numerous times as a guest artist, playing bassoon on a song called "Insta-boyfriend" and rapping about a beauty school. Leah works hard at it and has managed to book a small tour of the West Coast that leaves in two weeks. She doesn't want to go, and I am secretly scared to have her so far away.

"You have forty-three messages." Leah rolls her eyes.

I open a heavy FedEx package sent by Joe Miccio, a firefighter who researched the long history of firefighter salaries and wrote a fifty-five-page paper about it. I asked him to send me his paper so I could educate myself about the issues and speak authoritatively in press appearances. I am scheduled on Fox News, NY 1, and CNN. I lean back and begin to read the manifest. In painstaking and excruciating detail, Joe has explained the intricacies of the Fire Department's union and how it negotiates its salaries with the city.

Dave told me how the Taylor Law makes it illegal for police and firefighters to strike, so they have little to no negotiating leverage. As a result, for the past three years, unions have negotiated "on good faith," accepting 0 percent increases with the promise that a substantial increase would come in the future. That future never came. A probation-ary officer in the Fire Department with two children can qualify for wel-fare. After I finish reading, I lean back, thinking of Dave patiently waiting for the 3 percent pay increase, which was about to be settled be-fore he died. It was much less than what was promised, but the extra money would have paid off the washer and dryer and some of our credit card bills.

I close Joe's paper and plop it on my blue glass table, thinking of the money I collected at the Pier, checks from two dollars to twenty thou-sand dollars arriving daily from strangers, organizations, and fire de-partments all over the country. And there is more coming. Dave always said that he was worth more dead than alive, and the reality of this stings like winning the lottery on the day you've been diagnosed with an incurable disease. The death benefit, an oxymoron that does not elude me, will, along with the pension, make me comfortable for the rest of my life. I want nothing to do with it. I receive the checks with numb guilt, tossing them in random drawers without cashing them, hoping that if I get just one more, I can buy Dave back from wherever he is. I stare at the ceiling, where a dull gray light shines from the over-head fixture. Tiny black specks line the inside of the shade; bugs went out of their way to get inside, only to be trapped and burned.

Maybe I should have tried harder to convince Dave to sculpt full-time or move to a slower firehouse where he would be safe, but deep in my heart I know Dave would never have accepted that. He loved being a firefighter so much, he would do it for free. In fact, most good fire-fighters feel that way about the job and the city knows it, and that's why they refuse to pay them what they're worth.

I want to advocate for the firefighters, to get them more money how-ever I can. I will enlist other widows to help me. I will start an organiza-tion. I will call it the 9/11 Widows Association and we will talk about our lives and use this rare spotlight to help them. Joe is as excited as I am. We call Martha, who agrees to help, and when I collapse back on the couch I think of how Dave loved it when school groups visited the firehouse. It was an opportunity to share the job he loved with a popu-lation he adored. He used a running joke that most firefighters know. A little boy or girl would raise a hand and announce, "I'm going to be a firefighter when I grow up," to which Dave would respond, "You can't do both, kid."

*   *   *

"What are you doin'?" Theresa asks me every morning now. No matter how busy I am, her calls have become part of my new routine. "Can you get a babysitter for tonight?" I can tell she is excited.

"Why?"

"Can you?"

"Tell me!"

"Well, I know you were disappointed that U2 didn't play last week at the concert so I got two tickets!"

"NO WAY!"

"Can you go?"

"I'm going. There is no way I'm not!" I promise.

I hang up and smile, flooded with memories from college when U2 was the sound track to my memories. I think of the strange twist of fate that brought Dave and me together. Nineteen eighty-four was my senior year at Performing Arts High School, and the college admissions process was about to begin. I had planned on attending a music conservatory for bassoon or a progressive college like Vassar or Sarah Lawrence. I had auditions scheduled at Juilliard School of Music and Oberlin, and because bassoon players are rare, I had a good chance of getting in.

It was snowing hard all day on January 18. Dirty piles of gray snow were beginning to form on the edges of the bustling sidewalks as I headed home with my friend Melinda, carrying my heavy bassoon. Descending the stairs to the subway on 49th Street, we heard the familiar roar of an approaching train and ran. I followed Melinda through the special entrance quickly showing my train pass. A silver streak flashed into the station and we ran, trying to get to the front of the train. In an instant, I slipped, my leg flying out from under me, bouncing on the train and then wedging itself in the small space between the platform and the subway car. I screamed and pulled at my leg, which was being sucked underneath by a powerful vacuum as the train dragged me along. I saw my short eighteen years passing like a sped-up slide show. It was not the big moments you would imagine—no graduations or my first kiss—but small, insignificant moments like a stroll, family meal, my mother's face. I heard people screaming, saw the orange tiles on the walls, my jaw hit something hard. I pulled, nearing the end of the platform, until someone's arms reached under mine and pulled. I tried to ask who had saved me, but the crowd shook their heads and shrugged. My words were unintelligible, my jaw broken. Firefighters carried me out on a stretcher, their boots slipping on the snowy stairs. One of them said, "You are lucky," which seemed odd to say, but knowing now how Dave had gone to numerous subway accidents where limbs were amputated, I realize that I was.

I spent a week in the hospital, with a compound fracture of my leg and a broken jaw, and another month at home. I missed all of the auditions for college, except one that I had before the accident, at a small state school tucked beside Route 25A on the old estate of a cereal baron on Long Island, C. W. Post. It was my only choice.

C. W. Post was a commuter college for the local nouveau riche. Camaros and Trans Ams filled the parking lots, and a grand Tudor-style mansion was dwarfed by modern brick buildings used for dorms and classrooms. The male students wore sweatpants pushed up to their knees and baseball caps turned backward. The women had manicures, large shoulder pads, and teased hair. I lived in the arts dorms, where my roommate spent hours cutting photos of heavy metal singers out of magazines and gluing them onto our wall. I felt like I had landed on the moon, it was so different from anything I had ever known. I managed to make a few friends. We hung out in my dorm room listening to music, playing backgammon, smoking, and drinking gin and tonics.

It was in the parking lot of my dorm that I first saw "the trench coat guy." He wore a beret, sunglasses, army boots, and a long trench coat, in marked difference from the other guys. He was standing with an art major named Scott who lived off campus. Scott handed me a flyer inviting me to a party at his house. A week later my new friends piled into my 1977 Maverick and we drove to Scott's party, where almost everyone was so drunk they were leaning on furniture and kitchen counters to keep themselves up; a few art majors were painting on sheets, a girl was playing guitar, Scott was drinking out of a bong, and "trench coat guy" was nowhere to be found. I began to obsess about the mysterious stranger, searching for him on campus for weeks afterward. My girlfriends convinced me to forget about him and to focus instead on the preppie guy upstairs who had a crush on me. I told them he wasn't my type, too big and shy, but my girlfriends kept inviting him to our dorm rooms. The preppie guy sat quietly in the corner, never smoked or drank, and said little, until after about a month, when he asked me to take a walk. It was four o'clock on a bitter cold January morning and I would have preferred to be in bed asleep, but my girlfriends giggled, pushing me out the door and shoving my gloves onto my hands. I followed him outside, our breath making miniature clouds in the cold darkness, and it wasn't until we were standing on the frozen grass that I noticed he was wearing a trench coat and a beret.

*   *   *

Theresa and I walk into the Blue Ribbon, an expensive, trendy restaurant on 5th Avenue in Park Slope. We sit at a banquette in the middle of the room and read the eclectic menu, my eyes instinctively scanning the prices for the least expensive item.

"I'm getting the steak," Theresa decides, slamming her menu closed.

"That sounds good. Thirty dollars! Damn."

"Get it."

"It should come with a man for that price," I joke.

"Stop it! Order whatever you want. We've cried enough for this money."

But it feels strange. I never ordered what I wanted, only what Dave and I could afford. "A dollar a tear," I murmur, closing the menu.

"You and I are so different," she says, and I nod at the odd circumstance of our friendship. "I've always had money. In my first relationship, all we did was work, and I had everything: a big house, cars, pool. You name it."

"What happened to him?"

"Nothing! He was a great guy, don't get me wrong. He was a sweetheart. We're still great friends, but it wasn't enough. I really wasn't happy . . . and then I met Mike and we had so much fun. We laughed, we traveled, played golf. It was great. We didn't need all that stuff 'cause we were having such a good time just living, you know?"

"No . . . actually, Dave and I never had money."

"Yeah, but you were happy. He didn't work a second job so he could be with Aidan. You wrote, did your acting. It was the right choice, believe me."

"It's true. How much do you really need to be happy? I mean, money . . . when I think of all the time I obsessed about money, the what-ifs? It's like you're always trying to get to that next place instead of just being in the place you are in. I was so stupid."

"Yeah, but who lives like that all the time? I mean, life is hard . . . Look at us."

The waiter brings us cosmopolitans in pink triangular glasses. Theresa looks around the restaurant. She reminds me of a squirrel, her movements skittish and nervous.

"Don't you hate being around couples now?" she asks, eyeing a man and woman at the end of our banquette. "I can't stand it." We notice the waiter standing awkwardly, his pad poised in his hands.

We order steaks and toast to Dave and Mike.

"I've been getting so many signs from Mike lately," Theresa says when the waiter leaves. Her signs arrive every day, like the mail, and I listen halfheartedly, a nonbeliever. "I know you think I'm nuts . . ." she always begins.

"No, I don't," I insist. "I'd love to believe that every light flicker or song on the radio is him."

"Well, why not? How do you know it's not?"

I shrug. We have had this conversation a hundred times before. "I want something a little more clear. I want to know where he is and what he's feeling and everything I used to . . . I just want that so bad . . . I just . . . need . . . to know he's okay up there." I am suddenly crying, my tears dropping onto my bread plate.

Theresa reaches across the table and squeezes my hand, our secret handshake. "Listen, I was a nurse for fifteen years and spent a lot of time around dying people. I *know* they're in a better place."

"I wish I could feel that, but I can't help feeling like he's *supposed* to be here."

"I know. It kills me. *Kills me,*" Theresa says, her eyes watering, too. "Dying people all do the same thing. They call out for people that have gone before them, they get really, really serene, and if you saw that day after day, you wouldn't wonder where Dave is." I want to say something, but I stop, because the refrains of my wedding song are echoing through the speaker above us. Etta's distinctive voice crooning *"And life is just a ball. Oh, at last."*

"What?"

"This is my wedding song." I curl my lip into my mouth to keep it from quivering.

Theresa smiles, a cat with the mouse. "You see? Don't tell me that's a coincidence. You're just not open to seeing signs. They're all around us! I get the number twenty-two showing up all over the place. Mike's birthday was June twenty-second and little Mikey was born on his birthday and just everywhere I go . . . twenty-two."

I am considering this when our steaks arrive.

"Mmm. This is excellent. C'mon! Eat!" Theresa urges.

I cut myself a neat, square piece and pop it into my mouth. "Wow, that is good," I say, chewing guiltily. I let the steak sit in my mouth, savoring its salty richness. *Thank you, Dave.*

*　*　*

We climb to an upper tier of Madison Square Garden, which is completely transformed from the Heroes' Concert just a few weeks ago. The stage is wide and narrow now, and a long runway cuts through the center of the crowd. Bono slides along the catwalk, landing on his knees as he croons, his neck arching back, his blue-tinted glasses catching the colored lights that circle above him. Theresa and I hold hands, singing along as loud as we can. I can feel the driving drums and bass line making the floor below me vibrate and the teenage girls in the seats next to us watching us. We must look strange, alternately singing and crying and laughing to the music. Bono's expressive voice tumbles me through thousands of moments with Dave. The familiar montage of our seventeen years together, happy moments rising to the surface like oil.

Dave and I had just come back from our second walk together. Dewy mist that had settled over the campus made everything look like an out-of-focus photograph. Dave liked to listen, more a comfortable quiet than shy. I lit a drip candle stuck in a sangria bottle and turned on the radio. We sat on the floor, across from the fish tank, which cast a blue light onto the industrial carpeting. I wondered why he didn't kiss me, didn't press hard against me like all the other guys. "In the Name of Love" came on the radio, so I kissed him instead, his lips two small satin cushions. The first touch of the tongue came next. It made my capillaries swell with the rush of it. I pulled him on top of the brown polyester quilt, the geometric shapes hard to discern in the strange blue light.

"Teach me how to kiss," Dave said, stopping me from opening my blouse.

"What do you mean?" I asked, confused. Most guys would have been on top of me by now.

"Just teach me how to kiss. Show me what to do."

"You just kiss," I said, shrugging, but he kept looking at me expectantly. "Okay. You swirl your tongue around, I guess," I said, leaning in. "Like this." We kissed for a long time, making tiny circles in each other's mouth.

"That was nice," he said finally, collapsing back onto the bed, still holding my hand. I leaned next to him, my ear touching his denim shirt, and we fell asleep this way, lying on our backs, side by side on top of the blankets, the blue haze of the fish tank the only light in the room.

"You're the girls from *Third Watch!*" The two teenage girls next to us are now pointing and smiling. "We loved you!"

"That is too weird," Theresa whispers as the band exits the stage and the crowd bursts into earsplitting applause. The audience stomps their feet, shaking the risers we are sitting on until the band saunters back on stage for an encore. The crowd settles as the gentle chords of "Peace on Earth" begin, Bono striding up the runway. Theresa points at the walls where the names of the victims killed at the World Trade Center begin to roll up the walls of Madison Square Garden like the final credits of a film. Thousands of names float above us in every direction, and Theresa and I hold hands, shaking our heads. When it becomes too much, I watch the audience, thousands of necks in silhouette craning to see the names of someone they know or have heard of. The degrees of separation are small. It seems everyone knows someone else. The stories are in the air, floating like the names above us. I look for Dave but the names glide by fast now and I am dizzied by the sheer volume of them.

Theresa pokes me. I assume she has found Mike's and Dave's names, but when I follow her finger, she is pointing to a jersey hanging from the ceiling directly above us. She is crying hard, tears rolling past her freckled cheeks. The name "DeBusschere" is sewn in thick black letters arched across the back, and underneath the name in big bold numbers is 22.

14

Alone in the Crowd

Kenny Michitsch is writing the details for Matt Garvey's wake tomorrow afternoon on a dry-erase board in the kitchen. Kenny, short, with thinning hair and an impish face, is the kind of firefighter you often forget, always quietly puttering around the firehouse, a cigarette dangling from his mouth. At the company picnics, Kenny worked the hardest, flipping burgers and making hot dogs for the kids, telling jokes and smiling.

"How's Matt's mom doing?" I ask him, picturing Fran, her face racked with grief. I have heard she has not stopped crying since Matt died.

"Okay, I guess. They're not giving him full military honors, even though he was in the Marines, because there's no body. You need to have a body. I know she's disappointed about that."

There are three funerals up on the dry-erase board already. I remember how the board used to be filled with firefighters needing to switch shifts, birth announcements, retirement parties, golf outings, hockey games.

"Where is everybody?" The firehouse is unusually quiet.

"Joe O'Donnell took Kathleen Box to the site, I think."

"Oh."

"If you ever want to go, I can take ya," Kenny offers.

"Thanks." I have thought often about visiting Ground Zero ever since we passed it on the way up to Pier 94.

"I'm scared to go," I tell him.

"Yeah, I don't blame ya. It ain't easy to see."

I know I will have to go soon. There are rumors about the retrieval not being handled well. Tommy Butler's widow, Martha, and I stayed on the phone late last night. Her father-in-law told her that the site clean up is being rushed, that trucks are leaving with debris before the firefighters have had a chance to search them.

"Do you think they're going to find anyone?" I ask.

Kenny shifts in his seat. "Truthfully, I dunno. I'm not at the site that much. They say the firefighters have a better chance because they're in their gear. It's easy to spot, and, you know . . ."

"The bodies don't decompose as fast," I say. Timmy Rogers told me this weeks ago.

"Right." The phone rings and Kenny looks relieved to answer it.

"They found Matt," he says, hanging up.

"You're kidding!"

"Yeah, that was Jerry. They just found his body at the site. Now he can have full military honors."

"Wow . . . the day before his service. What are the odds?"

"Yeah, especially since he's only the third one." And I can't help but consider the odds of finding Dave after a month and a half.

*   *   *

At Matt's funeral the next day, I climb into a large bus that will take us to Calvary Military Cemetery, over two hours' drive east on the Long Island Expressway. Connor O'Brian, who has driven me here, promises that the bus will take us back to his car later. The firefighters sit in the back of the bus, pulling beers out of a cooler while Chief Hayde and John Suzulka tell jokes as we bump along. I have not been to Calvary Cemetery since Dave's father died. No one told Dave his father had cancer, but the signs of a withering man were hard to miss. Years later, Dave finally told me about the last night he spent with his father. He was visiting him in the hospital, where he discovered him asleep among blood-stained sheets, his catheter lying on the floor. Dave called the nurses, realizing for the first time how sick his father was. His father's face blinked red from the light of the machines as Dave sat next to him, scared. He wanted to tell his father that he loved him, he knew it was his only chance, but instead he talked about the rugby team, how he had fallen in love, that he liked the steel sculptures he was making in his studio at college. His father nodded and tried to smile. Dave didn't know why he couldn't say it. They were just three little words that would sink forever inside his father's disappearing heart. But Dave, never having heard the words himself, didn't know how to say them, and he left that night filled with infinite regret.

Matt is given a twenty-one-gun salute by a group of fresh-faced Marines in crisp white-and-blue uniforms. I stand in line with the other widows, our heads bowed as we strain to keep our heels from sinking into the soft earth. Matt's mother is sitting in a chair by the casket, her lower lip drooping as she cries. We are handed roses and one by one place them on top of Matt's casket. He was so young. I silently apologize to Matt for all he will miss. I kiss Matt's mom and line up again to watch the casket creak slowly into its hole. It is the first time we have gathered at a graveyard after a mass.

After the funeral, the bus takes us to a hundred-year-old home that was converted into an inn and catering hall. The reception is in a room in the back that looks like a greenhouse, with countless windows that fill the room with a hot, diffuse light. I sit next to childhood friends of Matt's, who tell me how shy and good Matt was. I nod, knowing that they are not talking about a generic version of "good" but one that means wholesome and kind, a Norman Rockwell kind of good that was Dave. That kind of good is as rare as pearls. It is the kind of man who opens doors for people, smiles at seniors, and reminds the waitress when she forgets to charge for something on the bill. Sometimes Dave's goodness infuriated me. He never honked his horn. He gave forty dollars to a Vietnam vet on the subway. I wish I could be that sort of good.

Jerry Smythe, Matt's best friend, is serving as unofficial host. I watch him scurry around the room, getting drinks for relatives and doling out tissues to Fran, who rarely stops crying. Jerry was responsible for bringing Matt over to Squad a few months before he died. The firefighters crack jokes about Jerry being hyper, his infinite energy always inspiring amusement and awe in the firehouse, but today I know why Jerry is running.

The volume crescendos as the plates are cleared and firefighters hover around the bar ordering more drinks. Most of the surviving wives have left to pick up their kids from school or to make dinner for their families, and I start to miss Aidan with an intensity that surprises me. I have been so focused on my own pain, going to endless funerals and wakes, that I have spent little time with him in the last few weeks. Guilt opens up like a valve as I make my way to an empty room and try to call home on my cell phone. The ring stutters and abruptly stops; "call was lost" flashes across the phone. I close my eyes and picture Aidan. I want to go home and tuck him in tonight. He needs me to be there, but I am trapped on Long Island with no way to get home.

The sun drops so low, the light points horizontally into the glass room. Martha, Theresa, and Debbie kiss me good-bye. They will share a ride to their neighborhoods of Suffolk and Ronkonkoma at the end of the Island. The firefighters show no sign of wanting to leave, so I pace up and down the halls. I wander into a small room on the side of the house that has been converted into a dark bar. Connor and Chief Hayde are sitting there, talking and smoking, beers in their hands.

Chief Hayde stands up when I come in. "Hey, Marian. Can I get you a drink?"

"No, thanks," I say sullenly.

"Whatsa matter?" Connor asks.

"I want to go home," I say, trying not to sound as upset and desperate as I feel.

"I'll talk to Jerry," Connor promises.

"Thanks."

At 7:30 P.M., the tables have been cleared, and Huey is singing rock-and-roll songs in the back of the room. Firefighters are singing along, sounding drunk and out of tune. I step outside and try to call home again. This time Leah answers and tells me Aidan is in the bath. I wonder if I should call my brother-in-law to come and get me, but I don't even know where I am and how far it is from his house. The farther away the firefighters float, the angrier I become. I don't blame them really. I am usually right there with them, practically running for the bar after a painful three-hour funeral, but tonight I am cold sober and I want to go home.

By the time everyone stumbles onto the bus, it is after nine. I have to kiss Aidan good night on the cell phone. "Love you, too," he says, the signal so weak, his voice sounds far away. I find an empty row of seats toward the middle of the bus and sit by the window, pretending to be asleep. When I open my eyes, I see Huey's wife, Kathleen, sitting next to me. She looks at me empathically, but the whites of her eyes look like glazed onions as she tries to focus on my face.

"You having a hard time?" she asks.

"It's been a long day."

"I understand," she says, but secretly I think *No, you don't* as she goes to the back, joining the crowd. I lean on the window, listening to Sean strum the guitar, singing Irish songs. His voice is surprisingly good, and the lilting Irish melodies quiet the bus.

Chief Hayde stumbles toward the back to listen, clutching the tops of the seats as if he were on a boat in a storm. Noticing me, he drops into the seat Kathleen just left.

"YouknowDavewantsyoutobehappy," he slurs. "Ifthere'sanything Icando."

"I'm fine," I lie. I want to tell him that I feel like I am in one of those dreams where you are completely alone, running from place to place and panicking because everywhere you go, there is no one there, no one at all, but I stare out the window instead.

I cry quietly, my reflection like a shadowy xerox in the window. I feel my breath stutter in my chest as I try to cry noiselessly. I imagine how Dave would be now; how, from across the bus, he would know how I felt, sensing my moods like a horse whisperer. I notice a tissue in my periphery. Sean is sitting next to me now, holding out a Kleenex. I have lost track of how long I have been crying.

"Thanks." He says nothing but sits there, staring at the back of the seat while I blow my nose.

"What do you miss most about Dave?" he asks unexpectedly.

I exhale loudly, trying to think of where to begin. "Everything . . . How he knew me better than anybody. So much really. The touching, the talking, the eating, the sex . . . not even the sex so much as that intense closeness you feel right after. The closeness that opens you up wide and you say things you usually wouldn't." I don't even know why I am saying this to Sean, but it makes me feel lighter, as if I have confessed something. Sean nods and I fall silent, dabbing my eyes with the already wet tissue.

"You know, I dreamed about Dave a few nights ago," he begins. I turn toward him to listen but Connor O'Brian has stumbled into our moment, smiling dumbly, his eyes bloodshot.

"What are you two doing?" he says. He leans over to kiss me on the cheek, but the bus lurches forward and he falls into my lap. "WHOA!" Sean steadies Connor so he can stumble to the back of the bus.

"He's supposed to be my ride home," I say, surprised at how angry I am that he's drunk.

"We'll find you someone sober to drive home with," Sean assures me.

"Good luck." I look down to see Connor's beeper in my lap. It must have landed there when he stumbled.

Sean sees me staring at it. "Are you thinking what I'm thinking?"

I look up and smile devilishly. "I think so," I say conspiratorially. Sean reaches over and lowers the window. I look over to him and raise my eyebrow, the beeper poised outside the window.

"Go for it." I hurl the beeper with all my might, listening to the plastic smash against the highway, surprised at how satisfying it feels.

"That felt good." I slide the window closed and in the next moment, I am consumed with guilt. Connor has been nothing but nice to me since Dave died. Why would I do that? "I can't believe I just did that."

"Did it feel good?"

"Yes, but—"

"It'll be our little secret then." We sit in silence, bumping along the L.I.E. A long silence relaxes the air between us until Sean says suddenly, "We're all going to die of cancer in a few years anyway."

"Don't say that!" I yell.

"It's true. All that crap at Ground Zero that we're breathing in, forget it."

"I thought you were trying to cheer me up."

"Sorry." But it is too late. We are both contemplating the future, the death of even more friends and the seemingly unending fallout from that infamous day.

*   *   *

I waited until the last minute to buy Aidan's Halloween costume, hoping he would change his mind and choose something less creepy. I had already talked him out of the Grim Reaper and a skeleton, so the Scream was our compromise. For months before Dave died, Aidan had told us he would be Anakin Skywalker from *Star Wars*. Dave was excited about making a pod racer with foam board and hot glue.

The phone is on its fourth ring when I dive for it. "Hello?"

"Did you go to the site to get your urn?" Martha asks, her voice flat and lifeless. The mayor held a ceremony the other day to present families with an urn full of Ground Zero debris. I have been receiving calls ever since from families worried that the retrieval is over or moving too fast. "Do you think that means they're giving up on finding anyone?"

"No. I've been making calls to find out what's going on. There's a lot of disturbing stuff."

"I know. My father-in-law is very upset." Martha's father, Bill, is one of a dozen retired firefighters who have shown up at the site to dig for their missing sons.

"I know," I say, thinking about Dave and Tommy being carted to a dump on Staten Island. "The guys at the site are calling it a scoop and dump operation now."

"We have to do something."

I keep the phone pressed to my ear all day as I shop for dinner and Halloween candy and clean my house, preparing for my first Halloween without Dave. I call chiefs and firefighters while I make chili for dinner, the mayor's office while I make cornbread, a steelworker at Ground Zero while I set out plates, trying to get a better sense of what is happening at the site.

By the time I pick up Aidan, my house is spotless and my head is spinning.

"This is the best holiday!" Aidan yells, bouncing out of his schoolroom door with a bag of half-eaten candy and his face covered in sugar. I try to act as excited as he is when he shows me a mask he made from a paper bag. I force myself to listen while he recounts what happened in school that day, the parties and bags of goodies.

At home, I help Aidan get dressed in his Scream costume, the face eerily resembling the Edvard Munch painting. I offered to make him an Anakin costume and even a pod racer, but he refused. Recently, Aidan has wanted nothing to do with *Star Wars*. Hundreds of figures and ships sit dormant, gathering dust in the corner, and the *Star Wars* videos that he watched every day have been pushed to the back of the video cabinet. Aidan and Dave would play *Star Wars* for hours, clicking toothpick-size light sabers into Lilliputian figurines. I would often tease Dave when I discovered him lining the figures up for battle, long after Aidan had gone to bed.

"I appreciate the way they're made!" Dave would rebuke and then, after a long pause, say, "All right, I was too old to buy them as a kid and I secretly wanted them," he confessed, smiling.

Aidan holds his hands up, trying to look spooky in his new mask. He chases me around the apartment, and I pretend to be scared, thrilling him with my shrieks and howls. Ever since Dave died, Aidan has been obsessed with masks. I try not to look embarrassed when I push him in a shopping cart through Key Food in a cracked skeleton mask. I feel like I am walking a rabid dog when he growls at people in a werewolf mask. I managed to coax it off him after he made a baby cry at Starbucks. His therapist insists that this behavior is appropriate considering what has happened. It is another way of hiding from it all, of scaring the world, the way it scared him when it took his daddy away.

Leah and Jason take Aidan trick-or-treating so I can finish cooking. Jason rolls his eyes at me as he leaves, knowing that, as usual, I have taken on more than I can handle. "Slow down or I'll be burying you next," he whispers, and I force a laugh.

"Put 'she was overwhelmed' on my tombstone, will ya?" I watch Aidan skip down the hall and disappear with Jason and Leah, who have been my lifelines since Dave died, answering my phone, calling people, cleaning my house, picking up Aidan.

Lieutenant Farrell arrives with green and red paint smeared in blobs across his face.

"What are you supposed to be?" I ask Dennis, laughing.

"I dunno," he says, shrugging, and I pat him on the back. It is my way of thanking him for being here, for knowing this holiday means a lot to Aidan and me. "I'm just a general spooky guy, I guess." He sinks onto the couch while I try to stir the chili, make salad, and take cornbread out of the oven at the same time. I wish I was with Aidan. I wonder why I chose to do all of this alone, today of all days. In my effort to make this Halloween like the others, I have forfeited the most important part of spending time with my son.

My mother arrives dressed as a mummy, with white gauze wrapped haphazardly around her pants legs. My dad is close behind her, wearing a pillow stuffed into his suit jacket.

"Nice hump," I say.

"Look." Mom points to a large refrigerator box she has made into a haunted house.

I'm touched by her effort to make something grand the way Dave used to. My father helps me lift the box into Aidan's wagon and we head to 7th Avenue for the annual parade.

Out on the avenue, the parade is in full swing. Mila and Joey, Leah, Jason, and my in-laws are all here. I walk slowly, filled with the profound ache of missing Dave again when I spot Nancy, in front of me, taking my picture for the *New York Times*.

"Not today," I say, but she ignores me, shooting more photographs.

"I don't think you heard her," Joey says, annoyed, stepping protectively in front of me.

"All right. All right," Nancy says, backing off, but before I can even say anything, I have lost Joey and Nancy and am walking alone. I stop and wait for my friends and family to catch up, and when they do, Joey is smiling widely.

"What?" I ask him, Mila giggling alongside him as he holds out his hand, revealing a roll of film. "I don't think she'll be bothering us anymore."

15

The Pile

The day after Halloween, Martha calls. "Marian, have you heard what happened?" It is only 8:00 A.M. and her soft voice is full of ire.

"No," I say groggily.

"Mayor Giuliani and Commissioner Von Essen cut the firefighters from Ground Zero."

"What?" I sit bolt upright.

"They took them off the site. There's only a few guys left, I think."

"*Why?*" I ask, feeling the familiar flush of outrage.

"I dunno. I thought *you* would know. That's why I'm calling."

"I don't know. I'm barely awake . . . I'll find out." I'm furious.

I hang up and start walking up and down the living room. This pacing has become familiar. It reminds me of the eleventh, when they tried to close Squad, and of all the waiting—this constant waiting. I imagine my brain is the center of a wheel, the thoughts flying with centrifugal force all around me. I try to pin them down, to put them in an order.

1. I will look for Dave myself. I will dig through the rubble with my bare hands until I find him.
2. I will organize the families. We will go down to City Hall and protest.

3. I will go from firehouse to firehouse gathering firefighters, and we will march together to the site.

4. I will enlarge all the photos of the victims and place them all over City Hall.

5. I will call the mayor's office and FDNY headquarters and arrange a meeting.

"They're saying it's because of safety," Joe Miccio tells me after he talks to the union. "But that's bullshit. No one's gotten hurt since the recovery started. I mean, these guys are doing a phenomenal job. You have firefighters *volunteering* to be down there. Fathers looking for sons. It's just not right."

"Well, no one knows what's going on. I have family members calling *me* for information. They're not telling us anything, and we have to hear from the *news* that they're taking firefighters off the pile?" I sigh loudly.

Joe O'Donnell calls from the firehouse, and I brace myself for more bad news. His voice is scratchy and tired, void of emotion. "We're goin' to City Hall tomorrow mornin' and we're marchin' peacefully to Ground Zero to say a prayer at the pile."

"I'll be there," I tell him without missing a beat.

"Naw, don't. It's firefighters. It's just the guys."

"So? I want to go. I'll bring a big picture of Dave. I can—"

"Listen, you did enough stuff already for us. You need to just relax, take care of Aidan."

"I feel better when I'm doing something."

"Well, you can do us a favor by calling all those press people you met and have them come down there."

"I will, but . . . I want to go."

"It's better if you let the guys do it."

I immediately call Mike Daly, the reporter from the *Daily News* I have become friends with. "Don't worry. I'll definitely be there. I'll even write you a story about it," he says.

* * *

That night I dream Dave is walking on a path. It is a bucolic country road, the kind you see in Merchant Ivory films, with ancient trees covering him like lush green umbrellas. My heart is light with joy.

"You're back! You're back!" I scream, skipping up to him. He is wearing his denim shirt and jeans, and he hugs me so hard I can barely breathe. I am crying on his shoulders, the joy and relief so intense, my heart feels like it has stopped. "Why did you go like that?" I scream, grabbing his arms and looking at him, but he is not looking at me, he is looking over my shoulder, and I turn to see my family: Luke, Leah, Mom, Dad, and Aidan. They are walking toward us in a slow, steady procession. It looks like a modern dance, the way they are staring forward, almost through me, and the terrible alone feeling returns, that horrible feeling that I am the only one left in the world.

Then, suddenly, I am on a hill, looking down at the same road, and I am on a swing. It has hearts carved in the back of it and I realize it is the same bench where Dave and I once kissed behind the Tudor house at C. W. Post. The bench was actually a swing between two magnolia trees, and I can still remember the sickly sweet smell of crushed magnolia flowers that stuck to the bottom of our shoes.

Then my mother is sitting between us on the bench and she is talking to Dave. I am mad at her because I need to talk to Dave. It feels urgent and immediate, like there is not much time, and she is taking it all. I keep leaning forward trying to see Dave and then, in a swift moment, he is gone, and my family is marching on the path again without me. I am alone on the bench, watching my father and Luke, who are now pallbearers and they are carrying a casket balanced on their shoulders. I am awash in a new sadness because I know it is Dave in a dozen pieces inside the coffin.

*   *   *

Later as Rosie O'Donnell's cheery face fills the television screen, I put my computer on my lap and turn it on, plugging in the phone cord. "You've got mail," the voice says as the computer chugs and hums, trying to list the 476 e-mails in my mailbox. I sigh and look around my apartment. The sun is shining on a pile of superhero figures lying in the center of the living room, plastic arms pointing in every direction. An old coffee cup has made a rubber-band-colored ring on the coffee table. Elvis is chewing a flower stem. *"Emotions flare as firefighters and police clash at Ground Zero . . ."* My eyes snap toward the TV as the screen fills with firefighters, their faces red. The camera shakes, focusing on what appears to be a fight in the center of the crowd, arms and legs flailing. I turn up the volume to hear the newscaster announce that thirteen firefighters were arrested for punching the police. As if on cue, Joe O'Donnell calls.

"What the hell is going on?" I ask.

"I guess you heard," he says, his voice frustratingly calm.

"I'm just looking at the news now!"

"A coupla guys got outta control."

"It looks like a riot from where I'm sitting."

"It wasn't like that, though. The press is blowing this completely out of proportion. It was real peaceful. There were mothers and wives with pictures of their loved ones."

"You see? I knew I should have gone!" I practically yell at him.

"I didn't know they would be there, I swear, but you know, everybody walked peacefully from City Hall to the site. Then we get to the site and we planned on goin' in there to say a prayer for the guys and they had police barricades there and they wouldn't let us onto the site. We have over three hundred forty-three brothers buried in there and they're not gonna let us onto the site? I mean, you gotta be kiddin' me. We just wanted to say a prayer! We weren't gonna do nothin'."

"So what happened then?"

"Well, I guess they got a coupla young cops standing there and I feel bad for them 'cause they really wanted to let us through, but the brass is standin' on the sides tellin' them to block us from comin' in. Some of the guys in the front were pushin' and gettin' pissed off, and then outta nowhere a couple of guys start swingin' punches, and then the news starts makin' it seem like we're all a bunch of animals, and I'm tellin' ya, from where I was standin', it was real nice and peaceful. A lotta the guys had their kids in strollers and everything . . ."

I shake my head in disbelief and sigh louder than I mean to. "This is not good." Then the phone beeps. Mike Daly is on the other line. "It was so reverent and peaceful," he tells me, promising to write a story about what really happened. I hang up and call Martha. I can hear her kids yelling in the background.

"I've never seen my father so upset," Martha tells me. "Bill was there all morning with a picture of Tommy on his chest."

"I think we need to try and get the families together right away."

"No kidding. It's ridiculous."

Joe Miccio calls. "This is getting totally out of control. I think the whole thing was a setup. It's a witch hunt."

"Yeah, but you can see guys punching the cops. It doesn't look good."

"I know, but they had brass there, and they were picking the union guys out of the crowd. Even ones that weren't even involved! Christ, they arrested Pete Gorman and Kevin Gallagher, the union presidents! They didn't punch anybody. You don't think that's a coincidence? Don't you think it's weird that all the guys arrested were union guys?"

I say nothing, because truthfully, I don't care if they're union or not. I want my husband found and I want his brothers to be the ones to find him.

After I tuck Aidan in, Jason agrees to watch Aidan so I can go to the firehouse to see if any news has developed. The bay door stays closed now and only a few buckets of flowers remain outside. To be polite, I ring the bell even though I know the door code to let myself in. The guys are sitting in the back around the table, having a late dinner.

"You want some chicken Parmesan?" Jerry asks.

"No, thanks. I'm not hungry."

"What, are you losin' weight?" Misera-Bill grumbles.

"Yeah, you look hot," Tony says.

"Yeah, what a freaking waste, right?" I say, plopping into a chair as Eric pours me coffee. I listen to the guys theorizing about the rally.

"I bet they staged the whole thing," Kenny says.

"Yeah, they knew when the guys got to Ground Zero, they were gonna want to go in." Tony's face is twisted in disgust.

"Von Essen's a pussy. Did you see him apologizing on the six o'clock news? Kerik is standing there right next to the mayor, and Von Essen is apologizing for our behavior. Fuckin' asshole." Jerry's leg is bouncing up and down.

"What, are you surprised? That guy's never stuck up for the guys. Ever. That's why nobody likes him," Tony adds.

The other men mutter in agreement as Eric plops a large crumb cake on the table and I sigh as Jimmy stands and writes in green marker "Mike Russo's wake" on the board.

*   *   *

Alone in my car en route to Mike Russo's wake, my mind is blank. I can't focus on anything. I don't even answer my cell phone, which sits on the passenger seat ringing and ringing. Things have continued to spin out of control. I stare ahead at an old Aspen station wagon in front of me. It has a Bush sticker on its bumper. I smile, remembering Aidan's therapy session yesterday. He had a puppet on each hand. One was a police officer, the other a gray-haired man.

"The policeman is telling him about the Twin Towers," Aidan told the therapist, who furrowed her brow and leaned forward in her chair.

"Who?" Mary said casually.

"The president."

"What is the policeman telling the president?" Mary asked.

"He's telling him about the towers," Aidan said, then announced, "My mom thinks President Bush is an asshole."

"Aidan!" I half scolded. Even Mary couldn't help but smile. "That's not a nice word." As Aidan shrugged and returned to his game, I made a mental note to speak more quietly on the phone.

The front foyer of the funeral parlor is wide, with faded blue carpet. Crooked white plastic letters spell MIKE RUSSO—ROOM 2 on a board in front. I pin my Squad patch on and follow some firefighters to a room on the right. Rows of gray folding chairs are set in the middle of the room, where a few people are having hushed conversations. I wonder why people always walk into funeral parlors as if they are entering a library—as if death requires quiet.

Theresa stands in front of the casket, carrying Mike Jr., who is now eighteen months old. He is a serious little boy with Theresa's small lips and stick-straight strawberry blond hair. The rest of Mike Jr. looks like his father: the wiry build and big blue eyes. Michael's parents stand next to Theresa, their faces long and sullen. Spotting me, Theresa signals me to come up to the front. I greet Michael's parents and Mike's older brother Tony, who looks so much like Mike that it is difficult not to gasp.

"You gotta see this." Theresa pulls me toward the back of the room where a wreath of golf clubs made from black and gray carnations stands over five feet tall. I cup my hand over my mouth to stifle a giggle. "Wait. Look at this one." She pulls me to another corner, where there is a wreath of a Harley-Davidson motorcycle so large it takes three easels to hold it up. Another wreath is squeezed in next to it depicting a football jersey the size of a blackboard.

A few weeks earlier, Theresa and I attended a wake that looked like a casting call for a *Sopranos* episode. We stood at the end of a long line of men in dark, shiny suits, greased-back hair, and gold chains. They were talking about meat in thick Staten Island accents.

"The ting is," said one, "people tink da fat is bad, but you gotta have some fat to grill it right."

"Yeah . . . marbelizin'," the second one said.

"What?"

"Marbelizing, the fat. Like you said, it has to be marbled."

"What the fuck are you talkin' about?"

"Fat! You was talking about fat and I happen to know somethin' about it. Dat's all."

"You gotta a fat freakin' head is what you got," the third one said, and Theresa and I tried not to giggle too loudly behind them. They went on and on like this as the line snaked through two rooms, until we finally approached the large room where the casket stood. Funeral wreaths as big as cars stood around the room in gaudy contrast to the staid mood. A giant fire truck made from red and black carnations dominated the corner. I had seen these wreaths at most of the wakes I had attended, depicting everything the lost firefighter loved: footballs, American flags, surfboards, baseballs, cigars, logos of bands and movies.

"I do *not* want these at Mike's funeral," Theresa had said, motioning to a soccer ball the size of a door on our right. We couldn't stop laughing as we made our way past twelve wreaths in all, a gallery's worth of overpriced, flashy flower art.

"I guess no one got the memo," I say to Theresa before I am laughing out loud, my stomach contracting as I try to control myself. Theresa is laughing, too—high-pitched and free as a little girl's.

"We're gonna get into trouble," Theresa says, pulling me into the hall as some white-haired relatives turn to stare. She leads me to where some widows are sitting in overstuffed chairs.

"What are you two laughing at?" Martha says, smiling. I dry my eyes and try to catch my breath.

"Those wreaths," Theresa says, wiping her own eyes with a tissue.

"Aren't they gorgeous?" Debbie says, and Theresa and I are laughing hard again. "You two are bad. They're nice! I like them."

"We're going to hell," I say.

"I already have my passport," Debbie says, laughing now.

Theresa chases Mike Jr. to a chair. "I don't know about you girls, but I am ready for another one of our dinners."

"Yeah, me, too," Martha says.

"Shall I organize a Merry Widows' night?" I ask.

"Stop! I hate that word," Martha says.

"Well, come up with something better then!" After a moment I gesture Martha to step away from the other women. When I have her in the corner, I lean in and whisper, "Martha, we have to talk."

"Yeah, what are we gonna do about the site?"

"I'm going to call all the media connections I know . . . and I think we need a meeting. We need to get the widows together."

"Stop saying 'widows'!" She pretends to cover her ears.

"I know . . . but . . . I think if we do, we can have some political clout and get the firefighters back working on the site."

"Yeah, whatever it takes. What?" Martha asks. She can see my wheels turning.

"I'm going to print up some flyers tonight and give them to whatever politicians are there at the funeral tomorrow."

"You can't do that! It's Mike's funeral!"

"I'll ask Theresa. She won't mind. We'll tell them the families are concerned and would like to dialogue."

"Marian!"

"C'mon, you have any better ideas?"

Martha shakes her head. "Okay, fine."

The next morning, I am speeding toward the church in Bayside, the flyers pressed into my bag, my veins pulsing from too much caffeine. The widows from Squad are lining up on the steps when I arrive. I tiptoe in between them, kissing their cheeks and handing them flyers. I spot my mother-in-law standing behind me, and she gives me a small wave. Across the street, the politicians have already taken their places in front of the firefighters lined six rows deep. The deputy commissioner, Lynn Tierney, catches my eye, and I break through the crowd and cross over to greet her. I feel the crowd watching me, but I don't care. I have to talk to her before she leaves.

"We need to have a meeting," I tell her, handing her a flyer.

"I heard you started a widows' group. I think that's great." I can tell she imagines a group of women sipping tea and crying over their husbands.

"We're all really upset about the firefighters," I continue, noticing the governor's wife, Libby, turning to listen. "I think we need to get accurate information out to the families."

"I completely agree," Lynn says, her blue eyes flashing. "Why don't I call you tomorrow to set it up, 'cause we've been meaning to do this, and I could use your help."

"Good." I hear the bagpipes begin in the distance, so I run across the street and take my place on the steps.

*   *   *

When I answer the telephone at 8:40 A.M. the next day, I recognize the deputy commissioner's voice immediately. It is as thick as cinder block.

"The mayor says he'll meet with you on Friday."

"Oh."

"Just a casual thing at my apartment, I think, since you're in Park Slope, too."

"Okay . . . that'd be perfect," I tell her.

"I need to know who's going to be attending though," she says gruffly. "We don't want people yelling and getting crazy."

"Nobody's there to yell. We just want some information," I say evenly.

"Well, we're trying our best. It's just been— Well, I'm sure you can imagine. It's been nuts."

"I understand, but you know . . ." I hear my call waiting beep, but I ignore it and continue. "It's been a while since we've heard anything— even if it's bad news. If you don't communicate, rumors start, and I can tell you, there's lots of them and they're very upsetting."

"No, I know, and we really want to hear from you guys."

I can hear phones ringing in the background and muffled voices and say, "I gotta go. I'll call you tomorrow to confirm."

I click the button to the waiting call. "Hello?"

"Hi. It's Mom," my mother says, her voice breathy. "There was an article in the *Staten Island Advance* today about a widow who's doing something about the firefighters and the site. It sounds like you should talk to her. Her name's Janice Pancini." I hear the papers rustling. "Her husband was a firefighter, too . . . How goes it?"

"I'm fine, I guess." There is a long, pregnant pause, and I know my mother wants more, but I am talked out.

"Okay, I don't want to bother you." She sounds hurt, and I hang up guiltily. I call information and, surprisingly, Janice is listed. I let the phone ring over and over until someone finally answers.

"Hello?" she says, sounding winded. I can hear kids in the background. "Who is this, please?"

"Hi. My name is Marian Fontana. My husband, Dave, is one of the firefighters—"

"Oh, yeah. I know who you are. I'm so glad you're not a reporter."

"I know. They're relentless, huh?"

"Oh my God! It's crazy."

"Well, I read about you in the paper," I begin. "I was trying to get some widows together for a meeting."

I hear a screech in the background. "Can you hold on a minute?" she says, cupping her hand over the phone. *"Excuse me!"* I hear Janice's voice muffled. "Mommy is on the phone! . . . I'm sorry," she says, her voice suddenly clear again. "I have twins."

"Oh." I try to picture having two Aidans to take care of. "I can barely handle one." She sighs. I say, "I thought it would make sense to combine our efforts and then maybe get more done."

"Definitely. It's too much for one person." She sighs again. "Definitely too much."

*   *   *

The meeting at Lynn's is not until 7:00 P.M., but we decide to meet at my house to make sure everyone is on the same page. Janice arrives with three women from Staten Island and a firefighter who offered to drive them. She is prettier than I pictured, with soft, pale skin and feathery brown hair. She introduces a heavily made-up blond woman with a tiger-print blouse and tight black pants who shakes my hand limply and sits down.

"I've been helping Janice with the case," she announces, her voice as confident as a lawyer's. "I didn't lose anyone personally, but my husband is working at the site, and I am a professional mediator, so I can facilitate this meeting to get your points across." Martha flashes me a glance and I bite my lower lip, a habit Dave hated.

"I think we can all speak for ourselves," I begin slowly, trying to mask my annoyance. "I think it's important that we all speak and stand united and firm on the firefighter issues—"

"That's why I think it would be good to have a representative do the talking," the blonde interrupts, crossing her leg. "I do it for a living so I thought I could help present what you want to say."

"Well, I think as long as we don't yell and get crazy and we state our case intelligently and clearly, then we can all speak for ourselves," I repeat.

"You should choose one person to open the discussion though," she says, her high-heeled boot waving up and down like a flag.

"Well, Marian arranged the meeting. She should start," Martha says.

"I agree," Janice says. "This is a family issue. The families should speak for themselves."

"I don't like that woman," Martha whispers to me as we walk to her car to drive the eight blocks to Lynn's apartment.

"I know! Why is she even here? This is just supposed to be families," I say, helping Martha clear the front seat of a diaper bag, crumbs, and toys.

She climbs into the driver's seat of her van, looking like a child stealing a school bus. "I'm nervous," she says, fluffing her hair in the mirror. "I'm not good at speaking, like you."

"You'll be fine. We're not politicians. We're grieving widows," I tell her.

"I hate that word," she says into the rearview mirror as she turns onto 6th Avenue.

"Sorry."

"No, it's okay, it's what we are. I just . . . can't get used to it."

Lynn lives on 12th Street in a large factory building that made clocks at the turn of the century. Her apartment on the fourth floor boasts exposed brick walls, dark cavernous rooms, and high ceilings.

"Make yourselves at home," Lynn says, unloading groceries from plastic bags. The statement is funny, since it looks like Lynn spends very little time here. The furniture is spare and unused, and there are hardly any pictures on the walls.

"The mayor likes red, so I bought more of that," she says, digging through an overstuffed drawer for a wine opener. Martha and I glance at each other wondering if she, like me, is thinking that this is all a farce and the mayor is not going to come after all. I mean, the city is falling apart, so why would he want to listen to a bunch of grief-stricken widows complain? Yet I can't help but feel the country behind us, arriving daily with support and comfort in an unprecedented display of solidarity. No, it serves the mayor well to listen to a few of us complain, to avoid being knocked off the pedestal New York has placed him on, or maybe, just maybe, he is coming in good faith and, like the rest of New York, was transformed by September 11.

"I guess he's late. He had two funerals today. This schedule is just so intense," Lynn says, entering from her bedroom, where she has changed into jeans and a long-sleeved shirt.

"Too many funerals," I say obtusely.

"Yeah, and it's terrible that we can't be at all of them. The mayor really wants to, but sometimes there are six or seven on the same day, what do you do? I mean . . ."

The buzzer interrupts her. I take a seat and help myself to a piece of salami and wait. The doorbell rings and two large graying men enter the apartment, looking past us. They walk into each room, opening and closing doors, wires hanging from their ears. They mutter into small microphones on their lapels, and in a moment the mayor enters, with Tom Von Essen close behind.

The mayor's forehead wrinkles as he smiles warmly, offering condolences and shaking hands with everyone. Von Essen plops into one of the chairs, his red face lined with fatigue. The mayor chats casually with Lynn in the kitchen and then helps himself to a glass of wine. He eases himself into a chair next to Tom and looks expectantly at me. I sit up tall and begin.

"Thank you for coming, Mr. Mayor. I'm sure you know this, but the families are concerned about how the site is being handled, particularly in regard to the firefighters." I stop and wait. "I think I speak for everyone when I tell you that we want the firefighters who were removed from the site last week to be put back where they belong. We don't want our husbands scooped up, thrown in a truck, and found at a dump when we know they can be found by their brothers on the site." I lean back to let him know I am finished.

"Well, first of all, we don't want any of your husbands to be found that way," the mayor begins. He speaks casually, as if we have been friends for a long time. "The reason we made the choice to remove the firefighters is that the safety organization we hired—"

"Bechtel," I say, to let him know I have done my research.

"Right. Bechtel deemed the site unsafe. Now, maybe they're wrong, but I don't want to lose any more men if we don't have to."

I consider this for a second. What if I fight for the firefighters to get back on the site and one of them gets hurt or, worse, dies? Will that be my fault?

I lean forward again. "I don't think any of us want anyone getting hurt . . . but these guys are trained to search. You funded them to learn confined-space rescue and collapse . . . and actually, except for a construction worker breaking his arm, there have been no injuries on the site since the recovery began."

The mayor shakes his head and continues. "I was at the site today and a grappler came within two inches of hitting a firefighter who was down in a hole and didn't know the grappler was there. Now, if I hadn't seen it with my own eyes, I would agree with you, but these rescue guys are fatigued and emotionally upset—"

"But no one's gotten hurt," I repeat, and Tom looks at the mayor with a combination of mild disgust and exhaustion. I feel my palms sweat and wipe them against the soft arms of my chair, uncrossing and crossing my legs. "I'm sure you know there is a long-standing tradition in the Fire Department that you do not leave a fire until every last man is out. You can't just remove these guys with all their friends still buried. Not to mention, we need them there. It's just not right to take them off."

"My brother is at the site every day and he doesn't want to leave. It's not fair to make him—" Martha says gently.

"The problem is," the mayor says, taking a sip of wine, "as the site gets smaller, you have the same amount of men working in a more confined space, and it's dangerous."

"But we think it's important that they're there," Janice says emphatically. "They know what they are doing."

"Listen, I don't think anyone understands that more than Tom and I about this, and we certainly would not have made this decision if we didn't feel like it was the right thing to do. Tom?"

The commissioner shifts in his seat, rolling his head back, his eyes droopy with fatigue. "Look, you got guys down there that haven't gone home since the eleventh, that are going to funerals and coming back to the site. There are fathers looking for sons . . . brothers looking for brothers. People aren't thinking clearly . . . It's just not safe. I mean, our guys are doing things down there that are . . . Look, I won't even go into it. They're not used to working in a paramilitary fashion the way police officers are."

I feel Martha bristle next to me.

"I completely disagree. The entire makeup and training of the department is paramilitary," I exclaim.

"Yeah, and half the guys in the Fire Department are in the Reserves," Martha says, sitting up. "My husband was in the Navy, and Tommy loved the Fire Department *because* it was paramilitary. He was a police officer, and for him, that wasn't military enough. He wanted to drill and train and work as a team and everything."

Two hours pass and we make our points over and over, refusing to back down. Tom grows silent, but the mayor rolls up his sleeves. We bring up health issues, communication, the need for a place at Ground Zero where the families can go.

"Look, the men we lost—these men will never be replaced. I feel a sense of duty to your husbands to protect these firefighters down there. They are my employees. I mean, I lost a lot of friends that day." The mayor looks at Tom, who is staring at the floor, his face tense. "I think we can safely put back some of the firefighters—Tom and I have been considering this—maybe fifty firefighters onto the pile."

"That's great." Janice nods, smiling.

"What about *all* of them?" I ask. "I think they all need to be put back."

"We'll start with fifty and see how it goes," Tom says.

"And what about the guys who were arrested?" I ask.

"Well," the mayor starts, "we have these firefighters on tape punching police officers."

"But there were hundreds of guys there that day that didn't. It seems like it's a witch hunt."

Tom is incredulous. "We didn't make them punch those guys. They were out of control!"

"They were blocked from the site they've been digging in for over a month!" I snap. "That was a recipe for disaster!"

Tommy sighs and throws up his hands. "They shouldn't have arrested Gorman and Gallagher, I'll give you that."

There is a long uncomfortable silence until Lynn leans forward. "Police and firefighters have always battled for turf."

"Yeah, but—" Martha begins.

"Look, it's likely we'll drop the charges against these men," the mayor says in a commanding voice that quiets us all.

"Good," I say, and the room is silent. "We really just want better communication, that's all. I mean, we have to rely on news from the firefighters . . . I think there needs to be a meeting like this with *all* the families."

The mayor nods, but before he can say anything, the woman sitting next to me, an older woman in her late fifties who has been quiet all night, speaks.

"The civilians don't have any communication at all," she says. "The Red Cross lost all my papers, and now I have nothing. They are about to foreclose on my house."

The mayor nods empathetically and looks to Lynn, who clears her throat and says, "I'll see what I can do. I mean, I'm helping the fire families, but I'd be happy to try to get in touch with someone who can help you." The woman nods appreciatively, folds her hands in her lap, and is silent again. I suddenly feel grateful for having the Fire Department to help me and guilty that so many do not.

"We're organizing a trip to Hawaii for the fire families," Mayor Giuliani says, looking at me, trying to lighten the mood. "We're working with the tourist board of Hawaii."

"Oh, how nice," the blond mediator says, smiling. She has been trying all night to get a word in, but the mayor clearly does not like her. "Can my husband and I go, too? He's working at the site."

"It's really for fire families," Tom says, unable to hide his disdain.

At about ten-thirty, the mayor stands to indicate that the meeting is over. He shakes hands, kisses Martha, Janice, and me hard on the cheek, and leaves, the two bodyguards following closely behind. Tom and Lynn remain in the kitchen, milling around the food and whispering to each other. I pour myself a glass of wine.

"That went well," Lynn says.

I nod, noticing Tom rubbing his eyes. "You look tired," I say to him. "It's been a long day."

"I read about you in the paper," Martha says, referring to a number of articles where Tom was quoted as saying "suck it up" to the firefighters complaining about the site. The firefighters were furious.

"That was taken totally out of context," he says, obviously tired of defending himself. "I'm not a politician. I'm a firefighter, and I'm trying to do right by these guys and they just don't get it." He shakes his head and then flicks his hand, giving up.

"I understand," Martha tries, feeling sorry for him.

"You don't know how I feel," he snaps, and then, softening, adds, "And I don't know how you feel, either."

Martha walks over to me and whispers, "Yeah, everyone doesn't hate me."

16

Ground Zero

Aidan's voice calls out. I have taken an Ambien, and waking up feels like trying to swim to the water's surface.

"Mommy!" Aidan yells again. I stumble through the dark, feeling my way to his bed, and sit, bumping my head on his top bunk.

"I'm scared," Aidan says rolling around, sweating.

"I'm right here," I say sleepily, my eyes adjusting to the dark as I wipe the wet hair off his face.

"I dreamed I saw Daddy and we were in the mall and there were smiley faces everywhere, but then he chased me."

"It was just a dream. Just your imagination. Try to go back to sleep." I rub his head for a long time, the way I used to, until my arm is throbbing. He tries to go back to sleep, but every few minutes, he flips over, trying to get comfortable.

"I saw Daddy wrapped in a blanket and he was cold." Aidan stares at the top of the bunk, and the feeling of sadness that has become as familiar as breathing grips my stomach. I convince Aidan to let me get him some warm milk. I walk on the cold floor, the silence of the apartment ringing in my ears. It is rare that this place is quiet, and I stand there, the hum of the refrigerator the only noise.

"Mommy . . ." Aidan calls out.

"I'm coming." I take out a pan and light the gas, the noises of life seeming loud and strange at this hour. I stir the milk, watching the tiny bubbles form on the edges, the simple task distracting me from this life that has become as dark as this hour of the night.

I bring Aidan his milk and sing his favorite song, and I can imagine Dave's voice singing softly, too, leaning his big body into the bunk and kissing Aidan's ear.

"Hush-a-by, don't you cry. Go to sleep, little baby. When you wake, you shall have all the pretty little horses. Blacks and bays, dappled and grays. Coach and six little horses."

I stare at Aidan's eyes, willing them to close.

"I'm scared I'm going to have another bad dream," he says pitifully, his bottom lip quivering. He is about to cry.

"You know, sometimes if you think about something before you go to sleep, you'll dream about it, so maybe if we think of some happy things, you'll dream about them."

"Okay," he whispers.

"How about swimming at the beach?"

"With Daddy?"

"Sure . . . and ice cream cones and Christmas trees."

"Popcorn," Aidan adds sleepily.

"Popcorn . . . and . . . sitting by a fire on a cold day, and snowball fights and sleigh rides and rolling down a hill in the grass."

"And toys," he says.

"Toys." The game only seems to make Aidan more awake, so I try counting, talking about his dream catchers. I even lead him in a deep relaxation exercise I learned in college, but nothing seems to work.

"Why don't you come into my bed?" I say finally, and Aidan jumps up and grabs his blanket. "But you have to stay still and go to sleep," I warn.

Aidan runs into my room, thrilled. He dives into the rumpled sheets on my bed and I climb in next to him, sighing. After Aidan was born, I became a light sleeper, one ear permanently tuned to his gentle breath. It was as if our umbilical were reconnected at night, tugging at my unconscious, preventing me from sleep.

I take deep yoga breaths, imagining the air filling my stomach like a glass of water, and exhale slowly, the glass emptying itself. Aidan is rolling around, his feet kicking like electric beaters. "If you can't stop moving, you'll have to go back to your room," I say sternly. Finally, I drift off.

Aidan kicks me hard in the back of the leg.

"AIDAN!" Fuming, I flip onto my back. "GO TO SLEEEEP!" I scream, spinning onto my side again. I stare at the intricate shadows the window gate makes on the shade, trying to calm down. *I hate you, Dave. I hate you for leaving me with this.* I squeeze my body tight so Aidan can't tell that I am crying. I am having a tantrum inside, but the mattress is perfectly still, as if I am asleep.

"I miss Daddy," Aidan's tiny voice whimpers, and he is crying now, too. I roll onto my back, wiping my tears with my pajama sleeve, and turn toward him. I exhale loudly, my anger floating away with my breath. I steady my voice and soften it.

"Do you want to talk about it?" I ask. It is dark, but I can see his silhouette. The shape of his head has changed, his features becoming more defined, more like his father's.

He has dark rings under his eyes and he clutches his blanket when he asks, "Why can't Daddy come home?"

"Because he's dead. He's up in heaven."

"Can he see us?"

"I think so."

"Is a plane going to crash into our house?"

"No, honey. You are very safe here and we are surrounded by people who love us."

"Why did that man crash into the building?"

"I dunno. He was evil."

"Why is he evil?"

"Because he didn't care if he killed people."

"Were there kids killed, too?"

"Yes, I think so."

"How do you get evil?"

"When people don't love you enough."

"Is that evil man in heaven with Daddy?"

"No. I don't think so."

"Where do they go?"

"I don't know."

"I think heaven is red and has clouds for steps."

"Really? Nobody really knows what heaven looks like."

"I do," Aidan says with certainty. He talks this way for hours, his giant eyes staring up at the ceiling. And when he has purged himself of the thousands of confused thoughts swirling around his head, his body finally relaxes. I watch his eyelids begin to droop, his shoulders sink deeper into his pillow, the tiny twitch of his fingers as he begins to drift off. I stare at him long after he is asleep, because it is as beautiful as watching a sunset.

The phone startles me awake. "Marian. It's Lynn Tierney. Did I wake you?" I look at the clock. It is already past eight, and Lee Ielpi is picking me up in less than an hour. He is a retired firefighter who lost his son and has offered to show me around the site for the first time.

"No," I lie.

"We're going to have a meeting with the families at the Sheraton next week."

"Next week? I think it should be sooner," I tell her.

"That's the best we can do," she says. "There's just too much going on."

"Can't you just send the families a letter or something?"

"I dunno. We'll see."

I hang up and stare at my feet, half asleep. I don't want to wake Aidan or see the site, but I must.

Aidan looks terrible, squinting in the light, his eyes losing the battle and closing again.

I coax him into his clothes, brushing his hair, washing his face, and gently ease him out the door.

I sign Aidan in late, avoiding eye contact with the security guard. Has it really been two months since our confrontation? Is that possible? The days have passed so quickly, and yet the time without Dave has felt like a life sentence. Aidan slinks into the circle in his classroom, giving me a quick wave good-bye. The gesture is so simple, I want to cry. I should have just slept in, made him pancakes, act like the mom I used to be. I watch him sit with his friend Charlie and start talking. I feel my jaw tighten, the prelude to crying, but there is no time. I only have five minutes to get back to my house before Lee picks me up.

He arrives late in a huge SUV borrowed from the Great Neck Fire Department, where he volunteers. He is shorter than I imagined, with small brown eyes that look like coffee beans pressed into clay.

"Hello, young lady," he says, opening the door for me. He puts a hand on my back and guides me into the seat. He is in his late fifties, mostly bald, with dark Italian skin. I have heard that Lee is the unofficial mayor of Ground Zero, befriending the volunteers, showing families around the site, and searching for his twenty-nine-year-old son, Jonathan, from Squad 288. With twenty-six years on the job, nineteen with the elite Rescue 2, he is highly respected by the firefighters. Lee received twenty-four ribbons and three medals before retiring five years ago from a shoulder injury he received at a fire.

"I've been watching you, young lady," he begins, and I feel myself tighten. I wonder if he is from the old school of firefighting that finds outsiders threatening, particularly a woman with a lot to say. "You've got these guys scrambling down there," he says proudly. "I heard about you getting the firefighters back on."

"It wasn't all me," I say.

"Well, I heard you're a force to be reckoned with."

I smile, embarrassed, and we fall into an easy rapport, agreeing that the families need to be given better information.

He tells me stories about the Department of Design and Construction and then stops and looks at me. "They're completely rushing. We've chased down trucks with debris and made them dump it out so we can search it . . . You've seen the site, right?"

"I've been too scared to," I say finally and he nods, sighing.

"That's okay. Your husband was with Squad One, huh? How many did they lose?"

"Twelve . . . How many in your son's company?"

"Only nine. Can you believe I'm saying *only*? It's actually nineteen because they were right next to Haz Mat, and altogether we lost nineteen. I think that's the highest number."

"Yeah. It is."

I shake my head as we drive into the Brooklyn Battery Tunnel. I imagine Dave on the rig that day, driving through this mile-long tunnel, pulling his turnout gear on, his heart racing with the possibility of a "good fire." I have been told by a number of firefighters that they were seen running through the tunnel on foot, Lieutenant Esposito leading the charge, Dave right behind him. With the truck mired in traffic, the guys would have reached the site before the driver parked on West Street. Did he have second thoughts when he reached the other side and saw the people waving handkerchiefs from the windows? Did he think of me at the muffin shop, waiting for him to celebrate our anniversary? I wonder what he was thinking when it all came crashing down.

I remember what Dave told me on February 26, 1993. He'd just returned from the Twin Towers after the terrorist bombing.

"I'm surprised more people weren't killed. There were hardly any stairwells for all those people, and if I stretch my arms out like this"— he reached his muscular arms wide—"you can touch each wall. That's how narrow it was." He was on a roll, his outrage making him talk fast. "Those fireproof stairwells are a fallacy. Every time a door opens and closes, smoke is getting in, and what do you think people are doing during a fire?" I nodded. My friend Amy had called that day. She worked on the ninety-eighth floor. I put the TV on after she called and saw thousands of people evacuating the towers, their faces covered with handkerchiefs, soot, and smoke. "You know what really pisses me off?" Dave was ranting now.

"What?" I said distracted. "The radios didn't work. They *still* don't work. They give Motorola millions of dollars and these guys can't make a radio that works?" Dave took a deep breath. I could almost see the temperature rising under his skin. "I tell you one thing, you couldn't pay me enough money to work or live in a high-rise, because I tell you right now, if the ladder can't reach you, you're not safe."

"You okay?" Lee asks me, jarring me from my thoughts.

"Just tired. Were you here on the first day?" I ask.

"Of course," he says. "As soon as I heard, I grabbed my gear and came down. I don't have to tell you this, uh . . . it was like . . . some movie set. I took one look at that pile eight stories high and, I mean, I've been in Vietnam and a firefighter at a busy company, and I have never seen anything like this." He turns to me suddenly, his forehead wrinkled with concern. "You sure you want to hear this?"

I nod quickly. I feel like I am rubbernecking at the scene of an accident, leaning in to see what happened but secretly hoping everything is fine.

"Getting there earlier on, it was quite obvious that this was—" His jaw juts out, his mouth fishlike, as it turns downward. "The mind cannot comprehend the devastation. It was surreal. Like a Hollywood set. The worst horror movie ever made. My main objective was my son. I was there about twelve or fourteen hours when I realized—" He gulps and stops. "Sorry," he says, squeezing the corners of his eyes. The gesture reminds me of my father. "There was no way," Lee murmurs, and I cry with him.

Lee turns in to a large parking lot on Greenwich Street that is now serving as Fire Department parking. The smell is overwhelming, as horrible as the men have described. Lee pops the hatch on his truck and we walk to the back. It is filled with bunker gear, helmets, and breathing masks. He hands me a white construction helmet with an American flag and a pink rubber breathing mask. "You better wear that," he says. "OSHA has been on our backs about wearing them."

I slide the mask on, grateful for an escape from the smell. "Let me guess. The guys aren't wearing them," I say sarcastically, and Lee just grins broadly, leading me down to West Street.

"It's hard to. They get in the way when you're down there." He grabs my elbow.

The streets are wet with mud. Countless dump trucks and small Caterpillar tractors pass by. I feel my heart racing the way it used to right before I went onstage, *thumpety-thump, thumpety-thump, thumpety-thump.* Lee walks briskly. He seems to know everyone, waving and greeting countless rescue workers and volunteers as we pass. Some men he hugs, clapping them hard on the back. The sense of community and purpose touches me, and I want to hug and thank these strangers for giving up their own lives to help mine, but I say nothing, trying to keep at bay the nagging thought that I am about to witness the grave of over three thousand people and the place where Dave died.

We pass an enormous white tent, a blinding sight in the landscape of mud and gray.

"That's the Salvation Army tent," Lee announces. "We call it Taj Mahal."

"The volunteers here are unbelievable. They've come from all over the country, cooking us food, getting us supplies . . . they're unbelievable." Lee guides me along the periphery of the site. I maneuver carefully around huge mounds of mud and debris, dump trucks, and large pieces of steel. As I climb, I avert my eyes from "the pile" that stands next to me.

We turn left onto Liberty Street and duck into 10 & 10, a firehouse directly across from the site. The firehouse, now empty, serves as a respite for recovery workers and a storage space for supplies. Lee introduces me to a few firefighters standing in the house watch.

I follow Lee up a narrow staircase in the back to the fourth floor. I can hear my breath amplified through the rubber mask as we approach the top stair and step out onto the tar roof. My heartbeat is even louder now: *THUMPETY-THUMP, THUMPETY-THUMP, THUMPETY-THUMP.*

It is the oceanic size that strikes me first, that makes my head shake back and forth. I take off the mask and the smell hits me like grief itself, an acrid mix of burning rubber and something decaying. Two gigantic piles of twisted steel and cement stand in the center of a sixteen-acre crater where minuscule rescue workers climb through the debris.

"They're taking down these walls today," Lee says, pointing to the cathedral-like skeleton of the lobby windows that have become the icon of Ground Zero. "You see that big red crane? Before we had—I dunno—six or seven smaller grapplers, and then they brought this red thing in, and it's a problem, 'cause the guys can't see what the hell it's scooping up." I watch the machine remove a mass of debris, bent beams hanging from its jaws. I squint hard inside the scoop, as if I might actually recognize something familiar, spot a piece of Dave. "It's unbelievable how fast they're moving this stuff."

I scan the periphery of the site, where the fronts of office buildings have been torn off, exposing the sagging floors inside, like cut-open fruit. The buildings left intact are covered in a thick layer of dust, their windows broken, exposing the nothingness beyond.

"Look, I don't know what you can control here, but you can go tell these people here that the whole thing has got to slow down. I don't know who's rushing this along. My feeling is it's the DDC, and they don't know anything about rescue. They're a construction company, and they have got to stop. It's too fast and we need to get closer. You see this guy?" Lee points to a tiny firefighter in the distance. "That guy is a spotter, and he's supposed to be watching what's inside this grappler." There's a small yellow grappler about seventy-five feet away from the men. "Those guys can't see that! They've got binoculars and they're trying to spot stuff. I mean, c'mon!"

I nod, becoming determined, my mind racing: *I have to do something.*

Downstairs, Lee introduces me to Chief Joe Downey. He lost his father, Ray, one of the most respected chiefs in the department. He has a warm face, and I like that he is a Special Operations chief now, handling things at the site. Lee also introduces me to Marty McTigue, a firefighter who was severely injured at a fire at a Con Ed steam plant. He gives Lee a hearty hug. He is startling to look at, with no eyelashes or hair, his voice barely audible due to the scarring in his throat.

On the way back to the car, Lee tells me how Marty was searching for trapped workers when he was enveloped in a superheated cloud of steam. Lee stood by Marty's bedside as he underwent months of operations and therapy. "I didn't think he was going to make it," Lee says.

I remember Dave talking about the ravaging effects of burns and how disturbing it was to see someone injured from a fire. "We call them roasts, because they really look like that, all black on the outside, like charred meat." Dave had volunteered at the burn center, where makeup artists transformed him into a burn victim to help the nurses with their training. "These nurses are incredible," Dave said. "I would rather die, though, than suffer from burns."

A washing station has been set up at the entrance of the Taj Mahal, and I follow Lee through the process of scraping the mud off our shoes.

"This is a joke," he whispers. "You think spraying a little water on our shoes is going to make it less toxic in there?"

The tent is warm and well lit, with round tables full of rescue workers slumped over Styrofoam cups of coffee. A long buffet table stands along the left wall, and volunteers smile and wave at Lee as we pass. Everyone seems to know each other, and I force smiles and wave at the volunteers. Lee finds two of the fathers, Ed Sweeney and Paul Geidel. They are three of a larger, tight-knit group of dads, mostly retired firefighters, who spend countless hours here looking for their missing sons. I sit with them while Lee talks about how he instinctively reaches for his cell phone, wanting to call his son. He and Jonathan spoke almost every day. The other fathers nod and I think of Dave's own father, long dead, missing from Dave's life most of his life. Dave began researching his father's brother after he graduated from college, an Uncle Ed who died during World War II in the Battle of the Bulge. After college, we traveled to find his uncle's grave in Luxembourg, the Rhode Island of Europe. The battlefield was a few miles outside of Bastogne, on a bucolic patch of rolling hills that were now covered with thousands of white crosses and Jewish stars. The sheer number left me breathless. Dave took out a pencil and paper and made a rubbing of his uncle's cross, adding it to a fat collection of letters and photos he'd spent years sifting through. In June 2001, Dave even attended the 105th Airborne reunion to meet the paratroopers who served under his uncle. Dave's research stemmed from honoring history, his uncle, and the sacrifice he made, but deeper down, Dave hoped by getting to know the uncle he never met, he would gain insight into his own complicated relationship with his father. The day after he returned from the 105th Airborne reunion, Dave carefully opened a fraying photo album set with small sepia prints of his father, tanned and happy on an island in the Philippines during World War II. Dave looked closely at the shining eyes of his father, a Hollywood-handsome man grinning confidently back, his arms wrapped around an unknown friend.

"That was probably the best time of his life," Dave said, staring sadly at his father.

"They're a great bunch of guys," Lee tells me as he climbs into the driver's seat of his truck. "I worked with John Viggiano for twenty years. Do you know John? He's got two sons that are missing. One's a cop. One's a firefighter."

"Oh my God." My hand instinctively cups my mouth. "That's horrible."

Lee nods, staring at the road ahead. "We've got a lot of dads down there."

"What do you think about what I said . . . about you helping me with the organization?" Since my decision to start the organization, Joe has helped me with the paperwork to start a not-for-profit, establishing a website and speaking to the media. Since the retrieval issues began, it became clear to us all that the organization needed to be about informing the 9/11 families—all the families—about the retrieval. I have been trying to convince Lee to help me. "I am opening it up to all families—not just widows."

"I dunno. I'm not big on organizations," Lee says cautiously.

"I understand. I just need someone I can call and check in with. Someone who's at the site every day, who knows what's going on."

"Yeah, I'm okay with that." Lee slowly considers what he has said.

He drops me off in front of Aidan's school. I kiss him good-bye and promise to call him. I spot Jason in the playground waiting—where I should be.

"Hey, what are you doing here?" I ask Jason, who dodges screaming children to greet me.

"I wasn't sure if you'd be back in time," he says.

"Jason!" Aidan screams. He looks disheveled, papers and notebooks sticking out of his open backpack.

"Take off your backpack before you lose something," Jason says, helping him. "He is such a mess!" We smile, watching Aidan tear through the playground as if someone pressed a release button. "I just left your house. You have so many messages, I am becoming phono-phobic."

"No kidding."

"I checked some of them. One of them was from the firehouse. There's this Royal Caribbean cruise that sounds kind of cool. I called, just to see."

"What'd they say?"

"Well, it was really funny, because I asked this lady, 'Where is it going?' Because I am thinking a tan, some beach." Jason changes his voice to sound like a bored secretary. " 'Nowhere.' So I say, 'What do you mean? It must go somewhere. Where does it go?' And she says, 'Nowhere. That's what it's called, A Cruise to Nowhere,' and I'm thinking that's the perfect name for a bunch of grieving families! And so I finally ask, because you need passports to get there, 'Where exactly is nowhere?' " Jason pauses, then resumes his bored secretary voice. " 'I dunno. You float out onto the ocean and then you come back. It's to nowhere.' "

"So," I say, laughing, "do you want to go nowhere?"

"Honey, nowhere's better than here," Jason says without missing a beat.

17

Cruise to Nowhere

Mike Esposito could have been a comedian, but he loved being a fire-fighter. All of the firefighters, especially Dave, respected his leadership as a lieutenant at Squad.

The Columns Funeral Parlor, on Hylan Boulevard in Staten Island, has been designed to look like a Georgian mansion. The home is packed with firefighters, friends, and family spilling onto the street. I press myself into the hot wake room. Timmy Rogers spots me and heads over.

"How are you doing?" he asks, kissing me on the cheek.

"I hate that question," I mutter, half joking. "Any word from the site?"

He shrugs, looking away.

"What?" I prompt, noticing how uncomfortable he has suddenly become.

"Ahh, nothing. How's your organization coming?"

Since my meeting with the mayor, I haven't stopped taking phone calls and meetings with Joe to create a membership form and a mission statement. I am overwhelmed by the response from the families. Their desperate calls flood the line as I try to juggle my time between meetings, picking up Aidan, and attending funerals.

"Okay. We met with the medical examiners' office today. I learned a lot about DNA and how hard it's been for them to test everything.

They're amazing guys. They're totally overworked and they're trying to get families to give better samples. Some families haven't even given anything. Can you believe that?"

"Yeah, I can." Timmy is staring at his shoes, the polish faded a bit on the tips.

"What's the matter?"

"Nothing."

"Timmay!" I joke. "C'mon, tell me."

"I'm not supposed to."

"What?"

"Naw. You don't want to know."

"Yes, I do."

"Nobody knows this," Timmy says, lowering his voice to a whisper. "We found Mike a few days ago."

"That's great!" I say. "Then Denise—"

"No. He was in really bad shape. We only know it was him because of the jacket and the list of guys working that was in his pocket. Other than that—it might take a while to confirm DNA, so we have to keep it quiet."

"You can't tell her?"

"Not until we get a positive ID." His mustache twists and I shake my head, wondering if Dave is somewhere close behind Mike, and if he will be recognizable. It is strange how my hopes have shifted from hoping Dave is alive, to hoping he will be found, to hoping he won't be found in too many pieces. I sigh, slowly picturing Mike's jacket, black and flat, like the Wicked Witch after she has melted away.

Timmy leads me by the elbow to the front of the line where Denise stoically greets the endless onslaught of well-wishers.

"Marian!" she exclaims, grabbing me into a tight hug, her glasses pressing against my face. "I'm going to kill these people," she whispers into my ear.

"Have you noticed the bad breath yet?" I whisper.

"Oh my God! I think everyone ate crap for dinner!" she teases, and I stifle a loud laugh as we release our embrace. I walk outside into the parking lot for some air, looking down at the wake card. It is a bookmark and, on top, Mike is wearing his class A lieutenant's cap, his dimples creasing like parentheses around his face, his glasses dimming the devilish glint in his eyes.

Mike's funeral is held at the same church as Eddie D'Atri's. All the wakes and funerals are beginning to blend together, like the days. More widows than I have ever seen are pressed against the front doors of the church. Tall speakers are broadcasting the chamber music being played inside. I greet Tim's wife, Tara Stackpole, Joanne Modaferri, and the wives from Rescue 5, where Michael Esposito used to work.

I sit with the widows from Squad, our patches pinned to our black jackets. From my seat, I have a perfect view of Denise, who sits regally in the front of the church, three of Mike's brothers behind her. They are darker and bigger than Mike was, with dark shiny suits and gelled hair. The only thing similar is their eyes, big, brown, and sincere as a Labrador's. Denise is flanked by her two teenage sons, Andrew and Mike Jr. Andrew, the eldest, has the fine features of his parents and thick spiked hair. Mike Jr. is softer-looking, with blond hair falling straight around his face.

In the center of the church, the Squad 1 firefighters sit gravely, hair pressed down from their uniform hats. Theresa sits next to me, and the other widows and wives stretch across the long pew. I spot my mother-in-law a few rows back, her chin quivering, and Dennis, as always, sitting stiffly next to her. I give a small wave hello and turn around when the music begins. It is a screechy violin to the side of the altar nearest to where we are sitting.

"Oh my God," Theresa whispers between her teeth as a large woman resembling Tammy Faye Bakker begins to belt "The Wind Beneath My Wings." I try to stifle a laugh.

"Don't start," Theresa says, smiling, and I try to ignore the singing. Anything can strike me funny, and once it does, I am lost, every muscle struggling to keep my laughter under control.

After the woman stops singing, Mike's brother Frank reads a eulogy he wrote. He is a large man, and it is painful to see him choke on his words, tears dripping onto his paper. Everyone in the congregation is silent, crying softly. Mike's brother Sal is next, continuing the chain of tears that seems to stretch on for hours. Everyone whimpers softly, except for Michael's family, who sit behind Denise wailing loudly. Denise tightens her mouth, her arms wrapped protectively around her boys. The wailing continues, the relatives clutching each other, their faces contorted. I feel as if I am no longer in a church but watching a play, the actors' emotions dramatic and huge. The wailing becomes so loud, it begins to drown out the eulogy. They are shaking their heads, sobbing to the skies.

"Knock it off!" Denise says sharply, stopping the relatives short. She leans forward in her seat to listen to Sal. I press my mouth together to stifle the laughter that traps itself in my mouth.

"Oh my God. I love Denise," I whisper to Theresa, who is suppressing a laugh herself. I take a few deep breaths to calm myself. Then firefighter John Kiernan is eulogizing Mike. He describes him as a combination of Peter Pan and Superman, and now everyone is laughing, because anyone who knew Michael Esposito knows this is true.

The youngest brother, Jojo, steps up to the altar next. He is even more distraught than Sal, crying freely in between paragraphs, pinching his eyes to stop the tears. For me, he is the most difficult to watch. In the middle of the eulogy he breaks off abruptly, consumed by his grief. I watch Denise leaning forward in her pew, her serene face concerned. She slowly stands up and walks up to Jojo, wrapping her delicate arm around his broad back. Denise's arm is so small, like a branch blown onto a fence, but she is holding the fence up and everyone knows it. Jojo collects himself and begins to read while Denise quietly tiptoes back to her seat.

I am proud Denise has chosen to eulogize Mike. She stands behind the microphone, her skin radiant, her small eyes shimmering with the same glint as Michael's. I know their love, like Dave's and mine, was unique and special, and the eulogy reflects on their life together, the way Mike made her laugh, gave her strength, kept his boys in his heart. As she reads, I can see Dave's face next to Mike's and they are laughing like two little boys. The image is so clear and intense it frightens me. I blink hard; am I so overwrought that I am seeing things? I close my eyes, trying hard to put the image away, but there they are again: Mike's and Dave's faces smiling beautifically together, as if they are right in front of me.

* * *

The following morning, I stand in the warm sun waiting for the car from Fox News. I listen to the familiar sound of wheels hitting the sewer grate. I am trying to squeeze in a few interviews before I leave for the Cruise to Nowhere this evening. I don't seem to ever get out from under the pile of messages from families, press, and organizations around the country wanting to help. I have begun to joke with my friends that I run an unorganization and that overwhelmed has become a noun.

Aidan taps in the window and pancakes his nose against the glass. I wave and smile, but his face is sad.

"Mommy, don't go!" he yells when I notice a sleek black Town Car gliding into view.

"I'll see you in a little bit, buddy," I say.

"I love you!" he yells frantically from the window. I wave to the driver and turn back to Aidan, but he is already gone.

After my interviews, firefighter Joe Miccio and I walk to 8th Avenue and find a restaurant for lunch. I usually don't trust places that are empty at lunch, but today it is perfect. We sit in a dark booth toward the back and I order a salad. Joe orders a cheeseburger. He looks tired today, the big circles under his eyes making him look like a football player.

"You did great today," Joe says, taking a sip of his seltzer. It is only 12:00 P.M. and I have already done four interviews. In the interviews, I made impassioned pleas for a dignified recovery, for the site to slow down, and for all the firefighters to be reinstated there. When I was finished, I was surprised to see Joe crying.

"Dave would have been proud of you," Joe said, wiping his eyes with a tissue.

I had almost forgotten that Joe had met Dave a few times when he briefly dated my sister. Joe was in a bar in an airport in Portland, Maine, when he spotted my sister and her friend. Joe came to a few of my sister's gigs, where he met Dave, drank beers, and talked about firefighting. One night, when we were playing at the Delmonico, Joe abruptly stood up and stormed out, never to be heard from again. It wasn't until after 9/11 that Joe confessed he had seen my sister kissing another man. I quickly realized he had mistaken Leah for our friend Dori. With the same dark hair and white skin, Dori was often mistaken for Leah, and that evening she had brought her new boyfriend.

During lunch, Joe and I finish the copy for a membership form to hand out at the family meeting on Monday. We write:

> *United in Love and Dignity—*
> *We are an information source for families, BY families. United by our deep loss, we can address the numerous issues facing us with strength and dignity. We strive to inform ALL September 11th families about resources, donations, tributes, identification, and memorials that will honor our loved ones. By uniting and supporting each other, we have become a powerful voice for our loved ones.*

And when we are finished, I meet Jason, Mila, and Aidan to go on the Cruise to Nowhere. The Royal Caribbean Cruise Line has allowed all rescue workers and up to five guests to attend the weekend cruise, and I am grateful to turn off the phone, to escape the mayhem, even for just a night. My parents will join us on the pier at 4 P.M. We stand in a long line of rescue workers and families waiting to get on the boat. We've already spent two hours parking our car and taking a bus to the pier. The tension is thick and Jason is trying to lighten the mood by making me laugh. "It looks like I'm going to be the only gay man on the boat," he says.

"No, there's the cast of the Ice Capades," I tell him, reading the brochure.

After meeting my parents and providing passports and IDs, we pull our luggage up a long steep plank onto the ship. We cross a grandiose lobby to brass elevators that lead us to the sixth floor. A blue-carpeted corridor runs the length of the ship, and we find our rooms at the far end, the equivalent of three city blocks. Our room is small but comfortable, with a queen-size bed and an oblong window. I slide it open, filling the room with the smell of saltwater, and watch the end of a sunset, deep oranges and purples dimming into a dark blue night sky.

"Your mailbox is completely full," the recording on my cell phone says as Aidan jumps on the bed. "Please discard any unnecessary messages." Aidan falls back, his legs flying up in the air. "You have thirty-six new messages and fourteen saved messages." I watch him jump, and wonder if I have made a huge mistake, starting an organization in the wake of our suffering. I know I want to fight to bring Dave home, but am I sacrificing too much at our son's expense? If I am truly honest with myself, maybe I have chosen to stay so busy to avoid the sad reality that it is just Aidan and me now. Being alone with Aidan reminds me of my lonely future, and the gaping hole left by the loss of Dave. I turn off my cell phone and dive for Aidan's belly, burying my nose in his stomach. He giggles and pushes my face away.

"Aidan! Look at the sunset," I call. He stops and looks out of the window. *WHAM!* I hit him with a pillow, and he falls onto the bed, laughing hysterically. He hurls pillows in my direction and I duck and dive, catching the pillows and throwing them back until I collapse on the bed, winded and tired but glad to be "nowhere" with Aidan.

For the formal dinner in the dining room that evening, I put on a black velvet dress that Dave bought me for Valentine's Day last year. I feel overdressed when Mila knocks on my door wearing a simple gray suit with a black silk shell. Her beauty has always been uncomplicated by makeup, her straight, dirty blond hair tucked neatly behind her ears. Her posture is slightly stooped, more from playing guitar than from the deep insecurity that dominated her in college when we first met. I am glad she lives so close to me in Park Slope and that our friendship has survived so much. Jason sidles up behind her, looking dapper in a designer suit and silk tie.

"You look so handsome!" I say, remembering how Dave always called Jason when he needed help picking out a tie or a suit.

The dining room is three mammoth floors, with crystal chandeliers like exploded fireworks in the center. A five-piece band plays on the landing of a large spiral staircase. A tuxedoed host leads our group to a round table. We take our seats, swiveling to look at the ornate carpet, the elaborate bouquets, the endless tables full of firefighters in their class A uniforms.

"Oh my God." Jason giggles as the band plays a jazzy version of "My Way." "I slept with the singer!"

"Isn't that a song?" I joke, craning my neck to see.

My mom chuckles and my father thumb-wrestles with Aidan. Waiters arrive with delectable food stacked high on large white plates.

"The food is delicious," my mother says, nibbling a piece of her rack of lamb. I poke my fork in the orange flesh of my salmon, thin asparagus flanking each side. My taste buds disappear from one minute to the next. Tonight they are missing.

As they clear our plates, I watch a firefighter father bouncing his son in his lap. His face is chiseled like Dave's, with a well-defined chin and wide eyes. The boy, no more than two, throws his head back, giggling, his straight blond hair dividing like curtains on his forehead. I am overcome with grief that seems to erupt from the corners of my jaw. Our table quiets as I sit and cry, struggling to reel my sadness back in. Jason slides over to rub my back, and I notice that he is crying, too. I squeeze his hand, loving him for understanding me as he does.

"Are you crying, Mommy?" Aidan demands, writhing in my mother's lap.

"Mommy's sad," my mother says softly.

The waiter arrives with festive-looking desserts, including an ice cream parfait for Aidan, topped off with cookies.

"Oooh, look what you got," Mila exclaims with forced cheerfulness.

Aidan takes a cookie out of the bowl and hands it to me. "Here, Mama," he says. "This will make you happy."

"You're so sweet." I gulp back my tears as I take the cookie from him.

"You don't have to take care of Mommy. Mommy takes care of you," my mother whispers, and I nod in agreement.

"No, Nonna," Aidan scolds. "Mommy and I take care of *each other*." He looks over to me and scans the table, and everyone promptly burst into tears. "Oh, man!" He rolls his eyes as our tears turn to laughter, and my father lovingly tousles his hair.

A number of other Squad families are on the cruise, too, and we meet them at a small bar on the top deck. I feel relaxed for the first time in weeks, and I sigh, taking in the unusual conglomeration of friends. Mila is in the corner, teaching Tony Edwards's daughters chords on a small piano. Aidan runs full speed around the room with Huey's three hyperactive boys. Dennis Farrell sits in the middle of the room with his wife, Donna, talking to Martha, who carries Patrick while her other two run around the room. My parents are at the casino and Jason is getting a massage.

A crowd has gathered outside on the deck, staring at the skyline as we cruise down the West Side of Manhattan. I pull my sweater tightly around me and step outside, the brisk air making my eyes water. We float past Ground Zero, the blinding floodlights glowing into the sky, as a firefighter bagpiper plays "Amazing Grace," the eerie notes drifting out and over the harbor. We are all silent and solemn again, remembering why we are all here tonight.

On Sunday morning, we say good-bye to my parents, and Mila, Aidan, Jason, and I wait for the bus to take us back to the parking lot. Two crammed buses pass and I sigh when the third one is full.

"Well, we're back from Nowhere going Nowhere," I say, annoyed.

The 57th Street parking lot is a mass of confusion, families lined up impatiently as two parking attendants run back and forth retrieving cars. I shift from one foot to the other, trying to keep warm, and listen to the transistor radio that sits in the parking lot booth. *"All news all the time. You give us twenty-two minutes, we'll give you the world."* I peel Aidan a banana I swiped from the breakfast buffet as he sits on my luggage playing with two green army men. *"Terrorism has not been ruled out as a flight bound for the Dominican Republic crashes over a populated neighborhood in Queens."* The crowd of fire families abruptly stops talking and turns to the radio. *"Hundreds of firefighters and rescue teams are struggling to extinguish the blaze. Witnesses say the plane was making its ascent over Far Rockaway when an engine appears to have fallen off the plane before losing control and plummeting into the small beach community still reeling from the loss of so many of its firefighters and police on September eleventh."*

A wave of panic passes through the crowd as families begin to scream, rushing forward to find out more information. "My mother is watching my kids in Rockaway!" a woman screams. "My house! I gotta get home!" another one yells. Aidan is standing up now, watching the chaos. Firefighters pace up and down the street, trying to contact people on their cell phones. Another woman I recognize is crying softly into her hands. "My kids are in school right there!" I bite my lip hard, trying to remember all the firefighters I know who live in Rockaway. I feel my own heart speeding up as I dial the firehouse. There is no answer.

Another busload of families from the ship arrives and a new wave of panic begins.

"What's happening? Why is everyone crying?" Aidan keeps asking, but I shush him to hear the parking attendant announce that all bridges and tunnels have been closed until further notice.

"Let's get him out of here," I tell Mila and Jason. I grab Aidan's hand and begin walking up to 9th Avenue, to the subway and away from the crowd.

When we surface from the subway station in Brooklyn, I dial the firehouse again.

"Squad One," a woman's voice says.

"Kathleen? What are you doing there?" I ask Huey's wife.

"We couldn't get across the Verrazano so we came over here with the kids . . . Donna's here and the guys went over to Rockaway to help with the fire."

"Is everyone okay?"

"I dunno. The plane was near George's house. We've been trying to call over there, but there's no answer." Dave loved George Ebert, a tall, lanky firefighter with the prominent brow of a boxer and the wide-open face of a little boy. He was in Dave's study group at the firehouse, and Dave was sad to see George go when he was promoted before him.

"We'll let you know if we hear anything," Kathleen promises, and I hang up just as we enter my apartment.

It's been completely transformed.

At first it feels as if I have stepped into the wrong home, until I recognize Aidan's art, hanging with clothespins on wires running the length of the hall, which has been painted a cranberry red. In between his drawings are blown-up photos of Dave, Aidan, and me in matted frames. I remember picking this color at Libby's house a few weeks ago.

"Everything's different!" Aidan yells. Our living room has been redecorated with wicker furniture, mushroom-colored walls, and new track lighting.

"I can't believe this." I sink into the couch, looking around.

"Do you like it?" Jason asks, his black eyebrows raised and expectant.

"It's incredible! This is . . ."

"Libby wanted you to have a fresh start."

"Libby did all of this?"

"Libby and Michael, and then John, Leah, Caren, Bates, Lori, and Maureen and Richard painted. Dennis Fontana redid the kitchen floor. I'm not sure. Do you hate it?"

"No! I'm very touched. I just have to get used to it."

Part of me is frightened, as if I have stepped through a looking glass where nothing will be as it was. The other half of me is relieved to have my things organized for the first time. I rotate my head back and forth, trying to take in the differences. My mother's large oil painting has been replaced with several small framed drawings I bought in Paris when I was eighteen. The blue glass coffee table Dave and I found downtown at a flea market has been swapped for a large wicker coffee table on wheels. I pull out one of its giant drawers to find Aidan's videos alphabetized in neat rows.

"Wow, I really can't belive this!" I say, shaking my head.

"It's organized and you *need* organized," Jason teases. Since Dave died, my mess has become bigger than ever before. Dave nicknamed me "Stop It and Drop It" for the way I entered a room, and now my chaos feels impossible to rein in, like the jumbled contents of my brain have spilled out into piles of clothes, papers, and books. I would sit embarrassed as my girlfriends complained about their sloppy husbands, expecting me to commiserate, but it was Dave who nodded knowingly, pointed in my direction. "Believe me, I know what you mean." I lay back on the couch, taking everything in until, like an overstimulated toddler, I fall asleep.

I wake with a start, remembering that tonight is the family meeting at the Sheraton Hotel that Lynn Tierney planned with the mayor. George Ebert had left a message that he and his family were fine, though the nose of the plane landed in their backyard. I call Lynn in a panic. Surely after today's traumatic events, the meeting will be canceled. When she answers her cell phone, I can hear sirens in the background. She is still in Rockaway at the crash site and she sounds exhausted, but the meeting will happen as planned. "There's no other time to do it," she says.

I sit at the edge of the couch, staring at the same spot until it blurs. Elvis rubs against my leg. I hear the door open and close; it is Jason and Aidan returning from wherever they went to let me nap. I don't even remember falling asleep, only the strange feeling of sinking into the couch as if I were disappearing into its worn cushions. I heave myself up to stand and ask Jason to watch Aidan so I can attend the meeting at the Sheraton and then pick up my car at the lot. He is as surprised as I was that it is still happening. "Those families are going to freak," he says, sitting on the floor to play with Aidan. I force myself to sit at the computer and write a speech about the organization for tonight, battling a weariness that refuses to leave.

Later, at the Sheraton, a simple carpeted room has been set with rows of folding chairs in front of a large blue dais. Joe Miccio greets me in the hall, and I follow him to a table in the back of the room where he has set up the stacks of membership forms we worked on last Friday. I am surprised by how many people have shown up tonight, despite the plane crash, though I can't help but wonder how many more have chosen to stay home. Families begin to mill around, asking questions. I meet Arlene Beyer, a young widow with compassionate eyes. She lost her husband from Engine 6. She introduces me to Donna Angelini, who lost both her husband *and* her father-in-law.

When the meeting is about to start, I sit in an aisle seat toward the front and feel a tap from behind me. I turn to see Lee Ielpi, his face stretched into a warm smile. He introduces me to his wife, Ann, a square-faced woman with short layered hair and small blue eyes, deep and full of anguish.

The mayor enters flanked by Lynn Tierney and Tom Von Essen. I recognize the bodyguards from the other night standing in the back. The mayor introduces Mike Burton from the Department of Design and Construction, a stern, mustached man with receding hair and a slight smirk. Then he introduces Tom Von Essen, Lynn Tierney, Dr. Kelly from the Fire Department Counseling Services, Dr. Hirsch from the medical examiner's office, and Maureen Casey from the Police Department.

The mayor apologizes about being late, then talks about the site. The speech is similar to one he gave to our group of widows a few weeks ago, except he speaks more softly now. I surmise he is either tired from today's crash, or perhaps he can see the families' faces, sad and angry, their nerves as visible as exposed wires. He tells us that everyone on the dais will say a few words about the site and there will be a question-and-answer session at the end.

"What is the most difficult to understand," he begins carefully, "as hard as it is . . . is that there are no whole bodies being found at this point, that they have been pulverized."

A short woman with blond hair jumps up, her blue eyes flashing.

"With all due respect, Mr. Mayor," she bellows, "my friend's husband was found intact yesterday. How dare you stand up there and tell me there are no whole bodies. They could see the dimple on his left cheek!"

"If you would just let me finish," the mayor says, but it is too late. All hell breaks loose. Hands shoot up like spears, and Dr. Hirsch stands tentatively, his voice weak. He is a skeletal-looking man with a long sallow face and tired eyes. Mayor Giuliani tries to settle the crowd, but most are standing now, too angry to sit.

"We are not saying that there are no whole bodies," Dr. Hirsch tries. "We are saying that we do not expect to find many whole bodies, since a majority of the samples we are receiving have been vaporized."

"You're lying!" another woman yells, and a murmur rumbles through the families.

"You look like a corpse yourself!" someone else shouts out.

"C'mon, people," the mayor pleads. "Calling people names is not going to help. Let's be respectful, and if you can just hold your questions until the end."

Another woman is standing now, her voice shaking with anger. "Are you going to tell my twin daughters, Mr. Mayor— Are you going to come to their birthday party tomorrow and tell my twin two-year-olds that their *father has been vaporized*?"

"Why are you in such a rush to clean the site up?" another shouts.

"I can't answer your questions if we're all going to talk at—"

"There are whole bodies being found at the dump—"

"That is simply not tru—"

"This is a scoop and dump operation!" a man with a brogue shouts.

The mayor tries to speak, but the room is in chaos. I can feel my heart beating faster. I am frozen, trying to handle emotions that are too big for the room to contain.

"We brought Dr. Hirsch from the medical examiner's office up here to answer any of your questions about the identification process."

The man with the brogue is standing up again. "We *demand* to know, Mr. Mayor: Did they find any large human remains at Fresh Kill?" The man pushes his glasses up his nose, his large face red.

Dr. Hirsch looks cornered, his small eyes wide like those of a trapped animal. "There was a woman's body found," he concedes. The crowd is grumbling. Giuliani's face drops and he turns to face Dr. Hirsch.

"Wipe that smirk off your face. This is not funny! You think this is funny?" A woman is standing, pointing at Mike Burton, who does indeed look like he is smiling.

"I'm not smirking," he exclaims.

Lynn locks eyes with me and I signal her that I would like to speak. The crowd turns in my direction as I stand. My hand is shaking as I clear my throat. I can feel a bead of sweat trickle and slide down my face. It feels like a tear, but it's not. The paper in my hand is shaking.

"My name is Marian Fontana. My husband, Dave, is among the twelve missing firefighters from Squad One in Brooklyn. Like many of you, I have been frustrated by the lack of information available regarding the retrieval efforts at Ground Zero. In the early days of the operations, I relied on daily reports from the firefighters as they returned dusty and exhausted from the pile. The recent decision to cut back firefighters working on the site not only made it difficult to get information, but took away the comfort of knowing that my husband's remains would be treated with the dignity and respect he deserves. As I attend funerals, I have spoken with hundreds of family members and firefighters who feel as I do. I found a group in Staten Island that had already begun to speak out. With the help of Joe Miccio, a firefighter assigned to Ground Zero, and Mike Stackpole, who lost his brother, Tim, in the collapse, the Widows and Victims' Families Association was formed. Our immediate goal is to protect the sanctity of the World Trade Center and to ensure the dignified recovery of our loved ones' remains.

"In the past, our nation has gone to extraordinary lengths to recover the remains of its citizens, civilian or military. New York City firefighters have the expertise to see this mission is done in a safe and reverent manner. Mayor Giuliani, Commissioner Von Essen, and Deputy Commissioner Tierney met with the members of our organization last week and gave us, for the first time, the opportunity to voice our concerns. I appreciate their decision to put fifty firefighters back on the site, but there is still work to do. Memorial services with empty coffins do not provide the closure we need. It is my hope that we continue to communicate with the mayor's office now and in the future to address the needs of the victims' families as they arise.

"I would like to thank the International Firefighters Association for their generous seed money," I say, then thank a few people by name. "Finally, I think I speak for all of us when I thank the firefighters whose tireless efforts to retrieve our loved ones have touched us all. Their peaceful protest was held for the same reasons you are all here tonight. Together, we will ensure that Ground Zero is handled as hallowed ground and help each other begin to heal. Please know that this organization is in its infancy and we need your help. We will be in the lobby with membership forms and to answer any questions you may have. We are working on a website to give you up-to-date information about the site, a chat room to discuss issues, and e-mail communication. Thank you for your support, and thank you, Mayor, for allowing me to speak here tonight."

The room is silent—only for a few seconds, but it feels like a lifetime. I keep my head down to stave off the emotion I feel from the applause that has erupted, the pat on the back from Lee, Joe squeezing my hand.

When the room quiets again, the mayor is at the podium again, and Joe and I walk into the lobby that feels like cool air on a hot night.

*   *   *

Aidan is wearing his Scream mask from Halloween to therapy today. We head up to 7th Avenue and turn the corner, dominated by high school students loitering and talking in loud groups.

A girl with cornrows pushing a stroller stomps her feet and points at Aidan. "*Yo!* You scared me!" I imagine myself punching her in the face, blood trickling from her nose. "Oooh!" All her friends scream and I squat, lifting my arms into fighting position like I am Bruce Lee. I fell them all easily, flipping them one by one until they are all writhing on the sidewalk, moaning quietly as I turn down 5th Street.

We ring Mary's bell and listen for her footsteps.

"Oh, my," Mary exclaims, opening the gate. "You look scary!"

Inside, Aidan walks immediately to an open closet where toys are stacked in plastic boxes. He chooses a Playmobil set of a doctor's office and hospital room and dumps the tiny pieces on the floor.

Mary watches Aidan as he sets up a tiny hospital bed with a tiny woman stretched on the bed. A doctor wearing a hospital gown and mask stands next to her.

"Is she hurt?" Mary asks after a few minutes.

"No. She's having a baby." Aidan arranges a father on the other side of the mother.

"Oh."

"The baby's coming out of the mommy," Aidan says, making an even tinier figure appear from under the blanket. "My daddy said he was going to give me a brother."

Mary considers this. "Oh. You must be very disappointed."

Aidan shrugs. "My family is too small." I feel my heart take the familiar elevator ride down into a sadness that I seem to visit often. I don't want to cry in front of him, though, and so I turn my head away, biting my lip.

"Well, families come in all sizes, but that is sad you won't have a little brother right now."

As quickly as a breeze, Aidan is done with this conversation and ready to move to the next.

* * *

Since I listed my telephone number on the flyers for the organization, calls begin early. I try to answer panicked questions from family members and quell rumors about seagulls flying off with body parts from Fresh Kills. One of the calls is from Jack Lynch, the Irishman from the meeting at the Sheraton last week. His brogue is thick and commanding. "I'll be honest witcha. I don't like what I'm seeing down there. I don't trust that they are doing the right thing at the site. I like what you said at the meeting the other night, and I've organized a bunch of families from the Bronx to join your group." His voice softens and cracks when he talks about his son Michael, a firefighter who was about to be married in October. Michael was one of ten children who grew up in the Bronx, where Jack was a bus engineer and where he still lives with his wife, Kathleen. "I'll tell you what," he says, "I know I probably won't get Michael back." He pauses for a moment. "But if there is something to get, I want it."

The more calls I receive, the more issues arise. The fiancées of firefighters have received no money. A fund has been set up in Washington to prevent the families from suing the city, the government, and the airlines, but the requirements seem unfair. The air quality at Ground Zero has worsened, and firefighters are getting sick. The Red Cross has been losing files. The fires are still burning at Ground Zero. The firefighters have begun to argue with the police. There are not enough supplies for rescue workers. There is not enough staff at Fresh Kills. The medical examiner's office is not getting adequate DNA samples. The families want a place at the site for the holidays. While I make lists and return calls and my planet spins so fast I can barely think, the thought of Thanksgiving, my first real family holiday without Dave, looms.

* * *

I arrive at the CNN studios early in the afternoon and make my way to the twenty-second floor. This will be my third appearance, and I have learned to arrive with no makeup on. I have even befriended the makeup woman, Margaret. A confessional intimacy comes with sitting in a black swivel chair and having someone dot orange pancake makeup on your face. Margaret told me about her mother dying recently after a long illness; I told her about Dave. I peek in the tiny room where Margaret always is, but tonight the room is empty.

"Do you know where the makeup person is?" I ask a serious-looking woman with thick bangs and shoulder-length hair.

"No. I heard them saying she didn't come in or something." The woman has a thick Queens accent and striking clear blue eyes exaggerated by thick blue liner and a matching suit.

"Oh, no. I can't believe I have to go on national TV with no makeup on." I touch my dry skin, the bags under my eyes, and start to panic. "Do you have anything?"

"I did mine at home," the woman says with no inflection. I sit down and dig through my purse. There is half a bagel, a notepad, business cards, wallet, Chapstick, and lipstick that is too red.

"You're Marian, right?" the woman asks me, her face round and sad.

"Yes."

"I'm Jennie. Jennie Farrell. I lost my brother James."

"Oh, I'm so sorry."

"I saw you at the Sheraton. I like what you said."

"Oh, thank you. What company did your brother work for?"

"He wasn't a firefighter. He was an engineer. We snuck into the meeting," she says without apology. "I've started a group called Give Your Voice, for the civilians who are not getting any information."

"Well, maybe we can exchange numbers. I'd be happy to share anything I know."

"That would be great because it's been very hard to find out things." Her face suddenly softens and she looks like she is going to cry. "This has been very hard."

"I know," I say. "Do you know what they're going to ask us?"

"Well, I'm hoping they ask us about the retrieval, but I know they're going to ask about some charities as well."

I shift in my seat miserably. Not only do I have to go on national television with no makeup, but I have to talk about money, something I have no interest in and know little about. It reminds me of the dreams I've had before my performances, where I am naked, onstage, in the wrong place on the wrong day, and I don't know my lines.

The intern seats us in a camera room I have been in before with Martha. It is a small booth with two chairs and two cameras that is always cold. Jennie and I sit in awkward silence.

We make small talk. I find out Jennie is one of five and she was closest to James, the youngest. We watch the small TV on the bottom of the camera. A woman is running, smiling through a field. The advertisement is for an antidepressant called Selexa. I try to recall when all the commercials became about medication. It seemed to happen overnight, when no one was looking—now the whole country seems to have depression, diabetes, allergies, and erectile dysfunction.

"Today we have with us two family members who lost loved ones on September eleventh and used their grief to promote change. Marian Fontana, president of the 9/11 Widows and Victims' Families Association and Jennie Farrell, founder of Give Your Voice. Thank you both for being here." Jennie and I are projected onto the news program in two small rectangles behind a handsome newscaster.

"Let's start with you, Marian. Your husband was a firefighter."

"Yes, he was working at Squad One in our neighborhood of Park Slope, and he is one of twelve firefighters that were killed."

"And what motivated you to start this organization?"

"Well, it began with the Fire Department trying to close my husband's firehouse two weeks after the eleventh, and I became active in trying to keep it open, and now my organization has very quickly snowballed into something much larger. Right now our biggest focus is to ensure that there is a dignified and reverent recovery at Ground Zero."

"Your husband has not been found."

"No," I say, my voice barely audible.

"And, Jennie Farrell, you lost your brother?"

"Yes. My beautiful brother, James Cartier, was a union electrician who was working in Tower Two when the planes hit. At that point he called my sister Michelle, who was working in Tower One, and told her to get out of the building and meet him at the Concourse. So my sister went down to the lobby where, in all the chaos, she remarkably bumped into my other brother John who worked in the area as well. They tried to find my brother James, but he never came out."

"I'm so sorry."

"Since then we have had a very difficult time getting information or even anyone to talk to us about what is happening down at the site. The families—the civilian families—are simply not getting any information, and so my brother Michael and I started Give Your Voice to speak for my brother and all the innocent people whose voices were silenced when they were brutally murdered on that day."

"There is a lot of talk about the charitable organizations not getting funds to the families. Have either of you heard of that happening, and are you dealing with this issue at all?"

"We have had a lot of families who are reeling from this loss and are unable to go through the paperwork required to receive these donations," Jennie says. The reporter asks me about money and how much the firefighter families are getting. I suddenly am racked with guilt that I am receiving too much money and the civilians are not getting enough and that this is somehow my fault. *I didn't ask for it!* I want to yell in my defense, but I briefly explain that firefighters have always had a dangerous job and so a system is already in place to help the families. I add that our organization is not really involved in the allocation of money, but in retrieval.

"That went well, I thought," I lie to Jennie, reaching under my shirt to take off my mike when it is all over.

"I guess so. It's never enough time," she replies. "I had a lot more to say."

18

Giving Thanks

I am speeding through New Jersey at 70 miles per hour, with Leah clutching the dashboard.

"You're scaring me," she says. She has always been a nervous passenger.

"It's fine," I say. She is right that I drive faster now, impatient to get where I'm going. The other widows drive the same way; we're easily agitated by bad drivers or people going too slow.

"I'm not even going that fast," I say, but reduce my speed anyway. Neil, Jason, and Aidan are in the backseat playing with plastic toy knights. We are on our way to Long Beach Island, in New Jersey, to stay in a beach house for Thanksgiving. I decided I could not do the traditional holiday at my parents' house, where we always played football in the leaves, burned cranberry muffins, drank Dad's homemade Baileys. I know that the absence of Dave would feel larger with these things, like staging a play without the lead actor.

Long Beach Island is an overdeveloped beach community at the end of the Jersey Shore. The houses are small and shuttered with quaint names like "The Sandpiper" or "Pirate's Cove," or family names like O'Callahan or Reilly. A lot of police officers and firefighters retire here, and it has affectionately been dubbed the Irish Riviera.

Today the whole island looks like a ghost town. There are boarded-up restaurants, and houses have their shades pulled down like closed eyes. The air continues to be unseasonably warm, as if winter has forgotten itself altogether. I roll down the car window to inhale salt air and turn onto a short street on the bay side of the island.

"There it is." I turn in to the driveway of a small blue house that was donated to us by the community. My parents and brother, Luke, have arrived already, the back of their wagon open like a wide mouth full of too much food and luggage. Leah's friend Allan and Dave's friend Cliff from Jones Beach will join us later.

Leah, Jason, Neil, Aidan, and I unfold ourselves from my car and help my parents unload the groceries into the small house decorated with shells and stained-glass lighthouses. The living room is tiny, its stark white walls covered with an oversize oil painting of a stormy ocean. A blue plaid couch sits below the painting, a cotton throw of a big lobster folded on its arm. We hoist the bags onto the speckled linoleum counter of a well-appointed modern kitchen that opens up to a small eating area. A bottle of white zinfandel holds a note that reads "Welcome to the Ashland house!" I try to picture the family that lives here, slightly overweight and happy.

"That is incredibly generous," my mother remarks, placing more bags on a dining room table that is shaped like a ship's wheel. "I sense they are a nice family. You can feel it in the house." I can tell Jason is stifling a sarcastic remark as he tries to fit the turkey and mashed potatoes he has brought into an already crowded refrigerator.

We make a simple meal. Afterward, my parents and Luke take a walk on the beach while Leah and Allan dance around the kitchen, imitating dance teachers and the bad choreography they learned as dance majors at Purchase College. I laugh watching them leap and fall, Allan's face pressed into an expression of mock emotion. Even Jason laughs, his deep voice climbing into another register as he watches Allan hoist Leah into the air. Neil joins in, dancing with both of them.

"What are you doing?" Aidan asks. He has been watching television in the living room. I pull him onto my lap and wrap my arms around his waist. He feels solid and strong, like Dave.

"They're being silly," I say, inhaling Aidan's impossibly sweet smell.

He leans back on my chest and I relish his weight, as if it is grounding me into the moment, forcing me to be still and present for the first time in weeks. Cliff arrives late and I show him the room he will be sharing with my brother, Allan, and Jason. "You okay sharing a room with a teenager and two gay men?" I ask, half laughing at the odd circumstance of it.

Cliff shrugs and laughs, the corners of his eyes wrinkling from too much sun, his red hair pulled back into a ponytail. "No worries," he says, chuckling and shaking his head.

That night I dream I am sitting with all the firefighters who died, in a vast auditorium or a church. I am in the back row, watching them laugh and joke in front of me. I peek above the crowd, craning my neck to find Dave, like an ant among giant flowers of uniformed men. When I finally spot him, he is sitting with Mike Esposito and they are playing with a gun and waving it around. It catches my breath and I scream at them, terrified, the way you only get in a dream, the panic visceral and intense.

"Be careful with that!" I yell, and they turn in slow motion as in a movie. I even think this in my dream. *They turn like this in movies.* When they finally turn all the way around, they look right at me. I can see the whites of their eyes, the ring of green around Dave's pupils. They have military haircuts and are both smiling dreamily, their dimples stretching, lighting up the room. I fill up with a sense of joy and lightness that I have rarely felt. Mike and Dave are laughing at me now, the gun waving in between them, and the terrible panic returns.

"Be careful!" I scream, but they only laugh. They want to show me something. I don't know how I know this, but I do. They are taking off their caps—the class A caps that firefighters wear at funerals. They are taking them off and turning around so I can see the back of their heads. There are two perfect circles in their hair, and I lean in closer to see what they are, suddenly frightened to realize that they are bullet holes.

"Mommy?" Aidan's tiny voice is far away. "Mommy?" I am being pulled from my dream. I don't want to leave. I want to see Dave.

"Mommy, are there bad people here?" Aidan is standing right next to me, his eyes glowing in the dark room.

"What? What's the matter?" I ask.

"Are there bad people here?" he asks again, and I sit up a bit, trying to focus.

"There aren't many people here at all actually."

"But are there bad people?"

"Here? No, I don't think so."

"Anywhere?"

"Yes, but I do know there's a lot more good people than there are bad people."

"How do you know that?"

"Because look how we are staying at this house. Somebody we don't even know lent us their home. Those are nice people."

"Because Daddy died?"

"Yes, and they know how hard it is for us without him and so they want to cheer us up. People all over the world are sending us cards and presents and wishing us well and doing good things so we will know that there are a lot more good people than bad. . . . Now you need to go back to sleep, sweetie." I want to go back into my dream, rewind the image, and freeze on Dave's face. I am scared I will forget it, the smooth arch of his cheekbones, the cleft in his chin. Aidan climbs back into his bed and leans on his pillow. His eyes are wide open but he is quiet. I listen to his breathing, in and out like surf, and it relaxes me. I remember leaning over his crib, his tiny sped-up breath making his chest rise and fall. He quickly falls back to sleep, but I am now wide awake, Dave's laughter echoing in my head. When I close my eyes, I can see the bullet wound, the small cranberry circle, deep gelatinous blood. Now my legs are awake, charged with energy as if some other part of my body told them it is time to exercise. I give up on sleep and sit up, turning on the light. I grab my book and try to read, watching the clock pass four and then five until the pink light of Thanksgiving morning seeps through my window.

It is irrationally warm, almost 70 degrees, with December peeking around the corner. Nothing makes sense. While the weather means the rescue workers do not have to freeze, the medical examiner's office explained that the heat is decomposing the bodies more quickly. The fires, which have at last burned out, didn't help, as many victims have been cremated.

We walk to the beach on Thanksgiving morning, crossing the empty main street, passing geometric, modern houses of cedar and glass. The sky is hazy and we set up our blankets near the water, the sand damp and soft. I lie on my stomach and listen to the dulcet sounds of the ocean, inhale the smell of the sea. Aidan runs directly to the water like a puppy free from his leash.

"It's cold!" Aidan squeals. I can't help but smile, watching him repeatedly throw himself onto the sand. We are lying in a row like seals in the warm sun. I am relieved that the ocean still feels like magic to me. I watch seagulls suspended like mobiles, floating on the currents. Neil is reading next to me. Allan is choreographing a dance on the beach. A lead dancer with the Doug Elkins Dance Company, Allan traveled the world, sharing his wild leaps and spins with audiences. When he became HIV positive, he began meditating, settling into a small apartment on 5th Street in the East Village. Leah gets up to join him and I rest my head on my folded arms, the breeze carrying a hint of winter as it blows my hair. The tattoo on Allan's arm undulates as he loses himself in the movement. He lost both of his parents too young and countless friends to AIDS, yet he is laughing hard, kicking up sand. Cliff turns and asks, "How about a massage?"

"I never say no to that. I'm a touch slut," I say.

Cliff's freckles bend into a smile. He kneels over me, and the pure sexual stance of it makes me ache for Dave, a chronic burn like an amputated arm that still imagines a limb.

"You're totally tense," Cliff says, kneading my shoulders.

"Yeah, I don't know why," I say sarcastically.

I close my eyes and play the film of Dave and me on the inside of my lids. He is sitting on my back, the camera closing in on every detail of his body, the muscular wave of his collarbone, the angular lines of his shoulders, the muscles on his wide, powerful back, the small scar on his right triceps, the freckle on his left hip. Farther down the beach, I see two teenage girls and their mother. They are setting up a large telescope and pointing it toward the ocean.

"What's he doing?" my mother asks, looking up from her book to see Aidan bouncing toward the family.

"I dunno."

"He's such a Tigger," Mom says. She has always referred to people by characters in *Winnie-the-Pooh*. If I am depressed, I'm Eeyore; anxious, Piglet; but for most of my life she has called me Pooh. Aidan is talking to some girls now, and they bend down to listen. I think I see them smiling.

"He's just like you," Mom says, referring to how friendly Aidan is. I like when she and I have these moments of mutual admiration for Aidan, when we row out to the middle of the ocean that keeps us apart. "You would go up to anybody." She smiles. "It was a little scary, actually, but I loved that about you. You just had to talk to everybody."

I walk toward the family, noticing that the girls are actually younger than I thought, no older than fifteen. One smiles, her braces flashing.

"Mommy! I saw a loon and a seagull!" Aidan says, and I smile at the mother, a plump woman in her mid-forties whose face is like a well-set table.

"He's so cute," she tells me. "We were just doing some birdwatching."

"I hope he's not imposing," I say, watching the girls struggle to hoist Aidan up to the lens again.

"Not at all. He's wonderful. Do you have a house here?" I tell her someone loaned us the home, wanting to avoid the telling of it, the story I will have to tell a thousand times to strangers I will meet in my lifetime. The words always catch in my throat, like something swallowed the wrong way.

"I am so sorry," she says, her voice lowering. "You're so young." I don't want to cry in front of a stranger, but when she looks up, her face softens. "We're actually out birdwatching for the first time since my husband died last year."

"Oh . . . I'm sorry," I tell her.

"He had cancer." We stare at the ocean, not knowing what to say. "Have you had the light thing yet?"

"What light thing?"

"After my husband died, the lights flickered all over the house and the phone would ring and no one would be there."

"It was creepy," says the older daughter, who has been listening in.

"I liked it," the mom says, smiling again. "It made me feel like he was still here."

"Actually, the lights in the house have been flickering since the towers fell," I confess. "I just thought it was the old brownstone wiring."

"No. I think there's this energy, if you're open to it. I didn't believe in that stuff before, but now . . . I mean, all those people dying together, there has to be this overwhelming energy on this other plane that we can't even understand."

I watch the tiny lines at the corners of the woman's mouth. Not crow's-feet or laugh lines—sad lines, I decide. Lines from crying and crying again, and yet there she is, standing as solid on the beach as anything else. I smile and nod, my mind filled with wonder at the odd circumstances of life, how the tide can push the sand into rippled patterns on the shore and then just as quickly change it into something else altogether. How, on this day, two widows washed up on this deserted beach to ponder the awesome energy of what is beyond this tiny life.

When we return, the house already smells of turkey and we fall into the tasks required for the holiday. Leah and Neil snap the ends off of string beans, my mother searches for matching glasses, Luke counts silverware, Jason bastes the turkey, Allan scrubs sweet potatoes, I fold the napkins. We all hum along to the Motown playing on the radio. I hate how all the songs are about love, leaving love, finding love, and losing it again. Aretha Franklin's "Baby I Love You" starts and I click it off, barking, "Jesus, can't these people write about anything else?"

"I love that song," Leah mutters, disappointed.

"Welcome to Grief 101!" I joke. "Where we've got your hottest hits to make you feel soooooo baaad." Allan cackles and I join in.

"Your favorite station for the first holiday without your loved one!" he says.

Allan and I step out onto the small deck that leads to a square backyard. I suppose that grass doesn't grow here, because every yard has concrete or the same round yellow gravel. Allan lights two cigarettes and hands me one. I look up at a sky that is covered in a thick gray roof of clouds.

"The first holiday is the hardest," he says, inhaling. I nod slowly, thinking about all the holidays lined up like dominoes, infinite, twisting into the future.

"I just want to pretend they're not there," I say, staring at the tiny shed with a rusty beach chair leaning against it.

"I hear you," Allan says, and I know he does.

I think of all the holidays I have spent with Dave: eleven Christmases, eighteen Valentine's Days, nine Easters, five Mother's Days, and fifteen New Year's. New Year's. New Year's Eve is only six weeks away. New Year's Eve became the holiday Dave and I spent alone. We stopped trying to find the perfect party or some grand place to be, deciding that being together was the best ticket in town. On New Year's Eves before Aidan was born, we had sex until late at night, luxuriating in the decadent pleasure of being in bed while the world passed by in the squeak of a shopping cart, the sound of footsteps crunching in the snow. Eventually, hunger would force us outside, where my skin felt taut and alive against the cold air. We ate at Inaka Sushi House, sipping hot sake while we watched the Japanese men slicing red tuna, fanning carrots into a perfect flower. At 11:30 P.M. we would walk to Prospect Park for fireworks. Dave's first company, Ladder 122, was always there, and we felt like dignitaries as the firefighters rolled back the fence to let us inside the big field where a large platform was set up for the fireworks. At midnight we'd crane our necks straight up to the sky. White lights fell like the branches of willow trees, red lights trickled down like rain. They were so close, I had to shut my eyes.

"Happy New Year," Dave would say, kissing me, his face sporadically lit by the fireworks above.

I was relieved when Dave didn't have to work on the eve of the millennium. Rumors of a terrorist attack were rampant throughout the firehouse. Mayor Giuliani was pouring tons of city money into the Special Operations Command, training the men for Sarin attacks in the subway. That year Dave and I broke tradition, attending a small party in the neighborhood. It was held in a prewar penthouse apartment with panoramic views of Brooklyn and the city. I could feel Dave's anxiety as he paced the apartment, his eyes wrinkled with worry. At midnight, the dinner guests clustered around the windows overlooking the park where the fireworks seemed to fall from the trees across from us. Aidan squealed with his little friends, stomping his feet, and when I went to kiss Dave, he wasn't there. I found him on the other side of the apartment, at a window in the dining room that faced the Manhattan skyline.

"I'm worried about the guys," Dave said. "I think if something happens, it will be at the Twin Towers."

I follow his gaze across the water to the two gleaming buildings. "Why?"

"I dunno. Just a feeling. Maybe it will be a subway. Times Square, even."

"Don't say that. C'mon, it's a holiday."

I could hear Aidan's delight squeezed out of him in a high-pitched howl that made Dave chuckle. "Happy New Year," he said finally, his warm kiss familiar and safe.

At dinnertime we sit around the cramped brown table laden with food. I am waiting for someone to make a toast, to address Elijah's chair, the missing presence at the table.

"Shall we say grace?" my mother asks softly, and everyone reaches for each other's hands.

"Grace!" Aidan says, giggling, and I remember making the same joke when I was his size.

"Aidan, why don't you say that poem you learned in school."

Aidan looks embarrassed for a moment, then begins, "Thank you for the food we eat, thank you for the world so sweet, thank you for the birds that sing. Thank you for just everything."

"Oh, that's nice," my dad says, grinning.

"I think it's 'Thank you, *Lord,* for everything,' " my mother corrects.

"No! It's 'Thank you for *just* everything,' " Aidan says.

"Well, when I was a little girl, it was 'God.' "

"It's public school." I try not to sound annoyed. I don't want to talk about God. I knelt to God for weeks, begging for Dave's life, asking for the little girl we were going to have together, for all the people in the towers to be safe, and it all fell on deaf ears. Like a spurned friend, I do not talk to God anymore. Yet I am sitting here breathing, talking, surrounded by friends who love me deeply and completely. When my dad raises his glass to talk about Dave, I raise mine, too, and I am thankful.

After dinner, I plug in my computer to find 386 e-mails. I start deleting the old mail first and then open one from John Viggiano, the retired firefighter who lost two sons: one a policeman, the other a firefighter. Lee had warned me that John was mistrustful of my organization. When I see the e-mail subject line marked "Young Lady," I sigh. John warns me to watch my step as I proceed through the quagmire of Fire Department and city politics. He tells me he has seen widows stronger than me stumble and fall. At moments his tone is paternal; at others he is warning me to watch my step when mentioning who I represent. At first I am defensive and start a letter about how I am a big girl with nothing to lose. I am about to press send when I stop suddenly, feeling nothing but compassion for this man who has served the department and sacrificed so much. I start the letter again, this time not as a spokesperson but as a person who has lost someone she loves.

I read the e-mail and shake my head, acknowledging how different I am only two months since Dave died. I used to cry when I left auditions, shake before shows, obsess about editors liking my work. More than failure, I feared rejection, not just of my work, but of *me* as a person, a human being who cares deeply about what other people think. If someone didn't like me, I would try harder to convince them, practically tap dancing in front of them until I proved that I was worthy of their friendship. Now, my numbness and shock have made me impervious to the opinions of others. I will say what I have to say because the world is listening, their ears temporarily poised to hear to my voice.

*　　*　　*

As we drive home, I say, "I think I'm in the *Times* today," as I listen to a message from a friend. I had been interviewed about the 9/11 Widows and Victims' Families Association before Thanksgiving.

Neil drives into a 7-Eleven and I buy three copies of the *Times*. As I slide back into the seat, my eyes fall on the front-page headline: "As the Widows of September 11th Unite, Grief Finds a Powerful Political Voice."

"Let me see," Leah says, leaning forward to grab an extra copy.

The car grows silent as Leah reads the story aloud, and my breath quickens with the strange feeling of being so exposed. There is a quote from Jennie, the woman I met at CNN. We have been sharing information nearly every day. "If Marian gets a phone call, I want a phone call," she is quoted as saying. I follow along in my copy. The story continues to the front page of the Metro section, where a large photo of me appears, sitting in the firehouse, my face determined and sad. The poster board of the men's photos leans on the dirty brick wall behind me, my eyes staring directly into the camera, caught in a half blink.

19

Fresh Kills

The phone rings so much, I unplug it from the wall and call Joe Miccio on my cell phone on my way back from dropping Aidan at school. The *New York Times* article has generated a new blizzard of interest, and I feel like I have just dug myself out from the last one. My ear is hot and sore from the phone.

"I can't handle this," I tell Joe, wanting to burst into tears. He is overwhelmed himself, his voice tired and scratchy. He has been trying to help Martha with the website, updating the number of bodies found and debris removed each day. I call Martha next. She tells me hundreds of e-mails are arriving and she can't even begin to answer them all.

"I can't do this. I got the kids!" she says, her one-year-old screaming in the background. My head is so swollen with information, messages, and things to do, I feel as if I will implode. At home, I make myself a cup of tea and sit at my desk, piled high with papers, photos of Aidan as a baby smiling at me, Dave's perfect profile as he tosses Aidan in the air. "Help me," I say to Dave. I rifle through the pages of messages from press, family members, firefighters, and strangers offering help, and my eyes fall on three people who have offered me office space. I call one of them, a man named Michael Spencer, who runs an organization called Hospital Audiences Inc. The organization helps sick and elderly people attend the theater. I feel like I am talking about someone else's life as I describe the shows I performed in, the concerts, the screenplays. He offers me a corner of his large office and I gratefully accept, checking one item off my long list of things to do: *Get the organization out of the house.*

Firefighters have begun calling me to complain about the site and how it's been divided. Tensions have escalated between the police and firefighters, and the grapplers are going unwatched. I call other firefighters to try to get a better understanding of what's happening. A police officer I know at the site calls to complain and I call Lee. I can hear the gigantic machines churning and squeaking in the background.

"Hey, kiddo. What's up?" He always answers the phone this way. I tell him what I've heard.

"Yes, yes. . . . Well, they keep changing the protocol here and it most certainly is not working." I can't tell if he is upset or yelling over the machines. "But we're still here. We found two people today."

I try to imagine the things he sees every day and grow silent. "That's good."

"That's salubrious! Every time we find someone, it's another family . . . well, you know. I don't have to tell you!"

"I'll call the mayor. You should come with me. Be our expert from the site."

"Naw, I'll stay here."

"C'mon, Lee. You don't even have to join my organization. Just come." He laughs hard from the belly and agrees to join us. I call the mayor's office and schedule a meeting for the following night.

Lee meets us at the gates of City Hall wearing his class A uniform, covered with numerous citations and medals. He trots across Broadway and greets Martha and me at the security gate, and I notice he is not wearing any socks. He notices me staring.

"I hate socks," Lee says, smirking, as he guides us through security.

City Hall is a stately Georgian building with a domed rotunda encircled by ten white columns. Martha, Lee, and I sit on low wooden benches off to the left side of the lobby, reviewing our agenda and information for the meeting. We decide who will speak when and who will cover what topics. I call Jennie Farrell from Give Your Voice. I ask her if there's anything she would like me to address. She is defensive and insulted that she was not included in the meeting. I try not to feel like a guilty five-year-old and promise to include her in the next one.

In a few minutes, we are hastily searched and led through a low gate. Richard Schierer, a cordial overweight deputy commissioner in his early forties, gives Lee a hearty slap on the back. Then we follow him through the mayor's office, a small simple room with a wide mahogany desk and Yankee memorabilia covering every surface, into a larger room where the mayor has assembled Chief Nigro from the Fire Department, Commissioner Von Essen, Commissioner Kerik from the Police Department, Dr. Hirsh, head of the medical examiner's office, and Lynn Tierney. The mayor begins the meeting with introductions and then leans forward in his chair, signaling me to begin.

"Mr. Mayor. Thank you for having us here again. We have been watching the site and have learned from numerous sources that a turf war between the police and fire departments has begun, and we wanted to suggest that we organize the site differently."

The mayor wrinkles his forehead, confused. "I hadn't heard anything."

"Basically, you have three sectors," I begin. "One has twenty-five police, one has twenty-five Port Authority police and ESU [Emergency Service Units], and then there are eighty-seven firefighters in one sector."

The mayor turns to Tom Von Essen. "Is this true? Because that makes no sense at all to me."

"Well . . . we were trying to divide the work," Tom says, looking weary, as usual. "The firefighters think they own the site down there."

Lee, who has known Tom for many years, leans forward. "C'mon, Tom, you and I know that there has always been animosity between police and fire, but there have been times, and I'm at the site every day, so I have seen it myself. There are times when there is no one in the police sector *at all*. No one watching the grapplers, and so a couple of firefighters will jump in there and spot for a while. When the police officers come back from wherever they've been, they are pretty pissed off that the firefighters are there." I nod at Lee as I watch the mayor's hands. He has incredibly short fingers that hyperextend so far they remind me of asparagus about to snap. The police commissioner bristles and starts to speak to the mayor, defending his men. Tom shrugs and nods, and Martha flashes me a glance, signaling me to get involved.

"The point is," I say, "we don't have time for a battle of the badges, and if I have to put a family member in every sector to remind all of these guys why they are there, then I will."

"I don't see why we can't we just move some guys into other sectors," the mayor says. "Tom?"

"Fine. Fine with me." He is staring at the floor now. The room is silent for a moment.

The police commissioner coughs. "There needs to be an equal division though. We lost a lot of guys, too," he says.

"Great." I shuffle to the next item on the agenda. "We still think the families are unclear about a lot of the retrieval issues. The DNA."

Dr. Hirsh, the sallow man from the meeting at the Sheraton, clears his throat. His voice is small and tired. "Well, we could use your organization's help in trying to get family members to donate better samples. The samples we are getting from the site are mostly small, so getting a good DNA sample is imperative."

"Well, maybe we can send letters to our list. We also have a civilian group we are working with that would like to help."

"Good. We really need swabs from the siblings or closest kin. Some of the hairbrushes aren't working, and we have an enormous amount of data to enter."

"The problem is," Giuliani adds, "there are only a limited number of forensics experts in the country. The samples we receive have to be sent out to a lab in Seattle and tested."

"And very often, more than not," Dr. Hirsh adds gently, "there is not a match. The samples are small and I'm sorry to be graphic, but they've been severely decomposed or burned, making it difficult to get DNA from them."

"Well, I think the families need to know this," Martha says softly. "It's been very frustrating not to know or to think that Tommy could end up in the dump."

"We're working on contacting every family. It's going to take a lot of time to identify these samples, and everyone just needs to just be patient," Dr. Hirsh says.

Six agenda items later, we are satisfied and quickly leave. The mayor kisses me good-bye, awkwardly smashing my face into his. Martha looks madder than ever, like a pit bull in a ballerina's body.

"I am so sick of everything," she says. "I'm glad we're doing all this, but we shouldn't even have to."

"What now?" I say as I step out onto the cobblestone walk in front of City Hall.

"I want to go to the site," Martha says, almost trying to convince herself to go. "Lee, do you mind taking me there?"

Lee guides Martha by the elbow across the muddy tundra of Liberty Street. A cold wind is whipping up West Street, the first hint of winter since the towers fell. A tall chain-link fence has been erected around the periphery of the site, where hundreds of cards, wilting flowers, pictures, and windswept teddy bears are woven through the links. I am amazed at how different the site looks now. The cathedral-like walls have been removed, and the six stories of debris are gone. The site is already below ground level, muddy from rain, and the workers look more fatigued than on my first visit here.

Martha presses herself against the fence, looking like a kid waiting to be invited to join a baseball game. She is more tortured than most at the prospect of having nothing of Tommy. She is the only widow in the firehouse who has made no plans to have a memorial for her husband. Lee puts his weathered hand on her back and patiently explains where the towers were, where some firefighters were found and where they think a lot of firefighters might be. Martha still doesn't want to leave after half an hour, so Lee agrees to stay with her while I head uptown to a meeting with Ken Feinberg, the special master assigned by the Justice Department to oversee the Victims Compensation Fund. The fund was set up to prevent the government, city agencies, and airlines from being sued by all the families affected. Recently, it has come under fire for its unprecedented restrictions that call for a cap on pain and suffering and deductions that will leave the middle-class workers, particularly rescue workers, with nothing. A number of family groups have begun to sprout up in response to this issue, and I reluctantly attend the meetings trying to get better information.

The meeting is held at a dark lecture hall on 3rd Avenue filled with families wearing 9/11 pins and hats. Kenneth R. Feinberg stands on stage, one leg up on a chair, his round eyes made bigger by large glasses, his hair nearly gone. The families are asking endless questions about why one death would mean more than another, why a man who worked his whole life toward his pension would now have that deducted from this fund. Feinberg answers in his thick Boston accent, his voice loud and arrogant. Halfway through the meeting, he looks utterly frustrated, practically screaming at the audience of distraught families. A woman in the center of the room with blond layered hair and pale skin stands up slowly.

"Mr. Feinberg, I just lost my husband, I have three children, and I am dying of cancer. My husband took out huge insurance policies on himself and me because of my condition, and under these restrictions, they will cancel out anything I would get from this fund."

"Well . . . Unfortunately, the restrictions require insurance reductions, and those are the standAHds we use to determine your payment."

"But I won't get a payment."

"UnfortunAHtly, some people will slip through the cracks."

"You're saying to a dying woman, I will slip through the cracks?" The room is silent. I can hear the pulse in my head. I almost feel sorry for Feinberg, who is standing now, shrugging helplessly, his voice lowered a few notches.

"I can't say that some people will not fall through the cracks."

*   *   *

At home that evening, a woman named Rhonda Shearer calls and introduces herself as the wife of Stephen J. Gould, a renowned evolutionary biologist. She tells me she is an artist who was using a warehouse on Spring Street to store her sculptures. After 9/11, she and her daughter, London, organized a volunteer group that doles out supplies to rescue workers. She tells me the Fire Department hates her, FEMA (Federal Emergency Management Agency) hates her, OEM (Office of Emergency Management) won't take her phone calls.

"They're mad because I just get the supplies and give them to the guys. The rescue workers wait for weeks of paperwork to be filed, and meanwhile, Marian, they are digging for remains with dining forks. It's ridiculous." Her voice is slightly angry and apple-crisp. "I read about your organization in the *New York Times* and heard about you from a number of the firefighters at the site. I thought you would be interested in some of the disturbing things I've witnessed during deliveries at the landfill in Staten Island, like firefighters' boots, just piled up and smelling like rotting flesh, smashed-up trucks that have not even been looked through, and I don't know if you know this, but there's a morgue out there, because they are finding whole bodies."

I feel my face burn, my temple throbbing against the phone. I want to dismiss this woman, her passion too intense for someone not directly affected, but deep inside I know that what she is saying is true. What if Dave is there, carelessly tossed like old chicken bones in a pile of garbage?

"Let me call you right back." I pace the living room, trying to order my thoughts in neat rows. I call Joe Miccio, Jennie Farrell, and countless firefighters and decide that I need to see the evidence for myself.

"Can you take me out there?" I ask Rhonda, calling her back. "I want to see for myself."

"I have a delivery there tonight. We'd have to sneak you in, though. They've gotten really strict."

"I have an interview on Aaron Brown tonight. If I can see it for myself, I can tell everyone on national TV."

"That would be great. Because people really need to know. No one seems to know what's going on out there. People know you now, so I have to be really careful. Wear your hair back and a big shirt or something, just don't look like yourself. . . ."

Leah and Neil arrive to babysit. I pace around the apartment, nervous and distracted. I pack Dave's old knapsack with a change of clothes for Aaron Brown, and some makeup, just in case, and get dressed in Dave's old flannel shirt, a loose pair of jeans, and a base-ball cap.

"You look like a lesbian," my sister jokes, and I smile and hug them good-bye.

Outside, Rhonda gives her horn a tap. She looks like someone who should be driving a Mercedes, not a white Ford pickup truck. She is a petite woman in her early fifties with a small, serious face, straight blond hair, and wire-framed glasses. I introduce myself and slide into the passenger seat next to her daughter, London. London shares her mother's fine features but has short black hair and wide, thick shoul-ders. London does not say much on the ride out, only nodding occa-sionally to confirm her mother's accounts of their visits out to Fresh Kills. "They are getting very suspicious of me and have gotten stricter and stricter about letting people in," Rhonda says. "Which says to me that they have something to hide."

I watch a light rain fall on the windshield and imagine Fresh Kills looking like the killing fields in Cambodia, the carnage too disturbing to see. I had heard from the firefighters and police that being assigned to Fresh Kills was the equivalent of toilet duty, the work tedious and slow.

The road gives way to high muddy hills rising on both sides. The powerful smell of garbage seeps through the window. We turn down a long, desolate road; the mud is illuminated in the headlights.

"Keep your head down and don't talk too much," Rhonda instructs me. "If they recognize you, I'm in big trouble."

London hands me a white hard hat and an ID necklace with her photo on it. We pull up to a security booth, and an overweight guard labors over to the window. His face reminds me of mashed potatoes, white and soft and blank. I put my hands in my lap to keep them from shaking.

"We're delivering some supplies," Rhonda says calmly. The guard leans into the window, glancing at the plastic IDs hanging from our necks. I try not to think of a hundred scenes in movies that are just like this—the tense moment when the audience doesn't know if the imposters will be caught or not. I concentrate on keeping my face relaxed and nonchalant, smiling slightly at the guard.

"Have a good night," he tells us, collapsing back into his chair as Rhonda steps slowly on the gas.

Giant floodlights peek out from behind the dirt hills as we turn in to a parking lot. Rhonda opens the door. While Ground Zero smelled of death and plastic, nothing can describe the stench that shoves itself at me, forcing me to cover my mouth with my hand.

"Don't do that," Rhonda instructs, and I force myself to take my hand away.

"It gets easier," London says, stepping down from the truck.

I jump off, my boots splashing into the mud and sticking there. I feel as if I am stepping off a spaceship onto another planet. Piles of debris lie everywhere like giant muddy haystacks.

"That's where the sifters are." Rhonda points to an open barnlike building with a green plastic roof. "And that's the morgue." Her finger aims at a darkened trailer. Baseball stadium–size lights shine down on the muddy earth that, upon closer inspection, is actually bubbling and popping like boiling soup.

"It's methane escaping," London says flatly, lighting a cigarette.

"It's quiet tonight," Rhonda says, walking quickly to the back of the truck. "Most of the guys working here are amazing, but there are a few that coop over there." She picks up a box, gesturing with her chin over to the police cars. I look back at her dumbly, not understanding the term.

"It's when cops sleep in their cars instead of working," London explains, handing me a box.

"But most of the guys are great," Rhonda reassures me, walking quickly toward a row of brightly lit trailers marked FEMA, NYPD, FDNY, FBI, MESS HALL.

"A lot of them are volunteers, like this guy tonight." She turns to the back of one of the trailers and knocks on the door. "He's a volunteer doctor." A tall Nordic-looking man, with thinning blond hair, a lab coat, and wire-rimmed glasses much like Rhonda's, smiles.

"Good to see you!" he says enthusiastically, as if he has been waiting for us all night. He steps aside to let us load in the boxes. The whole trailer is set up like a doctor's office, with shelves full of supplies and an adjustable examining table covered in waxy paper. He is so excited to see Rhonda, I surmise that he has spent too much time alone on the deserted island of this trailer. Rhonda returns his enthusiasm while London and I make a few more trips to the car. Each time we pass Rhonda, she is asking the doctor questions. I can tell she is grilling him for information, but he smiles steadily, revealing nothing.

"This place is hell on earth," I say to London while we wait for Rhonda.

"Wait till you look around," she says without inflection. She reaches into her army jacket and takes out a pack of cigarettes, offering me one. I'm not in the mood, but I take one anyway. It is something to do.

Rhonda tiptoes down the narrow steps and we follow her to the end of the trailers. I try to walk so my boots don't make any noise, but the mud squishes loudly. We duck past a darkened building around to the other side of the green-roofed barn. Two sifters are running, inclined conveyor belts that level off at the bottom like miniature roller-coaster tracks.

"You see, there's no one spotting!" Rhonda exclaims. "There's supposed to be two people there." She points to what looks like piles of dirt sliding down the sifter. The machines shake from side to side, loosening the debris and leaving chunks of twisted steel and garbage. "If they find something, they're supposed to stop the belt and mark it. Look at all this stuff going by."

I cup my hand over my mouth to hide my shock and get a reprieve from the sickening smell.

"What kind of stuff do they find?" I ask, unable to take my eyes off the belt.

"Everything. Photo IDs, jewelry, sometimes a part," she says carefully. I feel my jaw shift hard to the right as I try not to cry. I follow Rhonda back around the building. "The boots are supposed to be here," she says, pointing to behind the shed. "They're not here anymore." She is clearly disappointed, and I begin to wonder if this has all been a mistake, slogging through this wasteland. A drizzle begins again, and we follow Rhonda farther down the wide road. We see the lights of a truck and duck behind one of the piles, trying not to breathe as it passes. I feel like I have entered some strange life that is not my own. What am I doing here? How did I go from being a wife and mom to an investigator? I can't stop my eyes from looking everywhere, from taking it in and thinking, *This is no place to be found.*

The drizzle turns into a light rain and Rhonda is walking so fast, I can barely keep up. She is like a tiny dog, looking from side to side to make sure no one has seen us.

"Your mother is a spitfire," I whisper to London, who is lighting another cigarette, taking slow, long strides as she falls behind her mother.

"She's on a mission."

I watch Rhonda stoop down and pick up a long piece of fabric. "What is that?" I ask, catching up to her, but I can already see that it is a torn piece of bunker gear.

"You see?" Rhonda says, her forehead wrinkling. "This is *not* okay." I take the piece of bunker gear from her and look at it. It is a thin length of black cloth no bigger than a sheet of paper. It must have been sheared off of a firefighter's back to be that small. I hand Rhonda back the muddy piece and notice that we are standing in a fire truck graveyard. Mangled and crushed trucks are stacked in rows like laundry. Twisted ladders poke into the aisles row after row, some taped with signs that read FOR WTC MEMORIAL.

I spot the Squad 1 truck in the third row. As Tony said, the wheels are still intact, its roof caved in like a canopy bed. I peer inside the cabin, half expecting to see Dave sitting there, waiting. The emptiness is eerie, like a Ferris wheel in winter. I have never been near a fire truck without firefighters nearby. The narrow black compartments are covered in dust, walkie-talkies hanging like dropped phones.

"Look what I found." Rhonda hands me the muddy top half of a turnout boot. It has been sliced evenly, its two handles undamaged.

"They don't even bother to look in the trucks. This could have DNA on it," she snarls.

"That could be all someone gets," I echo, my voice rising with anger.

"Someone's coming," Rhonda whispers. She looks as guilty as a dog caught with his head in the garbage pail. "Let's go. Just tell them we got lost. Put that in your bag." She hands me the muddy boot.

"I don't want to take this!" I hand it back as if it were poison.

"It's evidence!" she says, determined. "You could show that to people if they question what you saw here tonight." I stare at the boot. When I look up again, London and Rhonda are already turning down another lane.

"C'mon!" London says, gesturing for me to follow. I frantically move my lipstick, wallet, cell phone, receipts, papers, and PalmPilot to the outside pocket of Dave's knapsack. I drop the boot in quickly, zipping the top. I can see headlights scanning the road we turned off of, like searchlights. I run to catch up with Rhonda and London who have ducked down another row. This one contains civilian cars smashed beyond repair: sedans, vans, SUVs half covered in mud like an archaeological dig. I can feel the weight of the rubber boot in my bag as we squish through the mud, the smell and guilt bringing on sudden nausea.

"I don't want this thing in my bag," I whisper.

"Don't worry about it," London says.

"What if someone finds out I have it?"

Rhonda is marching brusquely back, signaling for us to follow. She leads us back to the wider main road toward the trailers and the parking lot. I can feel mud splattering on my jeans and I am sweating. When we finally catch up, Rhonda is squinting at the sifting tent again.

"We need more spotters out here. Nobody wants to be out here and I don't blame them, but I mean, you've seen it. We need to get a lot more guys. Their eyes get tired fast, so they can only spot for about fifteen minutes at a time. Their eyes just get really fatigued."

"I'll see what I can do," I tell her impatiently. I want her to take this boot. I don't know why I have it. When I slide back into the truck, I hand the bag to her. "I don't want this," I say as she starts the engine and slowly backs up, the truck struggling to get a grip in the mud.

"Keep it, and the next time you meet with Giuliani, if he denies it, at least you have some evidence about the pile of boots."

"I saw a *piece* of boot. Not a pile."

"You might need it."

We arrive late to CNN headquarters for my Aaron Brown show interview. The interview is quick but effective, and by the time an intern leads me to a car service to take me home, my adrenaline has worn off and I am intensely fatigued. I sink into the black leather seat, the city spinning by in a streak of lights.

"How are you tonight?" the cabdriver asks the rearview mirror.

"Fine. Park Slope, please."

"Do you work for CNN?" the driver says. I don't feel like explaining but of course I do. Within one minute he is telling me about his 9/11. It is the story everyone wants to tell, like where you were when Kennedy was shot.

"I was parked right near City Hall and I saw the dust cloud," he says, stopping at a light, the red glare reflecting off his almond skin. "The city will never be the same. I can't go to the airport anymore because they pull me over and will arrest me and take my car."

"Why?"

"Because they think everyone with my skin is a terrorist. They arrested my brother. He was just sitting and waiting at the airport. He is not a terrorist. I am not a terrorist. I am an American, just trying to make a living." His accent gets thicker as he gets more annoyed. By the time he pulls onto 4th Street I know that my driver Depak is not Saudi Arabian but Bangladeshi, and he sends money home to his wife and two boys every month. He is trying to save money to bring them here, but after 9/11, getting them green cards will be difficult.

"I'm sorry," I tell him, and he smiles with his big white teeth when I give him a generous tip.

My sister is awake when I arrive home.

"Wow. What you said was pretty intense," she says hoarsely, sitting up from Neil's lap. "Aaron Brown was really interested. I'm glad he let you talk about everything."

"Yeah. Maybe it will help."

"It sounded scary," Neil says, looking at me intensely, and I nod slowly, trying not to cry. For once I succeed.

*   *   *

At the next scheduled meeting with the mayor regarding the landfill, I invite Give Your Voice. Jennie introduces me to her brother Michael who, although younger, has the air of someone much older. He has a serious face set into pale skin, and often furrows his brow as if quietly considering something.

The meeting is held in the conference room on the southwest corner of City Hall. It is a huge, airy room with a large round mahogany table dominating the center. Oil paintings of former mayors line the walls. I remember Dave telling me how, when they built City Hall, they never put windows on the north side of the building, because they never imagined the city expanding any farther uptown. Dave was always full of historical anecdotes; "useless information," I used to tease, but it was more than just a hobby for him, it was a way for him to give meaning to his world.

After Jennie complains about the civilians being excluded from meeting with the mayor, he explains that the firefighters and police were his employees first, but that he would be happy to help in any way possible to get victims' families the correct information and contacts. I can tell Jennie is not placated, but I know that she will tirelessly continue to advocate for her brother James. I bring up the landfill, and the mayor sidesteps the issue, saying they had tried a number of alternative sites, but that there was little choice, with tons of debris being removed from the site each day. He promises to increase manpower at Fresh Kills and to make sure someone from his office is overseeing the operation.

20

Hawaii

Nearly every week, the firefighters from Squad 1 call to tell me about free trips to California, the Bahamas, France, London, Germany. While I politely refuse, I cannot believe how people have mobilized in an endless ribbon of generosity that crosses borders and oceans, radiating out from this tiny island to everywhere on earth. And while the generosity is wonderful, the trips have caused gaping rifts in the firehouses. Some firefighters resent that they are toiling at Ground Zero, working weekends and holidays, while others are receiving royal treatment and exotic trips.

One afternoon, while frantically searching for the cordless phone, I place my hand on my heart to feel it racing. Did I drink too much coffee? Was I running too fast? Why has this feeling become so familiar? I pressed the page button on the phone base. Nothing. I sighed. Giving up, I go into the bathroom, the only room where I can get reception on my cell phone, and begin to check my messages: Charlie from the *New York Times;* Leo Bilken from Georgia with an idea for a memorial; Merri, can we do lunch?; Melissa, a widow from Cantor Fitzgerald; Mary Otti from CNN. I sit on top of the toilet lid to copy down the messages on a yellow legal pad: A firefighter from a Brooklyn engine has developed asthma; Japanese television wants an interview; Catholic charities; Theresa says hi; Congressman King's office; firefighters from Modesto have a check. When I stand up from the toilet and lift the lid, I notice the phone in the toilet bowl, a small sunken ship. I don't scold Aidan. I don't even tell him I know he threw it in the toilet. The gesture is an S.O.S. from a five-year-old. I call the firehouse. A bunch of the families from Squad are taking their kids out of school to go to Hawaii next week. I had originally said no, since Dave and I honeymooned there, but the guys reassured me we would not be visiting the same islands where Dave and I vacationed. "Put us on the list," I say. It is time for a break.

*   *   *

The night before our trip, it's almost 11 P.M. before I begin to pack. The small closet in Aidan's room is dark and I use a flashlight, tossing clothes everywhere until they are drooping from the chairs like wisteria. I pull down a storage box marked SUMMER CLOTHES and hoist it onto my bed in the next room. The shorts look too small for Aidan now. Is that possible? Could he have grown that much in five months? I have not been paying attention.

Staring at the open suitcase, I don't know where to begin. Dave was the packer. With the efficiency of a Boy Scout, he put only what was needed into neat piles. He prepared for rain and cold with one basic weatherproof jacket, for the sun with one pocketed pair of shorts. He brought a Swiss Army knife even when we weren't camping, and we always had an occasion to use it. Okay. One razor, two blades for shaving my legs. *Remember how I shaved the back of your neck while you smirked at me in the mirror?* Five T-shirts. *Not the purple one. It got a grease stain on the front from the fried clam I dropped at that dinner at Moby's Lobster House in Wellfleet last summer. That was our last summer. How can that be?* "Focus. Sunblock."

When the alarm rings the next morning at 4 A.M., the noise echoes in my ears like a scream. I walk into the bathroom, where the black and white ice-cube tiles shock my system awake. Everything sounds louder at this hour. I let the warm water massage my lower back, shave off a winter's worth of hair on my legs, and let myself experience the vague sensation of excitement. I am desperate for the world to stop spinning, for something to wake me from my grief-induced coma. Hawaii feels like the perfect solution, and yet the nagging nausea of guilt fills my stomach. How can I leave with Dave still buried in the rubble? Who will field the hundreds of phone calls, press conferences, and meetings? What if something happens while I am gone? And what if everywhere I go in Hawaii reminds me of Dave and our honeymoon, when the sunsets and flowers and fish were as bright as if they were painted by a child? Worst of all, what if they find Dave?

"It's the middle of the night!" Aidan says, excited and sleepy. "I slept an hour!" His eyes blink fast, trying to open. I kiss him on his warm cheek and reach for his pants. He's so tired it's like dressing a rag doll.

"C'mon, Aidan. Help me out here." I work his wide foot into the second pant leg when the car service calls. They are waiting outside. Aidan tries to carry his plastic *Star Wars* suitcase but gives up, dropping it halfway down the hall. I carry the bags out of the apartment in shifts, up the stairs and onto the stoop. I am sweating despite the frosty morning, wondering if single parenting will ever get easier.

The sun has started to rise, making the most run-down brownstones on Eastern Parkway look beautiful. Even Aidan, his eyes now wide, notices the pink light.

"The sun's coming!" he says, pointing.

"I don't think you've ever been up this early," I tell Aidan, peeling him a clementine.

"Yeeees! I stayed up the whole night when we went to Ireland on the airplane. Hey, where are all the cars?"

"Everybody's sleeping. It's so early."

The sun gleams off a speeding car like a comet.

"There's one, Mama!" Aidan points, bouncing in his seat. "Mama, how long are we going to be on the airplane?"

"About eleven hours," I tell him. "It's the longest ride you've ever been on."

"You going on vacation?" the driver asks, smiling at Aidan in the rearview mirror.

"We're going to Hawaii because the firefighters died," Aidan says, still staring out of the window. I watch the man's expression change, his mouth tightening in the corners. His eyes shift from Aidan's to mine.

"My husband was killed on September eleventh," I explain. I will never get used to saying this. "We're going to Hawaii with some of the other fire families."

"Oh . . . I am so sorry. Dat day was terrible. Just terrible. My wife and I pray for de firemen."

"Thank you."

Aidan looks small on the wide, black seat of the car. I rub his head and smile. It will be good to get away.

I find Leah at the back of the terminal, and after a long check-in, we board the plane. Hawaiian Air has chartered a 747 exclusively for the rescue workers' families. I scan the plane for families from Squad, including Tony Edwards, Huey Lynch, Mike Stackpole, and their wives and kids. I immediately spot some of the widows sitting toward the back. Theresa is with Mike Jr. and her two sisters-in-law. On the left side is Kathleen Box with her two kids, Debbie Amato and her four. The pilot's voice is so smooth he sounds like the host of a classical radio station. He announces that everyone in the crew today has volunteered to fly with us to Hawaii. The families burst into grateful applause as the flight attendants blush and nervously adjust their blue silk scarves.

When the aircraft taxies down the runway, we all fall silent. I know we are collectively thinking about our loved ones, how airplanes were the bullets that killed them. Fear quickens my breath again. I need something to do with my hands, so I tighten Aidan's seat belt and look across the aisle to Leah. She looks as frightened as I do, the back of her head pressed against the headrest, her fingers clenching the arms of her seat. We are picking up speed, running out of tarmac. Somehow the plane ascends, defying all logic as its massive weight climbs higher and higher into the air. The white noise of the plane is muffled instantly as my ears pop. It feels like all the families are holding their breath, waiting for the plane to reach altitude before exhaling.

"I see Daddy on the clouds!" Aidan yells as we coast above a blanket of white. "Look, Mommy! I can see him!" People turn to stare, their faces filled with pity. I bite my lip and look out of the small oval window. I half expect to see Dave standing there, waving at us, but all I see are clouds stretching like the ocean as far as the horizon. "See him?"

Aidan asks eagerly, and I am rifling through the files in my brain, trying to find the right thing to say.

"I don't see anything," I tell him, crying despite my efforts not to.

"He's right there," Aidan insists, pointing. A tissue appears on my armrest and I turn to see Mrs. Hetzel, the mother of one of the firefighters killed. She is sitting in the aisle seat behind me. Her daughter-in-law Diane, whom I have met many times, is sitting with her three-year-old daughter in her lap.

"Thank you," I whisper, and she nods, her gray eyes wet from crying, too. She reaches forward and extends her hand for me to take. The skin is loose and achingly soft, and we sit this way for a long time, crying together while Aidan waves to his imaginary father in the clouds.

*   *   *

We disembark to a welcoming committee of hula dancers and ukulele players, who greet us with leis and the soothing songs of Hawaii. They smile broadly, spreading cheekbones that are high and flat like those of Indian chiefs. When they finish singing, they divide us up into groups and direct us to a charter bus with our hotel name on the front. The bus bumps down a long main street of endless high-rise hotels lushly planted in front with palm trees and flowering shrubs. The beach is on the right, brightly lit in the midday sun. I adjust my watch to Hawaiian time.

Most of the Squad families are staying at the Marriott Hotel on a side street, a few doors in from the beach. Leah, Aidan, and I take the elevator to the seventh floor and find our room. It is airy and comfortable and overlooks a small pool and a giant palm tree that blocks our view of the beach. Leah slides open the door by the terrace, letting balmy breezes waft through the room.

"I love this place!" Aidan screams, bouncing from one bed to another. Leah laughs and smiles at me. She knows how hard it was for me to leave New York, but watching Aidan makes me feel lighter, and I know I did the right thing by coming here.

The next morning we arrive late to a welcome breakfast at the Hilton Hotel. After a plate of lukewarm pancakes, Tony's wife, Donna, and I walk Aidan and her son John, also five, to a conference room at the end of the hall. A striking Hawaiian woman with a thick black braid stands in the front of the room, demonstrating how to make paper leis. A large group of children sit cross-legged in front of her, craning their necks to see her thread bright paper flowers onto a string, dividing them with tiny pieces of straw.

"Any questions?" she asks, smiling broadly, her eyebrows raised. A boy no older than four, with a firehouse shirt and freckled cheeks, raises his hand. "Yes?" the woman asks.

"My daddy died," he announces plainly.

"Mine, too," a little girl says.

"My uncle died in the Twin Towers," says another.

A dozen kids are now raising their hands and the woman is visibly flustered, trying hard to maintain her smile. She just volunteered to make leis. She was not expecting to be ambushed by children's grief. Frantically searching the room, her eyes meet those of her coworker, who is cutting straws in the back of the room.

"Robin? Why don't you start handing those out," she says, trying to keep her voice steady. Robin is overweight, her head small and round like the top of a snowman. Donna and I tiptoe out, squeezing each other's hands so we won't cry.

"You should sign up for surfing," Tony tells me when we walk back into the dining room. He looks more relaxed than I have seen him in months.

"Yeah! It's going to be fun!" Donna exclaims.

"I don't think so." I remember my honeymoon in Hawaii, when Dave tried in vain to get me to surf. The waves were pretty gentle then, not nearly as big as during the winter months, but the ocean felt like a moody stranger that could turn at any moment. I never relaxed in the ocean, even when Dave, his brothers, and his friends, lifeguards all, surrounded me. Fear has always dominated my thoughts ever since I was young. Leah was the intrepid one, leaping easily across rocks, flipping in gymnastics, while I fixated on the horrible outcome should I fail. But Dave held my hand through my fear, beaming proudly when I mountain-biked down a dormant volcano in Maui and snorkeled above a colorful reef, and when I clutched his thigh on a helicopter ride over an active volcano, he put his hand on top of mine. I envied the rush Dave felt as the pilot flew fast and low over the coast. I could hear Dave's low and infectious laugh through the headphones that blared the *Miami Vice* theme song, and for a moment that laugh distracted me from picturing our deaths as we plunged into the Pacific.

"C'mon! Don't be a wimp," Tony tells me. "We're all going. Even the kids. Just come look."

I follow Tony to the back, where rows of tables have been set up to sign up for activities.

"These guys are firefighters and lifeguards and they started this surf school," Tony tells me. The table looks like the cast of *Baywatch;* three tanned, chiseled men smile at us as we approach.

"She's a chicken," Tony tells them, and I punch him in his large arm, newly covered with a Squad 1 tattoo.

"You're going to love it," an instructor says. He is wearing a sticker that reads DEREK in thick black pen. "It's really fun and safe."

"We'll all be there to help you," another one says, smiling, his teeth as white as eggshells. His name tag reads JOHN in capital letters.

"Okay." I shrug and lean over to sign myself up. "How can I resist?"

On the morning of December 6, the lifeguard/firefighter/surf instructors pick us up in a charter bus at our hotel. About twenty families board the bus, including most of the families from Squad. I sit in the back with Theresa, and we giggle at the handsome instructors shuffling papers and making announcements. John, the instructor I met yesterday, stands pointing out sights as we travel to the other side of Oahu. "The sunny side of the island," he says. I look out of the window, listening to his Hawaiian accent, and stare at the dramatic deep green mountains covered in an umbrella of clouds. I show Aidan three herons standing on a grassy patch beside the road.

"That's one of Daddy's favorite birds," I say, pointing at their long S-shaped necks.

"Daddy and I caught one when we went to Disney World," Aidan says. Lately he has been making up stories about things he and Dave never did, moments that did not exist. I am rattled by these stories that always involve Dave doing Herculean things—saving Aidan from the subway tracks, lifting boats from stormy seas, catching Aidan when he jumped from a window. In his last counseling session, Aidan told the therapist his last words with Dave. "My daddy called me and he said, 'Aidan, I have to go into the towers and save people,' and I said, 'Okay.' " After the session, I whispered to the therapist that they never spoke that morning, that Aidan was barely awake. I told her all the stories he had been making up, and she nodded. "It's normal under the circumstances," she said, and of course I know it is true because I have imagined that day differently, the way it would have been if I'd known. I woke up at 7:30 A.M. with a strange feeling in my chest. When Dave called I was upset and insisted he come home right away, leave the firehouse at once. Aidan was up already and pleading to talk to his father. Aidan would tell Dave about finding *Star Wars* figures at a stoop sale or recount a dream. I could hear Dave's voice, small and thin on the other end. "Okay, buddy. I'm going to come home now, okay? I love you."

"Love you, too," Aidan would say before handing me back the phone to hang up.

The other side of Oahu is, as the surfers promised, much sunnier than Honolulu. We follow John and the other instructors down a long winding path, flanked on both sides by tall, fragrant pine trees. Aidan kicks the small pinecones and needles as he walks, scraping his sandals, talking incessantly to Tony and Donna's son John. They have become good friends. The path opens up to a wide expanse of beach where white sand stretches for miles untouched, like freshly fallen snow. Small perfect waves roll onto the shore one after another. The surface of the water is quilted with patches of iridescent aquas and blues, hiding the coral reef below.

We set up our chairs and blankets close to the water, and Aidan immediately runs toward the ocean, Huey's and Tony's boys following. They pretend the water is a monster that can eat you up if it touches your feet. Screaming, they run back and forth, dodging the waves, laughing and collapsing when the water touches them. I smile, because for a moment, Aidan is exactly the same as them. There is no Ground

A Widow's Walk

Zero or missing father. They are just playing on a beach, the sun beating down on their bony backs as they try to escape the waves.

After lunch, the instructors dole out surf shirts, water shoes, and large Styrofoam surfboards and line us up on the beach. They stand across from us and demonstrate how to paddle the board and pop up in a squat, balancing in the middle of the board. I look in both directions and laugh at the wives and widows ogling the handsome surfers. We are divided into groups and given an instructor. Theresa pokes me in the ribs when we are given John. We lay our boards down and practice paddling, awkwardly flailing our hands in the sand. We pop up on our boards, sweating and giggling, posing in exaggerated *Hawaii Five-O* stances. Theresa chuckles and shakes her head when I pretend to run in slow motion in the sand, tossing my hair back like Pamela Anderson. I love to make her laugh.

Our group is last to go. Like ducklings, we follow John into the water, pushing our boards in front of us. My legs look white as porcelain in the water, the reef like an island of mountains below us. I once watched a film about a coral reef, thousands of years old, destroyed by the human touch in a matter of moments, thousands of vibrantly colored organisms fading to a bleached white. I try not to let my shoes touch its surface.

The waves seem bigger up close, and I have to tilt my board to get over them. Theresa has gone off with another instructor, so it is just Leah and me with John, the water splashing in our faces. My fear of the ocean returns, and I picture Dave in the water, his body becoming supple and light, swimming with the ease of a dolphin.

I paddle behind John, deeper and deeper, trying not to give in to my fear. John stops at a lull where the waves begin. "A break," he calls it. I am out of breath and my arms feel weak, the waves making my board rock below me. John takes Leah first, and I watch him push her, giving her a head start in the wave and yelling for her to paddle fast. She pops up and stands for a second, her graceful body teetering slightly before she falls, her long limbs poking up from the ocean. It is my turn next. John swims over to me and we wait for my wave. I tell him about Dave, how he surfed and swam and loved the ocean like an old friend.

"Paddle fast!" John yells, suddenly pushing me forward, trying to get me ahead of the wave. I swing my arms hard and fast, flailing them in circles. "NOW!" he yells, and I try to pop up, but my body feels heavy and weak, and so I slip off, the wave passing over my head, the water quiet and cold underneath. Paddling back is even harder now, the waves higher. John pushes me again and I can hear the wave behind me. We are in a race and the wave is gaining on me. "NOW!" John yells again, and I heave myself onto my board. I am too far to the front and can feel the board tilting up in the back. Just as I begin to slide off, I right myself and move to the middle. I am standing now, the board pushing me toward the shore. I can hear my sister cheering and the wave loud underneath me, but in my head, it is as quiet as night. I take a deep breath and smile, careful to stay balanced, to enjoy every inch of this feeling. I go again and again, until my arms feel like rubber bands stapled to my torso. John is patient and kind and lets me surf past the allotted hour I paid for. I don't want this feeling of lightness to end, the water like salvation itself.

"My husband would be so proud of me," I whisper to John.

"Why don't I take Aidan?" he asks. "He'll love it."

"I dunno . . . he's only five . . . he doesn't swim very well," I tell him. I don't want to tell him how scared I am of losing my son, that he's all I have left in the world.

"I'll get some of the other guys to help," he says, signaling one of the other instructors to join him.

Aidan learns how to paddle and pop up, and in less than five minutes, he is in the water with John. I am so exhausted I lie back on the blanket, watching the sun make shapes and circles on the insides of my lids. My limbs feel heavy, like they are on the cusp of falling asleep without me. I listen to the water, the muted yells from the kids, the voices of families being carried on the wind.

"Look at Aidan!" Leah yells, and I shoot up, cupping my hand over my eyes. Aidan is standing on his board, his arms outstretched, a slight smile on his face. I feel my heart racing with excitement and John is cheering him on. I grab my camera and run to the water.

"Go, Aidan, go!" I scream, and his smile widens into a half-embarrassed grin.

"Wow! He's good!" Lynn Stackpole says as I snap pictures, laughing and crying at the same time. It seems like every emotion you can possibly feel is filling my heart, stretching it like an overblown balloon. I can feel Dave everywhere in the warm beach air, his voice whispering on the surf. For the first time I listen to him, my ears poised to hear his reedy voice. "I am right here with you," he says.

We leave in the late afternoon when the orange light makes everyone look beautiful. I lean back in my bus seat, feeling like a sated queen, when Tony says, "Look." I open my eyes to see a giant rainbow stretched in a perfect arch across the landscape. Except for the tiny reflections in a sprinkler or the small colors in an oily puddle, I have never seen a real rainbow. It is larger than I imagined, covering at least a mile from end to end, with colors so clear, they look as if they were drawn.

"Aidan, look!" I say, but he is asleep on my shoulder, his lips rounded, his lashes fluttering. Everyone is quiet, watching the rainbow or dozing, and Tony is on the cell phone now, his face serious, his brow furled.

"Everything okay?" I ask Donna, who is sitting across the aisle from me, watching Tony.

"I dunno. I don't even ask anymore," she says. I nod and she turns to me, her eyes watering with concern. "He's so angry, Marian. It's like he's just . . . he's just not the same. I mean, I feel funny telling you, but he just . . . It's hard." I nod, trying to imagine what Dave would have been like had he lived. I know he would never leave the site except to attend funerals. I know I would be alone, tucking Aidan in each night, worrying about Dave's health as he inhaled the Ground Zero dust. I would listen for Dave, the familiar sound of the door opening, his heavy footsteps in the hallway, and when he crawled into bed each night, I know I would be as alone as if he weren't there. I would listen to his breath growing heavy, his body exhausted from work, and he would toss and turn, his dreams as haunted as his days, adrift in a sea of loss.

It is almost dark when we arrive at the hotel, the palm trees shadowed against the sky. We all agree to meet at the bar by the pool for happy hour at six-thirty, then disappear into our rooms to shower. Aidan insists on going swimming with John. From the moment we arrived in Hawaii, he seems to have been submerged in water. I shower last, laughing at the amount of sand that falls from my bathing suit in wet clumps. I tilt my head down and stare at my feet. There is a tan line from my surf shoes circling my ankles. I sigh, watching the sand slide into the drain, when Leah bangs on the door.

"What!"

"I need you to come out here."

"I just got in!" I say, annoyed. Maybe Aidan is back from the pool.

I swing open the door, dripping, my body wrapped in a too-small towel. Tony, Huey, and Mike Stackpole are standing in the foyer, their faces grim and serious.

"They found Dave, Marian," Mike Stackpole says.

I clench the towel tighter around me, to hold me together. "Where was he?"

"I dunno the details. It was in the South Tower, I think."

"Was he in good shape?"

The guys shift uncomfortably. Huey is twisting his mouth, trying not to cry.

"I dunno, Marian. We don't know any details. Joe O'Donnell was there, but he didn't know it was him. He probably wasn't in too good shape." Everyone is silent, watching me. Waiting for me to react. I stare at a piece of lint on the rug. I feel confused. I should be happy he is found. It is what I have worked so hard for, and yet the pain feels as heavy and hard as the day he died.

"If you want us to go back with you . . ." Tony starts.

"Yeah. We're here for you. Whatever you need," Huey says.

"We wanna do what's good for you," Mike says, and I nod. "This is a good thing, Marian."

"I know it's good." I am nodding because I don't know what else to do. "I'm glad you guys are here."

"I got the call when we saw that rainbow," Tony says, and as soon as my eyes meet Leah's I know I am going to lose it. I force my mouth closed and the tears to wait.

When the door closes, I cry with abandon, imagining Dave in parts, pieces of him scattered across the site like seeds. *"My beautiful husband,"* I wail, cupping my hands over my eyes so I can see the site, the rescue workers excavating Dave's shattered skull, his body parts rotted beyond recognition. Behind my lids, I can picture the pieces of Dave as they zip him into a body bag and place him on a Stokes basket. The rescue and steel workers and volunteers heed the silent ritual by removing their helmets and hard hats as Dave is draped in an American flag and carried out of Ground Zero while I lie in bed, thousands of miles away, wondering what to do next. That night I dream I am with Huey and Mike and Tony. They have terra-cotta pots in their laps and are planting Dave's bones in them, patting down the dirt. I want to snatch the pots away, but Tony doesn't let me. He hands me a pot of my own instead. I reluctantly take the pot and pick up a giant femur, cartoonlike in size. I try to put it in my pot, but it doesn't fit. Embarrassed that I cannot get it in, I try to jam it in, pushing hard on it. "It won't fit!" I tell the guys, getting upset. "It just won't fit!" They are shaking their heads, disappointed, and I am crying, not knowing what to do with the femur.

I wake up sweating, the room dark and boiling hot. I open the window and lie back in bed, wondering if I should tell Aidan the news and leave today for New York. The curtain billows in a breeze that cools off the room and dries the sweat on my skin. Everything feels worse at this hour, the strange shadows crossing the room like ghosts. The image of a carnival ride pops into my head, the pirate-ship ride that swings like a pendulum from one end to the other. "Go," one end says. "Stay," says the other. Aidan is snoring next to me, his crimson lips rounded into a perfect O. He has been sleeping through the night since we arrived here, and Leah can't stop remarking on how relaxed he seems. A million thoughts compete for my attention, preventing me from sleep, but the one I think of most is the feeling I had in the ocean yesterday, of Dave being all around us there, and how for the first time since he died, I felt peace.

The next day we sit quietly at a memorial for the sixtieth anniversary of Pearl Harbor. I have decided to stay here and sit among the veterans of war, whom Dave honored most in his life. I called my mother-in-law and told her the news; her voice was cracked and sad and relieved. I watch the veterans, their hats covered in pins and medals as they stand and salute, their thin lips quivering. I wonder if they remember their losses in the same way now, if it still aches to think of their countless friends, choking as they died in muddy trenches. I concentrate on the beads of sweat that trickle down my neck, hoping I have made the right choice. Everyone I am with seems relieved to not have the trip cut short. I can feel the firefighters leaning forward in their seats, stealing glances at me to make sure I am okay.

Families on the trip from other fire companies have heard the news about Dave and congratulate me, offer condolences. Some seem disappointed it was not their relative, others seem relieved. The light feeling I had yesterday has been replaced by a dark magma that sits in my stomach, churning and boiling, making me want to retreat even farther away. I ask a small group, including Huey, Tony, and their families, if we can spend an overnight on one of the other islands. I need to regroup, a quiet place to tell Aidan the news about Dave being found.

That afternoon we take a small plane to the island of Kauai. The ride is so short, Aidan announces, "You go up, have a Coke, and come down!" He has been a wonderful traveler, his exuberance contagious, a pinprick of light in my dark mood. Tony Edwards has finagled large condominium units for us on the eastern side of the island. Even though it is dark when we arrive, I can hear the ocean below us, and the wide-open comfortable rooms relax me. Aidan and I settle into a room downstairs, where a sliding glass door opens onto a small courtyard filled with tropical plants. I stand on the cold concrete and inhale the fruity smell of dark earth and look up at a small rectangle of stars above me.

After tucking Aidan in, Leah offers to stay home so I can go to Tony's condo for drinks. Their condo is on the second floor, with more bedrooms to accommodate their three kids.

"How you doin'?" Donna asks me, her large doe eyes blinking. I shrug. Lindsay, their sullen teenager, grabs a Coke from a six-pack on the counter, spilling some. "Go upstairs, will ya?" Donna says, wiping up the mess. Lindsay smiles at me awkwardly and clumps upstairs. "She drives me nuts, that one." Donna's tanned hand swipes the counter in that efficient way a mother of three has. "How's Aidan?"

"I haven't told him yet," I say.

"Well, you'll have a funeral when we get back, right?"

"Yes." I nod. I haven't even thought that far ahead.

"I lost my father very young, and it was rough." Donna picks up a Coke and opens the crammed refrigerator, trying to find room. "Can you believe we are only here for two nights! Look how much stuff he bought!" Her body is haloed by the light of the refrigerator. She takes out some limes and a bottle of tequila and puts them on the counter to make room for the soda.

"How old were you when your dad died?" I ask.

"Seven," she says, reaching for a pitcher behind the drainboard. "It was horrible, really. He died in a car crash. I thought we'd never get over it, but you do." She cuts the limes and squeezes them into the pitcher. "That's how Tony and I really got close, you know. He lost his father when he was eleven and he never really got over it. That's why it kills him seein' all these kids. He's just so . . ." She stops abruptly, as if waking up. "Jesus! I don't even know what I'm doin' here!" Donna says, laughing. "I don't know how to make a margarita. Do you?"

"Me?" I say, sliding off my stool. "I was born in Margaritaville!" I join her in the kitchen and begin pouring tequila into the pitcher. "I'm glad you guys came," I say, measuring out the triple sec. "I think we all needed a break." Donna puts her hand on my back and I feel myself tearing up when the doorbell rings.

Kathleen enters with Huey and the kids, who run upstairs to join the others. They open the sliding glass doors in the living room, filling the room with sea air and the muted sound of crickets. I stir the margaritas, listening to Huey sing, his face turning crimson. I sit and listen to covers of Creed and Led Zeppelin and the Beatles. Kathleen sits on the couch, her feet tucked under her, smiling at Huey, and for a brief second I am consumed with envy. Their love, while not overt, lingers in the recesses, like the tropical bugs pinging softly against the screen in the darkness.

In the middle of the night, my eyes snap open with fear. I have had another nightmare. It has started to rain hard outside, and I turn on my side and stare out the window into the courtyard. I left the window open a crack, and the raindrops are loud and furious as they plop onto the broad tropical leaves, making them glisten and sway. I lie awake for hours, replaying my life, my thoughts bouncing and crossing like telephone lines. My first boyfriend, Damon, pops into my head. He was a saxophone player from high school who turned me on to John Coltrane, Panchito's on Macdougal Street, and was the only man besides Dave whom I ever loved. On hot summer nights we would take the freight elevator to the roof of the old warehouse loft where his mother lived. We'd drink pints of Old English, eat Doritos, and lie on our backs, pretending the lights of the taller buildings were stars.

I squeeze my eyes shut and think about sex. It has been four months since Dave touched me. How can you make love to the same man for seventeen years and then have nothing? I wonder what it would be like to make love to Damon again, a man I haven't thought about in seventeen years. The rain finally stops and I roll onto my back, picturing Damon's long, bony fingers, his lean, thin body.

The lights flash on and I bolt upright, my heart pounding. I look around the room, but Aidan is snoring quietly on a mattress on the floor next to me.

"Hello?" I whisper, imagining that Leah has flipped a switch by accident from outside the room. I stand up, carefully opening the door into the hall, but it is quiet. I find the switchplate on the opposite wall and flick it on and off, testing the light.

"What are you doing?" Aidan asks groggily.

"Oh, nothing, sweetie. Go back to sleep."

I turn off the light and climb back into bed. Did I imagine the light turning on? Maybe I fell asleep and merely dreamed the light flicked on, or maybe it was on the whole time. I roll over on my side again. *Okay, Dave, I won't sleep with Damon.*

It isn't long before I give up on sleep and tiptoe upstairs to see the view from our window for the first time. A stunning mountain the color of green velvet rises as if it has been squeezed from the earth. The sun has begun to rise behind it, casting the sky in a thousand shades of blue and purple. I sink into one of the chairs, staring at the spectacle, and cannot help but think of God. I used to speak to Him every day. "Thank you for my health, for my beautiful boy, my husband," I used to say. I prayed for poor and sick people, for world peace, for people I had read about in the newspaper the day before. The sun glides up slowly and the beauty confuses me, sitting in defiant juxtaposition to all the death, destruction, and sadness I feel. I sit for a long time, trying to reconcile why this God, who created this magnificent sunrise, the mammoth green leaves of tropical plants, the balmy breeze, how he can also make a heart so sad.

Aidan's footsteps jar my thoughts. I bring my finger to my lips, signaling him to be quiet. I love the way he looks in the morning, his thick eyebrows making an awning over his tired eyes. "I want to take a bath," he whispers, rubbing the corners of his eyes.

"Okay," I whisper, standing and guiding him back downstairs. "Wait until you see this bathroom." I lead him to a tiled bathroom with a big Jacuzzi tub in the corner. I fill it up while Aidan gets the toys he wants to play with from our room. He eases into the tub, his body like a miniature version of Dave's, compact and strong, and hums while he lines his soldiers up along the tub's edge.

"Aidan," I say slowly, "I want you to know that the firefighters called me from New York yesterday to tell me that they found Daddy's body."

Aidan looks up from his soldiers, his brow furrowing. "You told me he was in the coffin."

"I told you his *spirit* was in the coffin."

"His body wasn't in the coffin?"

"No."

"You lied."

"Not really. I really felt like Daddy's spirit was in the coffin that day. I would have liked to have his body there, too, but they hadn't found him yet."

"Where's Daddy's spirit then?"

"Up in heaven and in our hearts."

"But where is Daddy?"

"Up in heaven and in our h—"

"No! Where is his *body*?" He is frustrated.

"I dunno. I guess the medical examiner's office."

"You lied," he says, not looking up this time.

"I didn't, I told you—"

"Yes, I saw it!" Aidan insists. I don't want to cry so I head over to the sink and throw some cold water on my face. If he wants to believe Dave was in there, why should I tell him otherwise? Does it make a difference at all?

"Well, if you want to talk about it . . ." I say, drying my face with a towel.

"Is Daddy a skeleton?"

"I don't know. Maybe."

"How do you know what he looks like?"

"I don't, really."

"Are you going to bury his skeleton?"

"I think Daddy wants to be cremated."

"What is that?"

"It's when they turn a body to ashes."

"How?"

"They put it in a fire until it turns to ash."

"Eww! I don't want you to burn Daddy."

"That's what he wanted," I tell him, exhausted from the inquisition. It is strange how I know what Dave wanted. We were too young to make plans like these. Dave and I loved the television show *Six Feet Under* on HBO. We watched faithfully every Sunday, and I remember Dave mentioning it during the opening credits. The strange music began, the violas plucking their eerie notes when they show in subtle close-ups the images of death: a toe tag, embalming fluid dripping through tubes, an eyebrow being swabbed in preparation for the process.

"Don't ever let them do that to me," Dave said that night. "Just burn me and scatter me to the wind." That is what I will do.

21

Given Up for You

Returning home feels like stepping into the scene of an accident. Jason has filled a two-hundred-page notebook with phone messages, and there are three shopping bags full of mail at the door.

"I'm shell-shocked. I hear a phone ring, and I jump out of my skin," Jason tells me, and I feel guilty leaving him with this mess. We sit on the couch and I tell him everything that happened, his brown eyes watering when I tell him they found Dave. He assumed as much from the phone calls from the medical examiner's office. After Jason leaves, I skim my finger along the list. I call the funeral director first. He tells me it will be a few days to identify Dave's body and then another day for cremation. I decide to bury him on December 20. I hate to make his funeral so close to Christmas, but I have no other choice.

I call Joe Miccio next and arrange to meet him at the office space that was donated to our organization. I left Joe in charge of running the organization while I was away, and while I trust him, his impulsive and intense nature makes me nervous.

Joe greets me at the elevator door, the rings under his eyes as dark as his suit. We pass a metal door and enter a warehouse-size space that we will be sharing with Hospital Audiences Inc. "Wow. You look like shit," I tell Joe as he leads me to the small corner we will be using as our office.

"Yeah . . . um, I haven't slept much. It's unbelievable how much stuff is going on. I invited some of the other groups to meet here. I know you wanted to work together, so I thought it would be good to introduce everyone tonight—so anyone who wants to work with us can."

"Tonight?" I am practically running to follow Joe to a desk in front of giant arched windows. It is piled with papers and exotic-looking photographs. A row of wide army green file cabinets line the wall behind it, and sitting comfortably in the chair is Michael Spencer, the man who offered me the space. He looks exactly as I imagined him from his voice, short, with gray hair sloppily combed over his head and thick, pouty lips. He stands up to greet us.

Joe says, "Michael. This is Marian—"

"I know who she is." He reaches over the desk to shake my hand.

"It's really nice of you to share your space with us," I tell him, and he closes his eyes, embarrassed, as a tall woman heads over to the desk. She is standing on a scooter, which she uses to get from one end of the office space to the other.

"I love that photograph," I say, pointing to a large color close-up of a tribal man with brightly colored beads around his neck and a stick running through his nostrils.

"I took that. I just got back from Papau, New Guinea. Here." He hands me other pictures of exotic brown faces with sharp cheekbones and yellow teeth, naked, squatting in huts, looking quizzically at the camera. I wonder if they know anything about 9/11. I envy that they live in a world with no Code Oranges and headlines. They float on strange-shaped boats and cross rickety bridges without ever worrying if they will be blown up before they reach the other side.

"I want you to meet Monica Iken," Joe tells me as we head over to my new desk. "She's a civilian widow who started a group to address the memorial." I arch my eyebrows, wondering how anyone could think that far ahead, but I suppose it is something that will need to be addressed. "I thought that since you were so overwhelmed with retrieval, instead of duplicating efforts, we can give the memorial stuff to her."

"Okay," I say slowly, "but I want to address this issue when it's time."

"Oh, yeah. We will when it's time. I called Jennie Farrell, too, see if she wants to set up Give Your Voice here, and I offered Monica to share office space here, too. Monica's group is going to use the space, but Jennie says she's happy working out of her house and that they have their own thing going. They're coming in about ten minutes, so if we can go over the agenda."

"Ten minutes! Joe! I'm still jet-lagged. I would have liked if you talked to me about this stuff first."

"You told me you wanted to reach out to all the groups and start working together—"

"How many groups are coming?"

"I think four. There's Monica. Let me introduce you."

A tall woman in a tight brown suit stands. She shakes my hand limply, her manicured fingers scraping against my skin. "Nice to meet you," she says, handing me a card and brochure.

"Monica lost her husband, Michael," Joe continues.

"I'm so sorry," I say, looking at the brochure adorned with a child's face. "Is this your son?" I ask.

"No. We were only married a few months." Sadness flickers across her face but she averts her large eyes. "But I feel strongly about the children. I am doing this for them, so they will have a place to go. I am advocating for all sixteen acres to be dedicated for the memorial."

"That's great."

Anthony from the WTC United Family Group marches in looking flustered. "Sorry I'm late," he says, plopping a bag onto the conference table where we are standing. He always enters meetings and press conferences looking as if he has rushed from somewhere else. He takes off his coat, his wide eyes quickly taking in the room. "This is nice," he tells me as Joe sidles up to make introductions.

"Anthony, this is Monica. Anthony runs the WTC United Family Group."

"Nice to meet you," he says, reaching into his duffel bag and extracting a button to give her.

Jennie arrives next, her large eyes red and tired. She is with her brother Patrick, one of the five siblings I haven't met yet. He is tall, with a cropped military haircut, glasses, and a green suit.

"Hey," I say, giving Jennie a hug.

"I heard they found Dave," she says, and I swallow audibly, trying not to cry. "It's really a blessing to have him home," she says, and I nod.

"I wish that for you, too," I tell her, and she pulls away from me to wipe her nose with a tissue.

We take seats at the conference table, Anthony still arranging papers in his briefcase.

*   *   *

The following morning, Leah and I walk to meet with the funeral director at Duffy's on 9th Street, a nondescript building I have been in only once. Leah and I meet Robert Amato in the lobby, a dark, low-ceilinged room with vases of plastic flowers. Robert seems too young to be a funeral director. He is a plain, soft-spoken man in his early thirties who wears gray suits and a permanent expression of sympathy. He leads us to an office downstairs and sits behind an oversize desk neatly stacked with brochures for caskets and urns and cards. *What a racket,* I think, feeling grateful that all my expenses will be covered. What do other people do when they have nothing? Robert clears his throat, jarring me from my thoughts.

"Leah tells me you would like to have Dave cremated."

"Yes."

"Okay, well," he says, standing. "Why don't I show you some of the caskets we have." I follow him to a room in the back where coffins line the wall. They are all made of wood in varying shades and types. They are all open and lined with white satin, which reminds me of a wedding dress or a christening outfit.

"Here are some of our more inexpensive ones, since you already had your viewing," Robert says.

"Why do they need a casket at all?" I ask, more out of curiosity than callousness, but Robert looks flustered.

"Well, most people choose our cardboard one back here." He signals me to a room even farther back. What looks like a large cardboard moving box stands against the wall. "Since it's not really used for a service."

"Is that okay?" I ask my sister, who nods.

"Yeah. Why would you pay three thousand dollars if they're just going to burn it?" Leah asks.

"Well, it's Dave," I say, looking at Robert, who stares at me blankly.

"It's really your decision," he says, and I shrug.

"I guess the cardboard is okay," I say, wondering if I am making the right decisions and why there are so many to make.

"That's two hundred fifty dollars," Robert says, jotting it down on a clipboard as he heads back to his desk and begins filling out the paperwork.

"Expensive cardboard," my sister whispers as we watch Robert retrieve another file from a drawer.

"I just need you to sign a few release forms for me. This is the death certificate. We will have other originals made from it for your records." I take the form and stare at it. It is the same colored paper as our marriage certificate, with thick black lettering and a similar-looking gold seal. My eyes scan the paper: Dave's name, date of birth, social security number, cause of death—homicide—*Blunt trauma to the head, neck, and torso*. I repeat the words to myself. *Blunt trauma*. The words linger on the page: blunt trauma. I hand the death certificate back, nodding, my eyes watering as I picture Dave getting struck in his head, his neck, his torso. Why is it so specific?

"What does he look like?" I ask Robert, who looks up from his paperwork.

"I really don't know."

My sister covers my hand with hers, and Robert looks at me, waiting for this wave to pass. I wonder how many times he has sat and waited for people to finish crying. I look up at him as empathetically as he looks at me; his is truly the worst job in the world.

He waits for the right moment and says, "Leah said you will be scattering Dave?"

"Yes, I need him divided into . . . um . . . five. Yes, five." Again Robert's face shifts and he says nothing. "Is that unusual?" I ask.

"Um, no . . . no . . . A little irregular, but entirely possible. You do know that since your husband was found, well, there was not . . ."

"Much of him," I say, nodding, and I feel my sister looking at me, confused. I haven't told her that no one at this late stage is being found in one piece, and I haven't had the nerve to ask Joe, the only firefighter from Squad who was there when they found him, just how many pieces there were. "It's just symbolic really," I tell him. "I just want to scatter him in his favorite places." Robert seems satisfied with this answer and makes a note on his clipboard, then hands me a catalog of urns.

"Did you want five urns then?" Robert asks.

"I dunno," I say, rifling through the pages. "This would be good for the cemetery," I say, pointing to a page of wooden urns designed specifically for firefighters and police. I choose a simple pine box with a Maltese cross to put Dave's badge number on. Robert opens his own catalog and copies down the item numbers while Leah and I look through the rest of the book.

"They're so big," I say, looking at hundreds of urns: ceramic, tile, metal, and more, in every shape. "I don't know . . . I mean, salt and pepper shakers would be fine." Leah giggles at my joke.

"Well, we do have some smaller ones." Robert reaches across the desk and flips forward a few pages. "Are any of these water scatterings?"

"Yes, two," I tell him, and he points to a small urn shaped like a UFO.

"This urn is used for that. It's light, so you can throw it and then it slowly dissolves."

"Yes, but if I'm scattering from the beach, I imagine throwing the urn and then the wave brings it back and then you throw it again and then the wave brings it back." Leah laughs at the thought.

"You're right. That would be more for a scattering off a boat, I suppose," he says, looking through the book for something else, but Leah and I are gone, laughing harder now, setting each other off in a fit of giggles. We have always had this problem when we are nervous or scared.

"Why don't I give you ladies some time," Robert says, standing, as Leah and I try to collect ourselves.

"I'm sorry," I manage to say as he nods and slides out the door. Left alone in the dim basement room, we let our laughter go until our stomachs ache, and then, just as quickly, we take a sharp turn into tears. It never ceases to amaze me how similar the emotions feel in my body, the stomach shaking, the shoulders bouncing, the tears falling. Even though laughing and crying are on opposite ends of the emotional spectrum, the similarities are difficult to ignore.

* * *

"Hey, kiddo," Lee says. "I heard about Dave." A long silence ensues. He is one of the few people I feel comfortable being quiet with. "It's hard. As much as you want it . . ."

"There's a part of you that doesn't," I say.

"Yup." Lee sighs deeply. "We found Jonathan last night."

"Where was he?" I ask.

"Right next to Dave," he says simply, and I fall silent again, considering the odd fate of this. "There were a bunch of guys found in a row, and they're guessing that they were right on the stairs with each other." Lee stops talking. He knows I am crying.

"That's so weird," I say between sobs.

"Isn't that something?" he says, and now my tears are audible, tiny staccato gasps of air.

"You're going to make me cry," he says, but I know he already is. I imagine his jaw protruding, exposing his small crooked teeth.

"I dreaded this day that— I didn't want to be there when they found him. I did, and I didn't." He pauses, searching for the right words.

"You didn't want to see your beautiful son that way," I say.

"Yeah," he says, exhaling.

"Were you there?" I ask him finally, surprised I did not know this already.

"I had been home from the site about two hours."

"Who found him?"

"Paul Ferrel from Engine Eight and a couple of guys from Rescue Two. . . . I got to the site last night after they called me. They had him in a Stokes and one of the first things Paul said, he came up to me and put his arm around my shoulders and he said, 'Lee, he's all there.' " Lee breaks off again, crying harder, his sobs audible as he struggles to regain his voice. "But I still had to feel him."

"You touched him?"

"Yeah." The image is as clear as if I am there, the wrinkled black body bag, the sad, dirty faces of the rescue workers, the drooping face of Lee standing over his dead son.

"Well, I went from his toes right up . . ." Lee is choking on his tears now, trying to talk. "He was in the bag, I didn't want to open it . . . I said to him. I spoke to him . . . I . . . um." Lee stops and swallows hard. I can imagine his Adam's apple rising and falling like an arcade bell when he whispers, "I apologized."

"For what?"

Lee chuckles suddenly. "It made no difference. I mean, he loved what he did, but I got him into the department."

"Oh, Lee. He would have done it anyway."

"Yeah, you're right," he says, blowing his nose. "I still had to apologize. I still apologize every time I look at his picture. Tell him 'I'm sorry I got you on the job.' " Lee sighs so deeply I can almost see the air traveling down. "His brother was there . . . Myself and some guys from Two Eighty-eight carried him out, and he was heavy." Lee laughs from the same place the sigh came from, and I can't help but smile. "I was so happy he was heavy because I used to tease him, you see, about putting on a little bit of weight. He wasn't fat, but I teased him, and when I picked him up I said, 'God bless, he's heavy.' "

* * *

Jack and Lee meet me in the lobby of Bellevue Hospital to attend the medical examiner's meeting. They wear the same baseball caps with red, white, and blue stars and their son's names embroidered on the front. We kiss hello and board the elevator to the eighteenth floor. Jack suggests questions to ask. We decide we will focus on where the families can go to visit their missing loved ones for the holiday. Over two thirds of the families have still received nothing, and Christmas will only intensify this pain. It is strange how the holidays feel ominous now, the words "merry, joy, and happy" glowing everywhere, in direct contrast to my mood.

In the large conference room, Jennie is already seated, taking notes. She is talking to Shiya Ribowsky, a lanky Sephardic-looking medical examiner with a thick beard and mustache. He begins the meeting, talking about the effects of charring in identifying DNA. I look out the window at a redbrick building across the courtyard and write "charred" on my yellow legal pad. I imagine bones with charcoal ends, their surface cracked and gray.

Dr. Robert Shallet, a rotund man with the face of a stern Santa Claus, talks about the process of air-drying the remains in a dehumidification chamber to keep the parts from decomposing and protect them from losing any DNA. I look around the table at Jack and Lee taking notes, at Jennie Farrell and her brother Michael, at the numerous medical examiners, forensic dentists, forensic anthropologists, many of whom were injured in the first collapse, having rushed to Ground Zero to help. They are faced with the unprecedented and daunting task of identifying over six times as many body parts as victims. I stare at the fading light outside, the words "remains, body parts, cheek swabs, procedure, samples, forensic" drift through my thoughts as I watch the sun fading.

Lee kicks me under the table. I was daydreaming, wondering how my life could turn so quickly from performing comedic monologues to talking about body parts. We are on the fifth item on the agenda, a form through which a victim's family can control how they are told about their loved ones' remains. Some families have had as many as two hundred body parts for a single victim, many others have received nothing. The form we are creating will allow family members to choose to be notified every time something is found, to be notified at the end of the process, to have their funeral director notified, a loved one notified, and so on. We brought up the issue with the medical examiner's office, a few weeks after I met a widow named Nicole. Her husband worked at Carr Futures, and his father was a retired firefighter. She was young and pretty, a former second-grade schoolteacher with straight black hair and luminescent skin. She told me she had been called by the medical examiner last week and told that her husband's heart had been found on the tracks of the PATH train, which ran under the World Trade Center. The heart stood alone and completely intact. I imagined it red and beating, an anomaly among the dust and twisted steel. "At least I got the best part of him," Nicole said. "At least I got something."

*　*　*

"I wanted to go to my class's holiday party!" Aidan whines as we arrive at the gates of Green-Wood Cemetery for Dave's funeral. I say nothing, feeling guilty that I did not choose another day for Dave's service.

I drive under the elaborate thin spires of the entrance that reminds me of the castles I made on the beach as a kid. A line of cars follow the twisting road to the Gothic chapel, a small elegant building of carved white stone and stained glass. At least I had insisted on making Dave's funeral a quiet, brief event with only the family, a few friends, and of course Squad 1. I see the widows first, their long coats blowing in the wind like black flags. I wave to Martha, her thin hair flapping in her face. My stomach shifts as I realize that she has not had a service yet for Tommy but has already attended two memorials for Dave. Princess Linda is here, too; Theresa and Debbie; and the survivor's wives, the unsung heroes.

The chapel is so small that only a few people can sit. Father Bartley recites a short prayer and we make our way quickly to the grave site. The cars snake past carved angels, crosses, and mausoleums, and I remember again the spring Dave and I hiked through this place, the dogwoods blooming and the billowy pink branches of cherry blossoms waving in the breeze. It didn't feel sad to me then, more like an outdoor museum than a cemetery, with so much beauty and history. I discovered a grotto tucked in the trees where a husband wrote a poem for his lost wife, and Dave showed me a beautiful sculpture of a thirteen-year-old drummer boy, the first casualty of the Revolutionary War. There was a large section dedicated solely to firefighters who died in the early 1800s, when Brooklyn was a separate city and firefighters died with alarming frequency. The gravestones were topped with sculptures of fire helmets encircled by a hose. I wanted this for Dave, but Green-

Wood stopped making them in the 1930s, when they became too expensive to maintain.

The heels of my boots sink into the soft earth as I make the awkward ascent to Dave's grave site. I keep my head down, the wind blowing hard in my face. I see firefighters from other companies, 239, 105, 122, who knew Dave. The funeral director hands everyone a peach-colored rose, and we stand around the small hole that has been dug. Dave's pine urn sits on the side, dwarfed by the vast hill behind it. Father Bartley whispers the prayer for the dead, his soft brogue traveling on the wind, mixing with the sighing of the pines. Leah is behind me, holding Aidan's hand, and I am sobbing hard. Toni and my mother are leaning heavily against me, two bookends trying to hold up a faded paperback. I try to ignore their weight and cry as I never have in front of a group, bawling without filters. When the weight of my two mothers becomes too much, I break free, stepping forward to the very edge of Dave's grave, peering into the dark hole. It makes me think of the fear I felt as a child, looking into the black unknown of the closet, the abyss under the bed, the shadowy shapes of the night. Aidan stands next to me, staring up at my face. I know he is feeling the same fear when he looks at me, wondering when his life will have some semblance of what used to be. I can see my face through his eyes, so I dry my eyes and force a smile.

"Let's say a prayer for Daddy," I whisper, sniffling, hoping no one will intrude on this moment as Aidan places his rose gently on the box and then watches as I do the same. We step back a few feet as the pine box disappears under a deluge of peach roses, everyone murmuring prayers for Dave. When the box is covered, we awkwardly make our way down the hill, my thighs clenching from the cold and the steep descent.

22

Last Words

December 22

"It's itchy!" Aidan complains as I pull the red wool sweater over his head. My mother-in-law brought it back from Ireland a few years ago.

"It's for the Christmas party," I tell him, trying not to sound as impatient as I feel.

When we finally arrive at Squad, the fire truck is parked out front, its new chrome sparkling. There are dozens of flowers perched in front of the firehouse door, white carnations and sprigs of pine. The familiar strains of "Holly Jolly Christmas" seep from under the firehouse door.

Christmas had been a painful time for Dave until Aidan was born, when he not only began enjoying the holiday, but became practically drunk with Christmas spirit, covering our small apartment with angels and lights and a tree so big he had to saw off its lower branches to make it fit. He took on the responsibility of organizing the firehouse Christmas party, too, constructing a Santa's chair and decorating the firehouse.

"C'mon, Mommy," Aidan says when I pause in front of the firehouse door, terrified to go inside.

The room is packed tight, the apparatus floor covered with long tables covered with red tablecloths and plastic plates of candy. Dave's family is sitting at a table toward the front. I kiss them hello and sneak Aidan's present under the oversize tree.

Squad has gone all out this year, hiring a DJ, clowns, face painters, a caterer, a chorus, and a Santa Claus with a real white beard. I, too, put on a good show, smiling at the kids, taking pictures. I hide the fact that my heart stops when I see the Santa's chair and the cardboard fire truck that Dave made. I tease Kenny Michitsch, who is dressed as an elf, the pointy rubber ears a shade lighter than his own. He wears a pointed felt shoe on one foot and a cast on the other, from a car accident he had two weeks ago. We corral the kids outside and watch as Kenny escorts Santa down from the roof in Tower Ladder 105, stopping the traffic on Union Street.

When the grief becomes too much, I tiptoe upstairs to the empty bunk room. Cots are lined up in two long rows on each wall, as in my favorite children's book *Madeline*: "In two rows of nine, the youngest one was Madeline." The cot creaks when I sit, and I stare at the white specks in the green tiled floor, trying to shake the feeling that something is terribly amiss. Then the cot moans under the weight of Sean Cummins, who sits next to me and hands me a tissue. "Did you see the bag for you? That one's yours," he says, pointing to a huge clear plastic bag overflowing with gifts, a new bicycle gleaming beside it. "Have you ever seen such loot?" I feel my lip quivering again, overwhelmed by everyone, the kindness and pain.

"It's pretty unbelievable," I say. He sighs and we sit for a long time, staring at the bag of gifts donated by firehouses and schools and people all over the country.

After a long silence, he says, "I had a dream about Dave, you know."

"Really?" It seems everyone except me has had nightly visits from Dave.

"I've had a few. I didn't want to tell you because I didn't want to upset ya, but I had one the day before they found Dave. I dreamed he told me where he was at Ground Zero. He kept saying these coordinates, these strange numbers, and I kept saying 'What the hell are ya talkin' about?' but then in the dream they suddenly made perfect sense. It was the far wall of the South Tower. And of course I woke up and none of it made any sense except that on that day they found him, he was on the far wall of the South Tower."

"Weird," I say, drying my lashes with the corner of the tissue.

"Pretty strange." We stare straight ahead, quiet again. "I'm sure you heard that I'm transferring to Rescue One." Dave had considered the move himself a few years ago.

"You do what you have to" is all I say, wondering if Sean knows how mad the men are at him for leaving before all the firefighters are buried. I don't want to admit that I am disappointed, too. There are so few of the original crew left now, with new guys appearing each day.

"Well, I put in for a transfer before the eleventh, but then of course I didn't want to leave so I canceled it, but I can't stay here anymore. It's not . . ." Sean's eyes squint and he lowers his voice. "I wouldn't tell the guys this, but this place is haunted. I can feel the guys walking around." He stares at his knuckles for a second and continues. "Like I'll go and close Dave's locker door and it will click closed, and then a minute later it's open again. It's not the hinge or anything, either. I checked that. It's just always open. All the guys are noticing it, too. I even put a chair in front of the door before we all left for lunch a few days ago, and when we came back it was open again."

"Maybe the guys are playing a trick on you."

"No, believe me, I am not a guy who believes in this stuff," and I chuckle, remembering how the owner of a B&B in Ireland told us not to sleep on the fairy circle or it will bring us bad luck. Ireland is full of ancient magic and folklore. "I wouldn't even have believed it if I didn't see it with my own eyes. I've been wanting to tell you, but I didn't want to scare you."

I want to tell Sean how skeptical I am, but then something inside of me stops. If it isn't true, what else do I have to cling to? A black void where Dave just sits for perpetuity? There is a part of me, larger than I like to admit, that has to believe Dave is not gone but is around me, floating like dust particles in a sunbeam, drifting everywhere. My brother, Luke, told me he was walking across campus and felt Dave tap him on the shoulder. My mother saw him surrounded in a pale yellow light, smiling. My friend Dede saw a vision of him during her yoga class; Louise from my writing group said he touched her face in a dream and whispered he was okay. And now Sean.

"I feel Dave a lot," I tell Sean. "Some days more than others. Some days I think that maybe I've lost my mind and I'm just too desperate, but deep inside me . . . I know it's him."

Sean nods and is silent for a moment. "Right after the eleventh, Dave spoke to me. It was sort of a dream." He turns and looks at me, checking in. "I don't want to tell you if it's going to upset you."

"No, go ahead, I'm fine."

Sean takes a deep breath, leaning forward. "I haven't told anyone, because I know they would think I was mad, but he visited me . . . your Dave. He told me his last thought before he died." Like a faucet being turned on, I am crying again, and Sean stops.

"He said his last thought was of you and Aidan. He said it to me like he wanted me to tell you. That's all he thought about, was the two of you. The last thought on his mind." He stops and the words sit like the pile of presents in the middle of the room. I nod heartily as huge tears fall into my lap. Sean puts his arms around my shaking shoulders. I want to tell him I know it's true, not because I believe in ghosts or visitations or signs, but because I knew Dave. I peeked inside his soul more than once and saw how clearly and deeply he loved Aidan and me.

* * *

A few days after New Year's, I walk along the cobblestone streets in front of City Hall for my last meeting with Mayor Giuliani. I hate to admit, even to myself, that I am genuinely sad to see him leave office. I did not vote for him in the last election and even joined a protest against him at the Brooklyn Museum when he tried to close an art show that he found offensive. Yet as suspicious as I am of politicians, particularly Republicans, he has endeared himself to me. I have heard of his penchant for being stubborn and dictatorial, but with our group, he has rolled up his sleeves to help us. I like the way he refers to the firefighters as "his men," even though I am often tempted to chime in, "Then why haven't you paid them what they're worth?" I find him charismatic and easy to talk to and I wonder if Dave would feel the same way. I can't even remember if Dave voted for him. Like everything else, in politics, Dave was always full of contradictions, joining me at a pro-choice rally in Washington while stubbornly maintaining that he was not pro-choice but pro-responsibility. He was registered as an independent, shunned partisan politics, but followed every political race and had quotes from FDR stuck to the refrigerator. At the firehouse, Dave never joined in discussions of politics, and when we stood together in the long line in the auditorium of John Jay High School to vote, Dave refused to tell me whom he was voting for.

The meeting is in the west wing of City Hall, in my favorite room, where oil paintings of former mayors line the curving walls. I have heard that the new mayor will convert this conference room to cubicles and office space to simulate a more businesslike environment.

I greet the usual group leaders. Monica is here today, clicking her long nails together. Mayor Giuliani enters with Tom and Lynn and all the staff I have become familiar with. Even Judith Nathan, the mayor's girlfriend, is here to say good-bye. Mayor Giuliani kisses me on the cheek, smashing me in the face as he usually does. I know it serves the politicians to be good to the families. Mayor Giuliani would not want to leave office with angry widows and firefighters yelling on the steps of City Hall. Yet I want temporarily to believe, even if it is naive, that the mayor was genuinely changed by the events of September 11.

It has been interesting to watch each politician adopt a family leader like a pet. Chuck Schumer and Governor Pataki chose the Cartier family. Eliot Spitzer likes Anthony Gardner. Hillary Clinton and Mayor Giuliani adopted me. Mayor Giuliani has invited me to benefits, and to serve on the advisory board of the Twin Towers Fund. Hillary Clinton asks me to luncheons and calls to offer her help. I graciously and cautiously accept the invitations, careful not to align myself with anyone in particular. Through all the speeches and press conferences and meetings, I can never quite shake the feeling that we have become diplomats of grief, the faces of 9/11, who will never return to the lives we once knew.

The mayor makes a long speech about his commitment to the 9/11 families, despite leaving office. He introduces us to the incoming Bloomberg staff, reassuring us that it will be a smooth transition to the new mayor. Despite this, we are all concerned that, having not been directly affected, the new mayor might not be as receptive to the families as Mayor Giuliani has been.

The following night I stand in a dark bar with Theresa Russo, Martha Butler, and Debbie Amato for our monthly Merry Widows' dinner. The original group has narrowed to a tight circle of women whom I call nearly every day. We are unlikely friends, as different as colors, and yet we have grown to love each other, attached by the same rope of loss, pulling each other up when one of us falls. Debbie was a suburban housewife who hadn't even learned to drive until her twins were three years old, but she was not by any means passive. She left her first husband, got a full-time job, and raised her son alone until she met Jim, sitting in front of his firehouse in Queens. Theresa was the career nurse, financially independent, in another relationship for seventeen years. She only met Mike recently, but it was true love for the first time. She never planned on having children and certainly not on raising them alone. Martha met Tom in high school. He was a police officer visiting the school, and she whistled at him as he walked across the cafeteria. By the time Martha was twenty-seven, they were married and had three young kids. Martha was quiet and shy, unused to expressing her emotions. But like everything else after that day, things changed. We are keenly aware that under different circumstances, we would have been polite acquaintances, seeing each other only at the annual picnic or the occasional firehouse dinner.

The smell of steak competes with the cigarettes, making it feel like a full-fledged French bistro. Toulouse-Lautrec prints hang on vanilla-colored walls. I look forward to these dinners, commiserating about the challenges of single parenting, the loneliness of an empty bed, the painful shock of seeing our husbands' shirts in the closet, the prospect of dating again, the helpless feeling of seeing kids grieve—and of course there are always surprises.

"I'm going to get a boob job," Debbie announces, cupping her hands around her breasts. At forty-two, her body is still taut and thin. Her husband was Captain Amato, whom I met only once.

"Get outta here!" I yell at her. "What's wrong with your boobs? They're perfect!"

"I hate them! They're like two coin purses with no change in them."

Theresa laughs hard. "I wouldn't mind just a little lift," she says, pulling back her jacket. She is well endowed, befitting her six-foot frame. "Just an inch up!" she says, hoisting her breasts from the top.

"I don't have anything," Martha says softly, her voice flat and sad.

"If you got a boob job, you'd fall over," I joke, and Martha actually giggles.

"I'd get black eyes if I didn't wear two jogging bras." I pretend to run, throwing my head back as if I am getting hit in the eyes.

"I'm getting my teeth done, too," Debbie says, laughing.

"What's wrong with your teeth?" I ask, astonished.

"I hate them!"

"You have beautiful teeth!" Martha says.

"I would get some lips. I have Irish lips," Theresa says, and then we are all confessing what we would change about ourselves: Botox, collagen lips, liposuction, porcelain inlays, face-lifts. I talk about the wrinkles under my eyes, the space between my front teeth, my round belly. And then I stop because I realize I have never considered these things before. I am a feminist, independent, opposed to undergoing surgery to please a man, and yet I realize for the first time, as much as I hate to admit it, that when Dave died, it felt like my self-esteem died with him. Wrinkles and moles I've had for years have become eyesores. I can see Dave watching me look at myself in the mirror, pinching the loose skin on my stomach after Aidan was born. "You're a woman. You're not a little girl. Women are supposed to have round stomachs. They're sexy, and it's beautiful, especially because it held my little boy." I watched him in the mirror and smiled because I believed him. The remembering makes a lump catch in my throat and my eyes fill with tears.

"Don't start that!" Theresa says.

"I just don't think I will ever be loved like Dave loved me." I start to cry, and now they are all tearing up. This is what we do, what the night will always eventually yield.

"I know I'm not. You're lucky if love comes around once in your life, and I know Mike was it," Theresa says.

"Stop it. You guys are freakin' depressing me!" Debbie says.

"It's true. I'm not marrying again," Theresa exclaims, handing me a tissue.

"Never say never," Martha deadpans.

"You really think you'd marry again?" Theresa asks.

"Me? Who's going to marry me? I'm so busy chasing around three kids. Who's going to want to deal with that? I know I wouldn't," Martha says.

"You're so young, though, to say that," Debbie says. "I know I want a man. Jim always said that I would find someone right away if he died. I hate being alone. It's killin' me. *Killin' me!*"

"I know. I feel desperate," I say. "How can you go from having sex four times a week for seventeen years to *nothing*?"

"Four times a week!" Martha yells, laughing. "What are you, a freakin' sex machine?"

"Jim and I did that!" Debbie says.

"Please! I was all over Mike," Theresa says.

"You were newlyweds," I say.

"I was too tired, with three freakin' kids," Martha says.

"I don't even miss the sex. I miss being held," I say.

"It's so true. I just hug my pillow at night and I'm like, 'Tom, how could you leave me like this?' " Martha's voice is so small, I have to lean in to hear her. I imagine her tiny body in her big bed, a rowboat in the vast sea.

"You girls are depressing me!" Theresa says.

"I know, right?" Debbie says, rolling her eyes. "I miss the sex."

"Me, too," Theresa says, biting her lip. "Let's stop talking about it."

"I can't take it. I don't like being alone," Debbie says. "I gotta have sex soon."

I nod, but to me it is like a paraplegic thinking about walking again. I cannot imagine sleeping with another man. "I feel bad for the first guy who sleeps with me," I say.

"Let's move her to the bottom of the list," Theresa jokes, referring to the bets we've placed, listing widows from the firehouse who will have sex soonest.

"Yeah, move her to the bottom," Martha jokes, sipping her drink. We laugh and I roll my eyes, but truthfully, I know that is where I am supposed to be.

*   *   *

When the phone rings at 7 A.M. a week later, I say, "This better be good," running for the phone before it wakes Aidan. I grab it on the last ring and let out a breathy and annoyed "Hello?"

"Is this Marian Fontana?" a voice whiny and slow asks.

"Yes," I say. "This is a little early to be calling."

"I apologize. This is Michael Bloomberg."

"Who?" I ask, confused. Michael Bloomberg. Why does that sound familiar? Did I meet him at a meeting? Is he someone from the neighborhood?

"Is this Marian Fontana?"

"Yes . . . wait. Where are you from?" I hope he isn't the press. I am too tired to think.

"The mayor's office," he answers.

"Oh." Then it hits me. This is our new mayor, the one who will be taking over for Mayor Giuliani.

"I just wanted to introduce myself to all the family groups and let you know that I am here and available to talk. We will be meeting next week, but I just wanted to say hello. I've heard about the work you are doing and I look forward to meeting you . . . Hello?"

"Thanks," I say lamely, hoping he didn't hear me smack my hand to my forehead. "I look forward to it, too."

Later that day, the wind surges up Broadway, swirling plastic bags in miniature tornadoes. It is so cold, I can't stop thinking about the rescue workers at Ground Zero. Still looking, still working. Every hour, every day. I pull the scarf more tightly around my neck and drop my head against the wind, ducking into the lobby of my office. I have been so busy attending meetings and press conferences, it is the first time I have been here since the initial meeting over a month ago.

Upstairs, Monica has completely taken over, setting up at the largest desk by the window. A young, balding man with round cherubic cheeks is slumped at a computer, entering data. He looks up when I walk over, shushing me with a pale finger and gesturing toward Monica, who sits in front of a television crew being interviewed.

My corner of the office is a complete mess, with unpacked boxes, computers, and piles of unopened mail. I tiptoe toward it and slowly sort through piles of packages and mail, the television crew shooting me dirty looks when a piece of paper ripping makes it onto their microphones.

I get a call from Diane, the wife of a firefighter and a public relations person we hired to handle the press calls. I can barely hear her on her cell phone, a loud white noise behind her. I make out that she's gotten another request from *Oprah* about the Victims Compensation Fund. I sigh out loud. I don't want to talk about money and defend myself to an audience of people who will call me greedy.

The Victims Compensation Fund, which was supposedly created to bail out the airlines from bankruptcy, was passed without the public's knowledge that it would change the tort system as we know it. For me, it was not about money, but it presented a classic moral issue. The middle-class worker—the firefighter, the window washer, the Port Authority Police—would be most adversely affected by this fund, essentially leaving them with nothing. I explain this to Martha, trying to persuade her to go on *Oprah,* and to five other widows, and finally convince Regan Vega, a raspy-voiced teacher from Windsor Terrace, the next neighborhood over, who lost her firefighter husband Peter on 9/11.

I wish her luck and then sigh in relief when I hang up the phone.

Back in Brooklyn, I take 6th Avenue to avoid bumping into friends. I need to be on time for my first therapy session with Dena. I am looking forward to the safe haven of Dena's warm office, but it will be strange to be there without Dave. Two years ago Dave and I had gone to couple's counseling with Dena, when the stress from his job seeped into our marriage like a toxic gas.

Skeletons of discarded Christmas trees rock in the strong winds, pine needles blowing into small piles by the curb. On Park Place, I look for the small bare tree in front of Dena's brownstone. The church bell chimes once. I am exactly on time. I remember watching Dave walk down the street, his pace deliberate and infuriatingly slow. With his yoga mat tucked under his arm, he would sidle up the steps, arriving exactly when the last toll sounded.

Today the office is darker as the sun dips behind some clouds. I climb the green-carpeted stairs to the fourth-floor office and sit on my side of the itchy gray couch. As I wait for Dena, I stare at the empty spot where Dave used to sit. I could see his profile, his back stick-straight, his hands on his knees, as he talked for the first time about picking up severed limbs on subway tracks, the sounds of ribs cracking like twigs as he did CPR, the smell of burned skin. He shared things there that I never knew. We talked about our families, the odd circumstance of our finding each other, and I fell in love with Dave all over again for being vulnerable, for wanting to know himself more. I know it took immense bravery to run into a burning building, but it took a different kind of courage for Dave to look inside himself. When we stopped therapy last June, I felt closer to Dave than I ever had, as if we were beginning life with a new perspective. I feel the burn of grief and force myself to read the book titles: *Codependency No More, The Journey Within, Adult Children of Alcoholics*. I notice how odd it is that these books are propped up in between fiction: *Of Mice and Men* and *A Heartbreaking Work of Staggering Genius*.

Dena enters with an empathetic smile and a cup of tea. She sits in her black reclining chair and pushes it back so far, I can see the bottom of her shoes. She is in her mid-fifties, with small close-set eyes, short cropped hair, and a colorful scarf. Seeing her immediately makes me cry and cry and cry.

"All that work for nothing," I say.

"It's good you and Dave were in a really healthy place," Dena says, and I know this is true, that our seventeen years evolved, the roots stronger and more entwined. There was nothing left unsaid, no feeling furled. Recently I had spoken with a widow who fought with her husband on the morning of the eleventh and she wore her regret like a leaden coat. Another confessed she was considering leaving her husband; still another thought her husband was cheating.

Outside, the wind hits my face and I begin to breathe slower. I walk to 7th Avenue toward the bank, and Mrs. Dumas spots me and waves. I taught her daughter gymnastics a few years ago. It's been five months since Dave died, and I thought I had seen everyone in the neighborhood there was to see, but there is always one more, one more genuine person standing awkwardly, not knowing what to say and so instead plastering on the face of sympathy and asking: "Is there anything I can do?"

"YES! WHY DON'T YOU BRING MY HUSBAND BACK HERE NOW, 'CAUSE, YOU SEE, I MISS HIM SO MUCH THAT IT IS UNBEARABLE AND I DON'T EVEN WANT TO LIVE! OKAY? THANKS!"

"No, thank you. I'm fine. Thanks for thinking of me," I say.

I actually don't mind seeing Mrs. Dumas. She was grateful to me for loving her daughter, Emily, a shy, bowlegged girl. Emily loved gymnastics and never missed a class, arriving early and waiting for me in the hall. I remember the day I was helping Emily with a back walkover when I felt a bump on her back, a tumor the size of a peach on her spine. It turned out to be benign and it was immediately removed, but after the surgery Emily was always in pain. Her mother suggested giving up gymnastics, but Emily refused, offering to become my assistant instead. She came each week, dutifully moving mats and beams while her friends flipped and cartwheeled in front of her. I know how Emily felt, the way I feel when I walk into a playground full of fathers pushing their kids on swings. Your heart twists up and you can't breathe because the yearning is so intense. I understand why Emily quit two weeks later.

23

State of the Union

I pull into the driveway of a small two-family brick house on Staten Island. Tony Edwards waves from his window, which looks like a picture frame around his giant build. His new home is much smaller than the colonial that he sold a few months ago so he wouldn't have to work a second job.

"It's about freakin' time," Tony jokes, hanging his suit bag in the back of his truck. He is wearing khaki shorts frayed at the bottoms, exposing his disproportionately small calves. The guys at the firehouse nick-named him "Chicken Legs," even drawing a face onto a potato, sticking toothpicks into the bottom for legs, and naming it Tony.

I have asked Tony to come with me to Washington for the State of the Union address. Hillary Clinton asked me to be her guest there tonight, but I didn't want to drive down alone.

I hoist myself into the truck's wide black seat and crack the window, filling the car with unseasonably warm air.

"You gotta map?" Tony asks.

"No."

"What, do I gotta do everything around here?"

"C'mon, you're my chauffeur. Get it together," I tease. The rhythm of our banter is comforting, and I am excited about the trip. I met Senator Clinton a month earlier when I witnessed President Bush signing the

Victims of Terrorism Tax Relief Act. I remember being struck by how much prettier she appeared in person, with striking blue eyes the same color as her silk suit, a flower among a sea of dark-suited, gray-haired men. She was seated in front of me and twisted herself around to ask me about Ground Zero and to admire the picture of Dave I wore pinned to my suit. I remember how Arlen Specter interrupted our conversation to make a joke about lawyers to Senator Clinton, who graciously smiled.

"All right, I got it," Tony says, folding a well-worn map back into its rectangle. "I-95 south almost all the way. I bet we can get there in four hours."

"No way. It's at least five," I bait him. Tony smiles and peels out of his driveway. Dave and I started countless vacations on this highway heading south, his hand resting on my thigh while he drove. After a long stretch, I would rub the back of his neck, his cropped hair feeling like fresh-cut grass.

"You all right?" Tony asks me, and I look out the window, trying not to cry. Tony says nothing. After attending fifteen funerals together, there is nothing more to say.

"This fucking sucks," he says. "We'll never be the same, you know that?" I nod, knowing this is true. "None of us will ever be the same."

I called Donna last night to make sure she was comfortable with Tony going with me, and of course she said yes.

"I'm actually glad to get him out of the house," she joked, a tinge of sadness in her voice. "He's been so upset. Ever since we sold the house."

"Well, he put a lot of work into that place," I say, remembering the tour he gave Dave and me when he had finished fixing up the house last year.

"Yeah, and now we're in a tiny place, living next door to his mother," Donna continues. "I try not to complain, because I don't want him to work a second job right now, but it's hard. You know, Marian, that last night in our house, I stood in the kitchen and I cried. I just . . . it's just too much change."

As Tony promised, we arrive at the periphery of Washington, D.C., in less than four hours. We pass vacant lots standing next to run-down row houses, the winding streets leading us past stoic federal buildings and manicured lawns to the circular driveway of the Hyatt Regency Hotel. The lobby is crowded with salty-haired men in pin-striped suits who eye Tony and me as we pass.

"I'll meet you in the lobby in an hour," Tony announces, finding his room first. My room is large and generic, with two double beds that immediately make me lonely. I have never been in a hotel room alone. In the bathroom, I turn on the shower to steam the wrinkles out of my suit. Clearing the mirror with my sleeve, I am startled by how I look. The stripe of gray has reappeared on my scalp, and the constant crying has made my eyes look small and tired no matter how much makeup I apply. *Who am I kidding?* I lean in closer and find a stubborn hair growing like wire from my chin. *What am I doing here?* Grabbing tweezers, I pull the hair out so hard my eyes water. Before I know it, I am crying again.

Later, Tony stands in the lobby looking impressive in his class A uniform. The suited men stare at us differently now, some even nodding fraternally in Tony's direction.

"You look nice," I whisper.

"I fuckin' hate this suit," he snipes.

I nod, recalling the firefighters, an ocean of white gloves and blue caps on the day of Dave's service. As clearly as anything that day, I remember Tony's face when I passed him on the church steps, his eyes filled with tears, his strong arm shaking in his salute, until I had to look away.

Hillary's assistant Patrick meets us at the front door. He has a young, freckled Irish face and wears a suit so large he looks like he borrowed it from his father. We follow him down corridors with high ceilings and rows of mahogany doors.

"Hillary is just down this way. It's not the nicest one. The newly elected ones get last pick, and Hillary and Chuck were at the bottom." He opens the door to a small room that looks like a college office, complete with fresh-faced interns who look up and smile when we enter. I have spoken to most of them on the phone and never imagined them to be so young.

Hillary's office is painted a gleaming yellow, and she stands to greet us, wearing a drab brown suit. We talk about curly hair, Sarah Lawrence, and Chelsea. She asks about Aidan and what it was like to be married to a firefighter. I tell her that when Dave died, we were living on $450 a week. She shakes her head and looks to Tony, who tells her that most of the men work second jobs to pay their bills but now are too busy attending funerals and helping widows to make any money on the side. I have brought along the Debt of Honor Bill in a paper bag and I hand it to her, chiding myself for not having something nicer to present it in.

"This is a bill my organization, the 9/11 Widows and Victims' Families Association, is backing," I say. It is a New York State sales tax, only fifty cents on a hundred dollars, and it would give every policeman and firefighter an extra fifteen thousand dollars a year. If nothing else, I had to come to Washington for this."

Hillary nods politely, promising to take a look at it, and hands the bag to Patrick. I imagine it stuck in a "to do" pile very much like mine, never to be read. I give the senator and her assistants Squad 1 sweat-shirts.

We take a long elevator ride and are led by Secret Service men to a small open tram, the monorail that runs under the Senate buildings to the Capitol. Hillary sits in the front seat and I slide in next to her. Tony starts to sit in the car behind us, but the senator insists that he join us in the front. I smile at Tony as he plops down, wedging me up against the senator.

"Sorry about my bottom," I apologize.

"You should be," Tony jokes.

"You're no fashion model, either," I mutter to Tony, elbowing him in the ribs.

"Neither am I," Hillary says, smiling.

At the Capitol, we are stopped by security guards who ask for our invitations. I tell the senator that I was unable to procure one for Tony. She smiles at the guard and he lets us through.

"Marian, I'm going to have dinner with a few of the senators before we start," Hillary says at the next checkpoint. "I'm so glad you came, and I hope you enjoy yourself tonight." She shakes my hand and kisses me on the cheek. She turns to Tony and puts her hand on his shoulder. "I'm so sorry. I tried to get you in, but every senator is only allowed one guest."

"Don't worry about it," Tony says. "I'm just her chauffeur." We wave lamely as she disappears into the crowd of politicians. Moments later, though, Tony runs into a friend, a former New York City fire captain, who is working security for the Capitol.

"You got any juice up here?" Tony asks him.

"Yeah, I can get you in," he says.

We follow him through the Capitol Hill lobby, a beautiful circular room lined with famous oil paintings of American battle scenes.

"This is the center of Washington, D.C.," the captain says, pointing to a glass tile marked with Roman numerals. "The middle of the wheel." I think of Dave and how much he would appreciate the rich history of this room.

"Dave would love this," Tony says, reading my mind.

Since Tony and I are seated separately, I make my way to a balcony behind the press box where all the guests of the senators are seated. I sink into my seat and watch the senators greet each other stiffly, waiting for the president to enter. Hillary enters, smiling and shaking hands. She is with Charles Rangel, and she turns and waves at me from below. When the president finally enters, everyone stands, giving him a hearty round of applause. He makes his way to the podium and I can see his black shoe scratching the back of his other leg. I feel like a hypocrite applauding the man whom I can't help but feel took advantage of my husband's death. His speech is long and filled with idealistic rhetoric that brings the audience to its feet, standing and sitting and standing again. My legs and mind grow tired and so I finally sit, refusing to rise as the crowd stomps their feet and cheers. People flash me dirty looks as if I'm chewing the Bible during church, but I don't stand.

After the speech, Tony finds me and we follow the crowd down the narrow circular corridors into the warm night.

"Did you see that lady talkin' to me?" Tony asks.

"No," I say.

"I was right across from you, but you were too busy talkin' to that cute guy."

"He was the husband of a congresswoman from Los Angeles. Too perfect for me," I joke.

"Yeah, well, this woman was a character," Tony continues. "She was countin' every time we had to stand up. Thirty-eight, thirty-nine. She was married to some senator. He died a couple of years ago. I told her about you."

"Oh, yeah? What did she say?"

"She said to cry in the shower so your face doesn't swell." It is the widows' secret. The warm water washes over us and we join in. And I nod, grateful that even in this strange place of pomp and politics, there is someone just like me.

"Let's go," I say. "I need some food and a shower."

* * *

Since I am meeting the new mayor at 7:30 A.M., Jason arrives at 5:30, wearing a baseball cap, with a Venti (the biggest) coffee from Starbucks in his hand. It is so big I have to laugh. If there were a Big Gulp at Starbucks, Jason would buy it. His eyes are swollen with fatigue as he enters, his deep voice groaning like that of Lurch from the *Addams Family*. I immediately feel guilty for making him come over so early. He probably waited tables until late last night.

"You okay?" I ask.

"Your gay nanny is a bit tired today," he says, slumping into the wing-back chair. He shuts his eyes while I scramble around, looking for a clean shirt. He has agreed to take Aidan to school so I can attend a breakfast meeting at Gracie Mansion. Aidan is still sleeping, and since my closet is in his room, I scan my clothes with a flashlight, trying not to make noise.

"How's this?" I show Jason a gray suit I have put on.

"It looks like the weather outside," he says.

"Why don't you go in and lie down? Aidan's not up until seven." Jason doesn't answer, so I cover him in the wool throw from the couch.

The cold outside is unrelenting, forcing my shoulders to shrug up to my ears. I turn on the car, watching the intricate crystals of frost melt away like a shaken Etch-A-Sketch. It feels like the whole city is still sleeping when I arrive at Gracie Mansion on the Upper East Side. I circle the blocks looking for a parking space. I turn down 90th Street, past the nondescript tenement building where I shared an apartment with Dave and Leah after college. We lived on the fourth floor, in a small apartment with narrow hallways and strangely shaped rooms. Dave and I shared a bedroom on the front of the building, where traffic blared into our window like a headache each morning. I had always wanted to live in Manhattan, to be part of that indescribable energy that hovers like heat above tar. After Dave graduated from C. W. Post and we traveled in Europe, I transferred to Sarah Lawrence College, where I managed to get Dave a job building sets for the theater department. He was truly talented at it, his precise thinking and artistic talent blending perfectly together to create stunning set pieces. After I graduated, Leah, Dave, and I found an apartment, and Dave reverse-commuted to Sarah Lawrence College, waiting to hear from the Fire Department. I waitressed in a Mexican restaurant in the Village that had a giant margarita clinging to the side of the building like King Kong. We always joked that we were serving dirty snow, since the margarita part of the sign had long been stained black from car exhaust. It feels strange to think of my life then, auditioning and performing, teaching part-time at the 92nd Street Y, taking acting classes. It feels like a film I watched about someone else's life. Not mine. It is too different now.

The dining room in Gracie Mansion is long and narrow, with a wide table running its length. An elaborate bouquet of wintery flowers dominates the center of the table that is set for more than thirty guests. Shining silver cups of fruit sit on top of white china plates. I sit in between Jack and Lee, who seem to always look like my bookends in their matching baseball caps. As usual, I tease Lee for not wearing any socks. Jack laughs robustly.

Everyone stands when Mayor Bloomberg enters, as if we are greeting a king. He is a small man, with long mouselike features, thin lips, and receding gray hair. We sit silently sipping coffee until Marie, Jennie

Farrell's sister, stands to begin the meeting. Last week, during a coalition meeting, we decided to prepare an agenda to show our unity and the broad scope of our concerns. We chose Marie to facilitate the meeting.

The mayor clears his throat, shifting from one side of his seat to the other, nodding and grunting approval. When we are finished, he sighs and sits up taller. "Well, thank you for that. I will certainly do my best to work with all of you." His voice is monotone and nasal, like the air being squeezed from a balloon. "I called this meeting to introduce a woman who I call a friend. She lost her husband, Neil Levin, and she will be serving in this administration as the family liaison to you all . . . Christy Ferer." We all clap weakly, and Christy smiles and stands, her eyes peering over her tinted glasses.

"She doesn't look too nice," Jack whispers to me.

"My name is Christy, and I am excited to be working for the mayor and for the families." She stands a little over five feet, with stylish shoulder-length hair, and she speaks with the aloof confidence of a politician. "Anything you need, I will be there for you. My e-mail and my phone number are on the agenda. I'm really looking forward to working with all of you." Her voice is thick and raspy as if she has smoked for many years. "One of the things we are working on is the six-month anniversary in March. There is someone trying to get the towers of light on for the holidays, two giant beams of light that will shoot up into the sky. It's really quite stunning, and I'd love to get your feedback on it, of course."

Edie Lutnick, whose brother Howard is well known from Cantor Fitzgerald, sits up tall in her chair. "Some of the families—particularly those who live in New Jersey and have a direct view of Manhattan—have expressed concern about seeing that image night after night."

"I personally like the idea," Anthony Gardner from the WTC United Family Group says.

"Me, too," I pipe in. "It seems like it is a very tasteful and touching tribute."

"I think the mayor's using Christy as a buffer so he doesn't have to deal with us directly," Lee whispers.

"I was just thinking that myself."

Outside, reporters cluster like pigeons waiting to be fed. Anthony,

Lee, and Jack take their positions in front of microphones and cameras as Christy pushes past a few reporters to greet me.

"I can't stand these reporters," she bristles. "And I am one." She rolls her eyes. "Listen, anything you need, just let me know," she says as the crowd of reporters presses against us and a microphone with ABC on it is thrust in my face.

"How do you feel the meeting went today?" the reporter asks me, a bright light shining in my eyes. Everywhere I turn, I see the family members I know doing interviews, and it strikes me as strange that this is what we do at the end of every meeting, press conference, event. I begin to answer carefully, always considering my words, but after the second question, Monica steps into the frame and begins to answer. At first I nod, waiting for my turn, but then, feeling foolish, I turn and walk away, the cold sleet falling at an angle into my face. Stepping away from the cameras, I immediately feel better and close my eyes to feel the cold drops of water on my skin. I have always loved cold water, the way it makes things crisper, clearer. When I was a child, my parents marveled at how I loved the frigid lakes of Maine and Lake Como in Italy. I can still see Dave's embarrassed smile as he stood on the shore of the Irish Sea while I jumped in, screaming so loudly, I could hear the hollow sound of my voice echoing off the jagged cliffs. My legs and arms were numb and as white as the underside of a fish, floating free, and I strain to remember if it was the cold black sea surrounding me or Dave's loving smile that made me feel so alive on that day.

Diane, the PR woman we have hired, calls me to tell me that E-Online has requested an interview.

"You can talk about the organization," she says. "By the way," she adds, "I saw you on the news, and Monica just stole your whole shot."

"I know."

"You can't let her do that."

The following day, a car service takes me to 57th Street. I head inside the Fox Television building where a long line of Spanish girls wearing puffy down coats are standing in line shivering. At the security desk, a bored-looking guard checks my identification, looking back and forth from my driver's license photo to the live, much older version of me. I have become used to the scrutiny since the anthrax scare two months ago. A red FOX TELEVISION sign hangs like a thought bubble over his head as he fills out a sticker.

"I'll take her, Roy," a squat young intern with a blond-streaked pony-tail says as if I am a package she is picking up. Without saying a word, she gestures for me to follow her through a labyrinth of halls, her tight black pants scraping noisily until she stops at a door marked MARIAN FONTANA—GUEST on a white piece of copy paper. In all my interviews I have never had my own dressing room, and I pause in the doorway, taking in the makeup lights, the phone, the fruit basket with beige slices of cantaloupe and waxy apples. "Someone will be here in a few minutes to take you to makeup," she says, tucking the clipboard under her arm and leaving.

I dial Jack's cell phone number. He and Lee are attending an Eliot Spitzer meeting on my behalf. I am leaving a message when another intern enters without knocking and signals me to follow her to a make-up room that is as big as my apartment. I am told to sit in a large swivel chair where a makeup guy who looks like a cast member from *La Cage aux Folles* glazes me with orange foundation and thick black eyeliner. He mutters, "Look up," and "Gorgeous," and something about Liza before handing me off to a scruffy-looking boy in a Led Zeppelin T-shirt and an oversize headset. He ushers me to the end of a line of people standing in the hall. I peek ahead to see if I recognize anyone, but the headset guy shushes us and leads us backstage. I can hear a comedian making dirty jokes and the sound of raucous laughter, peo-ple yelling, *"Whoop whoop whoop"* like they used to on *The Arsenio Hall Show.*

"What show is this?" I ask the woman sitting next to me, a redhead in a turquoise suit, and she gestures to a sign on the wall above the couches that reads "IYANLA" in giant cursive letters.

"Who is she?"

"She's sorta like the late-night Oprah." As if on cue, a short African American woman with tightly cropped hair and a moon-shaped face enters smiling, her huge white teeth gleaming. The audience applauds loudly, whooping it up for this woman I've never heard of.

"Welcome! Have you ever wondered what you would do if your world fell apart? Well, today our guests will share their journeys to hell and back!"

The audience applauds again and the lights brighten to reveal Tim, a short muscular man, looking half swallowed in one of the velvet chairs onstage. A television screen above them flickers as a montage of Tim as a teenager and Iyanla's smooth voice-over begins. "Tim Cramdon learned to medicate himself with alcohol and drugs at an early age." The camera lens looks as if it has been dipped in a jar of Vaseline as the music turns ominous and artsy close-ups of Tim glassy-eyed and drunk appear. "Filled with feelings of inadequacy and loneliness, Tim drank until he landed himself in prison for drunk driving . . . Tim would eventually triumph over his addiction, honing his restored vitality into a new pastime, competitive sports." Footage of Tim running marathons and triathalons is shown. "Tim decided to devote his life to keeping young people off of drugs and alcohol." The film ends, and the audience bursts into applause.

Iyanla is beaming, leaning forward in her chair. "Well, ALL RIGHT! God is a God of second chances . . . Am I right?" she says to Tim, who smiles and nods.

"Yes, ma'am. I was blessed to be given many chances to turn myself around, and I've been sober for eight years." The audience applauds again.

"When you hit rock bottom, that's good, because God made the rock!" Iyanla says, filled with a seemingly endless list of platitudes. Tim continues, his easy smile and Southern accent charming everyone, but I am distracted by wondering what exactly my role is here. I certainly have not been to hell and back. I am still in it. Right now. Right here at the Iyanla show.

In the next segment, an obese woman takes Tim's place in the velvet chair. "Four years ago," Iyanla says into the camera, "Fanny's twelve-year-old son was taken from her in a tragic accident. Let's look."

Everyone turns to the screen, where Fanny's thick Boston accent plays over footage of a handsome boy. "Mahk was a shy, beautiful boy with a spahkle in his eye . . ." She tells the story of how her son accidentally shot himself with the neighbor's gun. As one result, Fanny started an organization called A.S.K.—Asking Saves Kids.

I feel like everyone in the whole room knows what's going on except me. As they are about to go to commercial, I look up at the monitor, where I see myself looking exactly as I feel, like a deer in headlights.

The redhead in the turquoise suit is next. She is a therapist from Chicago who wrote a book about grief and life changes. I feel my seat vibrating and turn to notice a large black woman sweating and shaking in her seat. "I am so nervous," she says to me, fanning herself with a plump hand, as the headset guy makes his way across the stage. "I'm next," she goes on, looking like an animal about to be slaughtered.

"Good luck" is all I can muster as I watch her bright red suit stretch and pull as she lowers herself into the velvet chair.

"Yvette needs an act of faith to get over the death of her son, Earl." Iyanla dramatically tells Yvette's story. How her son was robbed and shot multiple times in the chest six years ago. Yvette was devastated. She had to identify the body. Instead of enlisting in a cause or starting an organization, she gained 150 pounds, never slept, and took up smoking. Iyanla slowly puts her hand on Yvette's knee. "Difficulties are our greatest teachers. You know Earl would want you to get over this."

Yvette nods. "Yes, I try, but I just can't stop seeing his face, the blood, his eyes rolled back in his head and . . . I dunno. I just want to know why." She begins to cry, tears cutting lines through her perfect makeup. The television monitor overhead plays a slide show of Earl. Iyanla lowers her voice to an empathetic whisper. "Sometimes there is no answer to why. It's the same for everybody, but you have to be willing to get that help."

Yvette nods, dabbing her eyes with a tissue.

"I am putting you on a forty-day plan," Iyanla says sternly. "In this plan, you need to have nine statements of forgiveness a day. You need to forgive God, you need to forgive yourself, you need to even forgive Earl for leaving you—am I right?" Yvette nods as Iyanla turns to the camera. "When we come back, we will meet a widow who lost her firefighter husband on 9/11. She's got some things to teach Yvette about healing.

After this . . . Was that okay?" Iyanla asks her producer, a dark-haired man with a Caesar haircut and designer glasses.

"Yup," he says tersely, ignoring me as I try to get his attention and find out exactly what I am supposed to be doing. Set people skitter around the stage, moving the velvet chairs to a raised platform in the audience. Headset guy signals me to sit in one of the chairs and weaves a microphone through my suit jacket and before I can even speak the cameraman is counting 5-4-3-2-1.

"Marian Fontana lost her firefighter husband, Dave, on September eleventh, her eighth wedding anniversary, but she has used her grief to help others. She began the 9/11 Widows and Victims' Families Association."

What the hell is she talking about? I am thinking when she turns to me. "Marian, you lost your husband, you're raising your five-year-old son alone. What message can you give Yvette about healing and moving on?"

My heart is pounding in my ears. "Well . . . um . . . It's only been five months so, um . . . I think that maybe keeping busy can help," I say weakly. Iyanla doesn't like this. She nervously shuffles through her index cards with her long, manicured hands.

"Marian, I believe everything happens for a reason. How did you know what to do?" Iyanla asks, and I hesitantly tell her the story about the recovery effort and working with the mayor and the Fire Department. Iyanla squints at me and nods. "Hmm. Any moment can be the moment," she says, shaking her head.

"Do you talk to Dave?" she asks, and before I can answer, she turns to Yvette, who has been trying fruitlessly to stop crying. "Do you talk to Earl, Yvette?"

Yvette nods and says, "I do. Every day. He calls me Shorty." She giggles through her tears.

"I want you to close your eyes," Iyanla commands. Yvette dutifully closes her eyes, and I try to hide my shock when Iyanla starts to speak as if she is Earl. "You know I'm in a better place, Shorty. Why are you doin' this? Why are you not lettin' me go?" She looks at Yvette like a stern parent. "Say this with me: 'I forgive myself.' "

"I forgive myself," Yvette says dutifully.

"For judging myself."

"For judging myself."

"And being angry at God."

"And being angry at God." There is a long pause.

"Any moment can be the moment," Iyanla says to the camera before turning to me again. "Do you have a special message for Yvette?" she asks me.

I look at Yvette, who is sobbing, her eyes red, her mascara gone, her face twisted with grief. "I think just trying to be around people who have shared a similar loss, um . . . and your grandchildren sound great. . . . My son is a great teacher because he still has so much joy."

"There's so much God in the children," Iyanla says, closing her eyes and smiling, and Yvette nods, looking like a house about to fall and I feel helpless and foolish, and when the red light on the camera finally goes off, I exhale for the first time, hand Yvette a tissue, and think, *I gave up* Oprah *twice for this?*

*   *   *

In early February, Joe Miccio and I meet at the office. He wants to introduce me to a woman he met at the site. She was a volunteer for FEMA and has offered to help organize and run the office when I am not there, which is most of the time. When I arrive, Monica is being filmed again by a news crew. She sits in front of a steel cross from the site that a firefighter had given me and I had put on the windowsill. The film crew shushes us and I tiptoe over to my desk. Monica's brother Chris looks up and smiles, his white face lit by the glow of the computer monitor.

"Hey, Chris," I whisper.

Joe enters wearing work clothes from Ground Zero. He has just come off a twelve-hour shift. He is standing with a pretty young woman with wide blue eyes and thin straight hair pulled back into a ponytail.

"It's been brutal with the cold," Joe says, taking off his jacket. "This is Jennifer Adams." She shakes my hand firmly, a smile opening up small round cheeks and a small pointed chin.

"I've heard so much about you," she says formally. She wears a silk blouse and business slacks.

"Jennifer has a business degree and was working on Wall Street when the towers fell," Joe announces.

"I worked in Tower Two for three years, too," she says, closing her eyes. "I lost a good friend. . . ."

"And she's given everything up to volunteer and wants to continue to help however she can," Joe continues.

"Well, we don't have much of a budget," I tell her carefully.

"That's okay," she says. "I mean, eventually I will have to get a job that pays . . ." She giggles, her blue eyes flashing. She eyes the piles of boxes and mail stacked in the corner. "You do need help though," she says, looking around at the mess, a high-pitched nervous giggle escaping.

"Yes," I tell her. "I run an unorganization."

"Well, that's why I'm here," she says in that perky way people from the South do, and I let my shoulders droop as if someone has taken heavy luggage from my arms.

*   *   *

The first meeting of the Lower Manhattan Development Corporation is on the twentieth floor of the Liberty Building. Lee and I have been selected for the Family Advisory Council, along with Monica Iken from September's Mission, Anthony Gardener from WTC United Family Group, Kathy Ashton from Give Your Voice, Mary Fetchet from Families of September 11th, and almost twenty others. We are one of eight advisory councils in all, big and small businesses, financial services, residents, transportation, and others. I have always feared that the overwhelming compassion shown to the families would dissipate over time. Being one small voice among eight big ones indicates that this is beginning to happen. The redevelopment seems all politics with Governor Pataki the voice of Oz behind the curtain directing it all. I find it hard to reconcile my personal loss with the big politics of all of this. I know in my heart that 9/11 changed people. I have witnessed the resiliency of the human spirit. I have watched people across the nation and world mobilize in an unprecedented display of unity and strength. Yet I can feel the tide inevitably shifting, and the events of September 11 becoming a powerful political pawn to rebuild and even start wars.

Since I am early, I decide to go to the "family room," a large office at the back of the building that overlooks Ground Zero. The walls are covered in missing posters, wake cards, pictures of families. An eerie wallpaper of smiling portraits, once-happy families glare from every corner. Lee enters wearing his trademark baseball cap and we stand at the window looking down at Ground Zero. The site is virtually unrecognizable now, with most of the gigantic grapplers gone. So much debris has been removed that the rescue workers are now standing six stories below street level in a vast pit. Lee points to a truck ramp being constructed on the west wall to give access to the huge crater. Everything looks so different that if you flew over it with a plane, you would never know what existed before. You could never explain that the sixteen-acre hole left in the grid of Manhattan, like a missing puzzle piece, was once two grand buildings that hovered protectively over the city's skyline for nearly thirty years.

At the meeting Lee and I sit at a grand conference table. A balding stenographer is perched in the corner preparing to record everything said, and a film screen stands next to a podium with a microphone. The topic tonight is the six-month anniversary of September 11, which will be taking place in a few weeks. To commemorate the event, a ferrety-looking man with a bowl haircut presents more specific plans for the "Towers of Light," two giant beams that will shoot up into the city sky like phantom towers for the six-month anniversary. The projections are eerie and beautiful, and I am amazed at this man's effort and even more stunned to hear that the man working alongside him had the same idea at the same time in an entirely different part of the city a few months before.

After the meeting, Christy Ferer, Mayor Bloomberg's liaison, sidles over, her tinted glasses pushed to the end of her nose.

"Marian, listen," she says, her voice raspy, her eyes squinting at me. "The mayor is putting me in charge of this whole event . . . Do you have anyone in your group who lost both parents?" The brusque way she asks causes me to stop to make sure she isn't joking, but as I watch her quickly jot a note in her PalmPilot, I realize she is completely serious.

"No . . . I don't know of anyone offhand." I try to think but then stop when I realize how ludicrous this is.

"I'm looking for an orphan or maybe a handicapped kid to throw the switch for the lights. Do you know any group who has that?" She looks at me expectantly from behind her tinted glasses and I bite my lip.

"No, actually, I don't . . . but I'll see if I can find out."

Christy disappears to ask Jennie Farrell the same question, and I watch Jennie's expression change as she listens to Christy, nodding, her face set in an almost imperceptible expression of disgust.

*   *   *

An icy breeze blows up Suffolk Street, making me shudder. While I have been firm in my commitment to only do media that promotes the firefighters and the organizations, I am being filmed today for a documentary called *Faith and Doubt at Ground Zero*. The documentary intrigues me. A few weeks earlier in a Victorian-era apartment in the West Village I met the director, Helen Whitney. She was a striking woman, with a square jaw, big lips, and a shock of dramatic gray hair, and her passion for the topic was contagious. Like my best professors at Sarah Lawrence College, the director asked well-considered and thought-provoking questions, and it made me miss that brief time in life when I could luxuriate in the profundity of knowledge and deep thought.

I finally find the building and Helen greets me with a firm embrace, her eyes sparkling. It is even colder inside, but Helen seems immune. I follow her upstairs to a choir loft where the television crew is setting up a chair in front of a stained-glass window. Two serious-looking crew members adjust the lights, click meters, and plug things in. Helen sits across from me, leaning forward intently like a therapist, squinting. I am so cold, I have to squeeze my jaws together to keep my teeth from chattering. I tell Helen everything about my loss of faith and my struggle to regain it. I tell her about the sunrise in Hawaii and how it had been difficult to reconcile that sunrise with Dave's death, wondering what kind of God puts these two extremes together in one domain. I tell her how I do not talk to God anymore, that Dave has become the spirit I speak to. I ask Dave to guide me, to help me make the right decisions, and to be with me through the long nights when the lonely dark seems as infinite as the pain of grief.

After the interview, I sit at a worn wooden table at Katz's Deli on the corner. It is packed with people on their lunch hour, eating thick pastrami sandwiches and talking loudly. I love Katz's Deli, one of the few places left in New York that hasn't changed. I am grateful to be here, and warm for the first time today. I am smearing extra mustard on seedy rye bread when I notice a plastic sign on my table that reads "This is where Harry Met Sally." I hear my cell phone in my bag and dig in to retrieve it; the word "Jen" is flashing across the front. My new volunteer/office manager and I speak regularly as she slowly pieces a working office together, managing the website, organizing my database.

"Marian, listen. I'm entering all the registration forms that families have been filling out and faxing over the last few months."

"Great," I say slowly, because she sounds upset.

"And I don't know if you knew this, but Monica has been taking the forms for *your group* and entering them into her database! For months, while you weren't here, she's been taking faxes and e-mailing your members . . . Can you believe that?" I put my sandwich down and take a sip of soda, trying to think. "Are you there? Marian?"

"Yes, I am here," I say, trying to stay calm.

"I said something to her and she played stupid, like she thought everything was for everybody, even though it clearly states that your registration form is for WVFA use only."

"Have you spoken to Joe?"

"Yeah. He said he had made it clear to her that the databases are separate when she first joined the office. She just had no families and so she took yours."

I sigh, shaking my head. I recall a few weeks ago when I tried to get to know Monica better. We were returning from a meeting with the governor, and I suggested we take the subway together back to the office. It was rush hour, but we managed to get seats. She was staring at her nails, a noticeable habit, saying nothing. I thought then about all the groups, how I knew so much about their lost loved ones. I knew that Anthony from the WTC United Family Group had a brother, Harvey III, who loved to cook and was great with computers. I knew that Jennie Farrell from Give Your Voice named her son James after the brother to whom she was so close. I know that Mary Fetchet's son Brad was shy. I know that Beverly Eckert's husband talked to her on the phone on the morning of the eleventh and Sally Regenhardt from the Skyscraper Safety Campaign had a strikingly handsome son who was a proby in the Fire Department. I knew nothing of Monica's husband. I have seen a wedding picture pinned above her desk, but otherwise she says nothing. Her press appearances are always about the memorial, and while she is well spoken, they seem devoid of emotion.

"What was Michael like?" I asked.

Monica's face shifted slightly. She sat up taller. "Every morning I see this flag in Riverside Park outside my window," she began, shaking her hair from her face. She never looked at me but faced forward. "We used to hang out at this park on the weekends. We talked about having kids and what we were going to do." She stopped and looked at her nails again. "I dunno. I can't stand it. I feel like if I wasn't doing this, I would die. I wouldn't know what to do with myself, because I just can't understand *how* someone can just be gone. Poof. There's nothing." She stopped and bit her lip. "I mean, you knew your husband could be killed. He had that kind of a job, but for me . . . I'll never understand."

*   *   *

It feels like everyone I have ever known is in the small bar on 5th Avenue celebrating my thirty-sixth birthday. All the widows from the firehouse are here. They have bought me lingerie in gift bags and toe rings and scarves to make me feel beautiful again. Three fire trucks are parked out front, and the room is filled with the smoky smell of bunker gear. Firefighters buy me drinks and wish me happy birthday while Jason and Leah, the behind-the-scenes hosts, put out food and collect gifts. Jason is always watching me, reading my emotional seismograph.

"How are you doing?" he asks me carefully. "Are you having fun?"

"Like a whore in church on Christmas," I joke, but he tilts his head. He knows I put on a good front. Everyone laughs when I light a cigarette with a candle from my cake. I crack jokes to friends and family, and everyone seems relieved to see me having fun. They want me to be as carefree as I used to be, and for them, I pretend I am.

After the party's over, some widows and a few firefighters linger in the back on mismatched couches clustered close together. A couple on the couch across from us is making out, oblivious to the other people in the room.

"I need to watch them?" Sally Siller says sarcastically. I am thrilled to have her here. I know it is difficult for her to come to social events. Stephen was the social one.

"I know, right?" I tell her, suddenly annoyed to have this couple here, reminding me of everything we don't have.

"I'll pay you twenty bucks to go sit next to them," Sally says, smiling, her teeth white and perfect. I stand up, giggling, and walk over, plopping myself next to them. Sally is laughing, and after a few minutes, the couple stops kissing. I light a cigarette and lean back on the couch, offering one to the woman. She is pretty, with white-blond hair swept to one side and dark red lipstick smeared across her face like an older, drunker Marilyn Monroe. She takes off her high heels and plops her feet in the man's lap. He smiles seductively at her and immediately begins rubbing her feet. I stand up and sit next to Sally again, sighing.

"Oh, man . . . I miss Dave rubbing my feet."

"I'll give you another twenty bucks to ask him for a foot rub," Sally says, giggling, and when the woman heads to the bathroom, I sit in her spot and plop my feet into his lap.

"I'll give you twenty bucks to rub my feet," I tell him. He cocks his head to the side, smiles, and, amazingly, begins rubbing my feet.

When the girlfriend returns, I smile at her. "Do you mind? It's my birthday," I tell her. She shrugs and sits with Sally, Martha, and Theresa. I know Theresa is telling her who we are because she always tells everyone we meet that we lost our husbands. I watch the woman's pale face shift and change shape, shaking her head.

"Give her an extra foot rub, honey," she yells to her boyfriend. "She needs it more than me."

*   *   *

It's March 4, what would have been Theresa's second wedding anniversary. She arrives at my apartment early. Lee is picking us both up to take us to the site.

"I loved your wedding," I tell her in the car.

"It was the best," she says quietly, looking out the window. I can read Theresa so well now, anticipating her moods and feelings the way I used to Dave's.

"It was at Russo's on the Bay," I say in a thick Brooklyn accent.

"That's your last name, isn't it?" Lee asks her.

"It was my husband's, yes . . ." she says. "I'm Irish all the way."

"I almost peed in my pants when you and Mike came up from the elevator," I say, smiling.

"I was so embarrassed!" Theresa laughs, leaning forward in her seat to talk to Lee and me in the front.

"Theresa and Mike came out of the floor in an elevator and there was smoke and music and lights and I just couldn't stop laughing." Theresa giggles from the back. "You looked like a scene from *Spinal Tap*," I tell her.

"I always knew something bad was going to happen," she says as the light on the other side of the tunnel beckons us forward. "I think that's why in all the pictures I have I am behind him, holding him, trying to keep him here because even though I was the happiest I have ever been, I felt this uneasiness . . . I just knew it would end."

We arrive at the site, scanning the landscape like generals surveying the battlefield.

"There's not much left to do," Lee says, and I notice that more chain-link fencing has been erected around the periphery of Ground Zero, making the site feel more like a fort.

"I don't think I can get us much closer," Lee says, annoyed, walking us past Liberty Street to the southeast corner of the site. "They've gotten so strict about people visiting."

"What am I looking at?" Theresa asks, her chin quivering.

Lee steps up and puts his hand on Theresa's back. He loves explaining the site. It has become his home over the last nine months, and he's not ready to move out. He points a short finger east. "That's the South

Tower. That's where Dave and my son were found. Your husband was never . . . ?"

"No. He was working at Rescue 5 that day." She stares into the pit.

"Yeah . . . we didn't find anyone from there."

"Part of me doesn't want him found. I want to think he just flew like an angel, up and away."

We are all quiet and she sighs.

"They don't even know where they were."

"They think they were in the Marriott," Lee says, pointing toward the western wall where a hotel once stood. Giant trucks still sit near the wall where engineers are now installing giant steel girders to keep the Hudson from leaking in. Theresa grows quiet and presses herself against the fence. Her whole body begins shaking, and I step up and put my hand on her other shoulder.

"This is horrible," she says, sobbing in the high-pitched way I have come to know. I hand her tissues, my eyes staring out at the cold subterranean catacomb the Twin Towers have become. I know that preserving this site will be difficult. Arguments have already begun over land and how much should be rebuilt. It has been less than a year and people are already returning to their lives, the way they used to be, and I realize I am crying for this, too. The only thing that made sense after Dave's death was that people seemed transformed. Priorities shifted, moments were savored. Now the site will become a chessboard for the players who want to rebuild. There is Larry Silverstein, the wealthy real estate mogul who took over the lease only a few weeks before the towers fell. There is Governor Pataki, the Lower Manhattan Development Corporation, designers, architects, politicians, businesses small and large, residents and community boards and survivors who will all need to be appeased. And then there is Theresa who has no grave, no stone, no cemetery to visit, and so she places her flowers along a chain-link fence and peers into a hole trying to guess where her husband died.

*   *   *

The late-afternoon sun dips low on New York Bay as the victims' families line the dock in Battery Park, waiting to board the Circle Line. A cruise has been donated to the families to see the Tribute of Light to commemorate the six-month anniversary. The Fire Department has its own boat, and there is a section of Ground Zero reserved for the families, but I have chosen to ride in the Circle Line with the other groups. I slide into a bench watching the television crews and cameras interviewing the usual family leaders. Anthony gestures with his arms, Monica tilts her head when she talks into the camera, Lee stands with his feet apart, his arms tucked behind his back. I am tired of the cameras and content just to watch them and hordes of people making their way to Ground Zero. It feels like I have lived a hundred lifetimes in this half a year, and yet it has passed as quickly as a breath, one day spinning into the next.

My parents, Leah and Neil, and most of my in-laws are seated next to me, and the boat is quickly filling up with family members. Martha Butler is here from Squad. She looks exhausted, carrying her youngest son in her arms while keeping track of the other two. I spot Lee and hug him and his wife, Ann, hello. Although I do not know Ann as well, I know she is the mortar keeping the family together at home. Lee told me that once when Ann was at the site, she became furious at vendors hawking postcards of burning towers and illegal FDNY T-shirts. Enraged, she dumped the tables, and I have admired her ever since. I greet Jack and his wife, Kathleen. She looks younger than her sixty years, with a face as open as the Irish Sea and a brogue to match. She tells me about her sixteen grandchildren, beaming proudly though her blue eyes are dull with grief.

I sit on a bench toward the middle, trying to keep track of Aidan, who runs in circles with Martha's son Sean. Leah puts her hand on my thigh as the motor roars to life, making a wake behind us. The sky is nearly dark, with only a few light blue clouds lingering. The lights of office windows begin to shine through the trees and the crisp air smells familiar. I have seen this sky before, taken note of the brilliant color in those rare moments when you become fiercely aware of such things. There was a sky like this on February 18, 1996, as Dave and I drove downtown in our beat-up Honda, which we named the "Fishbowl" because it leaked when it rained.

We had been sitting at a dinner party with old friends at my sister's apartment on the Upper East Side. I was eight months pregnant. I was imitating my eighty-eight-year-old grandmother telling me a dirty joke. Everyone was laughing, including me, when I felt a warm rush of water drip down my leg. I stopped.

"You guys . . ." I said slowly, squeezing Dave's strong thigh through his jeans. When everyone finally stopped, they stared at me with anticipation. "I either just peed my pants, or my water broke."

My sister broke the silence by rolling her eyes. "You peed in your pants. You always do that when you laugh." Everyone laughed again, but when I squeezed my muscles to make the gush stop, it wouldn't. I pushed away from the table and ran to the bathroom. I could feel Dave behind me.

"Are you okay?" I could tell he was scared because I wasn't due until St. Patrick's Day, a month later. Amazingly, I felt completely calm and even let Leah take pictures of me standing in front of a sheet she hung over the window. I can still remember the blue wool sweater Dave was wearing when our eyes met and Dave smiled at me, reassuring me that we would always face the unknown together.

As the night comes, the crowd on the boat drifts into silhouette, like paper cutouts. The motor has stopped and we are floating and waiting. Aidan is finally still, sitting next to me, leaning his head on my shoulder. My sister holds my hand. It is quiet, a somber version of the countdown to New Year's. Suddenly, a flicker, and two giant beams shoot straight up into the night, two towers of light. They are stunning, larger than I imagined, as tall as the towers but as translucent and gossamer as a dragonfly's wing. A ghostly apparition of what used to be. I can feel my parents' hands on my shoulders and my sister next to me and sense the distinctive smell of Aidan's hair, and am struck by the conflict inside me, the opposing ideas of beauty and death, light and dark. Monica is speaking loudly into her cell phone, but I don't take my eyes off the light. Aidan lifts his head and is staring silently at it, too, and I find myself watching him instead. He is as beautiful as the stars, the towers of light reflecting like filaments in his amber eyes, a thick awning of lashes blinking in awe, the way they did when he entered the world.

My midwife wheeled a light to the bottom of the bed and held up a mirror. After thirteen hours of back labor and two hours of pushing, the baby's head was finally out. Dave was massaging my hands, whispering "I love you" into my ear, and all I wanted to do was sleep. I felt leaden on the bed. The light above made me glisten with blood and sweat, and my thighs could not stop quivering.

"Look," Dave said, and I wearily lifted my head to see Aidan's wet shining skull poking from inside of me like some fantastic goiter.

"Oh my God!" I said, laughing and crying at the same time at the bizarre sight of a baby's head, hanging like some obscene Christmas ornament from between my legs, and before I could even rest, I felt it. The wave of pain rippling across my belly, tearing at the nerves in my back.

"Push!" the midwife commanded, and I heaved with so much effort I could hear the crack of my tail bone and my body stiffen and it felt like my insides were falling out of me, but when I opened my eyes, it was Aidan, sliding out of me like a wet puppet. The nurse grabbed his red body and dried him off. They lay him on my chest. He was sticky and warm, a thick, blue umbilical chord still connecting us. I stared at his face. His eyes were huge and absolutely gorgeous, and he was crying a throaty, small cry.

"Oh God." I could feel Dave hiccup the words as his big square hands reached across to touch Aidan's head, whose hair looked like black bird's feathers, wet and thick. "He's beautiful," Dave whispered, and he kissed me on my mouth, a kiss that was pasty and tasted like salt. Tears were falling from his blue-green eyes and I closed my own and lay back on the pillow, letting an ocean of fatigue and love wash over us.

* * *

A few weeks later, Lee and I walk over to Spring Street across from my office to have dinner. SoHo is crowded tonight, the air tinged with the hope of spring. Tonight was our second coalition meeting, an attempt by Lee, Jack, and me to join all the disparate groups together in order to have a more powerful voice in how the site will be handled. With the retrieval almost over and over half the families with no body recovered, the significance of the sixteen-acre site and what will be put there has become most prominent in our minds.

Lee and I are led to a booth in the back of a trendy restaurant, and I plop down onto a red vinyl seat, sighing. What I had hoped would be a positive step toward working together felt more like a meeting of the United Nations, everyone voicing different concerns and priorities. I was the facilitator and became frustrated with a select few who seem more interested in promoting themselves than any of the issues we are trying to address. Still others, always calm and intelligent, made valuable comments about how to handle the immense political football that the site has become. I tried hard to stay focused on the endless monologues, but I have grown restless and tired, weary of meetings and the thick fog of emotion that surrounds every topic we discuss. We accomplished little tonight, because while we are trying to operate like a business, the fact is, we are nothing like one, as encumbered by our grief as we are fueled by it.

Lee and I order red wine and scan the menu. I know Lee will order pasta and an arugula salad as easily as I know he will never wear socks.

"How's the little guy?" Lee asks, closing the menu.

"He's waking up at night a lot. It's like his little head can't shut off."

"Well, c'mon. It's too much."

"Yeah, I dunno, Lee. I feel so guilty all the time. I looked around the table tonight, and I realized I am the *only* person there who is a single mom and . . . that I've sacrificed so much time . . . and that maybe . . ." I shake my head with regret. "Was it worth putting in all this time and energy . . . to have over half the people not found?" I ask him. "I feel like I failed."

"Young lady," he says sternly, "I absolutely think that if we did not go in there and change things, some of these guys would not have been found." I nod, thinking about the site, the delicate choreography involved in this effort and the people, too many to name, who donated time, sacrificed their health and well-being searching for our loved ones. I can only shake my head over and over. It has become my tic of grief.

We talk about all the things that still need to be done, meetings and issues still not addressed even though the site will close in a month. Lee is on the committee for the closing ceremonies, and we talk about that day and how it will be handled.

"I can't believe it's almost over," I tell Lee, pushing my salad plate out of the way.

"You know, it has become such a part of the routine that I— I dunno. This sounds terrible, but sometimes I would be talking to the guys, and I'd have a femur in my hand and I never . . . it was just. I never stopped and went, 'This is unbelievable. I have a *femur* in my hand.' " Lee is trying to find the words when our entrées arrive. I order another glass of wine.

"There was this one night," Lee starts, and I look up to let him know I am listening. "It was around eleven or so, and I went back to the site and I worked. There was the smell, and you're always cognizant of the smell. It was not there all the time. So when there was a smell, I tell the chief, feeling like these poor people . . . they're calling to us with this smell. To me, it was their way of saying 'I'm here! I'm over here!' And this one was strong, and we looked and we looked, and then we heard somebody yell 'We got something' and we go 'Okay' and it's not like you run because it happens all the time." Lee shifts in his seat and leans in. I feel my heart racing and realize I have not taken a bite of my food. "So I walk up—there was a number of guys standing there—I don't know how old she was. She was caught up in the rebars—"

"What are those?"

"Reinforcement rods, long bars you put in the concrete." The waitress steps up with my wine and Lee stops. I consider how strange it would be for someone to eavesdrop on a conversation like this.

"You want to hear the rest of this?" he asks, always wondering how much I can handle and I nod. "So," he continues more softly, "this woman was badly decomposed. She was hanging upside down and she had long hair. This long hair just hanging straight down, and the guys get there and without speaking some guys step forward, others step back. It's kind of like . . ." Lee searches hard for the right words.

"They're using their body language to let you know if they can handle it or not," I offer, and Lee nods.

"So I move in a little closer and a little closer, and there's another guy and I don't know who he was. So I get up to this woman and I start talking to her. I always have. In my career with anyone like that, I talk to them." Lee stops, shaking his head in disbelief that he could possibly cry like this. "God damn it," he says, his head dropping. "The poor kid." He uses his linen napkin to dry his eyes. "Those are worse than finding pieces, because a piece is a piece. Finding an individual . . . Anyhow, in cases like this, you're supposed to get the body bag, so they don't touch you, and when the steelworker cuts the beam, they kind of . . . you know, fall into the bag so you don't have to touch the body. Well, this guy and I, we didn't say anything, it was a mutual feeling, and we knew we didn't want to do that. Who cares? So, she smells. So we were holding her and another guy yells, 'You don't want to do that!' but we didn't care. We held her and as they cut the bar and we gently laid her in the bag and I said, 'I gotcha. You're all right now.' " My jaw is aching from trying not to cry, and we sit in silence digesting our food and everything that has been said.

"I don't know if it made a difference," Lee says softly.

"It absolutely did, Lee," I say with a certainty that surprises me.

"I don't know."

"I do. You may not see why now, but it did." The waitress arrives with dessert menus and I order a cake with two forks.

"Yeah, maybe you're right. It made a difference for me anyway. Maybe for a lot of the guys watching, because even though they didn't want to be involved, maybe they're saying to themselves, 'That was nice. The way that person was handled.' " We sit in a contemplative silence until the waitress returns with dessert. Lee reaches across and helps himself in a gesture that reminds me so much of Dave that my heart constricts with missing him.

We eat for a while and then I say, "I'm worried about the guys from the site. What they're going to feel when it's closed." I remember one night when Dave came home from a fire somewhere in Brooklyn where a man had been killed. Dave was standing near the five- or six-year-old son as he watched his father being carried from the fire in a stretcher. The boy screamed and cried, searing the pain into any firefighter who heard it, most of whom were fathers themselves.

"We were silent all the way home," Dave said. "Usually, we would talk about how we handled the fire, who did what and how we could have been better, but no one said a thing all afternoon."

"There's a lot of guys from the job that are never going to be straight," Lee says. "No matter what kind of facade we want to put up. You're going to have loads of guys that are never going to talk or go to counseling, and they're going to take it out on whatever they have to, whether it's a bottle, their wives, their girlfriends, drugs. It's going to be there from now until time goes on, because that's how the mind works. I can remember Vietnam more vividly now than I did ten, twenty years ago." Lee lingers on this, his spoon poised reflectively in front of him. After a beat, I look directly at him and he is smiling, sadly, but smiling nonetheless, even through a life like his.

* * *

In my dream, I am being shown a beautiful apartment overlooking the city. The man showing me the apartment is a famous ballplayer, someone I have seen on television but don't really know. He is handsome and he introduces me to other good-looking famous people standing around the spacious loft with 180-degree views of Manhattan. I stand at the window, awed by the constellation of lights in other buildings stretching as far as I can see. I am thinking about the beauty of it, how amazing this city is, how proud I am to live here, when the ground starts rumbling underneath me. The cement cracks and shifts, and the building is collapsing beneath my feet, and I am falling, dropping with the speed of a roller coaster straight down, flailing my arms and legs to try to stop, but I can't. Cement is whizzing by, and pieces of steel, and fear and panic are surging through me because I know I am going to die and there is nothing I can do about it. I am falling backward, my face to the sky, and it is raining cement and steel, and I close my eyes because I am too scared to see my own death. I startle awake. The fear is vibrating in my body when I sit up, opening the doors to being conscious. Even when I am fully aware that it was only a dream, I cannot shake the very real sensation of falling. The words from Dave's death certificate resonate in my head: *blunt trauma to the head, neck, and torso.* Is it possible to dream someone else's suffering, to have a collective unconscious of death that makes the sensation of falling as real as if you were actually there, a chink of your DNA? I wonder if this is how Dave felt the moment he died.

*   *   *

The day they find Jack Lynch's son, I almost don't answer the phone. A cab is coming in five minutes to take Aidan and me to the airport. We're going to France to stay with a French firefighter's family for a week. Aidan is so glad to be missing school, he can barely contain himself, scooting around the apartment, bouncing on the couch.

"I got a call from the medical examiner," Jack says slowly, and I remember I missed the last meeting there. Maybe something happened. "They found Michael."

"Oh, Jack." I don't know what to say.

"It's wonderful really. I mean, this is what we wanted." He is quiet, his Irish brogue tapering off for a moment.

"Are you going to have a service?" I ask, wishing now that I wasn't going away, worried that I will miss Michael Lynch's mass.

"Well, you see, Marian, they found him embedded with another woman, and they think that either he was carrying her or maybe he threw himself on top of her. I really don't know, but it's going to take a few weeks to separate the parts."

"Oh my God," I say slowly. I can hear the cab beeping outside and Aidan's footsteps running down the hall.

"No, it's good. It means he was helping someone, and I know what he was doing." He breaks off and I know he is crying quietly, so I won't hear.

"Are you okay?" I ask.

"I'm fine. I just wanted to let you know. Listen, go and have a wonderful time. Lee and I will handle all the meetings here. So don't worry about a thing. I'll call you when you get back." Jack hangs up and I listen to the silence. Michael Lynch, two weeks from getting married, threw his body on top of a stranger, unaware that they would be welded together in death.

*   *   *

The trees in the neighborhood are sprayed with veils of bright green and the light has already shifted to spring, casting long shadows onto Union Street. The Merry Widows are meeting at Squad 1 before we go out for our monthly dinner. It has only been eight months, but it feels different to go to Squad now, the men falling back into their routines and new faces appearing daily. Fred Lawrence, Bobby West, and Timmy Rogers have retired. Sean has transferred to Rescue 1. Billy Redden works at headquarters. Even Dennis, the last surviving lieutenant, is having trouble with his back, and there are murmurs that he will be gone soon, too. Leaving is the last thing any of them want to do, but since a lieutenant's pension is based on his last year's salary, there is a mass exodus of firefighters retiring due to the unprecedented amounts of overtime pay at Ground Zero.

"If I stay," Dennis told me a few days ago, "I'm giving up fifteen thousand dollars extra a year for the rest of my life, and you know what, I'm thinking about it. That's how much I'm not ready to leave." And Dennis is not alone. The Fire Department not only lost 343 men but an incalculable amount of knowledge and experience, too. The face of the department is changing from salty experienced men to wide-eyed boys, many eager to learn, many others riding on the coattails of celebrity the firefighters gained after 9/11. "It's just not the same job anymore" is the mantra echoed throughout the firehouse, and I know it is true. When Dave joined Squad, you needed at least six years' experience to join Special Operations. Some of the young guys joining now have less than two. I imagine how hard it must be for the new men to step into the boots our husbands vacated. And while the new guys are friendly and kind, I am uncomfortable in the firehouse now, a stranger.

We sit in the back of the firehouse, and Theresa becomes uncharacteristically quiet. "I can't take being here," she whispers to me. She sees the table Mike bought for the kitchen with the names of the men written in calligraphy on top. She notices the engine door covered in a giant Squad patch that Mike gave to the firehouse before he left for Rescue 5. "I don't know how you come here all the time," she says to me. Martha is in the kitchen, speaking animatedly to the guys as they prepare dinner. Debbie is sitting on the couch across from us, giggling and flashing her new white teeth.

"You girls should stay for dinner," Eric says. "There's plenty of food." I thank them and stand up. It is time to go. I wait for the girls in the front of the firehouse, looking at the budding trees illuminated in the lowering sun. I stand alone in my aching, watching families stroll by, their new babies in slings or strollers, and I mourn for what I used to feel, what I imagined my future to be. I am so lost in thought that I am startled by an arm looping itself through mine. It is Theresa, smiling and ready to go out.

The weather is so warm we sit in the garden of an elegant restaurant where the branches of a black lotus tree canopies us from a low, blinding sun. We order a bottle of white wine, and Debbie talks about the breast job she will have on September 9.

"It's the last time I saw Jim and I just want to be knocked out that day." Theresa and Martha and I try to talk her out of the surgery. I tell her it was the grief that is making her feel ugly and unattractive. Martha tells her how you lose sensation in your nipples from the surgery. But Debbie is thrilled and determined and so we can't help but be happy for her.

"I'm going to love 'em," she says, dropping her head and looking at her breasts. "Now all I have to do is find a man." She smiles, her new teeth glimmering.

"Don't start," I warn her. "I am too lonely to think about it." We grow quiet as the waitress opens the wine. "Have you started thinking about having a service?" I ask Martha, one of only two widows at the firehouse who have not had a memorial.

"No. My father-in-law wants to wait for the end of the retrieval," she says.

"That's next month!" I exclaim.

"I know." She shrugs sadly. "He wants to wait, and it's fine with me."

"To the Merry Widows," I say, raising my glass.

"Yuck!" Martha whines. "You know I hate that."

"I can't believe it's been eight months," Debbie says.

"I still can't believe it, period," Martha says, suddenly turning sad. "I can't."

"How did you find out?" I ask, realizing that we have never spoken about that long, infamous day. The mood shifts and we are all silent for a moment.

"I was home," Martha begins. "We had Patrick's christening on Sunday, so Tommy took the second half of the tour. Otherwise he wouldn't have been working." She tucks a strand of dirty blond hair behind her ear. "I went to the store to return some things. In the car, I heard something about the planes hitting the towers, but I thought it was a joke and put on a CD. When I got home there were like fifty phone calls. The schools were closing and I panicked for the kids. I wasn't thinking about Tom at all because I was thinking 'no way.' "

The sun is nearly down now, a warm breeze floats through the air as our salads arrive. Martha sighs and continues. "My father-in-law drove to the firehouse with my brother-in-laws, and we called all the hospitals, and I still didn't think anything. I was just sure Tommy wasn't there." Martha chews a bite of her salad slowly. "Then my father-in-law came back. He said, 'It's bad Martha. It's bad. He went in and he's gone.' Everybody in my house started sobbing and shaking, and I just looked outside the window and said no. I just couldn't register it. I looked out the window the whole week waiting for him to come home. I just couldn't accept it. It took me four days to tell Sean. 'Where's Daddy?' he would say, and I just answered, 'He's helping the other guys. He's finding people.' But Sean is so smart after a while he said, 'I'm scared Daddy's not coming back.' And then I had to tell him and he cried and cried. 'I knew it!' he screamed. 'That's why everyone's in the house!' "

"Kids are so smart," I say, shaking my head. I know how Martha looked in the window because I had seen it at the site, the way she leaned on the chain-link fence, peering into the gaping hole of Ground Zero hoping to see Tommy.

Debbie's cell phone rings for the third time that night. "It's Catherine," she says, rolling her eyes. "I'm gonna kill them." She opens her phone. *"What?"* she says. "I'm with the girls and I'm eating. What do you want?" She pokes her fish with a fork, annoyed. "I'll be home later. I said I would . . . now stop!" Debbie hangs up and slams the phone down. "Those girls are gonna kill me," she says, frustrated with her teenage daughters. "I can't go to the bathroom without them calling to see how much toilet paper I used."

"That's hard," Theresa says, and we are silent for a moment. I think about Aidan and a dam of guilt bursts inside me. I have tried to spend more time with him lately, to read an extra book, to linger in his room, but I am distracted, unfocused, and tired.

"Where were you on the eleventh?" I ask Debbie.

"I was a lunatic that day," Debbie says, her dark eyes flashing. "I was so angry. The kids were hysterical and everyone was hysterical and I was like 'I don't want *any* negative thinking in my house! If you say or think anything negative, you can get out of my house! Everyone needs to calm down!' My brother-in-law comes over and I'm freakin' out now and I grab him by the collar like this." She squeezes her fist as if holding a collar. " 'You better go down there to that place and don't come back here until you bring Jim home.' " Debbie's nostrils are flaring and I remember seeing Jim's brother-in-law at Squad those first few days. I remember his eyes soulful and sad as he donned his brother's turnout gear to go find him at Ground Zero.

"Your poor brother-in-law," I say.

"I was so angry that day. I was serious. I was like, don't come back here unless you find him down there." More diners have joined us in the small graveled backyard and a cool breeze forces us to put our sweaters on.

"Who brought this topic up?" Theresa says, rolling her eyes.

"I did. We've talked about everything else. It just seemed weird not to know where you all were," I say, letting my risotto rest.

"Well, I was working," Theresa begins. "I remember my friend Mike Cullin called and asked me if Mike was working, and I just calmly said yes." She takes a sip of wine and laughs. "I don't know what I was thinking. Everyone I was working with left the building, but I kept working. I told everyone I had to wait for him to call me. I just wouldn't leave."

The waitress takes our plates. Debbie has barely eaten a thing. She seems to be disappearing these days, her face gaunt and thin.

"After a while," Theresa continues, "I went to Barbara's house to pick up the baby. Then, all of a sudden, I felt like I was burning. I started screaming and yelling. I really felt like my skin was on fire. 'Stop it! You're scaring the kids,' Barbara said, but I couldn't. It was so weird. It was like I really felt like I was burning. I got in my car because now I knew something was bad and I was going to drive into the city. Barbara got her neighbor to watch the kids and she got in the car with me. We ended up going to Fort Totten in the Bronx where they had set up a family assistance center for the Fire Department families. I was calling everybody I knew and I finally got John Ferri, a firefighter Mike knew. He was at the site, and he said, 'It doesn't look good,' and that was it. I was numb. I was just standing there blank. Barbara took me outside and I was shaking and I walked out onto the rocks by the water. It's beautiful up there . . . You ever been? I was standing on these high rocks that led to the water. I was staring at the water saying 'I can't believe he left me. He left me.' Barbara said it was the scariest moment of her life because I wanted to die. I was going to jump, Marian. I really was."

Debbie's cell phone is ringing again. *"What!"* she snaps. "I'm fine, now leave me alone."

"They're worried about you," Theresa says. "You're all they have."

"I know that, and believe me, I am with them *all* the time, but after a while it just starts to get to be too much. I mean, I can't do anything. Tara's the worst!"

"I know. Aidan won't even let me go to the bathroom alone," I say. "He thinks there's monsters all over the house." And I sit up taller to tell them a funny story. There is nothing I like more than making them laugh. "So it makes it very difficult . . . you know . . . in the bathroom . . . that time of the month, because he follows me in there! He'll cry if I close the door! So, I have to distract him and do my business while he's not looking. 'Look, Aidan! What's that!' "

"Oh, man," Theresa says, chuckling. "Is this what I have to look forward to?"

"It gets worse!" I am getting animated now. "So I dropped him off at school the other day and his friends are all talking. They are very curious about things now and I hear one of the boys say, 'My mommy made me cookies,' and his friend says, 'My mommy plays tennis.' And Aidan says, 'My mommy poops red candles!' " Martha's face looks completely different when she laughs, like a light being switched on.

"What did you say?" Martha asks.

"Nothing. I crawled out of the room and imagined all of Aidan's friends announcing my talent to their parents at dinner that night." Theresa laughs like she cries, high and short, her small blue eyes crinkling in the corners, her thick red hair shaking.

"Does Aidan talk about Dave?"

"All the time. He's very outgoing, always has been."

"Sean won't talk," Martha says, looking concerned. Sean is her eldest, the same age as Aidan, a handsome boy with Tommy's rich blue eyes, a rectangle of freckles across his nose.

"Have you tried counseling?" I ask her. "You get all those newsletters, right?" It seems like every counselor in the city is donating services.

"No, I don't think he would do it," Martha says.

"I don't know what I would do without my therapist," I tell them, and they all disagree. Theresa says that she can figure things out on her own, Martha says she doesn't feel comfortable, Debbie doesn't like talking to people she doesn't know. I want to tell them how vital it is, especially after what we've been through, but we were raised in different worlds when it comes to such things.

"This is therapy," Martha says, smiling.

After dinner, I walk Theresa to her new car, a gleaming new Lexus SUV. "Don't say it," she says, warning me. I have lectured her many times about how environmentally unsound these vehicles are, polluting as much as nine automobiles and eating gas as if it were free.

"I won't," I say. "If you want to support the Saudis that had a hand in

9/11 and killing Mike and Dave, that's fine by me." I smile, letting her know I am joking.

"You and I are so different," she says, shaking her head and hugging me good-bye.

"That's why you love me."

"I do, you bitch," she says, closing her window and the widows wave as she drives away.

24

Closing

It's only early May, but it feels like summer, the sun unmerciful, even at 7:00 A.M. I am listening to the rhythm of my shoes on the pavement as I pass Ground Zero, trying to make it to my interview at the Winter Garden, a low building across from the site. Dozens and dozens of reporters and cameramen have set up shop on the roof overlooking the site and I sidestep hundreds of cables and camera legs until I find George Stephanopoulos. He is much shorter than he appears on TV and squints into the blinding sun, as eager as I am to get this interview over with. A producer grabs my pictures and before I can even call after her, the cameras are on me, the lights like a second sun making me squint. I notice that feeling I get in the pit of my stomach and wonder why I am here. I turned down dozens of interviews for this morning, but somehow this producer convinced me, found my weak spot, and now the first bell is tolling for the moment that the first plane hit at 8:46, and I am not with my friends and the people I have worked with all year. I stop in midsentence. "I have to go," I say, leaving the hot lights of the camera and searching the roof for the assistant who took my photos. They are original photos of Dave and Aidan on the fire truck. The bell is tolling and I am still on the roof, late to meet Leah and make it to the site. The place will be packed with families today, and now I will be lucky to even get a seat. The camera crew follows me downstairs. They want to get a shot of me crossing the street. They practically push my sister out of the way.

My sister is furious as we tear across the West Side Highway. "You people are unbelievable," my sister snaps, and I feel like I am ten years old, the way Leah is protecting me. I berate myself for not trusting that feeling in my stomach the way I had all year, and then we are running, sweat dripping down the back of my neck, staining my black dress. The security is so tight every street is blocked with police telling us flatly to "Go around, go around." I try to call Lee, but he is a key player in today's ceremonies, carrying a symbolic Stokes basket out of the site with the other fathers probably at this very moment.

"I can't believe those people!" my sister is still storming and I run to keep up with her long strides the way I used to in high school where she carried her flute tucked into her backpack while I struggled with my cumbersome bassoon. We finally find an entrance on Liberty Street, but our seats are so far back, we can't even see the site. "This is terrible," my sister mutters, but before I can indulge my guilt the bagpipes fold me over like a punch in the stomach. My sister hands me tissues and I cry softly when I notice that a little boy, no older than two, is watching me from the row in front of us. His face is round and olive and framed with thick black hair looping into fiddlehead curls. He holds a picture of what I assume is his father, a man who, while balding, looks exactly like him. The mother is crying, whimpering softly into her hand. The little boy bounces in his seat oblivious to his mother's tears, waving the photo. I scan the crowd, noticing dozens of children patting their mothers' backs as they cry, the mothers' heads dropped down toward their chests as if praying.

"Marian. Marian Fontana?" someone says, and I turn to see a firefighter in his late twenties. His eyes are dripping with tears and his face is streaked red. He stands next to a hulking firefighter who looks embarrassed by his friends' outburst.

"I'm sorry to bother you, but I worked with your husband Dave at 122. I was a proby there for a little while before he transferred to Squad."

I nod and smile at him. "Nice to meet you."

He opens up his blue class A jacket and shows me Dave's wake card pinned carefully to the side. "Dave was the only firefighter there who welcomed me like a brother. He took me around. He never teased me. He taught me the ropes . . . literally. He was just so nice to me. I'll never forget how nice he was."

"Thank you," I say, feeling my own chin quiver, watching the firefighter drop his head to stare at his feet and try to collect himself.

"If you need *anything*," he says sincerely. "*Anything*. If you want me to help with that project Dave was working on with the plaques. Anything. You name it."

"Thank you," I say again. The firefighter nods once more, then drops his head, squeezing his eyes to try to stop the tears.

"I'm sorry," he says, and I pat his wide back.

"God bless you," he says. His friend leads him out of the gate, disappearing into the throng of people who have begun to leave the ceremony.

*   *   *

This June, I arrive early at the Society of the Americas on Park Avenue and climb a wide carpeted stairway to the second floor. I am being interviewed for a *Dateline* special that will air on the one-year anniversary. I stand in the doorway, watching a film crew flit around a stately room to adjust light stands, wires, and cameras. Two chairs face each other, the lights as bright as a stadium's, illuminating Beverly Eckert, one of the members from the Family Coalition. Her blue eyes look tired as she speaks with anchorman Tom Brokaw, sitting across from her. I know right away that Beverly is talking about her husband, Sean, who was on the phone with her when Tower 2 fell. Beverly is in her early forties with feathery blond hair and rice-paper skin that quivers as she struggles to keep back the tears that insist on falling. The cameras stop and Beverly is brought tissues. When she catches sight of me, she waves weakly, forcing a tiny smile. I met Beverly at a press conference in November for the Victims Compensation Fund and was impressed by her intelligence and insights. After Beverly is fluffed and relit and makeup is reapplied, the cameras roll again, and I can hear her describe how, after the plane hit, her husband was told to go to the roof. He was on the phone with Beverly when he arrived at the roof door and found it locked. Beverly describes how he was coughing then, his lungs constricting from the smoke. She was desperate on the other end of the phone, hearing her husband suffer, but Sean was calm, eerily calm, as he told his wife how much he loved her. There was a crack, a loud popping sound, and the line went dead.

Maggie, the producer, catches sight of me in the room and rushes over.

"I need you to wait over there," she says, smiling broadly. She is Asian American, with straight black hair cut in a trendy bob and the energy of a Jack Russell terrier. "Actually," she says, checking her clipboard, "we need you in makeup." I follow her to a small study serving as a makeshift storage area. Camera boxes and cables cover leather seats and most of the floor. A large mahogany desk sits by the window strewn with makeup that an African American woman is organizing.

"You can sit right here, honey," she says, gesturing to the chair behind the desk. I squeeze past a pile of steel boxes and step over some crates, finally easing myself into the chair. I watch the woman leaning over a Mary Poppins–type carpet bag and lay some makeup on the desk.

"How you doin' today?" she asks, her voice low and friendly. She is an attractive woman, sturdy-looking, with skin the color of cherrywood and square white teeth.

"I'm okay," I tell her as she takes my chin in her hand, scanning my face as if I am fruit she is considering buying.

"Hmmm," she says softly, and then she shifts her gaze to the makeup on the desk. "I'm going to trim your eyebrows a bit, okay?"

"They're like Chia pets," I joke as she reaches into the bag for tweezers.

"Some girls would kill for eyebrows like yours." She carefully plucks out a few hairs. She hums while she works, her voice vibrating in her large chest. She talks about the weather, her yoga class, her church. Her voice feels like the beach, rhythmic and deep, and it relaxes me.

"What are you talking about with Tom today?" she says, brushing powder onto my eyelids, and I say the words I have now said one hundred times but still can't believe.

Her tongue clucks as she shakes her head blowing on my eyes. "I had a good girlfriend in Tower Two," she says, and I lean back, listening. I have grown used to people telling me their September 11 stories. The degrees of separation are so small in this city, everyone has a friend of a friend who died, or can recount, in vivid detail, where they were and what they saw on that day. Every makeup artist, cabdriver, guest at a dinner party wants to talk about what happened. For some it is therapeutic, for others confessional, as if talking to me will help them make sense of the uncomprehensible. And I am the reluctant priest, listening, nodding, taking in their stories, awed by the strength and ultimate fallibility of the human psyche.

"You're going to like Tom," the makeup woman says. "I've been working for him for eleven years. Tom's real. You know, he is who he is . . . I've seen stars who think they are somebody else, not anyone from this planet, you know what I'm saying?" She stares at the line she has made on my eyelid. "Tom is real."

"That's good because I'm very nervous," I admit.

"Don't be nervous. He's real easy to talk to."

Maggie throws open the door and enters. She seems to operate as if something is on fire. "Tom needs a touchup before the next shot," she announces to the makeup woman.

"The only thing about Tom," she whispers to me. "He's got a big voice. A real big voice."

"Good to know," I say, and the makeup woman smiles, her face rising like bread in the oven.

Tom Brokaw enters. Unlike the other journalists I have met, he looks exactly as he does on television.

"Hello," he says softly to no one in particular, climbing easily into the seat I just vacated, smiling at the makeup woman.

"This is Marian. You're interviewing her today. She lost her husband," she says, patting a foam triangle onto a bottle of foundation.

"The firefighter, right?" Mr. Brokaw says, tilting his head back and closing his eyes while the makeup is dabbed across his face. "Thanks for coming," he calls so softly I can barely hear him.

Maggie leads me by the elbow to the chair Beverly just interviewed in. Today I will talk about the faulty radios the firefighters used on the eleventh, the same ones that failed in the 1993 bombing. My heart contracts at the thought that Dave might have left the building if he had heard the Maydays that were issued, and I have spent many dreamless nights wondering if it would have made a difference at all.

"You've obviously done this before," the soundman says, watching me slide a microphone through my shirt and clip it to my lapel. He looks disappointed that I took his one small job away. Maggie sits in the chair across from me, tapping her foot and reviewing the questions Mr. Brokaw will ask. Someone asks me to count backward into my lapel, and in seconds, Tom Brokaw is sitting across from me, reviewing his notes. "Oh yes," he says in his deep baritone. "This letter is quite something," he says, holding up a copy of Carolyn Leary's letter.

"Yes. She spoke at Dave's funeral," I tell him.

"Dave sounded like an incredible man."

"He was," I say.

We talk about yoga, and he tells me how he was practicing yoga on September 11 when the planes hit. I half listen to him talk about not sleeping for three nights covering the story, but I am distracted by the image of Tom Brokaw, the professional journalist, pressed into a downward dog on a yoga mat.

"Ready," a voice in the blackness behind us says. "Just count to ten please."

Tom puts his cards away and clears his throat, a pilot on his millionth flight.

"Ready," the voice says again. I can feel my hands sweating as I sit up in my chair and try not look nervous. "Three, two, one . . ."

"IT WAS DAVE FONTANA'S EIGHTH WEDDING ANNIVERSARY . . ." Tom's voice booms so loud I startle in my seat, like a cat jostled awake.

"Cut," the director yells as I cover my heart, trying to slow it down to begin again.

*   *   *

Squad 1 follows Theresa's SUV down Union Street to the Old Stone House on 5th Avenue in Park Slope. The house, built in 1699, was used by General Lord Stirling as his headquarters during the Battle of Brooklyn and is now a museum. Tonight, Squad will be presented with a community service plaque. The windshield wipers beat in time to Barry White blasting from the car stereo. Debbie is sitting in the back and we sing out loud, circling the block looking for a parking spot.

"This is sex music," Debbie says as Barry's bass voice moans.

Martha is missing from the Merry Widows tonight. She couldn't get a babysitter.

"Don't even talk about it!" Theresa says.

"Please. I have tumbleweeds in my underwear." I roll my eyes for effect. "I can't believe it's almost a year."

We find a parking lot and run as fast as we can through the muddy park and up the stairs of the old stone house. My friend Bernie Graham greets us, kissing me on the cheek. Bernie is the coach of Little League, and he insisted I sign Aidan up for his team; he's trying to fill the gap left by Dave. I didn't have the heart to tell him that Dave was probably the only firefighter in the country who had no interest in sports, but Aidan is a good hitter even though he runs the wrong way. At the last game I stifled a laugh when he yelled "Touchdown!" as he reached home plate.

"I need one of you to accept the plaque," Bernie says. His face is pure Irish, milky white with freckles and light red hair.

"Debbie and Theresa will," I tell Bernie, and he nods and disappears into the back.

"I'm going to kill you!" Theresa threatens, but Bernie is already at the microphone introducing them. Debbie looks as nervous as Theresa as they stand awkwardly in front of the crowd, holding the plaque while a local photographer clicks away.

After the ceremony, Debbie invites John Suzulka, a lieutenant from

Squad, to join us for a drink. I am disappointed that our monthly Merry Widows night is now including a firefighter, but I say nothing as we head across the street, the rain still falling in thick sheets, flooding the sewers. We sit at a picnic table toward the back of a bar on 3rd Street. I order a German beer in a strange, twisted glass while Theresa and Debbie sip vodka drinks and John nurses a glass of soda. The conversation is stilted. We talk about our kids and places we want to travel. John tells me stories about Dave.

"I gotta dance," Debbie says suddenly, closing her eyes and gyrating to imaginary music.

Theresa elbows me under the table. "They have dancing in Bay Ridge." In less than ten minutes, we are sailing down 4th Avenue, John and Debbie in the car behind us.

"She better watch out for him," Theresa says. "He's still married."

"I know . . . I don't like this. Why is he going out alone with a bunch of widows?"

"She's so ready to meet someone . . . I can't even think about it, to tell you the truth," Theresa says.

"I know, but I'm so lonely," I say sullenly.

"Oh, don't get me wrong, I'm lonely, but I'm not going to get involved with anyone in the state I'm in right now . . . Hey, where are they anyway? I thought they were behind us," Theresa says, looking in the rearview mirror.

We arrive at the club in Bay Ridge to find it filled with twenty-year-olds wearing low-rider jeans and tight tank tops. In the back of the room, techno music blares as boys with greased hair and thick gold chains posture, sneaking glances at the girls who stand in tight clusters around the room.

"I feel very old right now," I say, scanning the room for Debbie and John.

"No kidding," Theresa says. We find a spot at the front of the bar and order drinks.

After an hour waiting for Debbie and John, my blood is boiling and I want to go home. "You could have called," I snap at Debbie when she and John finally join us.

"I'm sorry. We were talking." Debbie says, and I roll my eyes. I am furious and I don't even know why. Debbie looks at me like a puppy who just peed on the carpet. "I swear to *God!*" she says, insisting. "We were just talking."

"Well, you could have just left a message," I say, taking a sip of my drink.

"I think I'm going to head out," Theresa says. She is doing a better job hiding her anger than I am.

". . . Are you comin' with me or not?" Theresa asks Debbie who lives near Theresa at the end of Long Island.

"Of course!" Debbie says, collecting her bag. "How else would I get home?"

"You have to take me back to the Slope though," I remind them.

"I'll take you," John volunteers.

"No. You're even closer to home than they are," I say, gesturing toward the Verrazano Bridge to Staten Island, where he lives.

We run to his car under my umbrella and I shiver as John opens the passenger car door the way Dave always did, and even though it felt so 1950s, I secretly loved it.

John asks me about Aidan and tells me about his kids, how they play hockey.

I watch rainbow rings settle around the puddles that have formed in the street as John speeds back to Park Slope. Turning down 4th Street, we double park in front of my apartment. Even though John's hair has receded, he is strikingly handsome with transparent blue eyes and sculptured good looks. He stares ahead as if he is trying to say something.

"I don't want you to think we did anything," he says.

"It's none of my business."

"I was just talking. I've been very lonely," he says.

"You should talk to your wife then."

"I've been trying, but she's so . . . She doesn't want to talk."

"Oh," I say, wishing I could escape the car.

"She hasn't kissed me in fifteen years."

"Well, that's not good," I say lamely. Why is he telling me this? Does he want me to kiss him? Or Debbie? I look at his profile, classical and handsome, the lines as even and smooth as a watercolor. I have never kissed a married man, thinking always of the wife, folding laundry, tucking in kids, shopping at Pathmark.

"You should talk to your wife," I say.

"I've tried. It hasn't been good for so long, I don't know what to do." He is deep in thought, speaking almost to himself. All at once, my whole body fills with an intense longing. I want to be held. I want to be kissed. I want to be told I am beautiful and worthy of love. I grab the door handle and say, "Well, whenever I questioned things with Dave, I had to stop and wonder what was going on in our relationship that had to be fixed."

"You're right," John says, snapping out of his thoughts. I open the door, which creaks loudly, breaking the silence.

"Thanks for the ride." He kisses me on the lips and I can smell Debbie's perfume on him. I get out quickly, slamming the car door behind me. I can feel John watching me as I descend the three steps to the gate, the rain dripping in my face. My mind races as I recall how much Dave liked John. They were in study group together for the Lieutenants' test, and Dave envied that John had his license to fly a small plane. I fumble for my keys, listening to the car idle, my heart racing. I open the gate and wave good-bye, the loud metal door slamming into its frame, and I lean back and listen to the distinctive sound of wet tires on asphalt as John slowly rolls away.

*   *   *

Sheila is one of a small but pervasive group of volunteers that I call the 9/11 groupies. They linger at every event wearing 9/11 buttons, clad in Fire Department sweatshirts and hats. September 11 has become their religion, firefighters their rock stars, something they can be a part of. I met Sheila at a rally a few months ago, and even though she is a pretty woman, with bright blue eyes and dark straight hair, there was something worn and fragile about her, like paper about to rip. She wore an FDNY hat and about thirty or so wake cards around her neck on a chain. She told me she lost her nephew and had volunteered at the site.

She named Bill Butler and Lee and most of the fathers and firefighters I knew. Recently, she started attending coalition meetings, often insulting other family members who began to question why she was there. Jennifer told me that Sheila had been kicked off the site and that it wasn't her nephew that had died, but her firefighter boyfriend's nephew. Even then, I found it hard to dismiss Sheila. There was something pitiful about her, like a three-legged dog whimpering at the screen door. I banned her from meetings, but she still called often.

"Marian. It's Sheila," she says, almost apologizing for her own name. "Have you heard about the Deutsche Bank business?"

"A little," I tell her. Like an old widow, the Deutsche Bank building on Liberty Street was swathed in a giant black veil when a twenty-four-floor gash was ripped in its facade when the towers fell. The building has never been searched, and the rescue workers believe human remains could have been blown inside.

"It's such bullshit. The Office of Emergency Management is saying there's a mold issue, health hazard, but c'mon! That whole place is a health hazard."

"The guys in Haz Mat are trained in this. Why don't they let them in?"

"I dunno. It's fuckin' bullshit. There's a big meeting today. I thought you'd want to know. The guys are really upset and could really use your help with this."

I wonder how she knows all this, but I do my research, calling a number of firefighters and chiefs at the site to verify the story. The Office of Emergency Management maintains that the plan for entering the building was not environmentally safe. The bank is worried about the mold and lawsuits, which could cost them millions of dollars. Other rescue workers claim Deutsche Bank just wants the building torn down so they can collect insurance money. As with all of these issues, somewhere in the middle is the truth.

I decide to attend a meeting at the site. Dennis O'Berg is there, Chief Spadafora, Chief Rasweiler, Captain Mike Banker. They have been at the site since the beginning, skirting the power plays and dirty politics to maintain a respectful and dignified recovery. They are some of the few firefighters left at the site to handle the minor details. An operational meeting is supposed to be happening at 11:00 A.M., but when John Odermatt, the commissioner of the Office of Emergency Management, hears that I am there, he promptly changes the location, moving the meeting to OEM offices in Brooklyn.

The Office of Emergency Management is located directly under the Brooklyn Bridge in a low, nondescript industrial building overlooking Manhattan. Security is strict so Sheila and I stand outside in the hot sun, trying to figure out a way to get into the meeting. After I convince Sheila to wait outside, I walk up to the desk and pull out my Fire Department ID. A bored security guard reading the *New York Post* looks up.

"Hi. I'm here for the meeting with John Odermatt." I sign in, noting the names of people who have signed in before me, and head through a glass door trying to find the meeting.

"Marian," John says, slowly standing. "You're not supposed to be here."

"And you're supposed to let them into the Deutsche Bank."

"This really doesn't concern you."

"Of course it does. I'd like to sit in on the meeting."

"I don't think that's a good idea."

"Why?"

We go on like this for some time, John's pale round face getting more annoyed. He reminds me of a college frat boy, his small eyes squinting, and when he finally relents, I follow him to a small meeting room a few doors down. Representatives from the Deutsche Bank are there, as well as fire chiefs and the Department of Environmental Protection. After a long and difficult debate, it is finally agreed that the firefighters can go into the Deutsche Bank building to search, wearing HazMat suits and supervised by the Department of Environmental Protection, who will be responsible for carting the debris away. Once I see that everything is being handled, I step outside, exhausted. It's almost time to pick Aidan up from school. Sheila runs over, and I am shocked that she has been waiting outside for so long. I can tell she wants to come home with me, but I make my excuses and find a cab. Once in the cab I call Jennifer at the office and tell her everything that has happened. We wonder where the firefighters will go to rest, now that the Salvation Army tent has been dismantled, and almost all FDNY personnel are gone.

"How much money do we have?" I ask.

"Two thousand dollars," she says glumly. While all the other groups have been actively pursuing funding, we have been operating with random and meager donations. "Let's set something up for them. There's O'Hara's restaurant."

"Yes, let's. Can you call there and see if we can set up an account for them? It's only about five guys who will be there for about a month."

25

Faith and Doubt

The sun looks like a comet reflecting off the hood of the maroon convertible I rented at LAX airport.

"Wow! It's so small," Jason says, but I think it's perfect. It is the car Dave and I talked about renting for our tenth anniversary. We were saving change in cans on top of our refrigerator to make this trip to California and drive up Highway 1 to see the coast.

A few weeks ago, Helen Whitney, the director of *Faith and Doubt at Ground Zero,* invited me to Los Angeles to speak at a television critics' conference. Her film was made for *Frontline,* which will be celebrating twenty-five years of documentary filmmaking. She asked me to join a few of the religious leaders interviewed for the film for a panel discussion, and I immediately said yes.

Jason tries to cram all of our bags into the tiny trunk. "We'll have to put one here," he says, hoisting a suitcase next to Aidan in the backseat. I find the button to open the roof and it folds back like a giant fan.

"Cool!" Aidan yells. "Can I do it?"

"Next time. Put your seat belt on!"

"I'll drive," Jason offers, and after he fiddles with a few controls and adjusts the seat for his long legs, we are off to the Pasadena Ritz where the conference is being held.

I study the map, deciding that Pasadena is only a short drive north on Highway 10 and then 101.

"Can't they use any other numbers beside one and zero?" I aks incredulously.

"It's the average dress size," Jason snipes.

An hour later, we enter the circular driveway of the Ritz-Carlton. The lobby looks pure 1940s Hollywood. A giant chandelier rains crystal droplets, and ornate floral bouquets are tucked into every deco recess. Italian marble floors soften the room, beckoning us down a long carpeted hallway that leads upstairs to a comfortable room on the second floor.

That evening, Jason babysits Aidan so I can attend a dinner with Helen, her producers, and other members of the panel. A van picks us up in front of the hotel and takes us to an expensive restaurant with a lush, verdant garden that makes me feel like an actor in *A Midsummer Night's Dream*. I am seated next to Lorenzo Albacete, a monsignor from Rome who was good friends with Pope John Paul II and writes religious columns for the *New York Times*. I immediately like him; his nature and build make him seem like a theological Santa Claus. Seated next to Lorenzo is Rabbi Hirschfield, a reform rabbi who wears a long ponytail, a crocheted yarmulka, and a suit. His quote in the film—"Religion drove the planes into the buildings"—has haunted me ever since I saw a rough copy at Helen's apartment a few weeks ago. Across from the rabbi are the producer, David Fanning, his two assistants, and a Muslim with a bodyguard because he has had several assassination attempts against him for his controversial view of Islam.

Dinner conversation is fascinating and lively, covering philosophy, music, politics, and food. Toward the end of the meal, Father Lorenzo leans back in his chair, placing his hands on his belly like a sated king. "Tell me about Dave." I show him the wake card I carry in my wallet and tell him everything I miss. He nods and grunts. I expect him to tell me that Dave is with God, an angel in heaven, or any of the other clichéd comments I have heard since Dave's death, but he says nothing. He just stares at the picture, nodding slightly.

"It was my wedding anniversary that day," I add for no particular reason.

I watch a bread crumb stuck to the side of his big lips as a low grumble emits from his mouth and, in a thick Spanish accent, says, "God is incredibly tacky." The comment is so irreverent and unexpected, I burst out laughing, nodding in agreement.

"I bet the gates of heaven are rococo gold. Completely over the top."

"And there are velvet couches covered in plastic," the monsignor continues, his belly bouncing as he laughs. I feel as if I am with a good girlfriend instead of one of the most respected men in Christian theology.

After the panel discussion, I find Aidan giggling in the pool with a six-year-old boy we met yesterday, also named Aidan. His mother, a documentary filmmaker, lives in Pasadena and uses the pool on weekends. She offers to watch Aidan so Jason and I can take a much-needed break and go for a run. We are thrilled at the prospect of exercise, since we have been ordering excessive amounts of room service.

"They put food under silver hats here!" Aidan yelled when the food arrived last night.

Jason and I jog through the winding streets of Pasadena, peering into the windows of greenhouses and the living rooms of sprawling mansions. The midday sun is dry and hot, and after the second mile, I stop to catch my breath.

I follow Jason down a steep hill where the lawns look like they have been mowed with a buzzer. Everything is pristine, perfect, and green, and we are lost.

"I can't remember how to get back," Jason says, giggling nervously. There is no one in sight and we have only seen one gardener since we began our run.

"Where the hell is everybody?" I ask, trying not to panic. I start to think of Aidan, how I have left him with a complete stranger who has no way to contact us. "I hate this place. I'm going to call it Lost Angeles."

"We just need to ask someone," he says calmly. My legs ache as I struggle to keep up with his long strides. Every driveway is empty, every home lifeless.

"This is weird," I say. "It's like *Dawn of the Dead.*"

"I know. It's like that airline commercial: *Where is everybody!*"

"Shit, shit, shit," I say, my heart racing with the fear that Aidan is now crying, and then I hear a woman's cough. Like two hunters hearing our prey, we run toward the noise.

The source of the cough is in her late sixties, her hair tied back into a neat braid. She is hunched in front of her garden, pulling weeds from a round patch of yellow lilies leaning toward the sun.

"Excuse me?" I say, trying not to sound panicked. "Would you happen to know which way the Ritz-Carlton Hotel is?"

"Oh dear. It's about five miles or so. Let me think." I grab my head with my hand, wondering how we possibly wandered so far from our hotel. Sensing my distress, she asks, "Would you like me to drive you?"

"Yes! Thank you *so* much," I tell her. "My son is back at the hotel and I'm worried he's going to get scared because I've been gone for so long."

"No problem at all," she says. "I'll just go get my keys."

"Thank you."

"That's so nice of you," Jason says as we watch her disappear behind a bright red door. Older people love Jason. He has that old-school politeness that they appreciate because it is so rare. He holds doors, pulls out chairs, and smiles easily.

Millie drives a dark blue Mercedes from 1986 and her husband is a composer for film. It seems like the entire city is in "the business."

"What are you and your husband here for?" Millie asks, stretching her neck to peer over the steering wheel.

"Oh . . . we're friends. We're here for the television critics' convention."

"Oh, are you an actress?"

"No . . ." Here it goes again. If all roads lead to Rome, then every conversation in my life seems to lead back to 9/11.

"Marian lost her husband," Jason says. "He was a firefighter killed on 9/11, and she was in a documentary."

"Oh." Millie scrunches up her face. "I tried to get tickets for *The Guys* and I couldn't. You wouldn't happen to know how I could get tickets, would you?"

I look in the rearview mirror at Jason, who is not even hiding his astonishment. *The Guys* is a play that ran in New York about a woman who helped a fire captain write eulogies for the men in his firehouse who were lost.

"No. I didn't even know it was playing here," I say as she pulls into the hotel's circular driveway.

"Oh, well. I really wanted to see that show," she says. I thank Millie and wave good-bye.

*   *   *

The following morning, Jason, Aidan, and I head out into the hot summer sun to find Highway 1. We pass through Santa Barbara and San Luis Obispo singing along to Cher and Madonna and, when Jason lets me, some Coldplay and Paul Simon. I sigh, identifying with the song "Graceland" as he sings. *"Losing love is like a window in your heart. Everybody sees you're blown apart. Everybody sees the wind blow."* We call ourselves "Thelma and Lewis," gliding our convertible along the coast. The landscape is so different here, the earthen colors of Italy combined with the rich greens of Hawaii and the jagged cliffs of Ireland. I point out hawks to Aidan as they circle above us. "DADDY LOVED THEM!" I yell to him, but Aidan has been complaining in the backseat since we left. "IT'S TOO WINDY!" he keeps saying, sinking into his seat, turning up the volume on his Walkman, which has been playing tapes of *The Chronicles of Narnia* since we left.

The highway gets narrow and small as we curve through the stunning landscape of Big Sur, snaking our way up to San Francisco, Jason's hometown. We are staying with his mom, Harry, who resides in Twin Peaks, a neighborhood that defies logic and gravity as comfortable-size homes dot the cliffs. Jason's house is as refined as his mother, with large, well-appointed rooms and picture windows overlooking the sparkling San Francisco Bay. I know Dave would have loved the dramatic slope of the streets, the ornate Victorian homes, the glittering bridges. Will I always wish Dave could experience the new things I see? Will my excitement always be dampened by the fact that he is not here? What I notice even more profoundly is how precarious everything feels. Instead of enjoying the view of the bay from Jason's room, I stay awake at night, imagining the earthquake that will tumble us down the cliff, shattering what's left of my life into pieces. Maybe it is because it is August and the anniversary is looming, circling like the hawks, crying, "It's been a year!"

For the last day of vacation, Jason, Aidan, Harry, and I drive to Napa Valley. Jason's mother sits in the front of the convertible, her hairdo carefully tucked underneath a silk scarf. I have enjoyed getting to know Harry these last few days. Her expressive face and wry sense of humor make me appreciate Jason even more. She is lovely with Aidan, patiently drawing him baths and listening to his long monologues about aliens and knights. There is nothing I enjoy more than watching Aidan from a distance, his expressive face billowing like a curtain with all the curiosity and sincerity of Dave.

"Have you been to Napa before?" Harry asks me, stretching her arm across the seat, her manicured hands covered in chunky turquoise rings. She smiles at Aidan, who is listening to *The Chronicles of Narnia* again.

"Never," I tell her. "I can't wait." We cross bridges and highways that eventually lead us down open fields of what looks like farmland. Upon closer inspection, I realize that these are actually vines hung heavy with grapes in every direction. "The wind is so strong back here!" I yell to Jason, my hair smacking me hard in the face. I am very uncomfortable and can't wait to stop.

"I told you," Aidan says, and I realize he has been suffering in the back like this for over two weeks.

"I'm sorry, buddy. I didn't know how much windier it was back here," I tell him, squeezing his thigh.

"It's okay." His legs seem to have stretched overnight, making him the tallest kid in his class; his straight brow is a carbon copy of his father's.

"I love you, buddy," I say.

"WHAT?" he says.

"I love you, buddy," I say louder.

"WHAT?" he says.

"Turn that down!" I tell him and I sigh, exhaling my annoyance into the wind.

"I love you, buddy," I tell him again.

"Love you, too," he says, and despite all my mistakes, I know he does.

26

Final Roll Call

On August 16, Tony and Donna Edwards drop me off at Theresa's house on their way to Tommy Butler's wake. He is the last of the twelve Squad 1 firefighters to have a memorial. I am relieved Martha has finally decided to have a service for her husband. The other widows and I were concerned that since he wasn't found, she might never decide to have one.

Theresa's house is on a corner lot of a suburban neighborhood on Long Island. I plop my bags in her small country kitchen and sink onto one of the bar stools.

"What are you moving in?" Theresa jokes, noticing my four pieces of luggage.

"I have an itinerary the FBI would have trouble following." I sigh, pulling out my overnight bag from the pile. I will be sleeping here tonight to attend Tommy's wake and the funeral tomorrow.

"Try me."

"Okay, I dropped my car in Staten Island for my sister's boyfriend Neil to drive up to Martha's Vineyard next week. My parents left this afternoon with Aidan to go to the Vineyard. After the funeral tomorrow, John Suzulka will drive Leah and me home, then pick us up at my parents' house in the morning to go to an airport in Teaneck, New Jersey, where he will fly us to the Vineyard in his Cessna plane."

"I don't know how you have the energy," Theresa says, shaking her head. "I can barely get up in the morning!" She wipes her already clean counter and grabs her keys. "C'mon. Let's take the Miata." I follow Theresa into the garage, where a beautiful red convertible sits, and we climb into the front.

"I just couldn't bring myself to sell this thing," she says, putting the top down and pressing the remote for the garage door to open. "Do you like convertibles?" I smile, thinking of Aidan in the backseat. The breeze blows my hair in a thousand directions as we wind our way through the back roads of the Island toward the wake at a firehouse in Kings Park where Tommy volunteered. Theresa pops in a CD and turns up the volume, drowning out the engine and the sound of wind in my ears. *"Hey, where did we go?"* Van Morrison sings, and Theresa throws her head back, singing along at the top of her lungs, her thick auburn hair flying back like flames. *" 'Laughing and a-running!'* Van Morrison reminds me so much of Mike," she yells over the wind. I smile at her, looking into the windows of the houses we pass, where I imagine couples pressed into their couches watching TV, the simple routines we all enjoyed before we spent a year attending funerals together.

The next morning I can see the heat waves hovering over the asphalt in the parking lot of the church. Theresa and I take our places on the steps for the last time. I wave to Lee and Ann Ielpi, Bill and Peggy Butler, John Viggiano and his wife, whose grief still hangs like a pulled shade over her face. The humidity hangs heavy on everyone, distracting us. We widows shift from one foot to the other, fanning ourselves with folded pieces of paper. As uncomfortable as I am, I feel worse for the firefighters, dripping in their class A uniforms, their wool jackets as ludicrous as snowshoes on the beach. When the bagpipes begin, breaking the thick air with their drone, Theresa moans. We have all grown to hate these songs, which have come to symbolize death as clearly as the Grim Reaper.

Inside the church, the cold stone walls are a welcome reprieve from the dense heat. I follow Theresa and Debbie to the pew reserved for us in the middle of the church, spotting my mother-in-law, Toni, and Dennis sitting in the back. There are memorial programs on the seat with a photo of Tommy on the front. Sliding in next to Theresa, I remember the last time I saw Tommy, at the Squad 1 picnic in August. Dave played volleyball with the guys and the women sat drinking iced tea and telling dirty jokes.

I squirm in my seat, the sweat collecting under my legs. Patrick, Martha's youngest, runs down the aisle of the church, smiling. He is eighteen months old now and looks like a miniature Tom, with wide cheeks and sharp blue eyes. He struggles to run in his tiny suit, teetering from side to side, savoring the attention as everyone smiles from their pews. Eileen, Tommy's sister, scoops him up and returns him to Martha, who sits in the front row. Tommy's friend Dean stands at the pulpit to deliver his eulogy that he improvises, meandering through the events he shared with his friend. As he digresses, I drift off in thought, staring up at the elaborate stained-glass windows where the stations of the cross are depicted. The first panel shows Jesus carrying a cross almost farcical in its enormity. Jesus' forsaken eyes are cast upward, droplets of blood forming around his thorny crown. In the second window, equally large, Jesus looks so anguished, I wonder if he questioned God the way I do, if he challenged why someone so good could inflict so much pain. And when Jesus inevitably falls in the final window, his followers rush to his side, looking equally pained and helpless, wishing Jesus could return to the man he once was.

When Dean finally finishes his eulogy, Martha stands. She looks bewildered, her face disappearing behind the microphone as she reads from a wrinkled sheet of paper. Her voice is as small as a whisper and we lean in to hear her express her grief, her love for Tom. Patrick escapes from Eileen's arms and runs down the aisle, when Martha stops suddenly, smiling at her son. Theresa, Debbie, and I beam at Martha, smiling like proud parents at our friend whom we have grown to love deeply over this last year. After she sits, our moods profoundly shift as a firefighter in front stands and yells. *"Please rise for final roll call."* Seats creak and papers rustle and soon everyone is standing, the firefighters replacing the caps on their sweating heads.

"Captain Jim Amato," a resonant voice in the back says as a bell clangs so loudly it startles me and makes Debbie burst into tears. *"Firefighter*

Brian Bilcher," the voice intones as the bell rings again. *"Firefighter Gary Box."* I can see Gary, his straight Caesar cut and distinctive smile. *"Firefighter Thomas Butler."* I watch Martha stare straight ahead as her kids lean into her chest. *"Firefighter Peter Carroll."* All the widows are crying now, their heads dropped, tissues pressed to their eyes. *"Firefighter Robert Cordice."* "I can't. I can't," Debbie says, shaking her head as if she is refusing to hear any more. *"Lieutenant Edward R. D'Atri."* The surviving wives behind us start to pass up tissues. Deirdre, Joe O'Donnell's wife, is crying, too. She has sent me cards for every holiday this year, including Aidan's birthday. *"Lieutenant Michael Esposito."* I see Mike's face, the dimples around his mouth when he smiled. *"Firefighter David J. Fontana."* The bell tolls, reverberating in my ears, waking up all my sadness and grief. It feels permanent now. There is no going back. Theresa holds my hand as the tears fall, landing in salty circles on my black skirt. *"Firefighter Matthew Garvey."* Now we are all sobbing with a pain that runs deep and organic, to the center of the earth. *"Lieutenant Michael R. Russo."* I squeeze Theresa's hand. "Oh, God," she moans, and I see Mike's eyes, blue and radiant as he stared at Theresa on their wedding day. *"Firefighter Stephen Siller,"* the man roars, and Debbie is turning from side to side, like someone trapped, the line of her jaw deepening as her teeth clench.

"I gotta get outta here," she says as the last bell tolls. She runs toward the door. Theresa and I follow her into the bright haze of the sun. I have never left a funeral before, and everything is so bright and hot, I can barely see as we chase Debbie into the parking lot, her crying muffled in the thick summer air. She stops at her SUV and we climb in, turning on the engine so the air conditioner will cool us. I slide into the backseat and put my hand on Debbie's shoulder. I have never seen her cry like this before.

"That final roll call—shit, I didn't know they were gonna do that!" she snaps, drying her eyes with tissues.

"I know, I know," Theresa says, calming now, her breath still staccato, like after a baby cries.

"How come Martha didn't tell us?" I ask, catching sight of my eyes in the rearview mirror, swollen and red.

"She didn't look like she knew. Did you see her face?" Theresa asks.

Debbie is looking in the rearview mirror. "She was crying hard, too. Oh my God. Look at me." She pulls makeup out of her pocketbook and dabs some foundation under her eyes. "You guys can go back in if you want. I can't."

"I don't want to. I'm just going to lose it again. Did you want to go back, Marian?" Theresa says, but before I can answer, she pats the underside of her eyes. "I don't even want to know what I look like." Soon we are all leaning in to mirrors reapplying the makeup we have cried off.

"Look at us," Debbie says, and I do. The widows who have survived almost a year's worth of funerals, and we are still putting on makeup, doing laundry, bathing our kids, changing diapers, paying bills, taking out garbage, writing thank-you notes, registering cars, getting haircuts and eye exams and new shoes, tucking in our kids. We are doing all of it. Alone.

After the funeral, John tells us he had to work and won't be able to pilot us to Martha's Vineyard. I am furious, but too tired from crying to argue, to ask why he didn't call to tell me the plans had changed. I know Debbie has been seeing him for the last few months, even though she vehemently denies it. Leah is also furious since we have no way to get to the Vineyard. At around midnight, John calls to tell us he found a pilot friend willing to fly us in the morning. "It will be expensive though," he said, and I don't care. I am desperate to see Aidan, to inhale his life-force as he runs through the waves. An old friend from Staten Island drives us to Teaneck airport, which consists of four folding chairs and a bathroom. The pilot, Bill, is in his early twenties with a five o'clock shadow and aviator glasses. He looks like an extra from *The Right Stuff*.

"I need to see your luggage," he says, looking at our bags. "That's too much. It won't fit."

After leaving the cooler and beach blankets in my friend's trunk, we follow Bill with our duffel bags onto the tarmac. He walks up to the smallest plane on the runway and opens a side panel with a key, jamming his knapsack through a small hole. When my duffel bag refuses to fit, Bill slams his body against the plane, forcing it in. I watch the wings rock back and forth as Bill repeats the same ritual for my sister's suitcase. Suddenly, a signal in my brain releases an alarm.

Warning. Alert. You are approaching a dangerous situation. You are a single parent getting into a Cessna. A Cessna. Those are always the ones that crash. John Denver, Patsy Cline, John F. Kennedy Jr. Christ! I'm even going to Martha's Vineyard like he was. I can't. I can't!

"You guys ready?" Bill asks, popping a piece of gum into his mouth.

"I just need a minute," I say, trying to keep my voice calm. My sister, sensing my panic, follows me into the bathroom, where I am hunched over the toilet, feeling as if I am going to throw up.

"You okay?"

"I can't do it. I just can't."

"It's going to be fine," Leah says, as if reciting lines from a bad movie.

"No really. Did you see the plane?"

"It's small."

"*Small!* It's a station wagon with wings. I can't do it. It's not fair to Aidan and *you*. You are my backup parent. We can't be on the same plane together."

"Stop it."

"No, seriously. We are like the president and vice president. We shouldn't travel together."

"You're being ridiculous."

"No. This is not good," I say sincerely, sitting on the toilet now.

Leah says nothing as I bury my head in my hands. I hear her sigh. It has been a full-time job being my sister this past year. "Okay, fine. If you don't want to go, we don't have to," she says softly, and I grab some toilet paper and blow my nose.

"I'm being ridiculous, aren't I?" I ask her.

"Kind of. I mean, you have to take a little plane from there next week for your *New York* magazine shoot, but . . . I dunno. Listen, I think it took guts to get on a plane, period, this year, and you've done that twice."

"Four times, actually," I say, tossing the balled-up tissue into the garbage pail on the other end of the room. It misses. "You're right. If it crashes, it crashes." I stand up. "Life's been shitty lately anyway . . ."

Bill is standing next to the plane when Leah and I walk onto the tarmac again.

"Everything okay, ladies?" he asks, and Leah smiles reassuringly.

"Just a little attack of nerves," my sister says, gesturing to me, and I feel like the mentally challenged sister as Bill turns and smiles.

"You're gonna love it," he says. "We better put you in the back though."

I fold myself into the backseat and press myself up against our luggage. Bill turns the key and the engine is so loud he gives us headphones to speak to each other. The sound crescendos as the plane taxis over to a runway in the middle of the airport. I am holding my breath, fear coursing through me, when Leah reaches her hand back to hold mine. I look out of the small clouded window and remember the helicopter ride Dave and I took on our honeymoon. Dave's face was set in an expression of pure joy as we flew low over crystalline waves. He laughed out loud as the lava flowed into the sea, making giant plumes of smoke, and I couldn't help but smile at his expression, which resembled that of a seven-year-old on his first roller-coaster ride.

Bill gets clearance from the control tower and begins to pick up speed on the runway. I am still holding my breath as the engine roars and the plane ascends effortlessly, weightlessly. It is so unlike commercial planes I have flown in, where the climbing altitude feels like someone hoisting the plane from below in sporadic spurts.

"This is amazing," I tell Bill.

"Pretty smooth, huh?" he says, smiling. The earth floats away, becoming a geometric collage of colors. We pass over Connecticut mansions and golf courses, cities and rolling hills of green. We bank right across Cape Cod, its boot sticking like a witch's finger into the ocean, and turn toward Martha's Vineyard I keep my eyes open as we descend, watching the low pine trees come into view as we bounce slightly and come to a stop as easily as a car at a red light.

"Thank you," I tell Bill, giving him a big tip for keeping me alive to see Aidan bounding toward me.

The firefighters on Martha's Vineyard have donated a gray cedar house for us to use. I have not been on this island in over twelve years, and the distinct smell of dune roses mixed with sand and grass floods me with memories. I spent almost every summer of my childhood here, my parents renting inexpensive cottages in Oak Bluffs and West Tisbury until the prices became too high. After graduating from Sarah Lawrence, I returned to Martha's Vineyard, living with a theater company: eighteen of us crammed into a weathered brown house in Vineyard Haven. The company staged mostly outdoor productions where mosquitoes and bad acting drove many in the audiences away. The alternative actors, however, were given a small black box theater in town, and that is where I staged my first one-woman comedy show, which Dave flew over to see. During the day I cleaned houses, drove a cab, and waited tables. On my days off, I went alone to the beach, where the ocean felt like a luxurious lover waiting for me. I would stay until the evening and buy fried clams and beer and a bag of Jelly Bellys and wait for the sun to set. A crowd would gather on Menemsha Beach to watch the slow-motion kaleidoscope of a sunset and applaud when the sky finally darkened.

"I miss being carefree," I tell Leah as our dad drives us up the Tisbury/Chilmark Road to our rental house.

"Me, too," she says, staring at the wide horse fields and stone fences leading to the house.

*　　*　　*

A narrow sandy path leads us to a cottage on top of a cliff. We are visiting some friends of Leah's at Gay Head Beach, my favorite place on the island. Whenever I have to imagine a beautiful place, I choose Gay Head Beach, pristine cliffs of yellow, red, gray, and black that never fail to make my jaw drop from their natural beauty.

The cottage is well worn, built in the 1960s, with plywood floors and a broken sliding door. Leah greets her friends and I slink in after her, feeling out of place, chasing Aidan around a houseful of strangers, none of whom have children. Sensing my discomfort, Aidan seems to behave awful on purpose, jumping on furniture and swinging too high on the hammock chair in the center of the room. I take him outside to walk him on the beach like an overactive puppy. He follows me on the narrow sandy path through a field of dune grass, leaning like modern dancers in the wind. The path opens up to a wide private beach that is nearly empty and scattered with seaweed and rocks. Aidan and I pretend we are on a deserted island, avoiding pirates. He is carrying the leash that belonged to my parents' dog, Vanilla, who died earlier this month. I wish I could take away the tide of death that seems to have swept over us this year, but I can only watch him staring at the leash wistfully. "I miss Vanilla," Aidan says, and I nod. I loved the way Vanilla greeted us at the fence and how my mom laughed when the dog chewed pinecones, letting them hang from her mouth like cigars.

"Me, too. She was a great dog," I tell him. We spot an old boat and Aidan directs me to run in fear from the skeletons of dead pirates. I scream and run, trying to look as frightened as I can, while he swings Vanilla's leash like a lasso. When we are finished with the game, Aidan hands me the leash to hold.

"How come everything dies on us?" he asks absently, searching for a rock.

"Well, dogs and cats don't live as long as we do, and Daddy . . . well, that's not usually what happens to people. Usually, people get old."

"Like wrinkled skin?"

"Like wrinkled skin," I say, smirking.

"Our family is so small now," Aidan says, and I nod, thinking of how I never imagined it being so tiny. I wanted the little girl with curly brown locks and eyes as wide and beautiful as Aidan's.

"Well, families come in all sizes," I say.

"Why don't you adopt a baby from China?"

"Well . . . not right now," I tell him. "How about we get a pet instead?"

"Really?" he says, turning to me. I stop, realizing I have offered something without thinking. What if he wants a dog? I can barely handle laundry. "I want gerbils," he says and I can't help but look relieved.

"A gerbil, huh?"

"Two gerbils."

"Two gerbils . . . Okay, I think that can be arranged," I tell him.

* * *

Aidan loves animals, surrounding himself with so many stuffed versions every night, he often falls out of his bed. "They are my kingdom," he announces proudly. "They protect me."

I have been taking Aidan to an old pet store on 9th Street since he was a baby, and he runs from aisle to aisle, squealing and pointing at tanks. The hamster and gerbil section is small, and I am immediately struck by how much they look like mice. My favorite pet when I was young was a gerbil named Squiggles, who electrocuted himself by chewing through an alarm clock wire. Amazingly, he survived, living an unprecedented seven years, his brown hair sticking straight up for the rest of his years.

"I want that one!" Aidan says, pointing to a white gerbil with beady red eyes and a long pink tail. I try not to appear as disgusted as I feel and simply nod, scanning the other tanks.

"Oh, look!" I say, noticing a soft, fluffy teddy bear hamster feeding a litter of newborn babies, as pink and small as fingernails. "Look at the hamster!" I hoist him up to see.

"No, I want that one." Aidan points down to the white gerbil, who is chewing paper into confetti.

"They have brown ones. The one I had when I was little was brown."

"No, I want him."

"He's an albino," the overweight owner says flatly, a cockatoo perched on his shoulder. He is carrying what looks like a Happy Meal box for the gerbil we choose.

"I want that one, too!" Aidan says, pointing to a brown gerbil desperately scratching the glass.

"No, honey, you have to take care of that one first and then we'll talk about another one."

"They have to be from the same litter or they kill each other," the owner says, wheezing hard from his trip across the aisle.

"Okay. The brown one, too, then," I concede, smiling despite myself when Aidan jumps up and down joyously.

"You have to take care of them though," I warn.

"Yes! Yes, I will. You are the *best* mom," he says, and I eye him suspiciously. "And I'm not just saying that 'cause you're buying me gerbils," he adds, his eyes wide with excitement. "Okay, that's a big part of it," he confesses, and I poke him under the arms to make him giggle.

At home, we set up the cage, the food, the water bottle, and Aidan stares at his new gerbils, who sniff and poop and scratch their way through their new cage.

"I love them!" Aidan says.

"You have to name them," I tell him, and he leans in squinting at them.

"I'm going to name that one Gerb and the other one Gerbie," he says, and I try hard not to laugh. I want to mumble "Original" but control my sarcasm and muster "Great!" instead.

It is difficult to persuade Aidan to leave his gerbils at home for our meeting with his new first-grade teacher. I was thrilled when she sent a letter asking to meet him the day before school starts. On the way up to the second floor, I bump into Aidan's kindergarden teacher, whose small eyes widen. For his last article on Squad for the *New York Times*, Charlie LeDuff interviewed Aidan. When I was in California, Charlie read me the article over the phone. It was a scathing indictment of his teacher, and I didn't have the heart to give him permission. "You have to tone it down," I said, and Charlie obliged.

"I am so hurt you said those things about me in the *Times!*" the teacher says as we pass. I want to tell her how she should be glad Charlie cut the meanest parts.

"He interviewed Aidan, not me," I say instead, which is true. Aidan took Charlie to the playground of his school and regaled him with stories about things his kindergarten teacher said and did. I felt sincerely sorry for her now, standing in the hall, incapable of seeing how difficult a year it was for Aidan and me. I ended up using my Red Cross donation to hire an assistant in the classroom to help Aidan through his difficult days, but the year was still undeniably hard for him. Now the teacher who had so much power over our lives stands before me, looking small and tired and helpless, and I realize she is not in fact a mean person, just emotionally ill equipped to handle Aidan's grief. "I'm sorry if it hurt your feelings," I say, and Aidan and I hold hands and head upstairs.

Eve Litwack's classroom is on the second floor at the end of the hall.

She is setting it up for the first day of school, stapling yellow construction paper onto a bulletin board in the back of the classroom. I immediately like Eve, who is self-assured, with a short pageboy haircut and an easy smile. Her room is cheery, with books and games and tanks filled with turtles, fish, and hermit crabs.

"I like pets, too," she tells Aidan, who has already told her all about his new gerbils.

"You're not going to yell, are you?" Aidan asks.

"Well, I can't lie. I lose it once in a while, Aidan, but I really try not to."

I smile, pleased with his new teacher who, if nothing else, is honest.

The next morning Jamie, one of Aidan's babysitters, arrives to start her new job as my assistant. I have hired her to help me organize the paperwork piled up in the apartment and respond to some of the hundreds of people who reached out to me over the past year. She is shy, the middle child in an Irish family who has lived in Park Slope for two generations. She keeps her thick brown hair pulled back in a tight ponytail and nervously sticks the stray pieces behind her ears.

"I'm really looking forward to getting away from death for a while," Jamie tells me, staring down at her thick-soled shoes. She has been working at a funeral parlor in the neighborhood for the last two years, after her father died suddenly from a heart attack. I chuckle at the irony of her remark.

"Well, this is pretty straightforward," I tell her. "I need you to go through all these letters and packages people sent and write down the addresses for the ones that have them. Unfortunately, there are a ton that don't have them because I was so overwhelmed." I give Jamie a purple pad and a pen to write down the names and head into my bedroom to write a speech on my computer. Tomorrow I am speaking at another fire rally, and I want to be prepared.

In less than ten minutes, Jamie calls from the living room. "Marian, something's wrong." I stand up, trying to hang on to the fragment of thought. "Something's wrong with the gerbil," she says, and I run into the living room where I see Gerbie hanging upside down, writhing in pain. He's wedged his foot in between the tiny bars of the cage. The gerbil twists in pain, blood dripping everywhere, as he tries desperately to gnaw off his own leg.

"Oh my *God!*" I yell, looking at the albino gerbil cowering in the corner, speckled with dots of blood. "Stop it, Gerbie!" I yell, shaking the cage, hoping the gerbil will fall and I can clean up what looks like a miniature set of *Helter Skelter.* I reach into the cage to try to free him, but he bites my finger hard, breaking the skin. *"Ow!"*

"Get me a glove and a box," Jamie says with authority. I find a leather glove in my sock drawer and dump some GI Joes out of a shoe box from Aidan's room. Jamie puts the glove on and sticks her hand in the cage, spreading the thin wires as Gerbie squirms wildly, biting, until he falls with a plop to the bottom of the cage.

"Is he alive?" I ask, watching Gerbie shiver, his fur wet with blood.

"I think so. Do you want me to take him to the vet?" she asks.

"I dunno. Can't I get another one just like him?"

"I think they have to be from the same litter," she says.

"Yeah, take him . . . This thing *has* to live," I say, grabbing a check from my bag. Jamie slides Gerbie into the box with such ease, I wonder how many times she has handled incidents like this one.

Around noon she returns, carrying Gerbie in a much fancier box. He is perfectly still, a tiny cast on his leg.

"Yeah, he just has to stay on antibiotics for ten days, and then the cast can come off. He might chew it off, but it's better if he keeps the leg still. It was three hundred fifty dollars because they had to take an X ray to see if it was broken."

"An X ray?" I say trying to imagine the tiny photo of Gerbie's bones, the size of little toothpicks. "Seems like it should cost ten dollars, he's so small." Jamie laughs, petting Gerbie gently. "You should be a vet," I say. "You were really good with him."

Jamie smiles, pleased with this idea.

On September 6, I wake up to the sound of rain drumming against the plastic garbage cans outside my window. I want to wake up Aidan but notice that his cheeks are fiery red and he is sweating. He stirs and looks at me, his eyes squinting in the light.

"My throat hurts," he says, and I head into the bedroom to get my flashlight. Dave kept flashlights everywhere, a buck knife under the bed, and an ax on the top shelf of the closet. I used to tease him about being paranoid, but now these things remind me of him and do indeed make me feel safe.

"Open up," I tell Aidan, shining the flashlight down his throat, where his tonsils look like the inside of a pomegranate. "I think you have strep." He falls back into his pillow. I run through the list of things I had planned today, my heart falling at the thought of missing another fire rally. I call the doctor who, after some prompting, agrees to call in a prescription of antibiotics. This is the fourth time Aidan has had strep this year, and his pediatrician thinks he will need his tonsils out. The thought of putting Aidan through surgery without Dave makes me wince.

When Aidan was five months old, he had to have inguinal surgery. The night before, Dave and I slept at my parents' house, which was located around the corner from the hospital. Aidan woke up three times that night smelling my breast milk and wanting to feed, but the doctors told us he couldn't eat. I put a pillow over my head to drown out his wails, which tugged so hard at my heart, my breast milk leaked all over the bed. Dave held Aidan the whole night, pacing back and forth, rocking Aidan, who screamed, his tiny face turning the color of an overripe plum. Eventually, Aidan fell back to sleep, his small head limp on Dave's wide shoulder.

That afternoon, while Aidan watches television, I set to the task I have avoided all year: sorting through Dave's large drawer under the bed. There are piles of clothes and sketch pads, a drawing book with designs for sculptures he would have started this year. There is a journal entry from when we had a fight, and it is hard to read how angry he was at me then. I don't even remember what the fight was about. There are programs from shows we have seen, love poems he wrote me in college, and between the leaves is a piece of loose-leaf written in his distinctive, blocky handwriting.

Today is my fifth day at the academy. One week down and seven more to go. Thirty-five more days. I'm one of one hundred new probies (that's proba-

tionary firefighters) in the third class of 1991. Up until now, my stay here has been busy mostly with paperwork and learning to stand and march in formation. Yesterday we were informed of the injuries sustained by firefighter Kevin Kane, himself still a probie of eleven months. He was severely burned in a fire. This morning, at 3 am, Kevin died of his injuries. The fire department sent Commissioner Kelly, a civilian in charge of public relations, to speak to us about Kevin's death and what it meant. He said that Kevin had been a group leader at the academy and that he was an excellent student and well liked. Commissioner Kelly told us that Kevin and his company entered the structure because they were told there were people inside. So they entered the building and began to search during which time Kevin was separated from his company and trapped in a room on the fourth floor. Commissioner Kelly said Kevin stood in the window calling for help while the room was in flames and the the men of his company tried to get a bucket to him, which only took a matter of minutes. During these few minutes, he received burns over 75 percent of his body. Kelly and other officers could not understand why he did not jump. But the fact is, he didn't. He stood in the window and waited for the bucket and when it was close enough, he jumped. As I said, he died this morning at 3 am. Commissioner Kelly tried to explain the job and what it meant, about the sense of family, commitment, and sacrifice. He quoted a chief he once heard speak. I can't remember the quote, but the gist of it was that this is the greatest and most dangerous job in the world and in a sense we do God's work . . . saving lives. When he was speaking, I can't imagine there was not one man in that room that didn't have to hold back tears. It was truly moving. I've never felt more proud to share any job or tradition or secure that my new family will take care of me and my old family as they did Kevin's. It reassured me of the fact that this is the job for me no matter what the danger. It gave me confidence to go on with my training without any doubts and to learn as much as I possibly can so that my fate will not be the same as Kevin Kane's. But in the end, I believe that when it is your time to go, you go and that ultimately my life is in God's hands, happily and forever.

I stop, unbelieving. Is it possible to know you are going to die? I read and reread the words until they begin to blur together, the way words do when you stare at them too long. I feel my chin quiver and the tears come again. I want to believe the pain lessens over time, the way everyone promised, but it has been nearly a year, and it hurts with the same intensity. Perhaps the pain lasts in direct proportion to how much you loved someone, and I will be crying like this for years to come.

27

One Year

I have decided against going to Ground Zero today. For me, it represents everything political I have fought for these past twelve months, and I want today just to be about Dave and me. The sky is as clear and blue as it was a year ago. I lie in bed thinking about the thousands of wives, mothers, fathers, sisters, brothers, uncles, sons, daughters, aunts, and uncles waking up right now and remembering this time last year. Everyone is remembering. I look at the tree in front of my house that my neighbor Bill planted a few years ago. The Block Association dedicated it to Dave, with a small plaque in front: "Dave Fontana: October 17, 1963–September 11, 2001. Firefighter, Neighbor, Father, Artist, Friend." The tree is bending in the wind, and I know it will be a blustery day. Of course it is a blustery day.

I bring Aidan to school for the morning while Leah, Jason, and I head up to Prospect Park. Since it is early and very windy, the park is almost empty. We walk across the big field, the green expanse faded in patches. Images of Dave and Aidan playing chase, eating bagels on the bench, Dave pulling him in the wagon, flood my head. It is so easy to live in the memories, to bask in the elixir of what once was. I find the clearing of pine trees where Dave proposed. It looks different now, damp needles carpeting the grove. At first I can't recall which tree it was that he knelt in front of, and then I spot it. It is the largest one, off to the left, with large green boughs that stretch like arms above me.

I have brought a spoon and a zippered bag of Dave's ashes. They look different from how I imagined them, and I realize I have never seen cremains before. You can see the pieces of bone and teeth hidden among the fine gray dust. At first I don't want to touch it, my stomach lurching forward. I slide the spoon in, but the wind whips the ash away onto the field before I can even bring it to the spot in the ground. I zip the bag closed again and dig a shallow hole with my spoon, my chin curling in an effort not to cry. Leah and Jason stand on the edge of the grove, watching me. I work the dirt around the stubborn roots and unzip the bag again, carefully sliding it inside the hole. I slowly ease the bag out, the ashes sliding in, chunks of bone clinking together. Can this really be all? Surely these seemingly insignificant granules can't be all that's left from thousands of moments, endless hours, a heavy arm on my side while I am sleeping. I quickly cover the hole with dirt and needles and sit hunched, watering it with my tears, until Jason steps up and squats next to me. His knees crackle and pop as he places a bouquet of peach roses on the makeshift grave.

"We need to go if we're going to be on time," Leah says softly, her voice nasal from crying. It must have been a horrible year for her, too, keeping her own grief at bay to make room for mine. Leah and Jason each take an arm, holding me up as if I am a hundred years old. They lead me slowly and carefully back across the field, out into the wide expanse, the wind blowing the hair onto my tear-streaked face, but I don't move. I don't want Leah and Jason to stop holding me, and yet I know someday they will have to let go and reenter their lives without me.

We keep walking this way until we arrive at St. Francis on 6th Avenue where Dave's memorial was so many months ago. Today it is a small gathering, with members of Squad, a few other firehouses, families, and some friends from the neighborhood. The stained-glass windows of the church have been cracked open, and a wind gusts through, making eerie whistling noises. Theresa, Martha, and Debbie are all here with their children. Mikey, Theresa's little one, has grown so much since I saw him last, his impish face the perfect embodiment of his father. My parents pick up Aidan from school and meet me at the church.

Huey has written a song, his sweet voice rolling through the church. *"I miss you, my brothers . . ."* He sings more softly than before, his hair grayer and sparser. *"My friends, my brothers,"* he crescendos, bringing all of us to tears, the wind rattling the glass. Theresa turns to me, raising her eyebrow, her signal to let me know that the rattling glass is all of them here with us. I nod. They are here. I give in to the divine cosmos that puts all these men into the air we breathe and around us in the lights, the butterflies, and the number 22.

That afternoon I drive Aidan out to Jones Beach for the second scattering. From inside the car, the world outside looks serene. You cannot feel the gusty winds, pushing clouds as fast as birds across the sky. The parking lot is almost empty except for a dozen or so lifeguards. I have asked Steve to make this simple and small. I want my life unfettered again. The lifeguards are all standing on the deck, red roses in their hands, as the wind blows their hair sideways.

"Field Six is crazy today," Steve says, stepping up to the car. I barely recognize the beach. The fierce wind has blown the water all the way up from the shore, making a small lake in front of the lifeguard shack. "I hope you're ready to swim," he says, his brown eyes flashing. I spot Theresa, who has come to say good-bye with me. I am so moved by her gesture, I run up to give her a hug.

"Thanks for coming," I say, squeezing her hard. I know it is not easy for her to be here, to see me scattering ashes she never had. Nobody from Rescue 5 was ever found.

"Don't get me crying. I'm a mess," she says to my shoulder.

"It means a lot though. I'm so glad you're my friend."

"Are you kidding? You got me through this year."

"You, too." And I know it is true.

Steve steps over with a large pair of Jones Beach lifeguard trunks. "You'll need these," he tells me.

"They're mine," Dave's good friend Don says, smiling, his mop of blond hair blowing over his face. I head into the shack and change into the trunks, which billow out like a fat suit and walk outside.

"You ready?" Steve asks, and I nod. We have to cross the tidal pool to get to the shoreline. "I don't want everyone coming to the shore, if that's okay," I say, and Steve graciously tells everyone that just family and a few friends will walk to the shore. All of Dave's family is here—Toni, Vicky, Ellen, Dennis, Brian, Ed, everyone but Hank. I have to laugh at the odd procession we make: rolled-up pants, skirts hiked up high, as we wade across the two-foot-deep tidal pool. Ed carries Aidan in his arms, and my mother-in-law, Toni, looks particularly fragile, her legs like matchsticks wading through the rippling water. Jason carries the ashes in a plastic Duane Reade bag on his head, making everyone laugh. When we reach the shoreline, the sand is blowing so hard, the granules hurt as they ping off our wet ankles. Everyone is waiting, silent as statues, staring out at the ocean.

"You ready?" Ed asks, taking my arm. Jason hands me the second bag of cremains. It is bigger than the first and just as disturbing in its texture. I examine the bag for a moment, deciding that this time, I want to touch Dave, to feel him between my fingers. I slide my hand in the bag and scoop out a small handful. The ash is surprisingly soft and gritty, and the chunks of bone and teeth dig into my skin. I squeeze my fist shut, take a few steps into the water, and throw the ashes as hard as I can into the wind. They fly high at first, the wind carrying them like a kite string across the sea. I pass the bag to Ed, who scoops a large handful and then holds the bag in front of Aidan, who peers cautiously inside.

"Is that Daddy?" he asks.

"Yes, sweetie. That's Daddy's body, and we're throwing it into the ocean that he loved to swim in." Aidan's face looks as young as a toddler's, his eyes wide as he reaches his hand into the bag. Aidan watches Ed throw the ash, fascinated by how it floats on top of the water before sinking.

"Your turn," I tell Aidan, but he shakes his head no. I know exactly how he feels, not wanting to let it go, and so I pass the bag around to my mother-in-law, to Ellen, to Vicki, her husband, Eric, Romi, my niece Martina, Dennis, Brian, Leah, Jason, Steve, and even Dave's friend Cliff, who is standing on the shore. When everyone is finished, it is my turn again. There so much ash left, I am surprised. I turn back to the ocean stretching out in front of me, as infinite as stars. I step deeper in, the waves rising up my legs, making the bathing suit billow up. I take a larger handful of ashes this time and hold it to my chest, savoring it like a kiss.

"You want to throw it together?" I ask Aidan, who still has not let go of his ashes. He nods, watching me, unusually quiet. I feel the tears coming, the sadness swelling like the gentle waves. "One . . . two . . . three!" I yell, and we throw the ash into the wind, which reverses suddenly, splattering us with a fine gray powder.

"I got Daddy in my eye!" Aidan whines, rubbing his eyes.

"What the hell," I say, and in a moment I am laughing hysterically as I turn the bag upside down until I am covered in Dave's ashes from my head to my waist. I can feel everyone on the beach behind us, watching.

"Well, he was all over you when he was alive . . ." Ed says, his giant shoulders bouncing, and my eyes are watering from laughing or the wind or crying, I can't tell which. I grow quiet and stare out at the ocean, the wind rippling the water like desert sand. I look down at my black shirt, covered with the powdery fragments of Dave, and I want to stand here forever, savoring him, pretending his large body is still pressed against mine, thick and strong. I don't want to say good-bye.

Ed and I grow quiet, staring out at the ocean. I wonder about all the things that can't be seen under the waves: the ancient fossils, infinite creatures, prehistoric sea grass undulating with the tide, and then slowly I lower myself into the water. It is surprisingly warm. I watch the powder rise up from my shirt and float to the top of the ocean. It hesitates for a moment, then disappears into the velvet deep.

Epilogue

Dave would have loved the high-beamed ceilings of this carriage house, the tall windows looking out on black lotus trees. The previous owner, Joe, a sculptor and historian, documented the 146-year-old barn's history as part of the Underground Railroad, where slaves were hidden in the crawl space below.

I never imagined leaving Park Slope, the watchful comfort of my friends and neighbors, my home for over twelve years. But I felt stranded in the land of families, my memories bumping into strollers at every corner. Small tasks that Dave and I used to do together took major effort as I circled the blocks looking for a parking spot, with Aidan sleepy in his pajamas in the backseat. Friends were shocked that I would move to Staten Island, the retarded second cousin to Manhattan and Brooklyn, but I fell in love with this house and its half acre of land, with a stream running through it and Japanese maple trees and an old dogwood that cascades white flowers in May. It is the house Dave and I always talked about, warm and wide open, and because of this, the house sometimes echoes as if something were missing. Even Aidan, who still sometimes has nightmares, notices the vast silence of the house at night. His wide flashlight eyes are filled with more questions about what happened on 9/11, and at nine years old, Aidan worries that he will forget Dave's voice. So I show him videos, I wrote him this book, and when he is scarfing down chocolate, I tell him how his father loved chocolate, too. I try to stay focused on Aidan now, relishing how he holds my hand when we walk to school or roller-blade in Silver Lake, because I know, like everything in life, it is fleeting. He is giant for his age, a Saint Bernard of a boy, his feet the same size as mine. He likes being the tallest one in his class and has made many friends at the same elementary school that I attended over thirty years ago. His teacher, Mrs. Colbeck, has been an unparalleled marvel, turning Aidan on to reading, and giving him the glorious feeling of having a teacher who adores you. There is much to be adored in Aidan, as my parents will attest. We live around the corner from them now and they pick up Aidan every Tuesday so I can go to my writers' group in Park Slope. I love that Aidan gets to have his grandparents so close.

When I moved, Jason helped me pack up the boxes, sort through Dave's clothes, and secure what was left of my blue glass with bubble wrap. Two weeks later, he got a job in Los Angeles writing for Madd tv, his first real paying job doing what he loves. I was thrilled that he could finally quit waiting tables and do what he was meant to do, but I cried for weeks after he left. Yet another loss to bear. We speak often, conversations on cell phones that echo and make him feel even farther away. The worst part of Jason's abrupt departure was that he missed Leah and Neil's wedding on August 23, 2003, at an heirloom-tomato farm upstate. It was a fine day; a heat wave had just broken and a slight breeze made the wildflowers brush against the chipped paint of the old red barn. The ceremony took place in front of a mammoth oak tree with two perfect branches on either side. Father Chris, the fire chaplain who had presided over hundreds of funerals, performed the ceremony, summoning Dave's name as the presence that brought Neil and Leah together. I tried not to cry, wanting the focus to remain on my sister for whom I felt so grateful. I stood in my sparkling blue gown, my now-blond hair piled on top of my head, and noticed how the sun made the edges of everything sharp, how crooked Neil's smile was, and how hawks circled above us, a sight Dave always loved. Aidan was the ring-bearer in a handsome gray suit, and everyone laughed when he walked through Leah and Neil's held hands, instead of around them, the way we had rehearsed. At the reception, Allan and I performed a skit Jason wrote, and there was uninhibited dancing, especially by the bride and groom. My parents danced to "Something in the Way She Moves," in that way only couples who have been together for forty years do. I had to admit I was jealous that their love would bring them through the years, but it also made me wonder what else was in store—if I could possibly be blessed twice in this life with love. I notice as the days pass and my heart heals, that it expands with the possibility that I can have love again. Most of my widow friends have found love already. Perhaps I am behind the curve of grief, or maybe it is not love but the unbearable loneliness making them settle for something less. I don't claim to know, but I imagine the joy of loving again.

I don't visit the firehouse much anymore, not only because we are no longer just blocks away, but because something has shifted there. The new guys are unquestionably sincere and warm, but the older guys, with a few exceptions, are distant. Perhaps we are painful reminders, or it is the inevitable tide passing, but I suspect, for reasons that I will never know, it was a unilateral choice to erase us from their consciousness. For Aidan, I attend the annual Christmas party and summer picnic, exchanging niceties, as if that monumental year never existed between us. Joe O'Donnell and his wife still call, send holiday cards, and remind me often that they care. It means more to all of us than they will ever know. George Ebert and some of Dave's old friends still drop by. I make sure Aidan remembers their names and shakes their hands. The Fire Department provides newsletters and activities for the 9/11 families, so we do not feel forgotten.

I still speak at fire rallies with Steve Buscemi, my former neighbor and good friend, who was himself a firefighter for four years. Firefighters never received the raises they were promised and the federal funds promised from President Bush never arrived. Even worse, firefighters were getting sicker. Even Joe O'Donnell was put on light duty for lung issues. And then Mayor Bloomberg began closing firehouses. I stood out in front of the old firehouses, locking arms with Steve Buscemi, neighbors, and local politicians. Everyone was arrested, except me. It wouldn't look good if they arrested a 9/11 widow and the firehouses closed. Everything was changing.

Amazingly, my organization is still thriving. In 2002 and 2003, we spearheaded the effort to unite the family groups to address the complicated issue of memorialization. We called it the Coalition of 9/11 Families and worked hard to ensure that the two squares called "the footprints" of the Twin Towers were preserved. Lee and I serve on the Lower Manhattan Development Corporation's Family Advisory Committee and never cease to be amazed at what an arduous, controversy-ridden task the rebuilding of Ground Zero is. It always seems a sad irony that Dave happened to be killed on the world's most expensive piece of real estate, and so the battle for us is always making sure business interests and politics don't override the reverence for what happened there. The endless meetings, the in-fighting, the bureaucracy are wearisome.

At the invitation of the Lutheran Disaster Relief Team of New York, we moved to Cortland Street to a small office on the twentieth floor overlooking Ground Zero. The site looks drastically different now, unrecognizably clean, flat, and sterile. A high fence surrounds the site where tourists flock, straining their necks to read signs that attempt to describe what was there before.

For a while, the organization struggled. While other groups had grabbed a piece of the charitable pie, our organization had no funding, and what we had went into funding the coalition. Lee loved showing visiting politicians, friends, firefighters, and family the view from the office, telling again and again the story of the recovery, pointing to where his son Jonathan was found. But for me, looking at the site day after day felt like picking at a scab. I missed Aidan, the theater, writing, my friends. I told Lee this, sitting on the small window ledge of our office, fighting back tears. I told him how I had been asked to write a book, how I wanted to document it all for Aidan and my grandchildren, and Lee smiled, patted me on the thigh and said what I expected him to: "Salubrious."

I know Lee and I will always be great friends, despite our different ideas. When President Bush used the image of a Stokes basket being removed from Ground Zero for his election campaign, the press called our organization for comment. Lee thought it was good to remind people about what happened that day. I was adamant that no politician should use 9/11 to promote him- or herself. I tried to make Lee see the hypocrisy of the president's using that image, while also censoring photographs of flag-draped coffins returning from Iraq. I was confused why Lee, firefighters, and so many of the families supported President Bush. Information was coming out daily about the mistakes made, the things that could have been avoided. Four widows from New Jersey have been tireless in their efforts to have the truth revealed. For instance, I read about the President having received an EPA report days after September 11. It said the site was not safe for the rescue workers. And every week there is more information, there are more fights, more battles—and we still don't know how to make ourselves safe from terrorism. I was saddened by how the world viewed our country now and felt the president squandered a rare moment when the world's nations came to support America in the wake of 9/11. Instead he shifted the spotlight to a country that never attacked us and began a war that seems impossible to end. But perhaps this is our organization's strength, that two people like Lee and I, with opposing views, can work together to ensure 9/11 and the people who perished there are remembered correctly.

On that same ledge, watching thousands of tourists walking aimlessly, with no clue of what really happened, my now executive director Jen Adams and Lee had the idea to open a temporary memorial at an office space next to the firehouse on Liberty Street. We will call the space "Tribute," and Lee and other firefighters, family members, and survivors will serve as guides, telling the story Lee loves to tell of how the world came together to help us—the true story of 9/11.

My niece, Gilby Grayce Mitchell, was born on December 26, 2004. I was supposed to be in the birthing room with Leah and Neil, but since Leah gave birth in only forty minutes, I didn't make it in time. Gilby, or Gigi as I like to call her, was nine pounds and three ounces, with thick black curly hair and eyes like shimmery black stones. It was snowing when Aidan and I arrived at St. Lukes Hospital. Aidan held her first, sitting her on his lap, his eyes wide, his smile unequivocally Dave's. "My family's finally bigger," he said, and Leah and I laughed and cried at the same time, as we are known to do.

April 2005

Postscript

It is hard to believe it will be five years since Dave died. Every day in the paper, 9/11 stories still appear: the Moussaoui trial, the memorial protests, 911 tapes of trapped office workers trying to escape the towers were released, and just yesterday I was called by some retired firefighters who told me body parts were being found by day laborers in the infrastructure of the Deutsche Bank building. The 9/11 stories seem unending. Movies are being made, and more books are being written about living in the "post-9/11 world." The war in Iraq stumbles on as more and more Americans realize how embroiled we are in something from which it seems impossible to extricate ourselves. Bush's approval ratings are at an all-time low and the American spirit seems to be following suit.

Yet, like a crocus in melting snow, I have hope and glimpses of the happiness I knew before. I am writing again, humorous essays about dating these last few years, and am returning to the screenplay I shelved before Dave died. More than anything, I miss the stage and have begun the long but exhilarating process of creating a new show. I am feeling for the first time, what Dave had always said, that "Life is good." For Aidan's tenth birthday, I took my brother-in-law Ed and his family to a small surfing town in Puerto Rico, where we unknowingly rented a house next door to Dennis Farrell, now retired. Dennis taught me how to surf, and I shared with Ed that I had finally found love again, to which Ed replied, "That's what Dave would want for you."

My organization, the 9/11 Families Association, is still thriving, with Lee and Jen at the helm working nonstop to create a visitors' center that is slated to open in June 2006. It is amazing to see the vision of Tribute come to fruition as the staff and board grow with the united goal of creating a poignant place for visitors to come and understand the profundity of what happened there. The docent program began in November, with guides volunteering from the 9/11 community offering tours seven days a week.

Jason still resides in Los Angeles despite being laid off from his writing job. He continues to write for television despite my constant pleas for him to return home. Aidan has surpassed five feet, with maple-colored surfer hair and a spirit that fills our home with humor and love on a daily basis. Our biggest addition has been our dog, Weazer, who we adopted from a shelter in the Hamptons last summer. My heart fills each morning when I enter Aidan's room to wake him, his thin white arm draped over Weazer's fuzzy body as they sleep.

Leah and Neil are still happily married on the Upper East Side, their small apartment full of diapers and laundry as they struggle to balance their lives with two small girls at home. My newest niece, Esme Geneva, was born exactly a year and a day after Gilby, on December 27, 2005. I made it to the birthing room this time, with not a moment to spare, arriving just in time to watch Esme's pink face press itself into the world. Aidan, once again, held her first, a look of consternation furrowing her brow as my giant boy smiled down on her.

Acknowledgments

Because of the nature of this huge event, I must thank all the people from around the nation and world who reached out to Aidan and me, sending us letters, cards, teddy bears, donations, vacations, organized memorials, made bookmarks, CDs, quilts, and acknowledged our loss. If I never responded to say thank you, please accept it now and know that it buoyed Aidan and me in our darkest hours. Thank you to all the 9/11 families, because while our loved ones were unique to us, our sadness and grief were not. To all the members and volunteers at the 9/11 Widows and Victims' Families Association, especially Jen Adams and Lee Ielpi for everything you do.

To my sister Leah, Neil, and Jason, who still hold me up on the bad days. To my parents for my creativity and for loving Aidan as much as I do. To all the Fontanas, especially Toni for bringing Dave's special spirit into the world, and my brother-in-law Ed for supporting me in writing about it. To the widows at Squad 1, especially Martha Butler and Theresa Russo for getting me through it all. To my friends in Park Slope, too many to mention, who make the neighborhood the amazing place I will always miss, especially 4th Street, Sarah Greene for her friendship, the plaque, and for bragging about me to friends, and of course the wonderful O'Connells. Thank you, Steve and Lucian Buscemi and Jo Andres for welcoming Aidan and me into your extraordinary family. Thank you

Acknowledgments

to my writing group, especially Louise Crawford and Wendy Ponte, for loving my words when I didn't. To the Brooklyn Writer's Space who gave me a quiet place to write, read, and the camaraderie of fellow writers, especially the talented Elissa Schappell. To the uncomparable Merri Milwe and Joan Greenberg, for your wisdom and for loving me like family. To Lorie, Robert, Jack Henry, and Cavannaugh Honor, for spending that amazing last vacation with us. To Mila Drumke for her beautiful music and friendship. To the Cox family, in loving memory of Peter Cox, for sharing the land of pointed firs with Dave and me. To George Ebert, Joe and Deirdre O'Donnell, Kevin Burns, and Dennis Farrell, for remembering.

In loving memory of Fiora Fontana, who sent her brother Ed Fontana's purple heart for me to give to Aidan some day. I never found the right words to thank you enough. To all the fire departments around the country and world that came to the funerals, Groud Zero, and the firehouses after 9/11. You make the brotherhood what it is, especially Ed Osborne and the boys in Modesto and Charles Boutroy and the firefighters in Plaissure, France. To the Field 6 lifeguards at Jones Beach, especially Steve Levy, who always goes above and beyond. To all the volunteers at Ground Zero, especially Angelo Guglielmo. Thank you to Lynn Tierney, Kids Connections, Enid Zucherman, Firefighter Johnny Finn, Joe Miccio, Jimmy Boyle, Dennis Smith, and Beth Danhauser and her husband, Stephen. To our friends far and near who reached out and shared their memories of Dave with me. To my agent, Susan Golomb, for persisting and reviving my creative life again, and of course, finally, my editor, Marysue Rucci, whose friendship and faith gave me the strength to write the hardest thing I have ever written.

About the Author

Marian Fontana was born and raised in New York City. She graduated from the High School of Performing Arts in music and Sarah Lawrence College in theater and writing. An accomplished comedienne, actress, and writer, Marian is currently president of the 9/11 Families Association, which opened a visitors' center across from Ground Zero at 120 Liberty Street in June 2006 (*www.marianfontana.com, www.911families.com, www.tributenyc.org*). She lives with her son, Aidan, in Staten Island.

SIMON & SCHUSTER PAPERBACKS
READING GROUP GUIDE

A Widow's Walk

by Marian Fontana

Discussion Questions

1. Marian's memoir is incredibly sad in so many moments and hilariously funny in others. What is the role of humor in her story? What is the role of humor in grief and in healing?

2. Marian experiences both a very personal loss, but also a public loss. September 11 was a national event and Dave's death became part of the history and legacy of that day. On page 114 Marian writes, "What happened to our husbands and so many others has made privacy impossible." In what ways is Marian's loss the same or different than if Dave had died on a regular day in the line of duty?

3. In the year after 9/11 Marian witnessed an astounding outpouring of concern and generosity from people all over the world and also encountered people who were insensitive and obtuse about her loss. How do you explain these wide disparities in people's reactions to September 11? Are some people genuinely compassionate and others not? Do you think 9/11 affected people who lived near the tragedy or had a connection to New York more than other people?

4. Marian and Theresa feel bad when they realize they are getting different treatment as widows of firefighters. Kathleen, who is with them, refers to their checks as "blood money." Do you think the

families of non-firefighters were treated fairly after 9/11? How do you think their experience differed from that of firefighters' families?

5. Throughout the book, many of the widows of Squad 1 reported getting "signs" from their husbands. Were there really signs, or did the women imagine them in order to reconnect with their husbands?

6. Were you surprised to learn about the closeness of neighbors, the strong community identity, and the outpouring of support demonstrated by the candlelight vigil that thousands of people attended in Prospect Park? Did you have impressions about New Yorkers that were either confirmed or changed by Marian's story?

7. Marian was raised by a Catholic mother and a Jewish father. She says she does not consider herself particularly religious, only attending church on holidays; but she thinks a lot about God after Dave's death. How do you think her dual religions informed her spiritual understanding of the events of September 11 and the death of her husband?

8. Marian is a writer, performer, and comedienne. The first thing she sat down to write after September 11 was Dave's eulogy. On page 158 she talks about the process of writing and the anticipation and insecurity of the creative act. What role do you think writing and creativity had in how Marian faced the months after Dave's death?

9. On page 199 Marian talks about the exhausting attempt to be both mother and father to Aidan. Discuss the difficulty of trying to be both parents to a child who has lost one.

10. Aidan's behavior is at times angry, stubborn, innocent, aggressive, and sweet. Discuss Aidan's reactions to his father's death.

An Interview with Marian Fontana

Q: How has writing this book affected your work as both a writer and a performer? What were the challenges in writing such a powerful and painful book?

A: I receive, and continue to receive, amazing letters and e-mails from people who have read my book and so for that, I am truly grateful. I never expected to touch people by sharing my experience, but from the letters I receive, I see that I have, and for that I am blessed. I am glad I have the book to give to Aidan as a document of this part of our lives. On the other hand, it has been a cross to bear. I have become identified as a 9/11 widow and so it has made returning to the life I once knew impossible. I don't blame anyone for this. It is what it is and so I feel both privileged and cursed by my role.

As far as writing the book, next to the experience of 9/11, writing it was truly the most painful thing I have experienced. Writing about it day after day, reliving it for two and a half years really made moving on impossible. Ultimately, I think it helped me process this painful time and helped me let go of Dave. As I wrote the last sentence I burst into tears, knowing that it was, in fact, the final good-bye.

Q: Can you describe how you blended your memories of your life with Dave into the story's narrative?

A: It happened very organically. In the first draft I made the memories distinctly separate, putting them in italics to let the reader know it was the past, but this felt contrived. Ultimately, it worked much better to weave them throughout the book.

Q: **In the months after September 11 you wanted so badly to receive a sign from Dave. Did the search for significance and meaning in small things disappear or do you still find yourself thinking about those types of messages? How have you come to understand the types of signs, communications, or coincidences that many of the widows reported receiving in the weeks after their husbands died?**

A: I will never know the answer, but I did feel Dave around me and continue to feel his presence. Now, it does not feel like literal "signs" but more of a feeling that he is around. I became estranged with one of the firefighters from Squad and have always felt very sad about it. Just last month I planned a surfing trip to a remote part of Puerto Rico. It is not commercial and has only one flight a day. I rented a condo from a former lifeguard on a remote hill overlooking the ocean. There was only one other house there and it turned out it was owned by this firefighter who retired a few years ago. We ended up healing our friendship and he even taught me how to surf again. I'd like to think that if it wasn't Divine intervention, that perhaps it was Dave intervention.

Q: **When John from *Third Watch* inquires about your screenwriting and offers to take a look at one of your scripts (on page 124), you say that your creative mind left you. How were you able to regain your creativity?**

A: By writing the book. As it says in the book, my creativity left me. I had no interest in anything and had to be convinced by my agent to write the book in the first place. I am grateful that she pushed me, because it helped revive something very important in my life. My husband always supported me, encouraged me to quit my day job to be a writer. He believed in my talent and so I continue to write and am even planning to perform again soon. I never did give John Wells any of my scripts, because I felt like all the scripts I wrote before Dave died were from a different part of my life. If I wrote one now, it would be very different.

Q: A lot of people found fiction, novels, and other forms of entertainment irrelevant in the months after September 11. People reported not being able to concentrate on anything other than the news and political books and articles. Do you think fiction and creative writing are important in a post-9/11 world?

A: Very. At first, it repulsed me. When I was considering writing a book, I went to a book fair at the Jacob Javits Center and eighty-seven 9/11 books had been sold to different publishers. I was disgusted and didn't want to be a part of that. Then the head of Simon & Schuster told me that it was natural for creative people to process this event through their art. I guess that made sense to me, but since I was directly affected, it took me longer to come to terms with writing a book. It was my brother-in-law who convinced me, who reminded me that it was Dave who encouraged me and believed in me as a writer. Most of all, my brother-in-law told me to write the book while the memories were fresh, so that Aidan would remember his father.

Q: In March 2006, construction of the World Trade Center Memorial began. Many families were opposed to the plan and the Coalition of 9/11 Families filed a petition in court to halt construction. How do you feel about the planned memorial? What would you like to see at the site?

A: I am on the Family Advisory Board of the Lower Manhattan Development Corporation. We are one of eight advisory boards guiding the memorial, which is to say, we have very little impact in what happens. I was touched by how many thousands of people submitted their ideas, but all in all, I felt the whole process was rushed and not forward thinking. Ironically, it is now stalled. I think if we had just slowed down and given the city and the families and the country time to heal and recover, the memorial would have been more poignant. It felt rushed and every great memorial I have seen in my life has had the benefit of time between the event and the memorial. I think this is necessary to do it well. That said, even though I was the impetus for bringing all the family groups together in the coalition, we are no longer members. I was tired of fighting and only feel good when I am being proactive, not arguing. Therefore, our organization, now called the 9/11 Families Association, is creating the Tribute Center, a visitors' center across the street from Ground Zero. We have been offering tours guided by the 9/11 community (survivors, family members, residents, etc.) to visitors, and in June our facility will be open to all. So while the memorial at Ground Zero could take eight more years to open, we are offering a place for people to go—to learn about 9/11, and learn from it.

Q: Dealing with the press and politicians added a complexity to your grieving process that not everyone who lost someone on September 11 had to deal with. What have you learned about politics and the press?

A: While I never planned on being public, I learned so much about the media and politicians. Both are incredibly powerful tools for dispensing messages quickly to the public. Controlling the message was difficult and I was sometimes misquoted, but in general, I met a lot of amazing journalists and politicians who really make a difference. There were others though, who used 9/11 as a tool for their own political gain. Watching the politicians, I learned how difficult it is—so many people wanting so many things. It seems easy to lose sight of who you are and what you stand for. Not to mention that politicians are beholden to so many who paid for their campaigns and got them where they are. It's a flawed system, but an amazing one, and I appreciated the access I was granted to get attention for the issues that were confronting the families.

Q: Have you stayed very involved with the widows and families organizations or have you stepped back some?

A: I am still involved in Tribute, the visitors' center mentioned earlier, but not full-time. The energy and effort involved are exhausting, and I realized that I would not heal if I kept going at such a pace. I tour with the book, work at my organization when I can, but it's important for me to step back and get away from 9/11. It was vital for my own health and for Aidan and I to start a new life. September 11 is everywhere around us. It's still in the paper every day. I turn down most media calls unless it promotes the organization or the book. I will always care and speak when I feel it is vital.

Q: What are you working on now? Are you writing? Performing?

A: I am working on my second book and am currently creating a new theater piece. It's been fun getting back to my comedy and a lighter side of my life. Right now, I am writing essays about dating and finding love again. I am happy for the first time in years, and while I still miss Dave every day, I am rebuilding a new life, spending more time with Aidan and my new nieces, and more time writing and performing. I love my life and feel a deeper sense of gratefulness for all that I am blessed with.

Enhance Your Book Club

1. Firefighters are unsung heroes. Visit your local firehouse or, if you are a parent, arrange for a school trip there. Bring them some homemade cookies. Think of ways you can support your local firehouse with a bake sale or other fundraising efforts.

2. Visit Squad 1 online at *http://www.nyfd.com/brooklyn_engines/squad1.html* and view an online memorial to Dave at *http://www.9–11heroes.us/v/ David_Fontana.php*. My website is *marianfontana.com*.

3. Visit the websites of Marian's foundations to learn more about what the families of 9/11 are advocating in the ongoing process to memorialize their loved ones: *http://www.911wvfa.org/* and *http:// www.tributenyc.org*.